A COUNTRY WITH NO NAME

ALSO BY SEBASTIAN DE GRAZIA

The Political Community

Of Time, Work and Leisure

Machiavelli in Hell (winner of the Pulitzer Prize for Biography, 1990)

A ★ COUNTRY WITH NO NAME

TALES FROM THE CONSTITUTION

SEBASTIAN DE GRAZIA

PANTHEON BOOKS

NEW YORK

Library of Congress Cataloging-in-Publication Data

De Grazia, Sebastian.
   A country with no name : tales from the Constitution / Sebastian de Grazia.
      p.   cm.
   ISBN 0-679-41977-2 (hardcover)
   1. United States—History—Fiction.
PS3554.E4227C68   1997
813′.54—dc20   96-31782

Random House Web Address: http://www.randomhouse.com/

Book design by Debbie Glasserman

Printed in the United States of America
First Edition
9 8 7 6 5 4 3 2 1

NOVEL: A small tale, generally of love.

—Samuel Johnson

CONTENTS

Foreword   ix

 1 MOCTEZUMA WELCOMES HIS ANCESTORS BACK TO
    THE OLD COUNTRY   3

 2 THOMAS JEFFERSON FOOLS WITH A FOOLISH KING   18

 3 A COUNTRY WITH NO NAME   47

 4 GEORGE WASHINGTON TO THE RESCUE   73

 5 THE COUNTRIES THAT SIGNED A CONTRACT TO
    BECOME A COUNTRY   112

 6 WE THE PEOPLE HAND OUT OATHS: YOU SWEAR,
    HE SWEARS, WE SWEAR NOT   143

 7 JOHN MARSHALL DEMONSTRATES THE POWER OF
    LEGAL RAZZLE-DAZZLE   177

 8 JOHN CALHOUN ZEROES IN ON THE FATAL FLAW
    AND ONE MILLION MEN FALL   216

 9 THOREAU PITS CONSCIENCE AGAINST
    CONSTITUTION   251

10 LINCOLN WANTS A NATION OF BLOOD BROTHERS   299

11 HOW HIGH THE TUNE: "THE STAR-SPANGLED
    BANNER" AND OTHER SOUNDS AND SYMBOLS   343

12 HOW TO GET RID OF A CONSTITUTION WITHOUT
    SAYING SO OR MEANING TO   379

Acknowledgments   417

FOREWORD

The pages to follow consist of the verbatim record of twelve talks
on American history by Claire St. John as tutor of Oliver Huggins
for two weeks this summer. St. John at the time was a graduate student writing a dissertation on the subject. Unknown to her, Huggins recorded, transcribed, and edited the talks, or "tales" as she
called them. They may be looked on as discourses in the history of
America, past and future. Huggins collected the illustrations and later
added the acknowledgments as dictated by Claire St. John.

C.St.J.
O.H.

A COUNTRY WITH NO NAME

1

MOCTEZUMA WELCOMES HIS ANCESTORS BACK TO THE OLD COUNTRY

MONDAY

"Good afternoon. I am Claire St. John, your teller of tales—"

"My teller of tales?" said Oliver Huggins, shaking the out-stretched hand. "I thought—"

"I did not finish. In future, if I am to tutor you in history, in American history, please do not interrupt." She waited a moment, then went on.

"My view of history is that it consists of tales. Tales must have a teller. I am your teller of tales. I have stored up a sequence of tales for our twelve sessions to come. Let's begin."

————One year many years ago—people who like to make rhymes say it was 1492—Lorenzo the Magnificent died, the Spaniards chased the Arabs and Jews out of Spain, and Columbus sailed the ocean blue. Many others before him sailed the ocean blue, or tramped over arctic wastes, or rafted out into southern seas, many that we know about, many we still don't know about. But Columbus's trips were special. In a way he did not think of.

"Do we have a map here, Huggins? No, I can see we don't." St. John dropped her formal tone. "Well, imagine you have in your hand an orange. Take a sharp knife and run it around the orange— thinly, mind you!—and peel it in one piece. Spanish waiters in restaurants and quite a few of their clients, too, were skilled at doing this in one long spiral. Suppose you, too, could peel the whole surface in two or three turns of the orange, and then would flatten the peel out on a table, this table here."

Oliver Huggins looked at the table top where St. John's beringed fingers and short, manicured nails were flattening out an imaginary orange peel, and said nothing.

"You would then have a flat representation of the planet Earth. If you do not want to bother with an orange, just find your old grammar-school variety of a map of the world."

————At this moment, she continued, the continents called America, North and South, stood apart like giant islands, separated by the Atlantic and Pacific oceans from the huge single landmass of Europe, Asia, and Africa. These continents and landmasses had not always floated in the same arrangement. Long before history began they disposed themselves differently, farther away or clinging closer to each other, lying deeper in the seas or higher above.

When Christopher Columbus made his voyages he did not know about the great Pacific Ocean. He thought he could reach the far other side of the great landmass of Europe, Asia, and Africa by crossing the Atlantic Ocean in big ships, as in a curve around an orange, sailing against the sun. He certainly would have done just that, had not there been a huge unexpected land barrier for him to stumble over. The odd thing is that to Columbus and the others who followed, the land and the people they found were a surprise, while to many of the people living there the appearance of men like Columbus was expected.

★ ★

"Am I going too fast for you, Huggins?"

"No, not at all."

"It must be a pretty familiar story. Now I shall begin with the tale of Moctezuma. So, draw up your chair."

"Thank you."

————Moctezuma was the Ninth Speaker of the Mexica, and on this day he was in trouble. "I think I have lost my mind," he said half-aloud to himself. Moctezuma Xocoyotzin, "Sun Burning Through the Clouds," son of Axayacatl the Scourge, had awakened in agitation, his heart pounding, his left arm seemingly paralyzed, the fingers of his right hand making little palsied movements. He looked down at them. In horror he recognized what his fingers were doing—making miniature signs of the cross! He wrenched his left hand over to clamp down on his right hand and straighten those blasphemous wriggling fingers, and brought them to a stop.

To clear his head Moctezuma shook it violently from side to side. He found himself sitting in bed upright. So, he had *not* walked in his sleep. It had just been a nightmare, a terrible nightmare. He shook his head again.

It was nearly the hour of awakening, he thought. He used to feel good in the morning. Now for a long time he had felt dead; he looked on each day with dread. It all began on the day that that fish-runner had come in, and to everyone's shock, asked to see him!, and told his fanciful story.

Moctezuma's eyes moved slowly to follow his servants as they quietly entered the room to dress him, their heads turned away, their eyes glued to the floor. For a few seconds they interrupted his thoughts, but then: Damn that day! Damn the day the Eagle Council had elected him Speaker! Damn the day his brother had died! That brother was the one who should have been chosen Speaker; he, Moctezuma, would have remained what he was raised to be, what he always wanted to be, a high priest spending his days in the House of Magical Studies.

The last day he had spent there was when those fishermen had brought in that bird, that crane, or whatever it was, with a mirror encrusted on its head. They had pulled it from the waters in a fish-net and the priests had put it on a table and tied it by its feet. In

the mirror he had seen a great army marching over a wide plain toward his city. In haste he called in the magicians. Shaking their
long hair and long faces, they saw nothing to confirm the Speaker's
vision.

But they did confirm the other omens: the great flames lighting
up the eastern sky at midnight, the mysterious fires that could not
be put out and burned down the temple towers of the great god
Huitzilopochtli, a bolt of lightning by daylight striking the fire-god's
temple, the evil three-headed comet that darkened the sun, the
churning and overflow of Lake Texcoco, flooding and destroying
houses all around the island-city. What did they mean? Nothing
good, certainly. Who could mistake the portent of the last omen,
that female voice surely belonging to the Snake-Mother, weeping,
"O my children, you are lost. Where shall I hide you?"

Moctezuma, ruler of a hundred cities, of a hundred tribes and
territories, whose troops could and would smash any one of them
at his mere word, shivered. Lately his dreams had turned into nightmares ever more terrifying, with upside-down, oblique, jumbled
pictures, distorted like those of the mushroom-eaters. Had he been
the priest he was cut out to be, surely he would be better prepared
to understand these dreams; just as surely he would not have had
them at all—someone else would have been sitting on the Speaker's
throne. Someone else would have awakened to twitching fingers
that made the sign of the cross.

Tears welled in his eyes. He wanted to howl and beat the palm
of his hand against his mouth, but that would upset the women servants. There they were now, holding vases of warm water ready for
his bath. His cousin Cacama moved alongside. Moctezuma rested a
hand lightly on Cacama's shoulder for support, stepped up on the
low bath platform, and then sat down inside the bath space. The
women poured the water over his shoulders and knees while he absent-
mindedly ran his hands over his body.

Details of the nightmare were coming back to him. He saw himself standing in the great temple by the sacrificial stone. The deep
wooden drums began their booming. A long line of fattened Tlax-
cala captives stood waiting their turn. The priests were moving in
a frenzied tempo. Two of them placed a captive on his back over

the humped stone, holding down his arms and legs. The celebrat-
ing priest raised the blade, held it up a second over the center of
the supine chest, then plunged it in and with a circular twist dug
into the gaping wound to tear out the pumping heart. Before the
shriek of the captive died out he held the smoking heart aloft in his
hand.

It was here that the nightmare went spinning about crazily. As
dark blood splashed the altar stone and the polished floor, slithering
down the temple steps, as the priests danced, waving entrails about
like snakes, as the people chanted to Huitzilopochtli, the great god,
Lover of Hearts and Drinker of Blood—Moctezuma's fingers, in his
nightmare, in time to the chant and the drums, over and over, wildly
made the sign of the cross.

He shivered again. In a flash the key to the dream came to him.
It was that spy, the one who had returned to report that he had
overheard a Tlaxcalan talking, telling about what the newcomer-
gods did as they witnessed a sacrifice.

"What did they do?" Moctezuma was impatient.

"Lord, they made what they call the sign of the cross. With their
right hand they touch their forehead, breastbone, left nipple and
right nipple, one after the other, like this"—he made the sign—
"marking four points of a cross."

"What is so special about this cross?" Moctezuma knew that they
raised crosses and kneeled to them in every city they passed through.
He feigned ignorance in hope of learning more.

"They say, Lord, that the son of their great god was nailed to a
cross, with outstretched arms, and died on it. They say that in the
name of the cross they will always win."

The ruler's interest in magic was aroused. He rubbed his thin
beard. "If the son of their great god died on it, how can it have
great power to win?"

"Lord, they say that the son after death went up to the skies to
join the father."

"I see." Moctezuma paused to think. "Then why do they make
the sign of the cross when watching a sacrifice?"

The spy hesitated, his eyes fixed on the ground. "It is not certain, Lord—"

"Speak up, fool!"

"Lord, the Tlaxcalan who was talking said he thought they made the sign to ward off evil."

"Evil!" The voice that issued from the Speaker's slender frame was like a roar. "Our sacrifices evil? Speak out!"

"Yes, Lord." The spy hung his head in shared shame. "Lord . . . ?" Again the spy wavered before speaking.

"Well?"

"They spoke of the sacrifices also with admiration."

"How is that? Speak up!"

"One of the newcomer-gods was heard to say that our priests could cut out a man's heart quicker than it took to make the sign of the cross."

Moctezuma sat back in his throne. For a moment he said nothing, then motioned to Teuzcleul, his ambassador. "Take him away. But hold him. I might want to talk with him again later."

A pretty woman-servant, her eyes looking at her feet, was holding the royal mantle ready to be draped over him. Wearily he placed himself to let it be dropped on his shoulders, while another servant held the sandals for him to slip on. He ignored the servant waiting to pass the necklace and pendant over the royal head and instead walked slowly to climb the steps leading to the terrace overlooking the city. Sunk in gloom, he spoke to no one.

The sun was rising fast. Moctezuma roused himself and walked back down the stairs. Today was a special day calling for a special dress. Already his lords must be assembled, waiting to dress him in full regalia and accompany him to the meeting place.

How he had hoped the newcomer-gods would not come to this city! He had not known what to make of them when he first heard of their arrival—within hours of their landing on the coast. The runner racing across the mountains to bring sea fish fresh for the royal table was the first with the news. The wretched man's tale, on top of so many omens, had disturbed him. Assembling his ambassadors and chief of intelligence, he pretended not to believe the man's story, and ordered them to investigate it. Later they all returned to report more or less the same things. Those who had spoken with the leader of the newcomer-gods said that he spoke a strange tongue.

"How could you understand him then?" scornfully.

"Lord, the Tabascans gave him a young slave-woman, who is always by his side. She speaks our language like one of us. She translated everything we said to him and everything he said to us."

"A Tabascan slave . . ." Moctezuma turned to his intelligence chief. "Did you try to reach her?"

The man moved a step forward, his gaze fixed on the floor. "Lord, we could not get near her when she was alone. We asked some Cholulans and they said that others had tried to bribe her to deceive him and she reported them immediately to her master."

"Some master," sarcastically, "hiding behind a woman."

"Lord, we learned also that she is his lover and uses his name. We cannot pronounce it the way they do—'Doña Malina.' Her tongue is his: their names are commingled—Malina, Malinche, Malintzin. But the newcomer-warriors call their lord 'Captain,' which means chief."

"Great chief that speaks with a woman's tongue." Then, dropping the sarcasm and wheeling to his chief of intelligence, sharply, "How many soldiers does he have? You should at least know that by now."

"He has about eight hundred fifty to nine hundred newcomer-soldiers." Hurriedly the man added, "Lord, they have hard, shiny swords and lances and body coverings and powerful bow slings, and those thundering fire slings, and the huge brutes that they mount and become like one great animal-soldier."

"I know all that." Moctezuma waved his hand in tired dismissal. "We have one thousand soldiers to every one of them."

The intelligence chief did not move away but stood in place, his eyes cast downward.

"Well?" surprised and annoyed.

"Forgive me, Lord, I have to report that some of my men have heard that he has made a pact with the Tlaxcalans."

"What!" Moctezuma could not suppress a start. "The Tlaxcalans?"

"Yes, Lord, I have heard only rumors so far, but they all tie together too well not to have a basis: thousands of Tlaxcalans are descending the mountains to join Malintzin's forces."

Moctezuma paled. "The Tlaxcalans? To join him?" Rage boiled

up within him. "Those traitors!" he spat. Composing himself, he murmured, "This changes everything."

Afterward he had tried every trick learned in years of warring and ruling. He had sent Malintzin the gold the newcomer-soldiers thought so precious. That just drove them on faster toward his beautiful city. He had arranged to have another tribe ambush and take them captive. Instead they had ambushed the ambushers and gained more allies. How he would have loved to take the brave Malintzin captive! Several times his soldiers had almost caught him, had him in their arms. Oh how the great Huitzilopochtli would have rejoiced to be offered Malintzin's quivering heart! But each time Malintzin's soldiers cut their way through and made away with him.

He, Moctezuma, Ninth Speaker of the Mexica, even offered to be a vassal and pay tribute to the great ruler who Malintzin claimed had sent him—if only the newcomers would stay far away. No, they insisted on coming to meet him personally in the great city.

Here now was his brother, standing at his side, patiently, holding the headdress, ready to place it on the Speaker's head, not the court ceremonial headdress but the royal military one.

His brother. His younger brother. Cuitláhuac. Eighteen years old. He could afford to risk the life of the city. From the start he had opposed the priests and their baleful interpretation of omens, had urged overpowering and capturing the newcomer-gods. He had talked with many survivors of the battles. Now whenever reminded of the power of the newcomers' weapons, he would answer, "They bleed, they die, just like us. Our swords are sharp enough to cut the heads off their deer-mounts. If we refuse to give them battle except in narrow passes, their deer-mounts cannot maneuver or outflank us. They lose their speed and weight. We can topple the men and sit on their armor until we are ready to sacrifice them to Huitzilopochtli."

Cuitláhuac could rise to fiery heights. "We shall flay their faces and make their skin into bearded glove leather; we shall butcher them like meat, roast and eat them with a sauce of peppers and tomatoes; we shall throw their heads and arms and legs into their camp and shout, 'Here, eat the flesh of *these* gods. They are your brothers. We are glutted with them. Stuff yourselves with our leftovers.' "

At each such outburst Moctezuma had looked at him reproach-fully. He loved this brother, and were it not for the priests, he might share his opinion. "Brother," he would soothe, "you know as well as I do about the great god Quetzalcoatl and the great ruler who took his name."

Cuitláhuac would reply with sarcasm. "Quetzalcoatl, Quetzal-coatl, Lover of Butterflies! He is not our great god. Our god is Huitzilopochtli, Lover of Live Hearts and Fresh Blood! Lord and dear brother, you associate too much with priests and wise men."

Moctezuma would then try a less priestly argument. "You re-member when you were young and I told you that the Lord of Texcoco had predicted that our country would be ruled by strangers? You remember that I challenged him to put the predic-tion to the ballgame test and that he beat me? That used to trou-ble you, too."

"Certainly. As a boy it troubled me, as a man it troubles me not a bit. What has happened to you, Lord and brother? You used to be a daring and victorious soldier. Now you seem infected by those wise men, the peace-lovers of the one-god, who turn their backs on war and captives and fresh hearts.

"Or have you been contaminated by the newcomers' god of peace? His heart is made of corn flour and they eat a little piece of him each day. Can you believe it? Such a stupid superstition! They eat their god instead of nourishing him. He is a god of peace, they say, and hates the spilling of blood. They burn their captives alive so that no blood oozes out, and thus he is not offended.

"Wake up, Lord and brother! Your throne and our city are in danger."

No denying Cuitláhuac's eloquence. The other lords in council grew restless whenever he spoke like that. Yet no matter how worked up Cuitláhuac might get, he would always take the Speaker's word as final.

Moctezuma looked first at his brother, then at the military head-dress he was holding ready, and again looked directly into his brother's eyes, to show him he understood the significance of the headgear. He nodded imperceptibly and Cuitláhuac settled the headdress on the Speaker's brow.

Cuitláhuac had not liked the idea of receiving the newcomer-gods in one of Moctezuma's halls. "We can lay a trap for them," he had argued forcefully. "When they come in to meet you, you go forward to meet them on the causeway to Tacuba. Stop at the bridge. We can pull the beams, block their advance or their retreat, and push them in the lake. Their deer-mounts will not be able to run, their armor will sink them in the water, we shall present their hearts to Huitzilopochtli, and be rid of them forever."

The maneuver could still be done and Cuitláhuac knows it, Moctezuma thought. The newcomer-gods would not understand what the headdress meant in any case. Militarily the plan was good, but the mere idea of carrying it out made the Speaker anxious.

Seated in the litter now, he waited while several hundred noblemen and chiefs went ahead to salute the newcomer-gods. Glancing down, he could see the heads of the noblemen carrying on their shoulders the litter that bore him, and alongside them the four noblemen holding aloft the royal canopy. Their eyes fixed on the ground, barefoot, they walked slowly and carefully. Far ahead he could see the plumage of the fore-party of his nobles bobbing up and down in formal homage. The first exchange of greetings was taking place and now the newcomer-gods were advancing toward the three officials preceding his litter with their golden wands.

The newcomer-gods looked just as his couriers and spies had described them. At their head was the bearded deer-god with a plume in his hat. Slightly back of him was a woman on foot, dressed in the style of a southern tribe. She must be the traitorous speaker-lover. They were followed by the party of deer-soldiers, the sun shining on their helmets, shoulders, and chests like bright mirrors. Behind these he could see several hundred men on foot on whom the sun also shone with blinding brilliance. Last of all—Moctezuma could see the plumage of their chiefs in the distance and rage churned up within him—marched an army of Tlaxcalans, traitors who chose to side with the newcomer-gods rather than keep their treaty with him.

The litter and canopy stopped. Moctezuma smoothed out his clothes and stepped down, leaning on his brother and on his cousin who had stepped up to accompany him. Attendants moved ahead, laying down the cotton tapestry to cushion his sandals. Persons of all ranks lined the edges of the causeway, close to the waters of the

lake, some prostrating themselves, all barefoot, their heads averted
or their eyes to the ground. Small boats teeming with people plied
the water along the causeway.

Moctezuma hesitated a moment and then decided to take a few
steps. The advancing newcomers stopped. The plumed deer-god
dismounted, and in the manner of a man walked toward him. So
did a few of the others; the woman, too, at the left side of the leader
whom Moctezuma knew as Malintzin. The woman looked at
Moctezuma. Suddenly she stopped and raised her right hand slightly.
Malintzin stopped. The entire entourage stopped as one man. In a
low voice the woman said something to Malintzin. Moctezuma
cursed under his breath. Of course! She had noticed his war headdress! Now what?

But Malintzin brushed the woman's hand gently aside and moved
ahead slowly. The procession resumed.

Moctezuma forced himself to move forward, his bearers moving
in step to keep him covered with the green-feathered canopy,
Cuitláhuac and Cacama supporting him delicately under the arms.
Just in front of Malintzin he stopped. Malintzin, with outstretched
arms, moved toward him as though to embrace him. Without a
word Cuitláhuac and Cacama laid hands gently on Malintzin's
shoulders to indicate that he should keep back. Puzzlement crossed
Malintzin's face.

Quickly, to prevent offense, the Speaker dropped to his knees,
put his hands to the ground, one atop the other, and as his preceding noblemen had done, licked the hand on top. Arising, he
spoke.

"Greetings, Malintzin, great ruler and highest priest. Greetings
and welcome to your home and your own country. From here you
have gone. To here you have returned."

Malintzin replied in tones and gestures of greeting. The slave-
woman crept forward to translate, but at a wave of his hand at his
side she stepped back.

Moctezuma continued, his head bowed low, his voice strong.
"Our Lord, you must be weary, Malintzin. The journey is tiring
but now you have arrived on the earth, you have come to your city
Tenochtitlán. You have come to sit on your throne, to sit under its
canopy.

"From the records that we have long preserved, that were handed down from our ancestors, we know that no one, neither I nor any other who inhabits this great valley of Anáhuac, is native to it. We are strangers, we come from outer parts."

The Speaker waited as if for breath, and the woman began to translate. When she had finished, Malintzin asked a single question. "Are you Moctezuma?"

"Yes, I am Moctezuma. And you, Malintzin, we know, are the descendant of Our Lord One Reed Quetzalcoatl. The rulers who have gone before me, your vassals, guarded your throne and kept it for your coming. Itzcoatl, Moctezuma the Elder, Axayacatl, Tezoc, and Ahuitzotl ruled for you in this city. Their swords protected and their shields sheltered your people.

"Yes, I am Moctezuma, and you, Malintzin, are the descendant of Our Lord One Reed. Like you he was fair-faced and thick of beard. He built a new capital in the Place of the Reeds. As high priest he worshiped the great god Quetzalcoatl, God of Learning, founder of agriculture and the arts, and adopted his name. He ruled wisely and prosperously, but was persecuted for years by a dark, powerful god and finally forced to flee. He burned his palaces, buried his treasure, and left the Place of the Reeds. He sailed away toward the east aboard a raft made of twined snakes, promising to return to us. It was so long ago that those who stayed behind married women native to the land, had many children, and built towns to live in.

"Our Lord One Reed was named One Reed because he was born in Year One Reed, the year he promised to return, and that is the year in which you, Malintzin, his descendant, have come in your city-ships from the land where the sun rises. Throughout this land you will be recognized, you may command as you wish, you will be obeyed, and all we possess is yours to dispose of."

The Speaker had stopped every now and then to let the woman translate. Now after she had finished he stood there not knowing what to do or say next. This Malintzin is big and strong, he thought. Perhaps the shining clothes he is wearing just make him seem so. His face is not much fairer than mine. Has the weather beaten it darker than the rest of his body? Unconsciously Moctezuma slipped his hands under his mantle to touch and feel his chest and arms, testicles and thighs. I am flesh and bone like everybody else. If anyone touches me, he feels me and I feel him. I die and so does everyone else. Can it be that this newcomer-god is the same? Now that he has dismounted it looks like I am even taller than him. What now? Oh god Quetzalcoatl, tell your servant what to do, tell him what to say.

Moctezuma sensed that his forehead was damp and his head light and that his body was swaying a little. Cuitláhuac and Cacama tightened their support of his shoulders but he shook his head, lowered his eyelids almost to closing, and began to speak again, more slowly, in a monotone.

"Do the Speakers of the past know the destiny of those they have left behind, their descendants? If only they are watching. If only they can see what I see . . ." Moctezuma's voice droned on. "No, it is not a dream. I am not waking in my sleep. Finally I have seen you! I have seen you face to face! I was in agony for five days, for ten days, my eyes fixed on the Region of the Mystery. And now you have come out of the clouds and mists to sit on your throne again. This was foretold by the Speakers who governed your city: From here you have gone, to here you shall return." The Speaker's breath deepened and his voice issued strong again.

"You have come back to us. You have come down from the sky. Take possession of your royal houses! Welcome to your land, my Lords!"

Moctezuma took a step backward. The bearers moved the litter forward and under him. He resumed his seat, glanced sideways at his brother, and fixed his look forward. Slowly his head fell to his chest.

The litter swiveled about-face. Cuitláhuac, head bowed, moved toward Malintzin and placed his hand lightly on the newcomer-god's shoulder, and as his honor-guard, led him over the causeway into the great city of Tenochtitlán.

Claire St. John took breath.

Oliver Huggins hurried to bring her a glass of water. "Ms. St. John, will you continue with Moctezuma tomorrow?"

"I doubt it, Huggins. These are not the Arabian Nights, you know. Anyway, I haven't finished today's session yet. You certainly are impatient for learning. Let me go on."

———As you have grasped by now, Malintzin is Hernán Cortés. The peace was short. Moctezuma was killed trying to placate his people. After ferocious battles full of heroism on both sides, the Captain and his men conquered and tore down this great city. They filled the lakes with debris. A new way of life was to begin in the old land that Cortés called by a fresh name—New Spain.

MEXICO $500

Vcentenario del
ENCUENTRO DE DOS MUNDOS

VALLE-MARTINO   T.I.E.V.   1988

It was a great world of powder and puffs, of warriors and priests gruff and gentle, of beards, bravery, and curses, of ladies and politeness, of the whip and the sword, the cross and the university.

The great god of the tribe that had ruled the land before Cortés appeared was Huitzilopochtli who, nourished on live human hearts, kept coursing through the sky. The tribe itself was the last of the nomad peoples sweeping down from arid highlands of the north into Anáhuac, the central valley to the south. They had come, they said, from a region named Aztlán. After wandering around for decades they had taken up temporary settlement in a barren land infested with poisonous snakes. Undaunted, they had eaten the snakes and hired themselves out as mercenaries to nearby city-states, showing themselves to be valiant, ruthless, thirsty for sacrificial blood, and incorrigible women-stealers. One day, in their ancient memory, their high priest had said, "Our god Huitzilopochtli commands us to call ourselves the Mexica and to leave here and find a place where an eagle will be perched on a mass of human hearts piled up so high and wide as to look like a luxuriant prickly pear cactus." Eventually they found this place—the eagle was there, perched with his wings outstretched toward the sun—on an island in a lake in the valley, and there they founded the beautiful city that awaited Cortés—Tenochtitlán or "the Place of the Cactus."

Hundreds of years later, after hundreds of plots and uprisings, the people here broke the rule of Spain and took back the name that Huitzilopochtli had given them—the Mexica. They were now Mexicans and their new old country was Mexico.

"That is that for today. Does all this sound exotic to you, Huggins?"

"It does seem—" Huggins started to say.

"Yes?"

"Well, it does not sound like American history to me."

"Of course not. And why should it sound like it when you've been taught to think differently? Remember it all happened just as two continents were being named America. Still, if not American history, what would you call it?"

"I don't know . . . I need time to think it over." Huggins looked down at St. John's silken ankles. "No, wait . . . I would call it pre-American history, I think."

"Good enough, Huggins. Let's go ahead this week and see how much more of American history is pre-American," and with that Claire St. John walked briskly out the door.

2

THOMAS JEFFERSON FOOLS

WITH A FOOLISH KING

TUESDAY

"Good afternoon, Ms. St. John."

"Good afternoon. What have you got there?"

Huggins looked down at his right hand. "Oh, just some mail I picked up from the mailbox."

"Not a notebook there, is there?"

"What?" Huggins felt his face flush. "No, there isn't." Had she seen him turn on the recorder?

"I was sure you grasped that I'd rather you not pen notes. Our subject is difficult enough and there are some stiffish fences to take. I want you to understand what I have to say as I am saying it. When I come in and say, 'Good afternoon,' I shouldn't care to watch you write it down in a notebook."

Huggins, relieved, permitted himself a smile. "Of course."

"For the same reason, I'm not assigning study nor asking you to bring any materials to tutorial. Any materials to read or quote from, I'll bring here myself." Claire St. John patted her calfskin envelope emphatically and opened it, drawing out a sheaf of papers.

"Yes," said Oliver Huggins.

"Do sit down." She sat down herself, crossing long, bare legs. "This story has been told to me many times in many ways."

————Once there were thirteen children who lived next door to each other but were separated from their mother by an ocean. As is customary for children of one family, they all had different names, like Carolina, Maryland, and New York. Some got their name from a mother, like Virginia, or from a father, like Georgia; some from the one who brought them up, like Pennsylvania from William Penn; some from whoever had lately snatched or first governed them, like New York from the duke of York, and Delaware from Thomas West, Baron De La Warr.

They called the peoples who lived there before them by the overall name of Indians or redskins. The Indians had their own names according to their different tribes, like the Mohawk, Mohican, and Narragansett. By and large the name of a tribe signified the same thing: the people. They were called redskins because their skin seemed to have more of a bronze tint to it than did the skin of the thirteen children. In return, the redskins called them palefaces, although many palefaces had rosier faces than the redskins. The palefaces spoke of themselves proudly as white men. (Their not-so-remote ancestors had painted their faces blue.)

Why the natives were called Indians is another matter, and curious. The first palefaces to arrive on their shores were sailing toward a land called the Indies. Naturally, when they sighted land, they mistook it for the Indies (a place much farther west) and so they called the inhabitants Indians. After a while it became clear that these shores were not the Indies and that the redskins had sprung from natives of another continent who called themselves the black-haired people. The Chinese, a black-haired people, when fighting the British in the Opium War of 1839, called them the "red-faced barbarians."

Some tribes, like the Mexica, as you've heard, told stories about the former presence and future return of white supermen, but most were much surprised to see such men. Some were pleased, some were fearful and angry. All were dumbfounded at first by the white man's tools and weapons, but quickly learned to use these tools themselves and then no longer regarded the whites as superior. Even so, sooner or later, the natives were conquered by palefaces from Europe. Spain, the Netherlands, Portugal, Sweden, England, and France became mother countries of colonies and settlements. The grandest mother of all was Spain, who dominated most of the great expanses the natives lived in.

The natives themselves did not have a name for these vast territories, and had little idea of their extent. They had names only for the territory that embraced their hunting and warring, fishing and farming life. The whites, however, having arrived in great island-boats, could sail around and in time get some idea of the expanse.

They sketched first a huge mass of land to the south of where the first navigator, Christopher Columbus, had landed. When reports of this vast zone got back to Europe, map-makers were greatly confused. Here was an enormous landmass not to be found anywhere. They didn't know how to label it in the new maps they were preparing. Another explorer, Amerigo Vespucci, was not only a skillful navigator but an accomplished letter-writer. His letters circulated throughout Europe and convinced map-makers that he was the most important explorer of the great expanse. One of them, Martin Waldseemüller, took this man's first name and made it into its feminine counterpart. On the face of his newest map, across the newly traced area, he wrote "America." He explained the novelty thus:

"Now truly these parts [Europe, Africa, and Asia] have been more widely explored. Another, fourth part has been discovered by Americus Vespucius . . . and I do not see why anyone should rightly forbid naming it Amerige—land of Americas, as it were, after its discoverer Americus, a man of acute genius—or America, since both Europe and Asia have received their names from women."

At the time, mostly the southern coasts had been sketched. So, the first to be named America was the *southern* half, which we now call America of the South or South America. A few years later, after Amerigo and two or three other Italian navigators in the service of England and France had charted enough of the northern coasts to show that there was another whole landmass to the north, mapmakers divided the name America into two and spliced it on their maps in this way: "AME" for the southern continent, "RICA" for the northern.

St. John placed her hands together flat on the table and drew them slowly, slightly apart. Then lifting them away, she scribbled an imaginary "AME" on the table over where her left hand had rested and a "RICA" where her right hand had rested.

Huggins looked with wonder at this parting of the continents.

St. John resumed her discourse.

————Later, prospective settlers, as they sailed from English and Dutch ports, did not think that they were bound for "the Americas" or "North America" or "America," but for more specific and attractive places, in particular Virginia and New England. Virginia was the first name that the English bestowed on the continent. Sir Walter Raleigh's report to Queen Elizabeth of his company's explorations contained a description of a sweet-smelling land across the Atlantic and gave a spelling of its name and that of the Indian chief's. The sound of these names and the thought of that territory lying far away, untouched and unpossessed, may have prompted the Virgin Queen's decree. "The King is called Wingina, the country Wingandacao, and now by her Majesty, Virginia"—virgin-land.

New England was named by the intrepid captain John Smith, who had drawn a map and published it together with a description of the territory in 1616. The Pilgrim immigrants used it to find their way in the wilderness. King James soon confirmed the name in the charter granting the land: "The same shall be called by the name New England in America." Thus he might hope to keep New Spain, New France, and New Netherlands at bay.

Eventually the English settlements grew into thirteen colonies. The inhabitants though subjects of the British monarch were not all Englishmen, and even those who spoke English or a form thereof were not all lovers of the Crown. Among the nonlovers were the Ulster Scots or the Scotch-Irish (as they began to be called here late in the seventeenth century) who made up the largest band of recent immigrants and whose politics was so lively in the back settlements that an English Virginian dubbed them the "Mac-ocracy."

Though they fought sometimes among themselves as children will do, the thirteen got along fairly well as a family whose parents protected them, treated them about as well and in some ways better than the children living at home. Part of this good treatment should be called neglect: their parents never provided schools or libraries or founded a university for them, as did Spanish parents to the south. After a while, the colonists, left to manage their affairs more or less as they pleased, began to get too big for their britches. From the 1740s to the 1760s while Britain struggled in wars, principally with Spain and France, some of the colonists, mostly New Englanders, took to illicit trading in the Caribbean islands with any and all foreign powers, including Britain's enemies. For every colonist engaged in fighting against the French in North America there was another trading with the French in the Caribbean.

Trouble bubbled higher as Britain tried to stop this trading and smuggling and then to get the colonists to contribute part of their gains to the family budget. The colonists took offense. Yet the sums levied hardly covered the cost of the motherland's protection of her children's trade on the high seas. They knew this of course, but were young and high-spirited. They continued to protest, making it seem as if what they objected to was their not having representation in London so as to vote on their fair share of family expenses. To be honest, they did not want to do this either, because they surely would have had to pitch in a lot more money once their brothers back home sat down with them and tallied up how much the thirteen children in America were getting away with. The colonies were too clever by half not to know that by depending on England for their military and naval defense and for other benefits as well, they were getting a bargain.

A Scotsman, Adam Smith by name, one of the most intelligent professors you would be lucky to find—

"I've heard of him!" broke in Huggins. "The economist . . ."

"No doubt you have," said St. John dryly. "Adam Smith, then, the very one who showed how many bored men, women, and children could work on the head of a pin, was also good at political science."

Finding this remark over his head, Huggins relapsed into silence. His tutor went on.

————Adam Smith reckoned that the mother country was fast losing money protecting this far-flung home of her children and that the most she, "the best of all mother-countries," was getting out of the deal was pride in family growth. It would be "mortifying to pride," he said, to let the thirteen colonies go; yet to do so might revive "parental affection on the one side and filial respect on the other."

A few of the colonies (Massachusetts in the lead) with the wind up their tail began to think that if they but twisted and kicked hard and fast enough they might unseat the rider. Using taxes as an excuse, they began in 1760 a decade and a half of protest, resistance, and terrorism that forced the British population in North America to take sides. The affair of the *Gaspee* illustrates the swift, irregular violence rebel elements handed out British regular forces whenever the occasion presented itself.

In the early summer of 1772, a British revenue cutter, the *Gaspee*, patrolling to prevent smuggling (smuggling had become a matter of pride for the rebels), chased a packet leaving Newport only to run aground in Narragansett Bay. That evening a drummer marched down Main Street in Providence beating out the news. Immediately, figuring that the tide would not refloat the schooner until about three in the morning, a group of men under the leadership of a resident merchant determined to destroy it. A young Rhode Islander, Ephraim Bowen, picked up his father's gun, powder horn, and bullets—the colonists all had guns and loved to cast bullets in the kitchen—and joined the gang.

In longboats with muffled oars they pulled alongside the vessel. A sentinel aboard hailed repeatedly, "Who comes there?" The raiders kept silent. The captain of the cutter, a Lieutenant Duddington, mounted the starboard gunwale in his shirt and cried out, "Who goes there?" When he hailed again, a Captain Whipple, the steersman of the longboat in which Ephraim was seated, shouted,

"I am the sheriff of the country of Kent, God damn you! I have got a warrant to apprehend you, God damn you! So surrender, God damn you!" During this edifying exchange, a man standing up to the right of Ephraim in the boat said, "Eph, reach me your gun and I can kill that fellow." Eph gave him the gun; he took aim, fired, and as Duddington fell exclaimed, "I have killed the rascal." So much for the rules of warfare.

The raiders then boarded the *Gaspee* without opposition, beat up the crew, set them on land and the schooner on fire, and dissolved into the night. The ship burned to the water's edge. Examination of Lieutenant Duddington's wound showed that the ball had hit him five inches below the navel.

The destruction of the *Gaspee* illustrates an unplanned kind of illegal violence. The participating "mobs" were often led and joined by men of substance. The planned and staged variety of threats and violence was the specialty of Sam Adams. He concentrated on the Massachusetts area. The news generated by his prodigious efforts spread throughout the colonies. It traveled by word of mouth, broadsheets, and the committees of correspondence and undercover resistance that Adams sponsored to keep sympathizers active, informed, and inflamed.

St. John stopped to sip from the glass of water Huggins had placed on the table earlier. "There were two grand, rebel incendiaries," she said. "Tom Paine the pamphleteer, whom we shall soon encounter as he makes his debut in the breakaway year of 1776, and Sam Adams the agitator, who began his work in 1760. Let me tell you a bit more about Sam Adams, Huggins. His role is not always fully appreciated."

————He was nearly middle-aged, poor, and in Boston when he began his seditious or patriotic activities. He organized gangs of waterfront thugs, eye-gougers, boot-stompers, and brawny Liberty Boys and put them on call. They provided the volatile mob element whenever shouts of "Kill the lobsterbacks" came in handy as a start, whenever a simple argument, brawl, or accident could be escalated into bloodshed and death. He then luridly described the dead and wounded—in broadsheets bordered with rows of coffins—as Patriot Martyrs and examples of George III's TYRANNY.

He devoted the whole of his middle age to overthrowing England in the colonies and in Canada, and stopped at nothing to succeed—at neither lies, violence, nor betrayal of faith. Wherever there was dirty work to be conceived and carried out, Sam Adams was Johnny-on-the-spot. There is hardly a mythic incident in history books, poetry, and songs of the period in which he did not play the behind-the-scene instigator and exploiter. You name it—the Boston Massacre, the Boston Tea Party, the Midnight Ride of Paul Revere, the Battles of Lexington and Concord. Almost single-handedly he managed to split the population into Patriots and Loyalists. Once his subversive tactics gained momentum, the colonists were polarized, without middle ground.

"Ms. St. John?"

"Yes, Huggins."

"What makes a man like Sam Adams tick?"

"I'm sure I don't know. He was a product of Harvard theology, he ran his father's brewery into bankruptcy, he was afflicted with palsy. Do these facts help?"

"Hmm . . ." said Huggins.

————"A tactic of terror"—that was the phrase John Adams, a young Massachusetts lawyer with a future, wrote in his diary to describe the hanging in effigy of a tax informer. The gallows rose twenty feet in front of a Maryland courthouse. (The lawyer was a distant and comfortably-off relative of Sam Adams.) Hangings in effigy, the forced swearing of oaths, lynchings, shootings, burnings, pilloryings, stabbings, confiscations, tar-and-featherings became the day's currency. And if you calculate that about one third of the population remained loyal to England, the "Tories" as opposed to the "Whigs," you can get an idea of the counterviolence that followed. New Jersey alone raised six Tory battalions. The War of Independence was not merely a rebellion, it was also a domestic war. Many great families splintered: Adams, Otis, Randolph, Lee, Washington, Rutledge, Jefferson, and Franklin.

Consider Benjamin Franklin's story. Born in Boston, the youngest son of a candle- and soap-maker's family, he was a well-known printer and journalist, a self-taught freethinker who, on moving to Philadelphia—Boston was too parochial for his tastes—threw his practical mind, roving intelligence, and excellent pen into colonial politics. He founded the Leather Apron Club and the American Philosophical Society. He, too, was a man with an assured future and the best sense of humor on the continent. People called him Doctor Franklin for his several honorary degrees. His experiments with electricity were ingenious and spectacular. His grandson was nicknamed "Lightning Rod Junior." To get to the point, Benjamin's son William, a bastard brought up in Franklin's own house, growing up tall and handsome, was appointed Royal Governor of New Jersey (then the Jerseys, East and West), the last of such governors in the colonies. Sadly for his father, William remained a loyalist, and an embittered one: when imprisoned for two years, his rebel captors would not let him visit his dying wife. Freed in a prisoner exchange, he joined the British army and became the brain behind Tory raids and a network of informers. Late in his father's life the two were reconciled, but just barely.

"You know, Huggins"—St. John got up from her chair and began pacing to and fro in an attitude of thought, not looking at him—"it's odd that no great American novel has appeared to dramatize the struggle between separatists and loyalists. I should have thought that a heartbreaking love story of two colonists . . . Say a girl whose parents are rebels, and a boy with loyalist parents, fall in love. You can set the story in New Jersey where Tory strength was strong."

From lowered eyelids Huggins observed the swish of St. John's skirt and its cause in the sway of her hips.

"Yes, a boy and girl . . ." St. John seemed caught up in a flight of fancy. "Tom and Becky, nonpolitical and in love. Tom's Tory parents flee the town in fear, dragging their lovesick son with them. Living now among people fighting to save their colony from radicals who have taken over, Tom joins a rough-riding band of Tory raiders. Becky, left with her parents and drawn into the enthusiasm for liberty and for death to tyrants becomes a water-and-cider girl in a rebel camp, a musket slung over her back.

"The camp gets word of a Tory raid to be led that night by the fearsome 'Colonel Tye,' a black leader of marauding parties, composed of both blacks and whites (among whom, Tom) fighting the rebels.

("Tens of thousands of blacks, Huggins," she explained, "had gone over to the British, relying more on the British promise of emancipation than on the rebel declaration that all men are created equal. Some reached Nova Scotia and England; some falling into the wrong hands were sold in the West Indies for rum, sugar, coffee, and fruit; most—tens of thousands relocated in English camps—died of camp fever and smallpox.)

"Just before news of the impending raid, Becky realizes that the odd feelings and slight belly bulge she'd been noticing all point to pregnancy. What to do tonight if her lover is in the attacking party (as indeed he will be) and in the dark and bloody skirmish is about to shoot her? Should she let herself be shot? Or should she, if she can, shoot him and save her child, and his?

"Or what if . . . ?" St. John stopped pacing, drew a deep breath, and went into a . . . well, into an act! She seemed to be playing a scriptwriter describing a scene to the film director, posturing excitedly and projecting her voice:

> Blood RED of GUNFIRE and burning encampment streaks the BLACK night.
> PULL BACK to show a MAN with a rifle moving cautiously on a stretch of field. PULL BACK more.
> WIDER: Ahead A WOMAN, pregnant, moving slowly in his direction, head down, burdened with a wooden bucket in each hand. They see each other, stop and stare. He shouts.
> TOM: Becky!
> He throws down his gun and rushes forward to embrace her. She—

St. John drew out of her trance, stopped posturing, and flopped back in the chair, looking exhausted. "Well, there you are, Huggins. What about it? Maybe not a great novel but at least a screen-play in embryo. Would you like to write it?"

The coup de théâtre left Huggins speechless. Where did she pick up such stuff?

"Would you like to write it?" pursued St. John.

"Sounds good to me," said Huggins, wishing she had proposed their writing it together.

"You could make it the start of a career. 'Young screenwriter takes Hollywood by storm.'" Still seated, St. John raised her arms to block the headline out in the air, using her hands as brackets.

Huggins didn't know what to say. Maybe he could be the pro-ducer, maybe he could coax his pa to kick it off with seed money and he, Oliver, could pick it up from there . . . Some of Pa's friends . . . He glanced at the photograph of his father among the others on the little table.

St. John was looking at him seriously. Was she pulling his leg?

Huggins pulled himself together. "There was a great love story and film about the Civil War," he managed, brightening at the thought.

"That's right! *Gone with the Wind*. But that war is some seventy-five years ahead."

St. John rose from the sofa lazily, moved back to the slatted chair she preferred, and picked up her larger story.

—The colonies, imitating one another, began to form assemblies and other governing bodies in violation of British law. Massachu-setts called for a single-purpose meeting of the colonies to discuss the stamp tax Parliament had put on legal and commercial paper, on newspapers, pamphlets, cards, and dice. Nine colonies sent del-egates and formed the Stamp Act Congress in 1765. The first General Congress, customarily called "Continental" to distinguish it from the local congresses sprouting up, met in September of 1774, the second in May of 1775.

You may ask, How could the Congresses be called "Continen-tal" when they represented little more than a two-hundred-mile strip of colonies along the Atlantic coast of North America, noth-ing to compare in size with the "continental" holdings of New Spain?

The colonies did not compare themselves to others on the continent. They compared themselves (living on a continent) to England (a petty island). England, said Benjamin Franklin, "compared to America, is but like a stepping-stone in a brook, scarce enough of it above water to keep one's shoes dry." The colonists were mainly English subjects living not in the motherland of England but on the continent of North America. In addressing English-speaking audiences the word *North* could be left out unless one wished to approach the Canadians or one needed an extra syllable or accent in versifying, as in "ready for the fray/for North Americay."

The word *continental* made headway. The first Congress passed a resolution not to import, consume, or export British goods. To enforce the bill it nominated a "Continental Association." Composed of local committees, town meetings, and county conventions, following the example of Sam Adams's musclemen in Massachusetts, they represented themselves as *the people* of the colonies, devoted to watching everybody else for violations of the rules. Whenever they found enemies of the people, they forced them by threats and assorted violence to recant, sign confessions of guilt (for sins like drinking English tea), and to swear oaths of attachment to "the people." During the war the troops the Congress raised were called "Continentals" and the paper money the Congress paid them with was called "continental" and was, the soldiers complained, not worth a continental.

Continental grew in use also because many canny speculators and new immigrants had an eye peeled for lands to the west. But more on that score in a day or two.

Almost from the start the English referred to the North American continent and their colonies there as British America, or America, for short. At the end of the sixteenth century the poet "Jack" Donne, future Dean of St. Paul's, sang of "His Mistress Going to Bed."

> *License my roving hands, and let them go,*
> *Before, behind, between, above, below.*
> *O my America! my new-found land,*
> *My kingdome, safeliest when with one man man'd.*

In his mistress's body the poet explores new land, comparable in "beautious state" to his country's new-found land, North America.

John Locke, the philosopher, in the late seventeenth century, wrote that "in the beginning all the world was America." He wished to evoke the primitive, the prepolitical, stage of life, and recall the wilderness, the camps and huddles of the North American tribes he had heard of, not the great, beautiful cities and urban civilizations of the Mexica, the Mayans, the Incas. America was that part of North America that was not part of New Spain or New France. Thus Tom Paine in the late eighteenth century indicated on the title page that his English language pamphlet "*Common Sense* [was] addressed to the inhabitants of America."

When the delegates of the opening Congress assembled in Philadelphia, the convention town of the day, on September 5, 1774, they had a good time, in spite of the heat, humidity, and black flies. They numbered some fifty or sixty, nearly half of them lawyers. Many knew each other only by reputation. As they arrived in the city from the various colonies, they would be welcomed and whisked away by gentlemen of large fortunes, Pennsylvanians mostly, some of them delegates themselves, and treated to the best the colony had to enjoy in the way of grand houses and plantations, conversation, blooded horses, charming ladies, gossip, food, and wine. Before and in between business sessions at Carpenters' Hall, some, dusty and fatigued, repaired to the tavern, others in the evening freshened up, dined elegantly at the home of Mr. So-and-So, a local lawyer, or breakfasted the next day with the local minister. Sam Adams was there with a new suit and money in his pocket subscribed to by Boston patriots. Some, like John Dickinson, the self-styled Pennsylvania farmer, came with coaches and fine horses, some with wives and daughters. George Washington (a rich Virginia planter renowned for his exploits in the French and Indian War) was the only one to show up in uniform, that of a Virginia colonel, with dangling sword bumping into everything. A Mr. What's-His-Name reported that earlier at the Virginia convention Washington had boasted, "I will raise one thousand men, subsist them at my own expense, and march myself at their head for the relief of Boston." Someone else, a gentleman widely known for his malicious tongue (I name no names), whispered to a companion that the colonel's wife must be very much a patriot too, as he seemed to be making rather free with her money.

Virginians were much in evidence. Some, after an early evening of reading newspapers and letters or of snacking on dried smoked sprats and punch, supped elegantly at the house of friends, drinking Burgundy and getting tipsy. Toasts abounded. The pamphleteer Tom Paine gave them, "May the collision of British flint and American steel produce that spark of liberty which shall illumine the latest posterity," a rather uninspired toast for so deft a phrasemaker. Others drank to "Wisdom to Britain and firmness to the Colonies: May Britain be wise, and America free," to "Union of Britain and the Colonies on a constitutional foundation," to "Union of the Colonies," "May Congress fulfill the expectations of the people," "The Colonies, one for all and all for one," and similar sentiments. Amid the huzzahs, the standings-up and sittings-down, no one remembered who gave the last sentiment—"To a Free Britain and a Free America." Most say it was some Virginia colonel or other. It brought forth a holler and general agreement that topped the evening and signaled time for bed. Whooping it up the night before never kept Congressmen from getting down to work the next day.

The second Congress, meeting in 1775, fired the opening salvo: a Declaration of the Causes of Taking Up Arms. The ones who had taken up arms were mainly Massachusetts men, on stages set by Sam Adams, at Lexington Green and Concord Bridge. The Declaration was an attempt at an excuse, to wit, self-defense. England did not wait for excuses. On news of rising hostilities in America, George III proclaimed a state of rebellion and sedition in the colonies.

Now came Tom Paine's moment. A self-taught Englishman, one-time corset-maker, sailor, teacher, low-grade crown servant, tobacconist, and grocer, he had emigrated from England in 1774 at age thirty-four. No one knew that in his traveling cases were pen and vitriol.

With the backing of Franklin, Paine had taken part in politics. It was January 1776. His pamphlet *Common Sense*, published in Philadelphia anonymously, swept the colonies off their feet. It claimed an American "continent" and "this new world" without an England. It reviled monarchy and "the Royal Brute" of Great Britain. "Europe not England is the parent-country of America. . . . Not one-third of the inhabitants even of this province [Pennsylvania] are of English descent. Wherefore I reprobate the phrase of parent- or mother-country applied to England only, as being false, selfish, narrow, and ungenerous."

Tom Paine didn't like the idea that the colonies were still children of the motherland. She was a bad mother; the colonies had drunk enough of her milk. They were grown-ups now and ready for meat, and by implication old enough themselves to suckle colonies, or indeed a whole continent. Wherever your eye alights on a page of this pamphlet, you can appreciate and sometimes smile at the rhetoric. "Can ye give to prostitution its former innocence? Neither can ye reconcile Britain and America." Or "As well can the lover forgive the ravisher of his mistress as the continent forgive the murders of Britain."

Common Sense sold hundreds of thousands of copies. Congress now agreed: it was time to burst the bands which connect. The Virginia convention had instructed Richard Henry Lee to submit to Congress a proposal for independence. On June 7, 1776, Lee stood up, tall and straight (as most patrician Virginians did when about to make a speech), and proposed a concise, three-pronged resolution.

As Huggins was to learn, from her portfolio his tutor usually extracted papers consisting of quotations. Now she had selected one sheet. "It went like this," she said, and read out loud:

> Resolved, That these United Colonies are, and of right ought to be, free and independent states, that they are absolved from all allegiance to the British Crown, and that all political connection between them and the State of Great Britain is, and ought to be, totally dissolved.
> That it is expedient forthwith to take the most effectual measures for forming foreign Alliances.
> That a plan of confederation be prepared and transmitted to the respective Colonies for their consideration and approbation.

Putting back the paper, St. John looked up and resumed discourse.

★ ★

————In deliberating, the Congress decided that something more was needed than these three clear and simple resolves, something more like a formal declaration to be broadcast to mankind. It appointed a five-man committee to compose such a statement. The committee included John Adams, Benjamin Franklin, and Thomas Jefferson. Jefferson said to Adams, "You ought to write it." Adams said, "I will not. You can write ten times better than I can." (Fifty years later both men, to their gratification, were to die on the anniversary of the Fourth of July.)

For such extravagant praise Adams did not have much evidence. Only once before had Jefferson written a long political piece by himself, at the time of the so-called Boston Tea Party when a group of Boston palefaces, Sam Adams's strapping Liberty Boys, colored and dressed as redskins and blacks, boarded three British ships and threw their tea cargo into Boston Bay. Exhilarated by the news, Jefferson, a new, young member of the Virginia legislature, took it upon himself to write *A Summary View of the Rights of British-America.* "Let not the name of George the Third be a blot in the pages of history," he wrote, and added a veiled threat, "Should the people take upon them to lay the throne of your majesty prostrate . . ."

This piece circulated first in Virginia, then in the other colonies, then in England, where some regarded it as treasonable. It established Jefferson's reputation for felicity of expression. Of more recent evidence had been the Virginian's work in Congress. Though not a speech-maker or debater—his voice from the platform was hard to hear—he was an excellent committeeman, serving on thirty-four committees between 1775 and 1776 and helping to write or rewrite major reports and resolutions including the one on taking up arms.

Thomas Jefferson was sandy-haired and good-looking, Welsh-Scotch through his father, English through his mother, six feet two, with deep-set eyes, a narrow long nose a bit pulled forward at the tip, a sensitive mouth. Complexion? "A red-faced barbarian" the Chinese, the black-haired people of the Middle Kingdom, would have called him. The color was freckled and reddish, true; the "barbarian" would have been false. Jefferson was the finest product of

Virginia plantation culture, a lover of the good things of this world—wine, olive oil, good cooking, panoramas, books, ideas, horses, women, dancing, singing, and playing the violin, solo or with the harpsichord. His taste in composers was impeccable—Purcell, Handel, Boccherini, Haydn. He fell in love with his wife-to-be over the keyboard of a harpsichord.

Jefferson's earliest memory was of being handed up and carried on a pillow by a mounted slave (who must have somehow become a reliable horseman). He dressed in the careless way and sometimes stood and walked in the careless slouch that befits a man to the manor born who all the same does not want to lose the common touch he never had. He did not mind getting his hands soiled by selecting seeds and plants or by tinkering with time-, space-, and energy-saving gadgets like the handy lazy Susan turntable. At home and outdoors in Virginia he would go about singing Scottish and Italian airs. If ever there was a man to enjoy leisure, it was Tall Tom. Everything in creation interested him. In his tastes more continental (European) than insular (English), he could read four or five languages, if you count Greek and Latin. He was the first to wear the French long pants.

Unfortunately, there lurked in him a chronic, visible itch for politics. When he gave way to it, his character sometimes lost its equable norm. Orderly in his habits, meticulous in his accounts, never stingy, he could not earn money, he could only spend it. It is surprising that he campaigned so hard in Virginia to abolish primogeniture wherein the legal right of inheritance belongs to the first son. Without the lion's share of his father's legacy going to himself, the favorite and eldest son, how would he have come to own the land that gave him the leisure to develop mind and taste? His short-lived law practice, though full, rarely broke even. Likewise his plantation. A Virginia estate, he wrote in a latter-day reflection, "managed rigorously well yields a comfortable subsistence to its owner living on it, but nothing more. But it runs him in debt . . . if he is absent, if he is unskillful as I am . . ." He died poor, humiliatingly poor, even poorer than he thought. Congress did nothing to tide him over.

Yet in Monticello, the home he built, he left a monument of what a villa in America might be and of what a gifted amateur in architecture could do with the help of slave labor and of great models like Hadrian (the Roman emperor who designed the Pantheon) and Palladio (the Vicentine architect who designed the Villa Rotonda). His sketches and the University of Virginia bear further testimony to architectural talent.

Except for rare periods of fierce headaches and for the sprains and contusions of falls from spirited horses, Jefferson was hale and hearty all his life. He was an early riser: the sun, he said during his last illness, had not caught him in bed for fifty years. I have noted he was no orator (unlike most other good people of Virginia). He was instead a voracious reader and a prodigious writer.

As a political thinker Jefferson was pretty good: his idea of yeoman farmers forming the backbone of a small republic is appealing. His lack of social, ethnic, and religious prejudice was most unusual and his frankness on the subject admirable. He had studied at William and Mary College and knew the classics. When he tried to assimilate the more high-flown ideas of the high-flown thinkers then in fashion, they got in the way of his prose. He didn't take time to digest. Once the troubles with England began, almost all the colonial luminaries of the day, especially the lawyers, took to cramming up on late seventeenth- and eighteenth-century English, Scottish, Swiss, and French thinkers, good and not so good, Thomas Jefferson reading more than most others; when it came to knowledge from books, no one could catch him napping.

Jefferson's writing style, unlike, say, John Adams's, did not allow for much versatility. To my mind, it was a bit stiff. Congress wanted to publish something with punch. Caught in the public excitement and the mood of Congress, Jefferson had to draft in two weeks something that would, he later confided, instruct mankind, command its assent, and justify the independent stand of the colonies before the tribunal of the world. He tried to do just that.

He divided the draft into four parts: a statement first of pertinent political ideas; second, of grievances committed by England; third, of colonial sufferance of these grievances; and last, a statement of the declaratory act. The outline was perfectly sound. Putting into lengthy prose the required indignation, however, skewed the proportions of the document, marring its nobility and force.

Actually, as far as declaring independence was concerned, Richard

Henry Lee's resolution, approved by Congress two days earlier, had done the job. Yet Congress wanted more: Jefferson obediently started with phrases conveying the universality of the conflict—"the Course of human Events," "Powers of the Earth," "Laws," "Nature," "God," and "Mankind." In the second paragraph he cast three or four sentences that his committee helped make smooth and rhythmical. I'll read the familiar lines.

> We hold these Truths to be self-evident, that all Men are created equal, that they are endowed by their Creator with certain unalienable Rights, that among these are Life, Liberty, and the Pursuit of Happiness—That to secure these Rights, Governments are instituted among Men, deriving their just Powers from the Consent of the Governed, that, whenever any Form of Government becomes destructive of these Ends, it is the Right of the People to alter or to abolish it and to institute new Government. . . .

Although Jefferson thought he had put the subject "plain and firm," some argue that from the start it remained unclear. Mouthfuls like "the Laws of Nature and of Nature's God," or "unalienable Rights" must have left the greater part of mankind in a fog, and to declare these truths to be "self-evident" and to hold that "all Men are created equal" when a large number of the delegates from the North as well as from the South, including the principal author, were slaveholders or slave-traders must have turned the fog into pea soup.

Take another perspective, "We hold these Truths to be self-evident: that all Men are created equal." "We hold" here means "We representatives assert." By "self-evident" the committee, if it was following Locke, meant—as my friend the philosopher Morton White points out—as evident as $1 + 1 = 2$. If that was the case, all that needed saying was: We representatives assert these truths to be as evident as $1 + 1 = 2$.

Jefferson may not have chosen the word *self-evident*. It may have been suggested by Franklin. Nonetheless, both the original draft, which said "sacred and undeniable," and the amendment, which said "self-evident," are in the Virginian's hand. The change does shift the ground of argument. The fact remains that Parliament and

George III would deny these truths to be either sacred and undeniable or self-evident, indeed would deny they were "truths."

Besides, is it as true as $1 + 1 = 2$ to say that "all Men are created equal"? Maybe he meant, "equal to Englishmen." There are so many ways in which men may be created equal or unequal. Who over the span of history has made sense of it? Fifty years later Jefferson himself explained the "palpable truth" by writing that "the mass of mankind has not been born with saddles on their backs, nor a favored few booted and spurred, ready to ride them." Put this way, in the horse culture of the times, the phrase might have better conveyed what he meant by equality. Equality is a marshmallow like Liberty: sometimes it is better not to say precisely what you mean, even if you happen to know what you mean.

These several fluid lines do contain snippets from the republican sentiments of the writers already mentioned and from a source often overlooked—the Levellers, the soldier orators and pamphleteers of Cromwell's army, and are much indebted to common law of the prior century. John Adams said that "there is not an idea in [the Declaration of Independence], but what had been hackneyed in Congress for two years before." Richard H. Lee charged the Declaration was copied from Locke's treatise on government.

Yet many persons believe that the political ideas of the colonial drafters are unique or came from nowhere or out of the bottle of a genie. Others hold that these ideas came mainly from one particular source, usually John Locke. I don't want to weigh things down with a heavy cast of characters. Briefly, these ideas begin with the ancients, chiefly the Romans; skip the Middle Ages; jump to Renaissance Florence, Venice, and the Netherlands; and march on to France and Great Britain in the mid-sixteen and seventeen hundreds. Long after he wrote his draft, Jefferson himself summed up by saying that he had sought neither to express original ideas nor to copy any particular one of those authors he had read, and added: "All the [Declaration's] authority rests then on the harmonizing sentiments of the day, whether expressed in conversation, in letters, printed essays, or in the elementary books of public right, as Aristotle, Cicero, Locke, Sidney, etc."

No doubt the members of Parliament, the prime minister, and his cabinet could understand the abstract, half-legal, half-philosophical jargon of the Declaration, but they were not mankind. Above all, the British monarch could understand that jargon, and resent as well its personal allusions. The second part of the Declaration leveled a series of gratuitous insults at George III as villain of the piece. Thomas Jefferson, having laid a philosophical basis for the right and duty of rebellion, then shifted toward a particularly strong right and duty against tyrants and devoted by far the longest section to turning "the present King of Great Britain" into a tyrant.

Taking as model the English Bill of Rights of 1689 (from which other colonial papers had borrowed, too), Jefferson set down a long trail of abuses. For a couple of years he had been keeping a "black catalog of unprovoked injuries," and like a composer scoring the same thematic material for different musical forms and instruments, had made repeated use of the list in his major public writings. The famous document of 1689 had blamed existing abuses not only on King James II but also on his "divers evil counselors, judges, and ministers." For his part, Jefferson laid all grievances, true and exaggerated, on the shoulders of one man, King George III (the only person he mentions in the Declaration), whose "cruelty and perfidy [are] scarcely to be paralleled in the most barbarous ages."

The third part of the Declaration of Independence was the briefest, a mere reminder of the angelic patience of the colonists in their sufferings under this despot and of the rejection of their humble petitions for redress.

Purists may say that Jefferson slopped over. The pitch of his attack on George III became strident and his attitude holier than thou. The Declaration of Independence was supposed to be an exalted expression, not a Tom Paine pamphlet or a Sam Adams rabble-rousing. But the rest of the drafting committee and the whole Congress had the final responsibility and actually did tone down some of the passages to a paler purple. Among other things, they excised the reference to slavery. Jefferson sat there wincing at every cut they made. It took Ben Franklin to calm him. Today no one reads or quotes the grievances-against-the-king section.

Back then everyone knew that early in his life, mother and the nursery had knocked George III off balance, that he had several bouts of madness—Tom Paine called him "His Madjesty"—that he often behaved like a stubborn fool. Otherwise he was temperate, conscientious, religious; he managed a farm of his own, loved sports and the outdoors. During his reign England laid the foundations of world empire in India and Canada, became mistress of the seas, and brought Napoleon to his knees. After all, the great natural philosopher and mathematician Sir Isaac Newton had his bouts of madness, too. Kings can be pretty silly at times, and at others pretty mean. So can scientists, presidents, councils, parliaments, assemblies, judges, and humble folk.

And what were Parliament and the cabinet supposed to be doing all this time? Sitting on their hands? Early in the game the colonists, to justify their resistance, had seized on the enormity of their being taxed without representation. Samuel Johnson, the celebrated English author and dictionary compiler, complained bitterly about colonial "croakers of calamity." Surely, he wrote, they do not think much of us "when they suppose us not to know what they well know themselves, that they are taxed [not by the King but] by Parliament." George III, however, like Lieutenant Duddington of the *Gaspee*, made too tempting a target.

St. John paused and took another sip of water.

"Did Thomas Jefferson hate the king so much?" Huggins spoke apologetically, as if he were crashing into a holy rite.

St. John did not object to the question. "Put it this way: His father's origins exposed him to generations of Welsh hatred of English dominion; it didn't take much for Jefferson to believe that a king, any king, George III, Louis XVI, no matter, was doomed to become degenerate. To him the kings of Spain, Naples, Denmark, Sweden, and Austria (as well as Napoleon when proclaimed emperor of the French) were either crazy, fools, or pigs. Men like Jefferson, you should remember, are republican. All republicans foam at the mouth when it comes to kings, and vice versa. A republic is a government without a hereditary king. A king is the main obstacle to a republic. You know the saying, 'Free as a king.' Well, in a republic each citizen feels free as a king. Of course, kings are never free, nor do they feel free. But that's another kettle of fish. The point is that people can get excited about these things. Just think of Patrick Henry's peroration in the Virginia House of Burgesses."

St. John hesitated. "Why are you looking at me like that, Huggins? Don't tell me you've never heard of Patrick Henry, the great rebel orator?"

"Sure I have, but I was wondering . . . It didn't seem like you were talking about 'Give me Liberty or give me—' "

"No, not that speech," interrupted St. John.

"That's the only line I know."

"This one you ought to know, too. It's a bit of republican history in a nutshell, a warning to kings that if they threaten to draw and quarter a Thomas Jefferson for treason . . . Let's see. I have it right here." St. John slipped a slim hand into her notecase and took out a sheet. "Are you sure you don't know it?"

Huggins shook his head.

"It took place in 1765 in the Virginia House of Burgesses. Thomas Jefferson was listening at the door. Patrick Henry was winding up his speech protesting the Stamp Act. From all reports the finale went like this: 'Caesar had his Brutus, Charles the First his Cromwell, and George the Third . . .' Cries of 'Treason! Treason!' broke out from the floor, drowning out Henry's voice. Coolly he waited for five or six seconds, then wrapped it up with, 'and George the Third may profit by their example!' "

As she quoted the last line, St. John lowered her voice ominously, and then concluded with satisfaction. "Well, that was too good not to quote."

"Who was Cromwell, may I ask? You mentioned him before."

St. John slumped back in her chair in disbelief. "*Oliver* Huggins, you ought to know who *Oliver* Cromwell was. In 1649 he beheaded King Charles I."

"No kidding. I guess I don't know much about my own name. English history seems to have slipped me by."

"Quite. Anyway, I think, Oliver, that the rebellion here went beyond this republic versus king business."

"It did? How?" asked Huggins, blinking. His first name had never sounded so musical.

"The colonists were spoiling for a fight."

"Really?"

"Yes. Rebellion builds cumulatively. Once irregular violence starts to spill blood, both sides, wild-eyed, see atrocities everywhere.

Soon each believes the worst about his brother, and killing and war seem just. In the heat of action, blood up their nose, men are apt to forget how small their complaints were at the start.

"The War of Independence was by no means a velvet revolution; it was not England's 'Glorious' or 'Bloodless Revolution' of 1688. Neither, thank God, was it the steel fist powered by the thirst for blood of the Jacobins, by the fiendish pleasure in parading with heads speared on pikes."

St. John waited, but Huggins didn't need to ask who the bloodthirsty Jacobins were. He was well-informed, having read in school *A Tale of Two Cities*. Besides, in a film club, he had once seen Leslie Howard in *The Scarlet Pimpernel*.

"Nevertheless," she resumed, "the colonies both before and after the Declaration should have paid more attention to compromise and diplomacy, especially with Britain's enemies and fair-weather friends, while biding their time and getting stronger. They could have explored treaty arrangements with other countries, struck further trade deals with the French, made overtures to Spain, tried corrupting an already corrupt Parliament. When the fighting was over, Franklin told his French friends that had he had one fourth the cost of the war for use as bribes in England, he could have *bought* independence for the colonists. He thought, and he was not far wrong, that every bewigged lord, every beefy squire, to keep himself in laces, snuff, and mistresses, had a price."

"Really? But they did make an alliance with France, didn't they?" contributed Huggins.

"Yes. During the war, and of critical help it was indeed. And a couple of years before the Declaration of Independence the colonies even sent a long, open letter addressed to the inhabitants of Quebec, inviting them 'with open arms' to join 'into a fellowship' and to send representatives of their 'province' to the Congress of 1775 at Philadelphia. Shouldn't the property honestly acquired by Canadians be as sacred as that of Englishmen? they asked piously, and liberally quoted France's own political thinker, Montesquieu. 'What would your countryman, the immortal *Montesquieu*, have said . . . ?' "

"What happened?" asked Huggins.

"Nothing. I guess the Quebeckers, lacking a Sam Adams and a

Tom Paine, didn't see King George as quite the very model of a tyrant."

"Are you French, Ms. St. Claire? I mean, Ms. St. John. Your name is so . . ." Huggins's question petered out in embarrassment.

"What do you mean?" Tutor sounded annoyed. "Why do you ask?"

"I'm sorry. I meant to ask about their speaking French. Really I meant to ask— The colonials weren't fools, why didn't they rely more on diplomacy?" faltered Huggins.

St. John held her fire, and then in tones of iciest logic, "Do you want a scientific answer?"

"Why, yes," mumbled Huggins.

"Here you are then—three reasons: amateur political thinkers . . . young and middle-aged hotheads . . . and guns a-plenty."

————The final paragraph of the Declaration (St. John returned to her lecturing voice) is a straightforward declaring of independence and of the authority in whose name the declarers were doing the declaring: "by Authority of the good People of these Colonies." There is some fuzziness about whether the good People are of these Colonies or of these States and about whether the Representatives and the independence they proclaim issue from the "United Colonies" or from the "United States." At the start of Congress the members were delegates of Colonies, at the end of the Declaration, they signed themselves (although they hadn't been chosen thus) as representatives of States.

There is some uncertainty also about who the "good people" may have been. Jefferson called them "the people," "our fellow citizens," "one people," "our people," and "a free people." Citizens under the laws of one colony or state might not have qualified under another, and in order to vote all of them had to be property owners, tax-payers, or members of a religious community. Which means that the majority of people were not part of *the people*. In any case, the Declaration had no proper name for these "good People."

After signing the Declaration, Thomas Jefferson's passion for politics subsided. He did not like the "mutilations" Congress had made in his draft. He headed home, riding horseback seven hours straight. He had been away four months, and worried about his wife's health.

Jefferson did not wear his heart on his sleeve. Little in his preserved words measures his love for wife and family.

As a young man he had kept a book in which he copied the literary gems he treasured. Many of the quotations show a concern with death, a not uncommon concern among the old and the adolescent. One of the verses comes from the last book of *Tristram Shandy* by the lately deceased, great novelist he admired, Laurence Sterne. In Martha Jefferson's final, lingering illness she turned to her husband's commonplace book. He was never out of call. When not at her side he stayed reading or writing or reflecting in a small room that gave onto the bedroom. He was then thirty-nine, she was thirty-three. The thought of inevitably leaving one another was ever present. On one of those longest days near the end, Martha took a slip of paper and started to write on it the beginning of the verse from *Tristram Shandy* as she knew it from Tom's literary commonplace book:

> Time wastes too fast: every letter I trace tells me with what rapidity life follows my pen. The days and hours of it are flying over our heads like clouds of windy day never to return more   every thing presses on

Here the faded ink stops. Her husband's hand in darker ink picks up and completes the passage:

> and every time I kiss thy hand to bid adieu, every absence which follows it, are preludes to that eternal separation which we are shortly to make.

The slip of paper, wrapped around a lock of Martha's hair, was found by his daughter in the secret drawer of her father's private cabinet, along with locks of hair and other small mementos of each of his children living and dead.

St. John glanced curiously at her tutee. Huggins, his face impassive, swallowed once.

★ ★

————When the Declaration of Independence appeared in the press, she went on, the public, wild with excitement, took to killing George III in absentia. In Manhattan under the disapproving eyes of George Washington (now commander in chief) a crowd containing some of his soldiers pulled down and mutilated a gilt equestrian statue of the king and smashed it to pieces. In several cities His Majesty was hanged, burned, and buried in effigy. Royal symbols on houses and stores were ripped away and demolished.

On the day of the signing, John Adams, in prophetic fever, wrote home to his wife that this day "will be celebrated by succeeding Generations, as the Day of Deliverance by solemn Acts of Devotion to God Almighty. It ought to be solemnized with Pomp and Parade, with Shews, Games, Sports, Guns, Bells, Bonfires, and Illuminations from one End of this Continent to the other from this Time forward forever more." Jefferson later quipped that if it hadn't been for the flies, the delegates would never have signed so quickly.

In the ongoing celebrations neither the name nor the person of Thomas Jefferson took part. John Adams knew and Congress knew but few others knew who the author of the document was. The public only learned of it almost a decade later. Before Jefferson died, however, public appreciation confirmed that he had written something great. At the end of his days, to his dearest young friend, James Madison, soon to become president, he wrote, "Take care of me when dead." He meant: Take care of the blessings of self-government, of the consent of the people, of the Declaration of Independence. His expiring words were, "This is the Fourth?"

The Declaration is no piece of history to be stuck in the archives. It lives on, for it did more than declare independence: it set out a political philosophy. Today people commonly confuse or combine the Declaration of Independence with another, later document, the 1787 Constitution. Two words stick in the heads of schoolchildren: everybody is created "equal" and has "rights" that cannot be taken away, and whether the words appear in the Declaration or in the Constitution doesn't matter. But we'll take this up later when we meet Abraham Lincoln.

The Declaration may not have turned out to be the broadcast to mankind that Congress had hoped for. My friend the historian R. R. Palmer says that the Declaration was never well-known or of any particular influence in France. If not in France, where else? It did affect King George. "I cannot conclude without mentioning how sensibly I feel the dismemberment of America from this empire." It was 1782; the king was writing a letter to the earl of Shelburne. "And that I should be miserable indeed if I did not feel that no blame on that account can be laid at my door." The king's next sentence recalls colonial smuggling and trading with the enemy; it recalls the committees of correspondence, the Liberty Boys, the persecuting of thousands of His Majesty's loyal subjects (about 100,000 of them, British Americans, too, who fled, mainly to Canada), the endless bills and declarations, and Thomas Jefferson and the Declaration of Independence. "I should be miserable," the king wrote, "did I not also know that knavery seems to be so much the striking feature of its inhabitants that it may not in the end be an evil that they will become aliens to this kingdom."

The king had his first little revenge when John Adams was ambassador to the Court of St. James's. Jefferson, then minister to France, was visiting London. Adams thought to take Jefferson to the royal court to introduce to George III the man who had written the Declaration of Independence. Whatever put this idiocy into Adams's head and whatever prompted Jefferson to accept are hard to imagine. Perhaps Adams thought the king was not such a bad sort after all and would welcome a chance to kiss and make up. The king's behavior shocked even his own court. With Adams and Jefferson before him he turned his back on them both.

The humiliation stung Jefferson. The British, he raged, needed "to be kicked into common good manners." Evidently that mulish being, George III, had had enough of the good manners of Thomas Jefferson.

"Ms. St. John?"

"Yes?"

"You said *first* revenge. Was there another?"

"Yes, during the War of 1812. George III was still king. The

British invaded Washington and burned down the new Executive Mansion."

"Oh."

"The king must have chuckled when he learned that, before setting fire to it (and the whole city), a group of British officers had sat down to enjoy a sumptuous spread in the Mansion dining room. Spits were still dripping with various joints over the fire, diverse wines were beckoning in their coolers, as President Madison and company beat a hasty retreat."

"Oh." Huggins squirmed uncomfortably.

"Come to think of it," said St. John, "I left something noteworthy out of Jefferson's character—humor. He once told a little story on himself. He was forty-two when Congress sent him to Paris to relieve Benjamin Franklin, then seventy-nine years old, of his post as minister to France. 'I remember in France when [Dr. Franklin's] friends were taking leave of [him], the ladies smothered him with embraces and on his introducing me to them as his successor, I told him I wished he would transfer these privileges to me.'

"Dr. Franklin, too, had a sense of humor. 'You are too young,' he answered.

"As it turned out, Jefferson was not too young to enjoy the favor of a few married ladies and to quote them *Tristram Shandy*, but quoting now in the lighter vein characteristic of its author."

St. John began to collect her papers. She added with the hint of a smile, "You must admit that George III took England away from the colonies just in time."

Huggins returned the smile with a bigger smile.

"Do you think I've made an even case for both sides?" she asked.

"Yes, I do," said Huggins in a rush. "I've never heard it presented so fairly before, but yes of course."

3

A COUNTRY

WITH NO NAME

"Good afternoon, Huggins."

"Afternoon, Ms. St. John. What was that tune I heard you humming, coming up the walk? It sounded familiar."

"It *is* familiar." St. John brimmed with health, good humor, and a Panama hat. "It's from *H.M.S. Pinafore*. Maybe you remember the words:

> *He is an Englishman.*
> *For he himself has said it*
> *And it is greatly to his credit*
> *That he is an Englishman.*

"No, I didn't remember them. They're good, aren't they?" said Huggins.

"These years I've spent in the States," she went on, "have rubbed away quite a bit of my native pronunciation, you know, but I too am English. I thought your father might have told you. By the way, the name England comes from the Angles, an ancient people, with a name old enough to rival the Mexica."

She was removing her hat as she spoke, in an odd way, thought Huggins. She raised her right arm and fist over the hat and with her fingers under the brim lifted it back and off.

"You may recall," she said, "that warmed up by Thomas Jefferson's heat, the representatives of the thirteen colonies along the North Atlantic coast repudiated their mother country England. So the Englishman of North America, no longer an Englishman, what did he change into? Good question, wouldn't you say? No longer a child of the mother country, whose child was he? Did a foster-mother adopt him? If so, what was her name? Was he saying he did not need parents anymore? If so, what name did he get or choose for himself? To the tune of *H.M.S. Pinafore*: 'It is greatly to his credit that he is an—' What? What would you say he was?"

"An American," prompted Huggins.

"Then you would parody the song by singing, 'It is greatly to his credit that he is an A-me-ri-can'?"

"Yes."

"Let's see whether you're right," said St. John.

————To *declare* yourself free and independent States is one thing; to *become* free and independent States is another. The signers of the Declaration of Independence and other colonial leaders said in effect, "We want to be free States; we will have constitutions for ourselves as States; and we will join together and fight to prove that we are and ought to be free States."

The self-declared States now started to rewrite their basic laws. Some had already written and adopted new constitutions. Most took the quick and easy way of writing the king out and the People in. But as states-declared-free they kept their old colonial names, a matter we'll look at in a moment.

In short order there were thirteen self-declared countries, each possessing a constitution and an old name for itself and for its people who, now that their constitution was republican, could call themselves "citizens" of their country. Each also possessed a lot of problems, the first and gravest of which was their spurned mother Britannia's anger against all of them. At the beginning of hostilities one lively cartoon, among many others, captioned "the Female Combatants," shows a fancy-dressed and periwigged "Britannia" saying to "Liberty," the opposing female figure, "I'll force you to Obedience you Rebellious Slut," aiming a blow with the right at Liberty's bare breasts. Liberty has bare breasts because she is represented as an Indian wearing only feathered headdress and miniskirt. "Liberty Liberty for ever Mother while I exist," Liberty exclaims, as she lands a right to Britannia's jaw.

According to the British, by taking up arms and declaring themselves free, the several colonies had broken the law, to put it mildly. Their assemblies and congresses, their acts of violence and terror, were illegal, unconstitutional, and treasonable. The thirteen naughty children had become thirteen nasty grown-ups.

The king, the ministry, and Parliament maintained that the good people of these colonies are subjects of the king, and have no authority whatever to become or even to declare themselves independent. That position of theirs—that they are bound by no laws to which they have not given consent themselves or through their representatives—is not confirmed by any authoritative record of the British constitution and intends the subversion of the English monarchy. Their acts are rebellious, to be put down by force of arms if necessary, and the participants in such acts to be executed as traitors. Thus was justified the king's proclamation of a state of rebellion in the colonies.

Samuel Johnson had said that the colonists "ought to be thankful for anything we allow them short of hanging." In truth, official punishment for traitors varied among different parts of the empire and was usually a lot worse than hanging. The penalty for treason in Merrie Old England, as read by British judges in sentencing Irish rebels in 1775, was as follows: "You are to be hanged by the neck, but not until you are dead; for, while you are living your bodies are to be taken down, your bowels torn out and burned before your faces, your heads then cut off, and your bodies divided into four quarters, and your heads and quarters to be then at the King's disposal; and may the Almighty God have mercy on your souls." I doubt the king would have insisted on the letter of the law for British America except perhaps in the case of Thomas Jefferson.

It must have been no small comfort to rebel leaders to know that only the word *hanging* was being bandied about. But a convenient list of candidates now existed from which to start the hanging—those good People who had signed the Declaration of Independence. Had they not at the end of that vile piece of paper pledged their lives, their fortunes, and their sacred honor? So be it. They had willfully forfeited their lives and their fortunes. Of sacred honor traitors had none. Let Fleets and Armies be dispatched.

The gentlemen subscribers to the Declaration knew that defense against the mother country was the first order of business, that money for it was priority number one, and that if they were to have a chance, the thirteen so-called states had better take more united action than just to assemble in Congress. Franklin had said they had better hang together or they would be hanged separately.

You may wonder why the moving spirits in these various declarations, conventions, and congresses were willing to take such risks especially since they were already well off. Thomas Jefferson had some ten thousand acres of plantation: how much more did he want? John Dickinson of Pennsylvania and Delaware was a rich farmer and landowner. His mother kept telling him, "Johnny, you will be hanged, your estate will be forfeited and confiscated, you will leave your excellent wife a widow, and your charming children orphans, beggars and infamous." Did he listen? He did, with one conciliatory ear. Which did not prevent him from becoming the drafter par excellence of some of the great public papers of the struggle.

Many have studied this question of risks. None have come up with a better answer than Adam Smith in the famous book *The Wealth of Nations* on sale in bookstores in that signal year of 1776. A learned man and a powerful thinker about money, trade, and manufacturing, he speculated about what men (including the leaders of the colonial commotion) were hankering after. Let's let him speak for himself.

> Men desire to have some share in the management of public affairs chiefly on account of the importance which it gives them.

Upon the power which the greater part of the leading men, the natural aristocracy of every country, have of preserving or defending their respective importance depends the stability and duration of every system of free government. In the attacks which those leading men are continually making upon the importance of one another, and in the defense of their own, consists the whole play of domestic faction and ambition.

So much for Smith's theory about men in general. He went on to apply his theory to the restive British colonies in North America. The leading men of America, he wrote,

desire to preserve their own importance. They feel, or imagine, that if their assemblies, which they are fond of calling parliaments, and of considering as equal in authority to the Parliament of Great Britain, should be so far degraded as to become the humble ministers and executive officers of that Parliament, the greater part of their own importance would be at an end. They have rejected, therefore, the proposal of being taxed by parliamentary requisition and, like other ambitious and high-spirited men, have rather chosen to draw the sword in defense of their own importance.

Blood had to be spilled and the war fought, a war of ambition. Congress had put an army in the field. Britain could ill afford to put a great many men and ships in this struggle: it was fighting battles on other fronts and seas as well, and its supply line for a land war in America was three thousand miles long. Nonetheless it threw in half of its great navy, fifty thousand regulars, and thirty thousand foreign mercenaries. The action developed into a bitter conflict. Both sides, the British and Tory versus the rebels, disregarded eighteenth-century rules of war. Remembering Sam Adams's dedication and skill, you can discount some of the stories of British troops bayoneting the aged and infirm in their rocking chairs, of murdering or burning up in their houses women in childbed or with helpless babes at their breast. You needn't discount some of the stories of the killing of prisoners.

War brings horrors: many are told wrong, many remain untold. General Washington, who spoke a lot about Providence and the Almighty Being, less about God, and nothing about Jesus Christ, surprised the hung-over Lutheran Hessians garrisoned at Trenton, on the morning after Christmas. On the English side General Charles, Lord Cornwallis, the last British commander, was of a different breed from the early commanders, the conciliatory and peace-seeking brothers, General Sir William Howe and Admiral Richard, Lord Howe. Cornwallis and his armies marched through the South burning barns, crops, towns, and devastating stores. In Virginia he took particular pleasure in ravaging Governor Thomas Jefferson's possessions, making off with livestock (which was cricket) and cutting the throats of colts (which was not). Jefferson accused him of a "spirit of total extermination."

The end of the war came in October 1781 after the battle of Yorktown where the rebel army with the aid of French ships, troops, and engineers bottled Cornwallis up. At the surrender, the British military band with a fine touch of sarcasm played a song called "The World Turned Upside Down."

"Huggins, have you heard of Niccolò Machiavelli, the great Renaissance statesman and writer?" asked tutor.

"I think so. Didn't he say the end justifies the means?"

St. John ignored the question and plowed ahead. "In his book *The Prince*, Niccolò claimed that if a country is centrally organized with a strong leadership, once you conquer the center, you can hold the country easily. But if the strength and authority of a land are dispersed among many local powers, though battles may be easy to win, new battlefronts soon spring up elsewhere. Conquest keeps slipping through your fingers. This was a great part of Cornwallis's difficulties, of the troubles of the British forces from the beginning, actually."

"You know," said Huggins, "I read somewhere once that George Washington lost most battles but won the war. Is that because the loose organization of the thirteen colonies gave them the advantage?"

"Yes, I'd certainly say that helped. If you want to follow this up sometime, you should read a book by a friend of mine, Sebastian de Grazia. You'll like the title at least—*Machiavelli in Hell*."

"Oh, I'll read it all right," he reassured her.

"Niccolò's writings were important in spreading republican ideas to America via Holland and England," she said parenthetically, and then added, "I have something here I want to quote."

————George III, sick and tired of these thirteen republicanizing grown-ups, announced that the mother country no longer recognized them as her offspring. He put his signature to the Treaty of Paris of 1783, which in part reads thus:

> His Britannic Majesty acknowledges the said United States, viz., New-Hampshire, Massachusetts-Bay, Rhode-Island and Providence Plantations, Connecticut, New-York, New-Jersey, Pennsylvania, Delaware, Maryland, Virginia, North-Carolina, South-Carolina, and Georgia, to be free, sovereign and independent states; that he treats with them as such; and for himself, his heirs and successors, relinquishes all claims to the government, property and territorial rights of the same, and every part thereof.

This long stroke of the pen turned rebels into citizens, self-declared states into real states. The hand that pushed the pen, though, had been forced by the sword. The argument in political philosophy over monarchy and republic had been decided not by reason, law, or weightier words but by force of arms. His Britannic Majesty, arm twisted behind his back, had agreed: the thirteen self-declared states were independent states. France, Spain, and the Netherlands agreed too. France had agreed earlier, in the treaty of alliance of 1778 between "the most Christian King and the United States of North America, to wit, New Hampshire, Massachusetts Bay, Rhode Island, Connecticut, New York, New Jersey, Pennsylvania, Delaware, Maryland, Virginia, North Carolina, South Carolina and Georgia . . ." *Mankind* now had thirteen new states, in fact and in international law.

Mind you, the term States did not refer to regions or large districts like counties or states in the weakened sense of the fifty "States" today. In the Declaration of Independence, "as FREE AND INDEPENDENT STATES, they [were to] have full Power to levy War, conclude Peace, contract Alliances, establish Commerce, and to do all other acts and things which INDEPENDENT STATES may of right do." Today the fifty States cannot do any of these things. The original thirteen claimed to be what we would today call thirteen independent countries. And each had a proper noun name.

I should also tell you that the frequent expression "the several States" does not refer to "more than two but less than many States." *Several* here takes its original meaning of *separate*. The several States are "the separate States," distinct from each other and from themselves as members of an association, government, or union.

How names came to fill in the uncharted maps differed from South to North America. In South America where the Spaniards prevailed, the process was more formal. The Spaniards seemed more aware that to lay claim to an unnamed land one has to find it a name. King Ferdinand gave pertinent instructions to his roving captains: "First of all, you must give a name to the country as a whole, and to the cities, towns, and places." Juan Ponce de León, even before disembarking, gave a name to what he thought to be a large island. Because it was the Easter of Flowers week and the land he could see was April-flowered, he named it Florida.

The Spaniards had developed naming-possession rites. In a simple ceremony, they set up a cross, held mass, paraded soldiers, fired off guns. The captain drew his sword, claimed the right of the king of Spain to the land, threw a few stones together, and hacked with the sword at a few trees. Sometimes they scooped water from sea or river and poured it onto the land.

The great French explorers, like René Robert Cavalier, Sieur de La Salle in possessing and naming the valley of the Mississippi "Louisiana," would also combine symbols of the cross, earth, water, and king.

England, appearing late on the stage, found many places already named and had to be content with renaming many to its taste. We've already heard about Queen Elizabeth and Virginia. John Smith and Prince Charles (later Charles I and as such beheaded) together made a lasting imprint on the land. Smith must have had a rather good ear for tribal speech. He put written names on Massachusetts and the Potomac and Susquehanna rivers. When he presented to Prince Charles a map of the features of New England (a name already confirmed by Charles's father, James I), he tactfully gave the young man first choice, asking that "his Highness would please to change their barbarous names for such English, as posterity might say Prince Charles was their Godfather." Charles Stuart, then sixteen, liked the game of names. After filling in thirty-odd names—the Charles River he named after himself, the tribal Accomack he changed to Plymouth—he gave the map back to Smith, who filled in the rest with the names of himself, his friends, and patrons. The map carries the inscription "New England" and the phrase, "The most remarkable parts thus named by the high and mighty Prince Charles, Prince of Great Britain."

The Carolinas owe their name to this same prince. Carolus (in Latin) means Charles. Later when George Calvert, Lord Baltimore, wished to get a name for his grant of land north of Virginia, he drafted a charter and presented it to Charles with a blank space for the name. When Charles (now king) asked him why, Baltimore said he had wished to name it after His Majesty but that honor had gone to Carolina. The king having already used up on maps the name of his mother and sister, proposed to name the territory "Mariana"— in honor of his wife, Queen Henrietta Maria. The learned Baltimore pointed out that Mariana, regrettably, was the name of the Spanish Jesuit who preached against royal tyranny. Not to be thwarted, the king ruled that the name be (and thus it stands in Latin charters) *Terra Mariae*, in English, Maryland. "So we name it and so we will it to be named in the future."

When a colony becomes a free country it often celebrates its new status by taking on a new name. It may re-adopt an old name (such as when part of the Viceroyalty of New Spain became Mexico, or more recently, when part of northern Rhodesia became Zambia, a name born of the Zambesi River). A colony may change the pronunciation or accent of its existing name, as the crown colony of Kenya in Africa, once freed, insisted on Kēnya. It may adopt a new name entirely, as part of Venezuela (itself a new name) became Bolivia, to commemorate the revolutionary hero Simón Bolívar. But generally names, especially old names bearing heavy loads of memories, resist change. India in or out of the British Empire remained India, Ukraine in or out of the United Soviet Socialist Republics remained Ukraine, Frisia in or out of the United Provinces remained Frisia, and their people remained Indians, Ukrainians, and Frisians.

So it was with the thirteen former British colonies in North

America. Now independent of England, not only in their own opinion but in that of mankind, they showed little inclination to change.
They held on to the names, some as old as one hundred years or
more, that they had as colonies—pretty much as George III and
Louis XVI had listed them—and their people retained the same
names they had as colonists—Marylanders, Carolinians, and the others, except that they were no longer subjects of His Britannic
Majesty but citizens of the republics of Maryland, the Carolinas, and
so forth. (Thomas Jefferson, going over his draft of the Declaration
of Independence, had crossed out "subjects" and inserted "citizens.")
As citizen-adults they kept the names they were given as subject-
children, and each country in its new status wrote its own constitution under its old name, keeping its separate self.

"So, Huggins, it doesn't look as if the former British colonists in
North America, once declared free of Great Britain, would pronounce themselves Americans," said St. John. "Let me be more
concrete.

"Take a case you must know something about. You remember
who Nathan Hale was, don't you? What can you tell me about him?
In two sentences, please. I don't want a speech."

Huggins replied with speed and confidence. "He was an American captain spying on the British. He was captured and hanged. His
last words were 'I only regret that I have but one life to lose for
my country.' "

"Good. You mentioned that he was an American captain. What
country did he think he was losing his life for?"

"Ameri—" Huggins stopped in the middle of the word, stumped.

"Well?" St. John jiggled her crossed-over left leg, the braceleted
one, up and down.

"You said there wasn't any America then," Huggins responded
lamely.

"I did not say that," she persisted mercilessly. "Never mind now
what I said. Think for yourself."

"I'm trying to remember," said Huggins bravely. "Maybe he was
thinking of his native land, of where his parents were born. I
think he was a graduate of Yale, wasn't he? Maybe he was born in
Connecticut."

"Suppose he was, and I don't know myself where he was born. What country then would he have lost his life for?"

"Connecticut?" suggested Huggins.

"Perhaps. Still, as Connecticut was almost always considered part of a larger whole called New England, it may be that he considered himself a New Englander and was losing his life for New England."

"That sounds more like it."

"Maybe, too," she continued, "the country or at least the model he had in mind was ancient Rome. In Joseph Addison's play of 1713, *Cato*, much admired by educated colonists, the Roman states-man declaims, 'What pity is it that we can die but once to serve our country!' But let me give you another case. Relax: I won't ques-tion you. You may have heard of the valiant commander of the Green Mountain Boys, Colonel Ethan Allen. He later wrote a mod-est account of his exploits that sounds at times like the autobiogra-phy of Benvenuto Cellini." St. John looked up. "By the way, you mustn't mind if I sometimes mention persons and places you've never heard of. I'm just showing off to myself."

"That's okay," said Huggins, a bit petulant.

"Ethan Allen with a small force, cheerfully undertaking to cap-ture Fort Ticonderoga, a British outpost on Lake Champlain, caught the garrison asleep. He ran upstairs where the captain slept and or-dered him to come out and surrender the fort instantly. The offi-cer came to the door. 'Surrender?' he said, sleep in his eyes, pants in his hands. 'By what authority?'

"I confess," said St. John, "that I don't know what I would have said, but to Ethan Allen the answer came in a flash: 'In the name of the great Jehovah, and the Continental Congress!'

"The action took place in May 1775. 'The authority of the Con-gress [was] very little known at the time,' Allen later wrote, and the captain began to demur, 'but I interrupted him and with my drawn sword over his head . . .' The captain gave up the garrison.

"Where the great Jehovah came in, I don't know, but 'the Con-tinental Congress' was not a bad reply," said St. John, "when rein-forced with steel."

————Certainly, a name for the rebels as a whole would have been useful, she proceeded. "Yankees" was not serious and applied only to New Englanders, not to Georgians or Virginians. It probably came from a European nickname for the cheese-making Hollanders—*Jan Kees*, or John Cheese. In the mid-1600s, the Dutch of New York applied it derisively to their northern neighbors, the English in Connecticut. Later, British troops stationed here followed suit. "Continental" was mainly attached to Congress, troops, and paper money. Neither "Yankee" nor "Continental" could be elevated into a name for a country.

By this time the English commonly left out "North" or "British" as prefixes in speaking of "America" and the "Americans." That "the Americans are able to bear taxation is indubitable," Samuel Johnson pronounced. The French, too, referred to their nationals in America as "les Américains." St. John de Crèvecoeur asked, "What then is the American, this new man?" Both writers thought of "Americans" in the abbreviated sense as North American subjects of the Crown, English or French.

"Wait!" Huggins could hardly hide his excitement. "Did you say 'St. John de Crèvecoeur?'"

"Yes," said St. John patiently, visibly bored, as if she knew what was coming.

"Was he a relative, by any chance?"

"He may be a relative, but so distant that you can't find a twig for him on the family tree. Uncle Gaspar is the family genealogist," she said in a tone of closure. "J. Hector St. John de Crèvecoeur, as he is remembered here, was a Frenchman and could not have considered himself a British American. He emigrated to Canada, served as an officer under Field Marshal Louis-Joseph Montcalm, and decided to remain on this side of the pond. He wandered south, became a citizen of New York, changed the spelling of his name from Jean to John and christened a town in Vermont after himself—St. Johnsbury. He married a Mehitabel Tibbett of a Tory family, and baptized a daughter Frances America. After the war he became French consul to New York, and then returned for good to his native France. He was a romantic in the manner of Jean-Jacques Rousseau."

As though that explains everything, thought Huggins.

★ ★

————Crèvecoeur, she added, claimed that settling and farming in North America would do worlds of good for the English and also for the Scotch, Irish, French, Dutch, Germans, and Swedes. "I could point out to you a family," he wrote, "whose grandfather was an Englishman, whose wife was Dutch, whose son married a French woman, and whose present four sons have now four wives of different nations." With "fat and frolicsome" wives and children they melt into a new race of men—Americans.

Colonials, too, wrote of America and Americans. John Dickinson, the farmer, lawyer, and writer I mentioned a minute ago, born in Maryland but educated in the Middle Temple in London, wrote newspaper articles entitled "Letters from a Pennsylvania Farmer" and "The Patriotic American Farmer"; it was clear that he wrote about colonials in Pennsylvania or broadly in British America.

But as separation from the mother country drew near, the names "America" and "American" went into a noticeable slump . . .

Oliver Huggins raised his hand to half-mast.

"What is it?" tutor asked.

"I don't get it. Why did the name America slump? I'd have thought it would have been more popular than ever."

"I'd have thought so, too. But think for a moment of the mounting anti-British feeling. And remember that America was shorthand for British North America, and American was shorthand for British American, useful in distinguishing a British American from an Englishman. America and American smacked of the English connection and just for this became the very names by which loyalists often chose to identify themselves.

"You know of that great soldier, Benedict Arnold, don't you? After military feats like his attack on Quebec, he turned into a swine and donned the redcoat of the Brits, a traitor to the cause of independence. He recruited a regiment of loyalists and named it 'the American Legion' (no relation to the present American Legion founded in Paris in 1921), while another Tory, Beverley Robinson, commanded a regiment called 'Loyal Americans.' There were also the King's American Regiment and the King's American Dragoons."

The news disturbed Huggins. "What name did the real Americans use, then?"

"By 'real Americans' I take it you mean the rebels," corrected St. John. "As I said, the lack of a name created something of a problem. The rebel Congress and army found themselves using 'Continental,' not so much a prophetic exaggeration as a term, common also among Europeans, of distinguishing themselves from England and the British Isles: There was England and there was the Continent.

"The growing agitation against England led to still another significant name. I'd better go into it in a simple time sequence, because I can see you're as perplexed as I was."

————You remember that the early map-makers, adapting the name of Amerigo (Vespucci) had overlooked Columbus. The English also had all but ignored the admiral: he had been in the pay of Spain. Ignoring also the voyages of Giovanni da Verrazzano (in the pay of France), England based her broadest claim to North America on the voyages of John and Sebastian Cabot, father and son (no relation to the immigrant Cabots of Boston), Italian navigators, true, but in the pay of Henry VII, king of England.

The colonists came to regard praises of the Cabots as so much English propaganda. They did not know much about Verrazzano. Though the Cabots, reaching northern Canada, had preceded him by twenty-five years, Verrazzano was the first to explore the Atlantic seaboard from Maine to Carolina, and the real mapper of what was to be the coastline of the thirteen colonies. The colonists had heard of Christopher Columbus, though. By this time the threat from Spain had diminished; Spanish patronage of Columbus bothered them less. They began to see the Admiral of the Ocean Sea with new eyes. Out of the changed vision came a new name—"Columbia"—Latin and feminine for Columbus.

Students of American place-names generally credit the poetry of Philip Freneau with the first appearance of "Columbia," in 1775, a year before the Declaration of Independence. But the bit of study I've done indicates that "Columbia" predates the Declaration by a century and a half and more. In England as early as the early 1600s Nicholas Fuller, an Oriental scholar, and others leaned to the view that Columbus's name should in all fairness be commemorated in the new world. A century later, still in England, the name Columbia appeared as a synonym for British America, sometimes used in derision. In the 1760s, the word appeared among would-be student poets at Harvard College. One of them, believe it or not, celebrated the crowning of George III. "Behold, Britannia! in thy favour'd Isle;/At distance thou Columbia! view thy Prince." In February of 1775 the *Boston Gazette* carried a poem by Mrs. Mercy Warren, a New England poet of some regard, employing "Columbia" as a term for North America. We are on the verge of the War of Independence.

Several months later, we see "Columbia" in print poised in opposition to Great Britain. Philip Freneau's long poem appeared in a New York newspaper under the title of "American Liberty." The first occurrence of "Columbia" in the poem—

> *What madness, heaven, has made Britannia frown?*
> *Who plans our schemes to pull Columbia* down?*

—prompted Freneau to add a footnote: "*Columbia. America sometimes so called from Columbus, the first discoverer." He addressed another pair of lines to Congress: "O Congress . . . On you depends Columbia's future fate,/A free asylum or a wretched state."

In October of the same year, Phillis Wheatley, born in Africa, the young slave of a Boston merchant, John Wheatley, wrote a forty-two-line poem addressed to General George Washington, the newly appointed commander of the Continental army, wishing him "a crown, a mansion, and a throne that shine/With gold unfading . . ." Washington in February of 1776 acknowledged receipt "of such encomium and panegyrick" and praised her genius. It was soon published in the *Pennsylvania Magazine*: "Columbia's scenes of glorious toils I write." The poem warned whoever threatened "the land of freedom's heaven-defended race" to beware of "Columbia's fury."

Surely 1775 may be considered the year of Columbia's coming of age. The name erupts all along the Atlantic seaboard, contemporary with the struggle against British rule.

In 1777, Timothy Dwight, a young congregational divine and future president of Yale, wrote the stanzas entitled "Columbia." The first two lines, inspired by mixed metaphors, go like this:

Columbia, Columbia, to glory arise,
The queen of the world and the child of the skies.

As a song it became immensely popular, first sung, apparently, by troops of the Connecticut Volunteers that Dwight served with as chaplain.

The names "Columbia" and "Columbian" and the phrases "Columbia's sons" and "Columbia's daughters" did not stay confined to verse. They were sometimes used in regard to the land and settlers of the West, won from former French territory. In 1791, President George Washington sent against the Indians north of the Ohio River a two-thousand-man expedition that ended in disaster. Almost one half the force was left on the field, killed or wounded. A Connecticut newspaper carried the headlines: COLUMBIAN TRAGEDY and BLOODY INDIAN BATTLE.

We have seen "Columbia" in verse, song, and the press. We have not yet recorded its official use as a name. In the War of Independence two warships had been christened *Columbia*, one in the Massachusetts navy, the other in that of Connecticut. When Washington was inaugurated president in New York on April 24, 1789, among the vessels escorting him was the schooner *Columbia*. Fittingly, our poet Philip Freneau was captain.

Ships aside, the prize for first official showing goes to the State of New York. An act of the legislature, passed on May 1, 1784, reads: "And be it further enacted by the Authority aforesaid, That the College within the City of New York, heretofore called King's College, be hereafter called and known by the Name of COLUMBIA COLLEGE," known today as Columbia University. A couple of years later "Columbia" became the name of the new capital of South Carolina.

These two official acts of separate States were followed by an official act of the United States. While George Washington was president the location of the federal capital—a place for Congress, the president, and the court to settle down—had been decided in favor of land on the Potomac River granted by Virginia and Maryland. Washington appointed three commissioners to plan the area's development. When the moment came to choose a name, the commissioners went to Wise's Tavern in Alexandria, Virginia, where

they were met by the mayor and officers of the city. After drinking a toast they formed a procession headed by the town sergeant
and composed of the Alexandria Masonic Lodge, large landowners,
and other interested citizens. The Masons laid a temporary stone
marker and the company repaired to the tavern again, this time for
a full round of toasts. After the occasion the commissioners wrote
a letter to the capital's planner and architect, Pierre Charles L'En-
fant: "Sir, We have agreed that the federal District shall be called
'The Territory of Columbia' and the federal city 'The City of Washington.' The title of the map will, therefore, be 'A Map of the City
of Washington in the Territory of Columbia. . . .' " The commissioners asked that ten thousand maps be so struck. Congress enacted
the name into law. The stone laid in Alexandria was later replaced
by a permanent marker which reads, "The beginning of the Territory of Columbia."

The following year (1792) Robert Gray, captain of the Boston
ship *Columbia*, plied the waters of the northwest Pacific coast seeking the mouth of a great river reported to lie in the vicinity. At the
same time, another captain and ship, Britishers, were sailing the same
currents and naming whatever they could find for Great Britain.
Gray found the river-mouth first and sailed up, anchoring the *Columbia* in fresh water. He named the great river "Columbia," thus
claiming possession and commemorating his ship.

"Did Jefferson or Washington ever use the word *Columbia*?"

"Yes, they were both well acquainted with the word, as you'll
see when we trace the subsequent adventures of *Columbia*," replied
St. John complacently. "*Columbia* was the thirteen States or their
land, I should say, conceived of as united, and 'Columbians' or 'sons
of Columbia' were her patriotic citizens. In pictorial images—draw-
ings, cartoons, and paintings—Columbia always appears as a handsome woman. Her only pictorial rival is 'Liberty,' another, almost
identical beauty."

St. John paused to pick up her glass of water.

"Are you saying that America was first named Columbia?" Huggins had just sighted land.

"Easy does it, Huggins. Whether that unity you call 'America'
really existed is as yet problematic. All I'm saying is that Columbia

seems to have been the first female name and image applied to the thought or feeling of unity of the thirteen countries and of their lands to the west and was beginning to be used in an official sense. How's that for being precise? And cautious."

She seemed amused. "If troops or ruffians of the Sam Adams variety had climbed through the meeting-hall windows of Congress and put pistols to the heads of the delegates, shouting, 'Pick a name for this country right now, or else . . . !' I do believe they would have voted for 'Columbia.'

"What I've been talking about is a search for a name for something hoped for (by some, not by all), for one country unified out of thirteen. But we must not get ahead of ourselves in the way most historians have done."

"Historians?" Huggins was doubtful. "In what way?"

"Well, if you want to know . . . I'll give you an impromptu quiz. Where did you learn that Nathan Hale was an American officer?"

"In school, I guess. From the history books they gave us to read."

"All right. What war was he caught and executed in?"

"The American Revolution."

"What do you celebrate with illegal firecrackers on the Fourth of July?" St. John pressed further.

"The signing of the Declaration of Independence." Huggins's forehead was beginning to feel damp.

"Independence of whom from whom?" the prosecutor shot at the witness.

"Of America from England," replied Huggins.

"What is the name of the aborigines of this land?"

" 'Indians.' 'American Indians,' or 'Amerindians.' Or maybe 'Original Americans' or 'First Americans.' Or, yes, 'Native Americans.' "

"End of quiz," she pronounced. "Your American history professor would have graded you one hundred on the quiz. What would I have given you?"

"Zero." Huggins managed a mournful look, followed by a smile.

"Right you are, and for that last word of yours I'd have changed your grade to one hundred," said St. John, smiling too.

"Technically what the historians are guilty of is the cardinal sin of anachronism, here a mistiming of names. Thinking of themselves as 'Americans' they extend their own identity too far back in time, and others have copied them. Take another example you've not heard of, I'm sure.

"One critical night in the War of Independence, the story goes, General Washington ordered his guard contingent alerted. 'Put none but Americans on guard tonight,' he told an aide-de-camp. This makes a nice vignette, don't you think, Huggins? There must have been other soldiers in camp, French probably, or recent English, German, or Dutch immigrants. But the general felt secure only when his own trusty countrymen, who were already 'American,' guarded his life. However, the story seems to have been Americanized from a command the general gave for his guard on that night of April 30, 1777: 'You will therefore send me none but Natives.' he ordered, 'and Men of some property, if you have them.'

"We have a bit of a problem here," said St. John changing tack.

————The principal names that historians of this period use today are "America" and "the United States" or "the United States of America" for country and "Americans" for its people. The people of the time themselves sometimes used "Yankees" or "Continentals" but most prominently "Columbia" or "Columbians."

Now, no one could count how many times these names and others were used in print and orally over a period of years by at least two and a half million persons of various national origins, noting in what context, with what intensity, and with what contradictions they appeared. But one can indeed reexamine whatever records are available.

We have loads of newspapers and pamphlets, diaries, stories, tons of letters, books, heaps of clothing, tools and weapons, cartoons and paintings, songs, speeches, vestiges of parades and festivities, party platforms, notes and documents ranging from floor debates in colonial legislatures to law cases, treaties, and constitutions. I base my remarks on several of these sources; I've examined many of them, and in continuing I'll put somewhat heavier but far from exclusive reliance on major public papers like resolutions, declarations, constitutions, and official speeches.

Another point about the method we'll use in our madness: If we discover that there is no proper name for "country," we must assume that others may have noticed this too. Perhaps many made the observation but for one reason or another did not mention it, or if they did their words did not survive to reach us. What I am saying is: We shouldn't be satisfied with an apparent omission. If we can find no name for country, we should not neglect to see whether others have made the same observation. I'll refer to one or two persons in a minute, but I hope to tell you tomorrow who was the first to decry this curious and important deficiency.

So far the most likely names for the territory and inhabitants of the seaboard and adjacent lands to the west are "Columbia" and "Columbians." These names seem to have gained widespread usage in the period extending from the rebellion to the end of George Washington's presidency, which is as far as we will take them today. It's a good moment to turn to the line of major official papers—the Declaration of Independence, the Articles of Confederation of 1777, and the Constitution of 1787.

St. John looked directly at Huggins. "Certainly there we'll find what country, if any, these documents were written for or about, and perhaps a clue to how you got the idea that it is greatly to your credit that you are an American."

Feeling challenged, Huggins stared back at her. Dropping eye contact, St. John went back to her exposé.

————According to the closing lines to the Declaration, its signers were representatives of the "United States of America." In 1643 a number of colonies had formed a union entitled the "United Colonies of New England." But Thomas Jefferson knew of a more recent phrase in the "Declaration on the Causes of Taking Up Arms" of 1775 whose authors (Jefferson himself shared the drafting honors with John Dickinson) signed themselves as the "United Colonies of North America." That document justified as self-defense certain acts of the Continental Congress, of which the most aggressive was appointing a Colonel George Washington as commander in chief of the "Army of the United Colonies."

The transition from "Colonies" to "States" was easy. Spain, France, and England were states. People here were already using "States" in discussing frames of government or constitutions for their particular ex-colony. Jefferson might have used "countries," but "States" better fit the philosophical and legal jargon he was using, much of which he found in Blackstone. The ambiguous term "nations," as applied to Indian tribes, seemed too small in compass, and as applied to empires, seemed too great. "Provinces" had a precedent in the United Provinces of the Netherlands, but in English it sounded too territorial. "Republics" referred to a form of government rather than to the first and firm objective of the Declaration—independent statehood.

No, *States* was a good term for the time being. The Declaration of Independence's primary purpose was to announce that the colonies had resolved to separate from Great Britain and to say why. In itself it had little to do with forming a new union or a big country. It was more a separation document than a unity document. As such, it didn't need a name for a new country. Neither did it need a name for the "good People of these Colonies" in whose authority it was drafted.

The year 1776 marked the first time the phrase "the united States of America" found its way into print. For the record: Congress on July 19, 1776, had "*Resolved*, That the Declaration passed on the 4th, be fairly engrossed on parchment with the title and stile of

The unanimous Declaration of the thirteen united States of America.

It was not a name but a description. The "united" and "States" were two common terms, the one an adjective modifying the other, a plural noun. The preposition "of" indicated a point of location or a whole that included the part specified by the preceding word. Less technically, "of" here means "located in" or "part of," as in the "United Colonies of North America." The only proper noun is "America," as the location or the inclusive whole. The phrase appeared also in the 1778 Treaty of Alliance with France, this time as the "United States of North America." If you want to keep in mind what the conception of the time was, the simplest way to do it is this: Whenever you come across the phrase the "United States of

America," put "thirteen" before a lower-case "united," change the "of" to "located in," and put "North" before "America." Thus: the thirteen united States located in North America.

When on June 7, 1776, Richard Henry Lee moving for Virginia had proposed and the second Congress had accepted the brief motion for independence, part of the resolution, you remember, had called for the framing of a confederation. Congress did later draw up and approve a plan, and called it the "Articles of Confederation and Perpetual Union." This document had a different purpose: it intended to form a group of some kind, a confederation (Lee's term) or a confederacy or a union (the Articles' own self-descriptions). A name for the group therefore would have been appropriate and useful. Instead, Article I reads, "The stile [that is, title or mode of address] of this Confederacy shall be The United States of America." The authors did not choose a name, but following the Declaration of Independence's example used a description, the same description. Throughout the document it appears in lower case—the united states.

A number of problems involving two or more of the thirteen countries (such as common war debts, common waterways, and separate state dealings with Spain, France, and even England) soon brought confusion: Are you one country or thirteen? For that once-a-year when the Congress was in session the countries seemed united; afterward they were their thirteen individual selves again. It would have made things easier had there been one proper name, like Spain, France, or England, to refer to a unified country and to a unified citizenry, assuming that in this case such things existed.

Dissatisfaction with the Articles of Confederation led to a convention at Philadelphia and the drafting of a document described as a "Constitution for the United States of America," the great written constitution in existence today. Tomorrow I'll go into some of the circumstances leading up to it. Having come this far, though, let me note a few points on the question of names.

The new constitution must have helped out a little, one would think. Surprisingly, as far as a name went, it helped out not at all. Following the example of the Articles of Confederation it left things as they were with the separation document (the Declaration of Independence), speaking at the opening of "the United States of America." Which leaves us with the several States located in North America united in a confederacy, and with no proper name for all of them as one country.

"So, Huggins, if you thought that your country got the name 'America' from the constitution or from any of the presumably American documents we have been looking at, you have another think coming. They all mention 'America' to specify geographical location, but none of them cite 'America' as the name of your country or of any other country."

Huggins was frowning. St. John was waiting for a reaction, jiggling her leg again, to speed up his thinking or to make him even more nervous or to make sure he noticed her gold slave anklet?

"How can that be?" said Huggins finally. "Maybe constitutions don't mention whatever country they're written for. Maybe they take it for granted or maybe at the time it was legal practice to take it for granted and not mention the name."

"Good thinking, Huggins, but it won't wash. It's the legal practice of lawyers to take nothing for granted, isn't it? And most difficult, almost impossible, for them to write a constitution without mentioning the country or the people they're writing it for. It happens that a number of constitutions were written shortly after this one and each of them identifies by name the country it was written for. Take the constitution written in Paris in 1791. Its title is the 'Constitution of France.' Take the constitution written in Warsaw in the same year; it promises the free exercise of religion 'throughout the extent of Poland.'

"Let me open, and close, another possibility," said St. John.

————Although the new constitution did not name a country, perhaps it did name its people or body of citizens, in that way identifying a country, as "French citizens" would identify "France." The people of Mexico are Mexicans, the people of Brazil Brazilians, the people of France Frenchmen. Take the French constitution again: one of its clauses declares that "there shall be no privilege or exemption to the common law for all Frenchmen." Or the Swedish constitution of 1789 titled the "Act of Union and Security": it states that "the Swedish people have the incontestable right to discuss and reach agreement . . . with the King."

If the Framers of the constitution by mentioning "America" in the phrase "We, the People of the United States of America" were not referring to a location but to a country, why didn't they designate its citizens "American citizens"? Does this constitution mention Americans anywhere? It does not. It mentions "citizens" and "free persons" and persons counted as three fifths of a person, that is, slaves, but they are all nameless. They are not Canadian, French, Brazilian, or Mexican citizens. Neither are they American citizens.

"Therefore, Huggins, the possibility for this constitution is closed. Neither, incidentally, will you find an American mentioned anywhere in the Declaration of Independence or the Articles of Confederation. These documents are un-American, wouldn't you say?"

Huggins shifted nervously in his chair.

"Oops!" St. John's lips dissolved in a smile. "I see the word unsettles you. That's why I used it, to make you squirm a little. But it carries too many inappropriate associations. Let's say these documents are non-American or American-less. Or if you prefer, as I do, pre-American. We are still at the stage we were in at the time of Moctezuma—pre-American history."

————The advantage of a name is great. The leading members of the Philadelphia convention had some trouble working without proper nouns for country and citizens. Most of them were advocating a stronger central government and must have sensed the lack of name for the unified country they fancied. A name would have expressed unity, staked out a claim in diplomacy, provided a symbol around which identity and sentiment could cluster. These men wrote and spoke of "our country" or the "general government" or the "national government." To have a national or "consolidated" government—and such was their aim—one ought first to have a country or a nation. But if there was one, they never spoke its name.

Later, when trying to get their draft of a constitution ratified in their respective states, a few of them wrote a famous series of newspaper articles (now titled *The Federalist*) urging adoption, but they still had no name for the country they were proposing a government for, or for its citizens. One of the three authors of those articles was the eminent jurist John Jay. Years later his grandson wrote that the disadvantages of "the want of a distinctive national appellation" were "very generally admitted." And an English observer reviewing the scene at the same time concluded that "it does seem as if the founders of the Republic forgot to give it a name."

"You have not fully experienced what it means to be an American citizen, have you, Huggins? I mean, I don't suppose you're old enough to vote yet."

"Oh yes I am!" Huggins's voice rang out. "I'm nineteen, actually nineteen and a half, almost twenty, to be exact."

"Really?" St. John's eyes widened. "How does it happen you're entering college late?"

"Well, Pa had legal work to do in Ethiopia for nearly two years. We all moved there. Before that I went to the usual schools."

"All male, I presume."

Huggins was puzzled. "I guess so. Why do you ask?"

"No reason. Please go on."

Huggins shrugged. "Anyway, that's why I'm supposed to prepare for university this summer. I'll get advanced standing here because I went to college in Ethiopia, but they offered no courses in American history. I had some private lessons. I learned French and Italian. I learned how to ride."

"You did?" St. John's voice rose in surprise. "In Ethiopia? What kind of horses do they have in— Never mind. Let me finish the day's work."

————The Framers of the 1787 Constitution were good, clever men. They had an opportunity (we can say in hindsight) and missed the boat. Slipping back to colonial days, they used a collective, common noun title. Instead of the United Colonies, we have the United States, as clumsy and cold as only a makeshift name could be. Surely one of them could have said, "What shall we call this new country of ours?" Someone could at least have turned a suggestion over to the Committee on Stile and Arrangement. "Columbia" for one possible choice was not bad as a name: short and sweet, unused before, easily taking "Columbian" as adjective or noun.

Or suppose the committee was unimaginative or undecided: it could have left blank spaces as John Smith and Lord Baltimore did with Charles I. Then, if the convention as a whole liked the name "America," for instance, as the name of their prospective country, there were lots of places in the constitution where they could have filled in the blanks.

Rather than starting off with "We, the People of the United States of America," they could have written more simply, "We, the People of America," or "We, the American People." Both sound good. Or in writing about citizens, they could have inserted the single word *American* at any number of appropriate places. In Article IV, Section 2, they could have filled in a blank thus: "the citizens of each state are *American* citizens and shall be entitled to all privileges and immunities of citizens in the several states."

"That too sounds good to me." St. John picked up her Panama. "It was not as simple as it seems, Huggins. There's a tale or two behind the scenes. George Washington saw this clearly. You'll have to wait till tomorrow. But I'll give you a clue. The Framers didn't dare."

4

GEORGE WASHINGTON

TO THE RESCUE

George Washington
Gouverneur Morris
James Madison
Alexander Hamilton
Charles C. Pinckney

USA 14

Constitutional Convention, 1787

THURSDAY

"Here, Huggins, smell this," pushing some papers under his nose.

"What is it?" said Huggins, taken aback.

"Don't be afraid. It won't bite you. Just some paper, as James Madison, father of the constitution, said. It's a copy of the present constitution of the United States." St. John thrust it closer. "Come on. How does it smell to you? In its prime, immature, ripe, over-ripe?"

"I don't know," said Huggins, still baffled but sniffing at the pages. "It smells okay to me."

"To me too." St. John withdrew the paper from the vicinity of

Huggins's nose and sniffed it herself. "Smells like it has quite a few years to go.

"Now smell this." She thrust in his face a few pages she was holding in her other hand. "This is another constitution of the United States of America. It smells just as good, maybe a bit creamier. Which smells better? Take your pick. Which do we keep, which do we drop in the shredder?"

"I don't know which is which and what is what," Huggins complained. "What is that other constitution?" pointing to the one in her left hand.

St. John immediately straightened up, put her right hand behind her back, and focused on the pages in her left. "Have you ever read the constitution of the United States of America?"

"Of course I have," said Huggins. How could she believe he hadn't? He began to recite, "We, the People of the United States of—"

"That's enough, thank you," cut in St. John. "I meant, have you ever read the *first* constitution of the United States of America?"

"That *is* the first constitution. There is only *one* constitution. Oh, I see, you mean the first *draft* of the constitution."

"Your agility surprises me," said St. John. "But in fact you were quoting from the final draft of the second constitution of the United States. There was a previous constitution. It was titled and is now invariably called 'The Articles of Confederation and Perpetual Union.' "

"Didn't you mention it yesterday? But I never heard it was the first constitution of the United States."

"You wouldn't hear it. Nobody does. It's a case of national amnesia. The document was called *the Constitution* just as Constitution number 2 is called today, and just as Thomas Jefferson in the Declaration of Independence referred to the English constitution as 'our Constitution.' Had we counted that one too, the present one would be number 3."

"What happened to number 1?"

"It was overthrown."

"Overthrown?" said Huggins, unbelieving.

"Overthrown," intoned St. John.

"When was this?"

"Not long after King George signed the peace. A group of men struck a clever, risky, and illegal blow overthrowing the first constitution of the United States of America in the space of a year."

St. John brought her right hand back in front of her and laid both sheets on the table—Constitutions 1 and 2.

"Who were these men, conspirators?" Huggins began to see cloaks and daggers.

"That's what a lot of people called them, obliging them to deny the accusation publicly as wanton, malignant, and calumnious."

"Were they ever charged with treason?" Huggins wanted action.

"If they were, you'd have heard of it, wouldn't you?"

"I don't know. I'm beginning to think there was a lot going on I haven't heard about."

"Good, Huggins. We're making progress. This may come as a shock to you, but those who overthrew the then existing constitution are now called the Founding Fathers or the Framers. You wouldn't want to try and hang them for treason, would you?"

"No, just a minute. I didn't say that. I just asked whether they were ever put on trial. I didn't know who they were. I just thought—"

"You just thought," mimicked St. John. "I can see you'll make a good lawyer. What difference does it make who they were? Treason is treason, is it not? Unless you reason as I do that treason when successful is not treason but heroism or patriotism. That's why it's said there is no such thing as successful treason."

————I had intended to spend some time on presenting the arguments and the men on both sides, those who wanted to keep the existing constitution and those who were striking out for a new one; both sides had good arguments. They were all men, part good, part bad. On both sides there were farmers, debtors, creditors, merchants, mechanics, shippers, and landowners, many more of the farmers and mechanics, laborers and debtors opposing a new constitution, many more of the others—creditors, land speculators, shippers, merchandisers, and manufacturers—favoring it. And as always, on both sides a generous ration of lawyers.

James Madison, behind the closed doors of the State House (now called Independence Hall) in Philadelphia, confided that the strongest motive among those who pushed for the convention—and he should know: he was one of the prime movers—was the fear of "popular license" spreading through the newly independent states. "License" meant "too much liberty"; "popular" meant "of the people," or again in Madison's terms, "democratic excess." It wasn't so much that Constitution 1 was weak, as that the new state governments were springing debtor relief laws, issuing cheap money, confiscating property (that of the loyalists to start, but heaven knows where this would end)—in short, threatening property, contract rights, and the repayment of debts with specie, with hard money that made a noise when you slapped it on the counter, that added weight to your money bags.

Madison's conclusion is as accurate as any, and will hold us for the time being. As we go along over the next couple of days, you'll grasp its significance.

When the first constitution of the United States of America was ratified in 1781, celebrations broke out in all the States—fireworks, parades, receptions, dinners, and cannonades. Conceived in 1776, it was part of the same resolution in the Congress that proposed independent statehood. Drafted in the following year, it began a new calendar that dated all public events from the Declaration of Independence, from when the United Colonies of North America emerged as the united States of America, in General Congress Assembled.

Every so often one meets with this dating practice among revolutionaries. They hold their revolution to be of such importance that they make all time begin with it. The French were soon to do that, starting with the republican calendar of 1792. Typically, the changed calendar lasts a short while and then, except in little-noted officialese, goes back to dating exclusively from the greater happening—the birth of Christ. The nonreligious date on which the delegates underwrote Constitution 1 was "the Second Year of the Independence of America." *America* here is short for *ex-British* America, now (after the Declaration of Independence) the America prospectively independent of Great Britain, the territorial location of the thirteen Atlantic ex-British colonies, the already named States. And alongside ex-British America there were still French and Spanish Americas.

Obviously, if 1776, the year of the revolution, of the Declaration of Independence, was the first year, 1777 was the second. Though official, the wording of this new calendar has not been consistent. At the close of the Northwest Ordinance of 1787 these lines appear: "Done by the United States, in Congress assembled, the 13th day of July, in the year of our Lord 1787, and of their sovereignty and independence the twelfth." A more recent presidential formula reads thus: "I [the president] have hereunto set my hand this 24th day of December, in the year of our Lord 1992, and of the Independence of the United States of America the 217th." In the year of our Lord 2000 the political year will be the 224th.

Constitution 1, close in time and origin to the Declaration of Independence, is close also in its spirit of free and independent States. The Articles were to frame a confederacy or union, one that would not impair the autonomy of the several states and their own separate constitutions. Throughout the document, we saw, the title was written in small letters, "the united states," indicating that it was not a proper noun. Article II states that "Each state retains its sovereignty, freedom and independence, and every Power, Jurisdiction and Right, which is not by this confederation expressly delegated to the united states in Congress assembled."

This plural title of "the united states" for a confederacy or union posed no threat: it could not be the singular name of a superstate that might drain the thirteen states of their freedom and powers.

When Constitution 2's turn came around in 1787, its drafters (today called the Framers) had to cope with the ever-present fear of the States that a large consolidated state would sooner or later deprive them of their power and independence. If the opponents of such a state hadn't realized it at the beginning, it soon became clear that the most influential and aggressive delegates at the drafting convention in Philadelphia were aiming not at an amendment to the existing constitution but at a new constitution that would indeed take vital powers away from the States and lodge them with a central government.

Sensing the opposition, the Framers became wary of words that might convey that Constitution 2 was setting up one consolidated government. They sugarcoated their vocabulary, resorting to "the government of the United States" instead of "national government," and following Noah Webster the lexicographer's coinage and the Framer Alexander Hamilton's lead, took to calling themselves Federalists, thereby begetting a confusing, parochial meaning: A federalist is one who in a system nominally federal promotes a strong, central government. Their opponents, the true federalists, advocating a decentralized federation, protested this usage to no avail: they were dubbed the anti-Federalists.

Had the Framers adopted a name for the unified country they desired—and they could surely see that a name would have given them inestimable advantages—they would have thereby revealed to the States their radical objective and the extent of their transgressions. This fear in the States of an overpowering single government was reason enough to keep the convention from proposing, or even thinking about proposing a national name, whether America, Columbia, or anything else.

More than this, Constitution 1 already existed and by its own title and text was declared to be perpetual. It did have provisions for amendments, but the advocates of Constitution 2 calculated that they lacked the political support to amend it and that even if they did manage to get that support, the basic structure of Constitution 1 was such that they could not within its limits achieve the power over the States they wished a national government to have. What to do?

Masking their intentions, moving with urgency and secrecy, these "artful men," as their opponents called them, took their chances and struck the blow I just described as the overthrowing of the first constitution of the United States of America—in a rush of meetings, conventions, over-dinner and behind-closed-door understandings. Patrick Henry, the famous Virginian orator, called it a greater revolution than that against England.

When the Committee of Detail of the Convention laid before the delegates the first draft of Constitution 2, its first article called for the same cautious phrase as that in Constitution 1—"The stile of the government shall be, The United States of America." The Committee on Stile and Arrangement in preparing the final draft deleted this article and transferred the phrase to the preamble: "this Constitution for the United States of America." The only progress the convention achieved was to capitalize the *u*, making it the

"United States," but retaining its plural sense throughout. There is no use of the phrase in this constitution that cannot and should not be read as "these United States."

"It's hard to believe," said Huggins. "Do you want me to read Constitution 1?"

"What for? It's deader 'n a doornail, ready for the shredder." St. John waved the document in her left hand and made the motions of thrusting it up and down into a machine.

"Well, if Constitution 1 was not legally abrogated, it should be restored as law, shouldn't it?"

"Not a chance," said St. John.

"Can you tell me more about how this happened and who was involved?"

"What good would that do?"

"If our present constitution is Constitution 2, there might someday be Constitution 3, right? Constitution 2 is legal, right? I'd like to know how from one legal constitution you can arrive at another legal constitution—illegally. It sounds like I want to learn how to be a revolutionary, but that's not what I mean." Huggins paused for a thought. "My idea of law must be Pollyanna-ish, I guess."

"I'll see what I can do," said St. John. "You asked earlier who these artful men were. There were three who took the important steps at three places: Mount Vernon, Annapolis, and Philadelphia. Hear ye now, the Tale of the Artful Trio."

————Scarcely had the ink dried on Constitution 1, the Articles of Confederation and Perpetual Union, when opposition arose. Noises of discontent began to be heard in high quarters. George Washington, Robert Morris, John Dickinson, Gouverneur Morris, Alexander Hamilton, James Madison, and others began dashing off letters of worry and fear over the existing constitution.

The first of the Artful Trio is George Washington. In his early fifties, he had left the command of the Continental army and returned home to Mount Vernon where his land ran for ten miles along the Potomac. His wealth came largely from his wife—fifteen thousand acres of land and three hundred slaves, not counting Bank of England stocks and specie. Two generations earlier his ancestors

had emigrated to Virginia from England where they had had a hard
time as supporters of the ill-fated Charles I. Here, though busy in
buying and selling land, they did not do particularly well. George
Washington had to work for a living. He grew to over six feet, with
roan hair, big hands and feet, "the best of constitutions," he claimed,
and great strength—he could bend a horseshoe with his bare hands.

Perhaps fortunately, Washington had not had the social background of most of the other delegates to the Philadelphia convention; their riches were older. He was an Anglican, though, and did
become a Mason. He did not study law at the English Inns of Court,
or for that matter at any other school. His education was limited to
reading, writing, arithmetic, and the elementary geometry needed
for surveying. A fellow Virginian, who had been his early mentor,
once called him the "upstart surveyor." That occupation, however—maps and geometry—helped him in his second occupation:
soldier.

George Washington was a surveyor and soldier all his life. If you
understand this you have the key to most of his career.

Honest in public affairs, he was not averse to cutting corners in
official expense accounts or in buying horses, land, and slaves. Surveying stimulated an interest in land speculation, a disease of many
of the great British Americans. It gave him advance notice of pur-
chasable and profitable land. His passion for acreage had already revealed itself when he was sixteen and bought five hundred acres of
wild land. By age twenty-one he had picked up over fifteen hundred acres through payment for his surveying services alone. Washington's military experience in the French and Indian War, where
he demonstrated great bravery, led him to appreciate the value of
opening traffic to lands to the West. He later collected a sizable
claim in the Ohio Valley, due him as a bonus for his service in that
war.

In those days land was still the great source of wealth and prestige. Speculators and settlers drove ever farther west, where land
could still be had cheaply, through claims often disputed by both
redskins and fellow palefaces. By charter Virginia's western boundaries extended as far as the Mississippi, but George III had halted
all settlement in the western section, presumably to prevent land-
grabbing and gain time to prepare a plan that would benefit him,

his friends, his creditors, and the empire. Colonial resentment at land containment was one of the sorest points in colonial relations with the mother country. The Revolution won these lands from Great Britain. They were now up for the taking. At home and abroad huge land companies were lobbying Congress and would have liked nothing better than a government strong enough to give them title against the claims of the States.

A tenth or so of Washington's income came from selling good whiskey. He made money building and renting houses, too, as well as buying and selling slaves and horses. A letter of his of 1766 to a slave-trader gives some idea of relative values in Virginia plantation life of the time. "With this Letter comes a negro (Tom)," it begins,

> which I beg the favour of you to sell in any of the Islands you may go to, for whatever he will fetch, & bring me in return for him
>   One Hhd of best Molasses [hogshead: a cask containing from sixty-three to one hundred forty gallons]
>   One Ditto of best Rum
>   One Barrl of Lymes—if good & Cheap
>   One Pot of Tamarinds—contg about 10 lbs.
>   Two small Do of mixed Sweetmeats—abt 5 lb. each.
>   And the residue, much or little, in good old Spirits.
>   That this Fellow is both a Rogue & Runaway (tho, he was by no means remarkable for the former, and never practised the latter till of late) I shall not pretend to deny—But that he is exceeding healthy, strong and good at the Hoe, the whole neighbourhood can testifie . . . which gives me reason to hope he may, with your good management sell well, if kept clean & trim'd up a little when offerd for Sale.

Washington took pleasure in a gentlemanly husbandry and farming. But his accounts show his main business by far was speculation in land. He was held to be the wealthiest man in the several States. His will disclosed a land estate of over sixty thousand acres, much of it acquired by buying up cheap the land entitlements of soldiers.

Washington could be pleasant, and never forgot his manners. The marriage of his half-brother Lawrence into the Fairfaxes of England and Virginia gave George a valuable connection. To Sally Fairfax, a young woman already married into that baronial family, he declared his love even while engaged to his future wife Martha. Sally taught him the civilities—how to bow and kiss the lady's hand. He usually drank a pint of Madeira at dinner and did not refuse rum, cider, punch, or brandy. He kept to his limit, which was enough to put today's social drinker under the table. Temperamentally reserved and phlegmatic, when he became a celebrity he didn't care to shake hands. The handshake is a gesture signifying equality, however minimal. Washington would try to keep gloves or something in his right hand to discourage prospective handshakers. It took a lot of champagne to bring out his conviviality.

He could or would not bring himself to laugh at jokes or even to laugh with children playing around his knees, although he loved children, or with the bevies of admiring young beauties that gather around a gallant captain—and he loved being surrounded by belles of the ball. Whenever he smiled in public, the press reported it. He did not tolerate being teased, except perhaps by his small plump wife, who could sometimes coax him out of injured dignity by twisting one of his vest buttons while looking up at the mountain height, hazel eyes meeting blue-gray. Teasing and practical jokes were threats to his dignity. Clothes preserved dignity. Washington was always careful about his lace ruffles and cuffs, his shoe buckles, his coats and knee breeches, his wigs and pigtails, and silk stockings.

At the Philadelphia Convention the naughty Hamilton bet the naughty Gouverneur Morris (more about them later) that he wouldn't dare go up to Washington, clap him on the shoulder, and say something like "How goes it, George?" Gouverneur, so the story goes, did just that, came back and collected his bet, announcing, however, that he wouldn't make *that* bet again. Washington had turned on him his fiercest countenance, drilling him with icy eyes. Someone present, maybe Hamilton himself, later remarked over rum punch, "You'd have thought that Gouverneur had reached for his crotch."

Critics of Washington's dignity do not understand that gravity, as the ancient Romans called it, is especially necessary in a republic where the ceremonies of authority are scant, that in his case, luckily, there was a proper meeting of the necessity of the job and the character of the jobholder. Washington liked pomp. If there was anything in monarchy that would have won him over to the Tory cause, it would have been a uniform of the highest rank, horse guards, trumpets a-trumpeting. When elected president, he rode to New York in state in his gorgeous coach-and-four, postilions in white and scarlet, harness buckles engraved with the Washington coat of arms.

To make sure that the importance of the chief executive was recognized, the first draft of Constitution 2 had decreed that the president should bear the title of "His Excellency." The final draft wisely ruled this out. The story is told that when President Washington let it be known he preferred to be announced as "His Mightiness the President of the United States," the Speaker of the House laughed out loud. Washington never forgave him. "The President of the United States" became his official title. "His Mightiness," though, suggests what was appealing to Washington about the presidency— its punitive and war powers, and occasions for pomp and ceremony. Lots of people spoke of His Excellency, even of His Majesty, and of Martha as Lady Washington.

You can see Washington protecting his dignity at an early age. As a young man he went swimming in the Rappahannock River. One day two girls made the mistake of running off with his clothes. Somehow he got home. One likes to think of him skulking back with fig leaves girdling his groin. Anyway he had the girls arrested: one was let off, the other convicted of theft, her back stripped to the waist, and given fifteen lashes. Years later, Nathaniel Hawthorne imagined that Washington was born with clothes on, hair powdered, ready to bow gravely. "Did anybody ever see Washington naked?" the great writer asked. "It is inconceivable."

We do not know whether he ever flogged anyone himself or left all flogging to his overseers. Certainly he oversaw the execution of many whippings, not only. of slaves but of his own soldiers. I doubt that he himself was ever flogged. He did put great store in discipline and punishment. Floggings were dished out freely in the Continental army. The commander in chief informed Congress that if there was to be discipline, he had to be permitted to inflict more than the regulation limit of thirty-nine lashes for the ordinary offense. Congress raised the limit to one hundred. Bite the bullet, boys.

There were several mutinies in 1780–81. In January of 1781

troops of the New Jersey Line mutinied, demanding to present their complaints to the legislature. Their commander told them that their grievances would be corrected and promised the mutineers a full pardon, but once the men returned to duty, he wrote Washington for advice and assistance in the matter of mutiny. Washington sent Major General Robert H. Howe to the camp with six hundred men picked from the best regiments at West Point, ordering Howe to enforce unconditional submission and to execute a few of the principal incendiaries. One man was taken from each of the three mutinous regiments: one was pardoned by the intervention of his officers, two were shot by weeping members of the mutinous regiments.

Washington believed that such action could teach necessary lessons. After the execution of the "pardoned" mutineers, he wrote Friedrich von Steuben, the Prussian baron serving as a major general in the Revolution, that it was lucky that the mutiny occurred when it did; it put an end to rebellious spirit before it had gone too far. Nonetheless, mutinies did continue.

Having mutineers execute their own comrades may have been a disciplinary practice of revolutionary forces. Just before departing Virginia, twelve soldiers of the Pennsylvania Line stepped out of ranks and persuaded their comrades not to march until they were paid in "real, not ideal, money." (The prevailing ratio was 40 continentals to 1 specie.) General Anthony Wayne later wrote that he had these men arrested, tried, and sentenced to be shot. The firing squad, whether by design or accident, was made up of the particular friends and messmates of the culprits. A first group of mutineers was executed, except one who fell to the ground wounded. Wayne ordered a soldier to step out of rank and to bayonet the man who lay moaning. The soldier protested that he could not do it, the man was his comrade. "Mad Anthony" Wayne then put a pistol to the soldier's head and threatened to blow out his brains. The underpaid, underclothed, and underfed soldier thrust the bayonet into his $6.66-a-month friend's chest and throat. General Wayne then maneuvered the regiment about the corpses and ordered five remaining mutineers to be hanged. So ended that ruckus.

Huggins couldn't contain himself. "God!"

"Yes, I know. War is hell," soothed St. John.

"But where is the consent of the governed the Declaration of Independence talks about? These soldiers were not ordinary soldiers. They were fighting for liberty and the right to govern themselves. If they had lost faith in their leaders, why couldn't they say they could no longer give their consent and just leave like the officers? I don't understand you, Ms. St. John. You're a girl . . . a woman, a young woman—and you can look at men bayoneting their friends lying on the ground, wounded, and say, 'Tsk, tsk, war is hell; boys will be boys.' "

"What does my being a female have to do with it?"

"I've always thought that women hated violence more than men. And in this case there's violence and injustice. Maybe women don't have faith in justice. I don't know, maybe I'm wrong."

"I can't speak for my sex, but I feel the same as you do. For me the field of honor is there, on the ground, where the wounded and dying are crying out for their mothers. This is not the moment to talk of patriotism and consent, particularly since we are not sure what there is to be patriotic about. Perhaps later. You caught me forcing myself to be fair to Washington. Let's move on."

————You've got to take into account that save for his intimacy with the play *Cato*—"O liberty, O virtue, O my country"—Washington was not a literary man. Nor was he a man of ideas. His intellectual contribution to the Revolution was nil. On matters of policy he relied on the thinking and writing of others. His neighbor George Mason was his mentor before the Revolution; his writing aide, Alexander Hamilton, was his mentor afterward.

Where he could trust to instinct was in military matters. Washington the surveyor wanted to be a great general. Soon after his marriage he sent an order to London for a half-dozen busts of great men: Alexander the Great, Julius Caesar, the duke of Marlborough, Prince Eugene of Savoy, Charles XII of Sweden, Frederick the Great of Prussia—all illustrious military captains. Now one thing Niccolò Machiavelli in *The Prince* says about a military captain is that he has to have the reputation of being cruel, else he can never keep an army united or disposed to battle. I'm quite sure Washington's reputation for cruelty has been handed down to us as a reputation for just severity. As for the treatment of mutineers, Niccolò, who wrote a famous book on the *Art of War* (John Smith carried it in his knapsack in company with the Bible), says that to keep a brake on armed men is not easy.

"Look at it from the captain's point of view, Huggins. These are men armed with lethal weapons. If you are not prepared to cut their heart out, they'll cut out yours."

Huggins stared at her, his eyes wide with incredulity.

She pushed on unperturbed.

————I might mention another of Niccolò's mottoes: Keep soldiers punished and paid. Washington kept his troops punished; he could not always keep them paid, and this as we saw was a cause of mutiny. Washington's distaste for the Congress was largely due to its inability—time and again he wrote pleading letters—to send pay for the soldiers.

A crisis arose near the end of the war when parts of the army refused to demobilize without first being paid their arrears. By a trick, giving the troops a furlough, Washington and Congress defused that powder keg. The troops left to go home and never returned except individually, to present their claims. A month later Pennsylvania troops of the Continental army surrounded the Congress assembled in Philadelphia. Congress fled to Princeton.

A few months before, early in 1783, another crisis had emerged when the officers refused to budge. Washington appeared at their meeting. As their senior officer, they had to let him speak. He took out a written speech, and then searched for and slowly put on his spectacles to read it. "You see," he confided to the assembled officers, "I have grown not only grey but also blind in your service." This remark so moved the officers that they decided to wait for their pay.

One of Washington's few weaknesses was self-pity. His aide, Lieutenant Colonel Alexander Hamilton, was alert to cut signs of it out of the General's speeches. In this case it seemed to have helped. I have not verified the text; there is something fishy about it. Washington did not read much: why should his service to his officers have put a strain on his eyes? Persons of normal vision almost all need reading glasses at age forty-three. Washington was then fifty. He must have begun to need glasses before he had even begun his "service," as he put it, to the officers. He might as well have hinted at his teeth, which had begun to give trouble in his twenties, or at the signs of tremor and deafness that were creeping upon him now. That phrase, too, "in your service," while lining him up on the officers' side, leads one to overlook that in fact he was in Congress's service.

But Washington managed to pull off this piece of theater successfully. His six-foot-three-inch frame, his uniform, his reputation, his perennial gravity, would have helped. I don't know. Soldiers in his army mutinied or deserted; officers resigned. Continental troops suffered long periods of cold and hunger; Washington and his staff of officers, judging from his written expense accounts, never suffered much more than having to switch from Madeira to brandy. Perhaps he had a motto of his own: "Keep officers contented and troops in fear."

In brief I'll conclude: Though Washington contributed few ideas, he did stand for something—the opening up of western lands and the consolidation of the States under a government strong enough to keep a standing army punished and paid. His record was convincing. He speculated in land, came on strong for discipline and order, and was contemptuous of a bankrupt Congress. His traits of stiffness or gravity and of pleasure in dress and pomp lent solemnity to any meeting and later, as some say, helped hedge the presidency with majesty.

During the war Washington had formed a few close attachments to younger men who had worked under him. One was to the young, handsome, courageous Major General Marquis Marie-Joseph de La Fayette, who had joined the rebel cause and in later years signed his letters to Washington—"your adopted son." Another was to Lieutenant Colonel Hamilton, who shared the General's opinion of the weakness of Congress under Constitution 1 and became the second member of our holy trio.

Born in the British West Indies the illegitimate son of a Scotsman and a woman jailed for adultery, this precocious lad Hamilton found at age eleven a clerk's job in an accounting firm with shipping interests between St. Croix and Manhattan. He made rapid headway in the company. With its support, and thanks to help from a maternal cousin and his Presbyterian connections, he arrived in New York at age sixteen, to study at a New Jersey academy and at New York's King's College, which you now know as Columbia University. His studies interrupted by the war, he earned a commission as an artillery man and conducted himself so intelligently and bravely that he came to the attention of Colonel (later General) Henry Knox, the best artilleryman in the Continental army, who introduced him to General Washington. For four years (1777 to 1781) he served as Washington's private secretary and confidential aide, where his command of French stood him in good stead.

Fair-haired and ruddy in coloring, slender, and narrow of shoulder, dignified and graceful in carriage, Hamilton possessed an agile mind, clear and logical, bent toward economics and law. Add to this a warm temperament, generosity, ambition, nervous energy, and violet-blue eyes. He was a fighter through and through, outspoken and impulsive. His unrelenting persecution of Aaron Burr, thwarting that great general's ambition for the governorship of New York and for the presidency of the United States, led to the duel that cost him his life. He confessed that his heart was ever the master of his judgment. When his heart took command, his self-confidence became arrogance, his arguments opinionated and uncompromising. Sarcastic rather than humorous, his tongue was often impolitic and indiscreet. Not long after his marriage to Elizabeth, daughter of Major General Philip Schuyler, a New York patroon, he took offense at a mild reprimand from Washington and resigned from the commander in chief's staff. "The Great man and I have come to an open rupture," he announced to a friend. Hamilton wanted more action in the field anyway. He applied and obtained a command from Washington and led his column gloriously in the final assault against the British at Yorktown.

Washington had full confidence in him, prized his courage, integrity, honor, and brilliance, and continued to seek his advice and help more than from any other quarter. As early as 1776 Hamilton was advocating direct collection of taxes by agents of a central government, and soon after the drafting of Constitution 1 was remarking that a convention should be called to frame a new constitution.

He had to wait six or seven years for some prominent people to take him seriously.

James Madison (whom I already quoted on Constitution 1), the third of our threesome, another young man to whom Washington took a shine, was a fellow Virginian whose first North American ancestor had disembarked over a century earlier and whose father owned big estates in Virginia. At the College of New Jersey (now Princeton University) young Madison seemed bent on acquiring a living in the ministry; for a while he pursued studies in theology and Hebrew, serving as tutor to the younger children of the extended Madison family. Just five feet tall, slight of frame, small of face, he was quietly dignified, cool, and precise in his ways. He liked conversation, loved to tell a good story and have a good laugh. He married the widow Dorothy "Dolly" Payne Todd, a plump beauty, whose grace, charm, and lavish hospitality made the social life of his household sparkle.

The rebellion against England drew Madison into politics. He became a delegate in 1776 to the Virginia constitutional convention and in 1779 to the Congress. After the war he took up the study of law and was soon elected to the Virginia legislature. When Jefferson went to France as minister, Madison—always studious—plied him with requests for books on political ideas. His wide reading in constitutional history and theory laid the ground for his fame as the Father of the Constitution, number two, that is. The young man's concern for rights and religious freedom solidified his friendship with Jefferson; his belief that Congress should have power to collect revenue from the States linked him to Washington and Hamilton. With Jefferson abroad, Madison felt more drawn to the General's orbit, although he continued to report his activities and views in a stream of letters to Jefferson in Paris.

So much for a bit of background on the three men. It will guide us through the subject you asked about earlier, how the constitutions of the United States went from legal number one to legal number two, illegally.

In 1785 the Virginia legislature decided it was time to attend to disputes with Maryland over navigation of the Potomac River and Chesapeake Bay. Madison proposed that commissioners chosen by the two legislatures meet at Alexandria to "frame such liberal and equitable regulations concerning the said [Potomac] river as may be mutually advantageous." The commissioners would conclude their deliberations at Mount Vernon.

Why Mount Vernon? Because General Washington had invited them. The game is afoot.

Washington's home was a village in itself. Arriving at the serene, grandly colonnaded porch one did not see the cottages, the stables, the shops, the beehive of industry behind it. The trail starts here, at Mount Vernon.

Huggins saw Claire's eyes go dreamy. "It's easy to imagine the setting," she murmured.

It was first of all a lovely late March afternoon, white clouds piling up to the west. Crocuses, daffodils, and forsythia were out, buttercups covered the meadows, dogwoods shimmered with tiny red buds, honeysuckle and jasmine climbed up trellises and fences, the air smelled of warming earth still dry enough for a good gallop. Martha Custis Washington looked out a tall window in the hall.

Yes, there he was, cantering up to the road, tall in the saddle, turning into the serpentine driveway to the house at an easy trot, hounds scrambling forth and back and around happily. No one looked better on a horse than her Old Man. Everyone said so, and they were right. A magnificent rider, that hulk of his glued to the saddle. He and the new big three-year-old—what was its name? Oh yes, "Speedo"—they made a perfect picture as they came in on the grass at a slow walk, the hounds tumbling over each other, the stallion halting at the portico. The General took pride in those lofty, two-story columns. She had to admit it was pleasant to sit out there and pour tea and through the glass watch the boats on the river. Of course, in good weather one could be doing the same thing from an ordinary porch. But the General liked to turn out in brown jacket, satin knickers, purple cravat and lace jabot, with his hair powdered and tied at the back in a silk bag, to greet his guests from the portico. Somehow its proportions and his went well together, like horse and rider.

She went out the door to watch him. At the side of the house, waiting, stood Glover. The General dismounted gracefully and handed the groom the reins. She waited until he reached the porch steps.

"Did you have a good run?"

"Found and killed a bitch fox. Chased it nearly three hours, and treed it three times."

"George, you looked a picture, coming up so tall in the bright sunlight."

"Humpf," muttered Washington. "No different from what I do every day, come rain, come shine."

He did not relish compliments about his fine figure on horseback. She knew this but sometimes could not resist the temptation to tease. He used to be pleased by such compliments but not since that verse of "Yankee Doodle" made the tavern rounds in New England: "And there sat Captain Washington, upon a slapping stallion." There was more to it.

> And there was Captain Washington
> And gentle folks about him.
> They say he's grown so tarnal proud
> He will not ride without 'em.

Washington sat down on the long bench. Clem sidled up to it, turned his back to the General, and expertly pulled off his boots. The General stood up, began stomping around in stocking feet, regaining his land legs. The boy started to carry the boots away.

"Hold on, Clem!" Washington raised his voice. "The stitching is breaking loose around the ankle on that one again. Get your pa to sew it up right this time or I'll have him by the heels."

"Yes sir, General," Clem chimed. He moved off, examining the stitching on the boots indifferently as he walked.

Washington turned to his wife. "He's a good animal. Has a nice easy canter and a good fast walk." He had switched topics from boots to mounts. "He can get into a fast run for the money. I bet he will be right for the two-and-a-half miler come autumn."

"Dear, you had better dress before settling down. The commissioners will be here soon, you know."

"I know, I know. The weather's good. They may get here a little early. Is everything set for supper, dearest? You don't know them. It's just an impromptu sort of thing but . . ."

She smiled to herself at the apologetic tone. She ought to know how to arrange a little supper party for eight or ten persons, she who called herself the Landlady of Mount Vernon Tavern. In all their married life they had dined alone perhaps a couple of dozen times. No one in all Virginia, probably no one in all the Colonies—Heavens! she still thought of them as colonies now and then—could afford such frequent hospitality. It was a surprise and a blessing that dear Daniel when leaving her a widow had left her as much money and property as he did, or they might be as poor as poor Mr. Jefferson. Of course she and George did not have children; so she had time for a busy social life at home. Steady as a clock, busy as a bee, cheerful as a cricket, that she was. Too bad about the children. It had bothered her a lot at first, and him, too. But you learn to live with it, what else can you do? You couldn't help wonder, though, sometimes, how life would have been if they had their own children, together. The General loved children. His pockets were always full of presents for them. He loved Daniel's and her children as if they were his own, and no matter what you say, that is uncommon in a man. Their friends imported Irish or Scottish schoolmasters for their children. Not George. He would not accept a tutor from Scotland; the children had to have an English accent. And think of the love he had for young Marquis de La Fayette, and for the Marchioness too. Just recently, Martha remembered, he showed her the letter he was writing to the Marchioness in Paris, inviting her to come, too, on a visit to Mount Vernon. "Will you My Dr Marchioness deny us the pleasure of accompanying him to the shores of Columbia?" Now if *they* or some other persons from abroad were coming, she could understand his fretting about table and all, but these tonight were just a few Virginians and Marylanders sitting in the small dining room, not the banquet hall.

"I do know that you've been looking to their coming for the whole week," she replied, "and the meeting has been on your mind for a long time." She spoke matter-of-factly.

"A great deal hinges on our little talks tonight and tomorrow," he answered patiently. "The value of our western property, my dear Patsy, depends on our preparing some plan, and now, before it is too late, is the time to put our heads together."

"Of course, Papa. I *know*." Mrs. Washington matched his air of patience. He was always so apprehensive. "You have been saying that ever since you gave up the army." He liked being head of the army. He liked uniforms so much, he used to wear his colonel's uniform and heavy sword on every possible occasion. Sometimes he was the only one there dressed like that; he was on all the military committees. Naturally they thought of him when they had to pick a commander in chief from Virginia. Those were good days, going to Morristown by carriage, wrapped in furs, with family and friends, to stay with him in camp. He had to order two log buildings for the servants, but he didn't mind. She liked the balls. She liked to ride by His Excellency's Guard. So tall they all were, stiff at attention as she passed. Those thighs! Rows of them in tight buffs and . . . Please! Not to dwell! And he was more active physically in the army than he is at home. You would never catch him spending hours reading books. If it were not for hunting and overlooking the plantation, all day in the saddle, he would be bored. Just port and cards every night. He did write about plants and things in that journal of his, and he was forever writing letters . . .

"It is all part of the same thing," her husband was saying. "The States and their puffed-up ideas of independence, always prattling about sovereignty, their darling sovereignties. Why cannot they bring themselves around to realize that we must be *one country*. Each of them has to sacrifice *some* rights."

"I *know*, George. It was clever of you to invite them here." She giggled to herself: that empty-headed Mrs. Banting had told her one day that somebody (she forgot who) said that asking a state to give up part of its sovereignty was like asking a maiden to give up part of her virginity.

The General continued. "You are acquainted with most of the company tonight from Virginia—Mr. Madison, Mason, and Edmund Randolph. And there's the Maryland party. They will be coming directly from their meeting in Alexandria. I told you they were not bringing their wives, didn't I?" He had quit stomping his feet and began to walk inside the house toward the stairway. "In a way I am glad: we can pay more attention to the project. The ladies, though, do brighten up the hours, I must say."

She thought so, too. One of the things that had surprised her a little when the war was over and won and the victory celebrations and balls under way, was his excitement—hidden (but not to her) under his mask of gravity—at seeing the ladies decked out in all their finery. He was quick to the dance. How he could be so light on those big feet when tripping to quadrilles and minuets was a mystery. She had always known he was a good dancer, not as good a dancer as he was a horseman, but indefatigable—yes, that was the word, indefatigable, riding or dancing for hours. She never worried about his straying from the path, however. She was not jealous when he danced the feet off Kitty Greene at camp that time, three hours without stopping. It would not have been so bad had she not had to sit through most of it with a smile and everybody watching, and there sat General Greene with his limp. You cannot blame her for being cross. About appearances, that was all. A lot of women did worry about their husbands. What they said about tidewater Maryland was just as true of Virginia (she almost giggled aloud this time): a virgin was a girl who could run faster than her uncle. Surely, the closeness of Virginia families produced more than a tight little cousinage, but her grave and awkward Old Man was not your typical Virginia gallant, no. He sprang from English blood, of course, but his forebears had little to recommend them: his father . . . his grandfather . . . the further back you went, the worse it got, dealers as sharp as any Yankee. If the Fairfaxes had not taken him under their wing . . . yes, including Sally Fairfax. *Mrs.* Sally Fairfax. Tall, slender, graceful, elegant Sally Fairfax. That was nothing more than puppy love. Only thing left of that romance was *Cato*, that play he and Sally read together years ago. Sally's stage voice still rang in her ears: "Believe me, Prince . . . I did not know myself how much I lov'd thee." Many years ago. How she had hated that Mrs. Fairfax and her sapphires. Well, it wasn't hate, it was jealousy, of course it was. Still, it *was* silly of him to buy Sally's pillows at the auction of the Fairfax things. She had known just what to do with those pillows: Amy's woolly head still slept on them every night. He never seemed silly when talking about horses or cards or racing or cockfighting or breeding hounds or soldiering or farming. She marveled that he rode over the farm like clockwork each morning and filled his journal with details each afternoon. But that *Cato*, and that Sally. Well, flirtatious he was when he met her and flirtatious he is now, as flirtatious as the next one, and a spark in his eye for some ladies more than others—but never did he follow up, of that she was certain. As for Sally, she was in England now. Not likely to return with all the Fairfax property in Virginia gone, confiscated, auctioned. And it was she, his dear Patsy, whose cameo likeness he carried around his neck on the gold chain peeking out alongside his cravat.

"The evening will be bright enough." She walked through the door after him. "The card tables are ready for some lively play. It will not be all talk of the Potomac and the Pocomoke, will it, dear?" Her husband's mouth relaxed a little, and she knew her sally was successful, as he put on his amused-at-the-little-woman's-ignorance look.

"It will be little play and much work, I fear." His voice lifted in answer as he climbed the stairs. "Is Will upstairs?"

"Yes," she called back up to him. "He is laying out your clothes now. Will you take the commissioners out on the horses in the morning? Do you want me to let Will know?"

"Yes, don't bother, I have already told him." Her husband's voice was trailing off.

"I have set four bottles of Madeira and four of champagne on the sideboard," she all but shouted, "and you know where the brandy is."

She walked slowly back into the hallway, glanced at herself in the long mirror, a plump, gray-haired little lady dressed in hazel to match her eyes, not at all displeasing; three years older than the General, she was holding up her end. One thing about being older, the good Lord would probably take her before him. She could not bear to be a widow again, no, not after being married to the General. She gathered her skirts, she knew just what she would wear, the mauve silk gown with a blue sash, the Brussels cap with black ribbons, just a few pearls, the blue and white brocaded slippers with heels and the diamond circle on the instep. Tonight's little party of eight—a trifle. Sam and the other houseboys knew just what to do, though she would never acknowledge it.

After dinner the men stayed in the dining room to smoke and drink. She should remind him not to drink too much port, the doctor said that was what made his teeth black, but she would never nag him publicly, certainly not today, and anyway they were deep into discussing whether something or other was altogether proper. ". . . Revision of the federal system is a delicate matter," she heard a familiar voice saying. ". . . The present constitution will bury us in its ruins."

When she walked into the room George was cracking nuts, as usual between thumb and forefinger.

She bid them a cheery "Good night, gentlemen."

They jumped to their feet, returned her salutation and bowed. So did he, but she could see he was distracted; he sat down quickly, cutting the little ceremony short. She hoped the game would be worth the candle. As she was leaving she heard him continue: "I don't know about the pragmatic side of this, gentlemen . . ."

Whatever the pragmatic side, Martha knew the General would take his time deciding whether to have any hand in the business. "George Prudence Washington" she used to tease him when they were courting. If anything, he was more cautious about things now, never moving an inch if a doubt lingered, but once his mind was made up . . . he was always right.

Martha started up the stairs to the bedroom. Where was Amy? Honestly that girl will be— Oh, there she is.

Amy was behind, following her mistress to the bedroom.

"Girl, why are you always underfoot? I'm going to trip over you one of these days."

————Martha Washington's hospitality and the Mount Vernon meeting were successful, said St. John, shaking her head a little as if to clear it of pictures. Among other proposals the group drafted a compact which their two States later approved and acted upon, forming the Potomac Company, with George Washington as president. Was such a compact between the two States constitutional? Constitution 1 in Article VI states that "No two or more states shall enter into any treaty, confederation or alliance whatever between them without the consent of the united states in congress assembled." The question hinged on whether the agreement between the two states constituted a treaty. Congress did not object. Neither did anyone else.

The eight Mount Vernon commissioners further recommended that their respective States (with the blessing of Washington) call for a convention of all the States "to take into consideration the trade and commerce" of the Confederation.

The second meeting was to be at Annapolis. Less than a year after the Mount Vernon gathering, the Virginia legislature invited all the other States to a convention to draw up a uniform system of commercial regulations, nominating five commissioners of its own. The invitation, drafted by Madison, sustained that if the State legislatures then ratified the convention's resolutions "unanimously," the united states in congress assembled would be empowered to move on the proposed system. Nothing wrong with calling for a confederacy-wide trade convention. Madison must have known he was putting the cart before the horse: according to Constitution 1, Article XIII, an amendment had to be *first* "agreed to in a congress of the united states," and *afterward* "confirmed by the legislatures of every state."

Madison, the constitutional expert, was already thinking of resorting to unconstitutional steps. The invitation scheduled the meeting for September 1786, in Annapolis. Nine state legislatures liked the idea. Commissioners from five of the States arrived in Annapolis. Madison was there; so was Hamilton, representing New York. Madison had asked George Washington to attend, but the General, sensing that the undertaking was irregular and doubting its success, gave only his moral support.

The other four State commissioners hadn't arrived yet. Those from Massachusetts and Rhode Island were due in a couple of days. Hamilton moved to adjourn and the group closed the meeting down in three days, claiming that they constituted too "partial a representation for the business of their mission."

The move to adjourn was a ruse. Hamilton had written to his

wife that he planned to stay only a few days. Four days—September 11 to 14, 1786—as it happened. Quickly before the other commissioners arrived, those present devoted their time to composing a clever letter which they called a "report." They sent it not only to their respective legislatures but also to the united states in congress assembled in New York and to the governors of the several States, out of "motives of respect" while admitting that this extended mailing went beyond "propriety." They then adjourned *sine die*.

Most likely at this Annapolis meeting Hamilton planted the subversive idea of a convention that would overrule the old and draw up a new constitution. The twelve commissioners from five states—all experienced in committee politics—proposed "unanimously" (a much used word in these meetings) that a convention of commissioners for all the several States "meet in Philadelphia on the 2nd Monday in May next" (note the specificity, a tactic these men were to use throughout) to form "a plan for supplying such defects as may be supposed to exist" and "to devise such further provisions as shall appear to them necessary to render the Federal Government adequate to the exigencies of the Union, and to report such an Act for that purpose to the United States in Congress assembled" and then to the legislatures of every State for their unanimous confirmation.

So, the third meeting was to be held in Philadelphia. Hamilton drafted this "Annapolis Report." From a meeting in which two States amicably discuss their joint river traffic, we have gone in a few steps to a project in which all the States are to assemble and propose remedies for a supposedly defective and inadequate government (that is, the confederated government framed by the first constitution) and to report to Congress, although Congress has not asked them to do so. Hamilton had upped the ante.

The beauty of the scheme is that the schemers advise Congress that by proposing changes in the constitution they intend to take over Congress's job.

Huggins didn't see the beauty. "Why did they have to do that? Why not just go ahead and meet in Philadelphia? Why create unnecessary problems?"

"You see," St. John spelled out, "the advocates of what among themselves they called a national government faced a huge problem: they lacked authority. Suppose you and I, with George Washington and Ben Franklin, got together to write a new constitution and proceeded to do so. What would we do with it? Publicize it, of course. A few persons might read it and like it, a few more might be impressed by Washington and Franklin, the great mass might never hear of it, or if they did might shrug and say, 'Looks like the old boys have gone dotty.' For the bicentennial celebration of the 1787 Constitution a number of writers including some respected constitutional lawyers individually composed new constitutions of the United States or proposed changes. So what? What authority did they have? Nobody paid attention." She pressed on.

————In 1786–87 the key to everything was Congress. The united states in congress assembled was the legitimate government. The two tasks of the national government advocates were 1) to destroy the authority of that constitution from which Congress's legitimacy sprang, and 2) to establish an authority for themselves: in other words, to subvert and supplant the existing regime. To achieve the first goal they intensified a campaign against Constitution 1, calling it weak, defective, and inadequate. For the second goal of gaining at least a temporary authority for the proposed constitutional convention, they had to secure the approval or the semblance thereof from the united states in congress assembled. Congress could either ignore the proposed convention or at the other extreme accuse the schemers of attempting to subvert the constitution. What the three-some and their followers wanted, though, was for Congress to acknowledge their convention plan as not improper, or better yet, to make it official by saying that Congress had requested or recommended it. Their main tactic was to claim that their aim was not to propose a new constitution but simply to revise or amend the one in force or to supply it with provisions or remedies.

Congress did not answer. It received the Annapolis letter, referred it to committee, adjourned without further action.

Many in the State legislatures were suspicious. So were individuals. Sam Adams of Massachusetts, R. H. Lee and Patrick Henry of

Virginia shied away. "Methinks I smelt a rat," explained Henry.

Everyone—not just Madison and Hamilton—knew that the existing constitution permitted only one way of amendment: the united states in congress assembled had to propose and all thirteen States had to approve.

Washington, asked again and again to attend the scheduled Philadelphia meeting, balked. For good reasons. If he went, he would be president of the convention. But the convention was, to say the least, irregular. What good would it do to be its president if Congress or even a group of State legislatures denounced it as illegal? It would turn into a fiasco. His hard-earned reputation would thereafter be that of a has-been or worse. With typical caution Washington asked the opinion of a legal giant, his friend John Jay, whom we met yesterday and whom he would later appoint first chief justice of the supreme court. Jay warned him: the projected Philadelphia convention lacked authority.

Washington wrote back that though the convention might be illegal, Congress by recommending it might give it "protective colouring." Yet even that might not be enough, he reflected.

"It sounds like a soccer game to me," disapproved Huggins. "Hamilton passes the ball to Congress, Congress dribbles, some State legislatures steal the ball from Congress, other legislatures shout 'Out of bounds!' Patrick Henry tries to intercept the throw-in which goes to Washington who dribbles, then feinting a pass to Congress kicks laterally to Madison who back-passes to Congress; Congress dribbles . . ."

"Wait, wait!" St. John cried out excitedly in the voice of a sports announcer. "Something's going on out there. People are erupting from the stands! They're charging across the field . . . They're trying to uproot the goalposts!"

With a wink at her pupil, St. John shifted down to her tutorial tone and explained.

————1785 and 1786 were depression years. By the fall of '86, in about half the States farmers and small businessmen were hitting courts and legislatures for debt relief and cheaper money. Infuriated by foreclosures through debt collectors, lawyers, and courts, they prevented or broke up court hearings. In central and western Massachusetts rural resistance was mounting. Less than a month or so after the Annapolis party had sent out their "report," some 500 embattled, indebted farmers demanded that their Massachusetts legislature print more money, enact stay-laws, abolish imprisonment for debts, apportion taxes more fairly, and restore *habeas corpus*. Getting little response, they dragooned Daniel Shays, a destitute farmer and a former captain of some distinction in a Massachusetts infantry regiment during the Revolution, to march with them on the State supreme court.

The governor of Massachusetts called up 600 militia to confront them at the Springfield courthouse. The court, evidently still feeling unprotected, adjourned. In January, a few months later, the governor, with money supplied by prominent merchants, raised the call to over 4,000. The rebels had targeted the arsenal at Springfield. There the militia met and routed them.

The uprising might not have caused so much fanfare—it was called Shays' Rebellion—had Congress kept its nose out of it. Under Constitution 1 it had no authority to intervene in State disturbances. Yet it authorized Henry Knox, the guzzling, intrepid, three-hundred-pound secretary of war, to bring together a force of 1,300 troops to protect the federal arsenal at Springfield, and meanwhile led the public to believe that the mission of the troops was to fight Indians along the Ohio River. Knox supplied arms from the arsenal to the Massachusetts militia. His troops were never needed, never used, but their illegal presence and aid aroused public protest.

In his report to Congress and in his letters Knox estimated insurgent forces at 12,000 to 15,000 and described the aims of the rebels. Here is what he wrote Washington:

> Their creed is "That the property of the United States has been protected from the confiscations of Britain by the joint exertions of all, and therefore ought to be the common property of all. And he that attempts opposition to this creed is an enemy to equity and justice, and ought to be swept from off the face of the earth."
> In a word, they are determined to annihilate all debts, public and private, and have agrarian laws, which are easily effected by means of unfunded paper money which shall be a tender in all cases whatever.

Thomas Jefferson, cool as a cucumber in Paris, wrote some time later that the "rebellion in Massachusetts has given more alarm, than I think it should have done." It was on this occasion that he wrote the ever since oft-repeated, oft-misquoted sentence: "The country should have such a revolution every generation."

But merchants, investors, large property holders and creditors, among them members of Congress and State legislatures, seized upon the uprising to scare themselves and others like them out of their wits. "Do you want another Shays' Rebellion?" they challenged. Anyone who doubted the wisdom of the proposed Philadelphia convention they stigmatized a "Shaysite." The insurrection found a welcome place in the oratory of convention supporters. "Our government," Knox had continued to Washington, "must be braced, changed, or altered to secure our lives and property."

In earnest, State legislatures began appointing delegates to the convention. The irresolute Washington decided he would go to Philadelphia after all. Madison wrote a memorandum entitled "Vices of the Political System of the United States." Congress called for the report on the Annapolis letter it had turned over to committee five months before, and began a passionate debate.

Upon a flurry of motions from the floor, Congress rushed to reply, demonstrating that it too could weasel words. On the twenty-first of February 1787 it "transmitted" to the State legislatures the Annapolis recommendation for a convention in Philadelphia which was to meet, Congress had resolved, "for the sole and express purpose of revising the Articles of Confederation and reporting to Congress and the several legislatures such alterations and provisions therein as shall, when agreed to in Congress and confirmed by the states, render the federal constitution [i.e., Constitution 1, the Articles of Confederation] adequate to the exigencies of Government and the preservation of the Union." At first glance it seemed to say to the States: Go ahead, appoint delegates to Philadelphia, but stick to revising "the federal constitution," that is, the Articles of Confederation.

Historians in general have interpreted this to mean that Congress was sounding a warning not to propose a new constitution. They have overlooked that Congress was authorizing a convention not merely to consider revisions, but actually to revise the Articles. Anyone could consider and propose, but constitutionally, only Congress and all the State legislatures together could revise. Such language appeared to delegate to another body, a convention, Congress's own unique power and that of the State legislatures. Congress had no authority to delegate the power to amend to anybody. If this was not a careless slip of the pen (uncharacteristic of a group of lawyers), it was acting unconstitutionally. Congress should have said, Go ahead, meet and let us know what you *propose*.

Moreover, while it seemed to be using Constitution 1's language—"when agreed to in Congress and confirmed by the States"—Congress deviated significantly by avoiding the exact phrase "confirmed by the *legislatures* of *every* state"—thus opening up the possibility that State conventions might be substituted for State legislatures and that less than all the States need confirm. These two slip-ups, if such they were, proved important.

Congress's response was assurance enough. It was the "protective colouring" that Washington hoped for. Congress could not now warn the delegates that they were engaged in acts bordering on treason. From this point forward advocates of the convention knew that whatever they might propose, they had little to fear from Congress.

The Virginia delegation—Washington, Madison, and Governor Edmund Randolph, arrived in Philadelphia on May 14, early enough to meet in the house of Robert Morris, a notable land speculator and financier, where Washington was to stay, and go over a plan drafted by Madison. The plan contained fifteen articles, not for a revision of the existing federal constitution but for a new constitution.

On May 25 the convention opened. Robert Morris proposed George Washington as president and he was unanimously elected. The first order of business resolved "that nothing spoken in the House be printed, or otherwise published, or communicated without leave." Then Randolph arose, was recognized, and presented the Virginia group's plan. As the delegates immediately understood, the plan went beyond Congress's instruction to hold to the existing constitution. This time it was not Congress but the convention that was exceeding its authority, was assuming powers it did not have and an objective that was subversive.

Since Randolph, the governor, stood up and made the proposal, the delegates of Virginia as a body were proposing to get rid of the constitution of the United States of America.

No one outside the convention protested (although some inside did). No one outside knew what was going on. Secrecy prevailed. George Washington, the Mason, saw to that.

Some three and a half months later, on September 17, 1787, by "unanimous" order of the convention, Washington submitted "to the consideration of the United States in Congress assembled that Constitution which has appeared to us the most adviseable." By another "unanimous" order Washington informed Congress that it was "the opinion of this Convention, that [the enclosed draft of a constitution] should afterward be submitted to a Convention of Delegates, chosen in each State by the People thereof, under the recommendation of its Legislature, for their assent and ratification; and that each Convention assenting to and ratifying the same, should give Notice thereof to the United States in Congress assembled."

Note that Washington and the convention openly submitted not amendments but another complete Constitution, asked not for Congress's agreement but merely for its "consideration," asked for confirmation not by the legislature of each State but by a Convention in each State—three unconstitutional proposals in violation of Congress's original instructions and of the constitution.

Washington's report of the convention's outcome also proposed procedures for putting the new constitution in force. The procedures themselves are unconstitutional. Washington and the convention sought authority for constitutional change by ratification through the conventions (not the *legislatures*) of nine (not of *all* thirteen) States.

Off goes the draft of a new constitution with covering letter. Addressed to Congress assembled in New York.

The moment was critical. The course should have been clear. Congress should have rejected the report and reported to the State legislatures that the convention signers had exceeded their authority and, by trying to push through a new constitution by unconstitutional procedures, had opened themselves to charges of treason and disloyalty both to their respective States and to the united states in congress assembled. Implicated also was the violation of their oath to the existing constitution, a matter we shall take up next week.

Without saying so, Congress indicated it stood ready to abdicate.

Instead of deliberating about the plan and approving it, or rejecting it and bringing charges as was its duty, Congress had "100 copies of the new Constitution" printed and transmitted to the several legislatures and governors—without sign of approval or disapproval.

Worse than that, in two little phrases it left itself open to future accusations. In transmitting the Philadelphia draft, Congress attempted to whitewash the convention of any wrongdoing. It certified that the convention had acted according to Congress's own instructions, that it had acted "pursuant to the resolution of Congress of the 21st of February 1787." We have just seen that the convention had instead flagrantly ignored Congress's instructions. To put it bluntly, Congress lied.

To top this, Congress indicated that it had succumbed to the authority of the Philadelphia convention, that *Congress* was now acting pursuant to the *convention's* instructions, serving as the convention's vehicle of transmission. The convention had resolved to and did lay before Congress its "opinions" about the submitted constitution and the procedure for its ratification. Congress called these opinions "resolutions" and "resolves" and stated that it was acting "in conformity with the Resolves of the Convention . . ."

No clearer evidence, if evidence is needed: in February, Congress had meant to give the convention unconstitutional authority to act in its stead; in September, it was certifying this "unanimously." So all its members, too, were guilty of attempting to overthrow the constitution of the United States of America.

The frequent claim of unanimity in these proceedings, one suspects, was useful to ensure that if any of these men, conventioneers and Congressmen, were later accused of illegal, unconstitutional, or treasonable proceedings—some Congressmen *had* tried to move for censure—they all would be in the soup together.

The more obvious advantage of using "unanimously" was to convince opponents and others that they were in the presence of a united front. Let me mention one little trick which you may regard as unworthy of the noble aspirations of the Philadelphia convention. At the moment of signing it was clear that unanimity was not to be had: some members, and at least one State, would not sign. Rhode

Island, having refused the invitation, was not present. Two of New York's three delegates had left in protest against "the consolidation of the United States into one government," leaving only Hamilton. The eighty-one-year-old Franklin made a plea for all members present to sign, but George Mason and Edmund Randolph of Virginia and Eldridge Gerry of Massachusetts stubbornly refused to sign with their respective State delegations.

Gouverneur Morris came up with the solution. (It's hard not to admire the fellow.) He passed it on to Franklin, who moved that this formula be used: "Done in Convention, by the unanimous consent of the States present . . ."

It was signed as usual with personal names bracketed by State names.

One little flaw was that New York could not properly be said to be present: of its three-men team, two had gone off in a dudgeon, Hamilton alone remained but attended irregularly. So the huge State of New York appears on the document with a sole signature, incongruously without brackets: "New York . . . Alexander Hamilton."

The much, much larger flaw resulting from these shenanigans was that this constitution that begins with "We, the People" ends with the "consent of the *States*."

Huggins was puzzled. "I don't get it. Why was Congress so stupid? It was signing its own death warrant. A new constitution meant a new Congress would take over, wouldn't it?"

"That's just it. All along, the Confederation Congress in New York was in favor of the 'national government' men. Yet it owed its very existence to the Articles of Confederation. Once it thought it had support for sharp change—after Shays' Rebellion—Congress moved, showing its true colors."

"But they moved themselves out of a job," protested Huggins.

"Maybe I didn't make something clear in my talk of all these meetings, caucuses, State legislatures, and Congresses. They interpenetrated themselves. To take a few examples: James Madison was a member of the Virginia legislature, a participant in the Mount Vernon and Annapolis meetings, a delegate to the Philadelphia convention, a member of the united states in congress assembled then in New York, and soon to be a member of the new Congress. Similarly for Washington and Hamilton, of course. Many Congressmen and many of those who framed this constitution or were instrumental in getting it ratified by the States became the new elected and appointed officials, moving into the supreme court, the federal district courts, the president's cabinet, and fifty-four of them into the new Congress alone. Almost all belonged to the brotherhood of public creditors. They were not leaving their jobs. They transferred from one government to another."

————The advocates of a new constitution, St. John carried on, were known for their admiration of the English system of government, Hamilton being the most candid and fervid. During Washington's presidency their party was dubbed the "Anglo-Monarchists." The English were the ones, you remember, to favor the names *America* and *Americans*, the shorthand for British North America and for British subjects in North America.

When George Washington left the presidency he wrote a farewell addressed to "Friends and Fellow-Citizens" and turned it over to the press. He had thought of retiring after his first term and asked Madison for suggestions in drawing up the farewell. Madison did write a draft, which Washington laid aside to pick up again at the end of his second term. This time he called on Hamilton for help. He used the suggestions of both men, but his own sentiments prevailed.

Among the sentences in the address that are clearly Washington's is one of special interest. The president was telling newspaper readers that they should properly estimate the immense value of their "national Union," and went on to say: "The name of AMERICAN which belongs to you in your national capacity, must always exalt the just pride of patriotism more than any appellation derived from local discriminations." The word *American* in Washington's script is double-underlined. *Appellation* is an alternative for *name*. Washington is urging people to shift their patriotism and change their name.

At the moment he was writing, it would seem, the peoples of the several States, Kentuckians and Virginians in particular, did not regard these names of theirs as mere local discriminations and did not feel a greater patriotism for the name *American*.

Yet, finally, someone has unequivocally identified the problem of names, and named the people, those members of a country with no name. The statement is strong: the name "belongs to you." It echoes an earlier phrase of Washington's. As president of the Philadelphia convention he had transmitted the draft of Constitution 2 to Congress—whose hands were already deep in the pasta—with many phrases sure to irritate opponents. It was "obviously impracticable," his letter read, "in the federal government of these States to secure all rights of individual sovereignty to each." In the convention, he claimed, "we kept steadily in our view that which appears to us the greatest interest of every true American, the consolidation of our Union, in which is involved our prosperity, felicity, safety, perhaps our national existence."

There it is: "every true American." George Washington is again a hero, the great Nomothete. He gave Americans their name.

Huggins had heard of an "athlete" but never of a Nomothete. It must mean a name-giver, like those people in the advertising business who spend their time naming cars, soaps, soups, and things.

———In both these instances, St. John was observing, Washington links the name with the term "national," thus subordinating the names and patriotisms of the States. Presidents, politicians, and demagogues today still find use for the phrase "every true American."

A little doubt of authorship creeps in. One mustn't forget that at the convention there was that man with a wooden leg who was always jumping up to speak, Gouverneur Morris. If Washington, Madison, and Hamilton constitute a holy trio, Gouverneur Morris makes it a sacred quartet. Washington's covering letter to Congress is in Gouverneur Morris's handwriting. So is the final draft of the constitution itself. According to Madison, Gouverneur Morris gave that constitution its style and arrangement. Gouverneur himself said as much.

On the other hand, Washington had sometimes praised his troops as "brave Americans." What else could he have called them once he could no longer use British Americans? Did Washington dictate or mention "every true American" to Gouverneur before the letter was written? Highly unlikely. The Committee on Stile and Arrangement handed him Gouverneur's letter to sign. Did the phrase come off Gouverneur's pen first and later reverberate in Washington's head when he came to composing his farewell address? More likely.

One thing is sure. The signature at the bottom of both letters is George Washington's. If he did not invent the term "true American," he liked it, it corresponded to his nationalist sentiment. He had the greatness of stature to make the name stick.

Wait a moment . . . *Did* he make the name stick? What happened to the name "American" after Washington's farewell? Did it cross the land from New Hampshire to Georgia like wildfire? Did the peoples of the several States, having been given a national baptism, know who they were, and look upon Washington gratefully?

A half-century later, a famous New York writer, Washington Irving, author of *The Legend of Sleepy Hollow* and of a satire of George Washington, and soon to become ambassador to Spain, wrote an essay "On Nomenclature," on the subject of the lack of a name for country. "We want a national name. . . . I want my own peculiar national name to rally under." He derided "the United States of North America" as a "collocation of words" that gave rise to "circumlocution." He dismissed identifying himself as an American. "The title of American may serve to tell the quarter of the world to which I belong, the same as a Frenchman or an Englishman may call himself a European."

No, Washington's "Friends and Fellow-citizens" continued to use their old pre-independence names. "Americans" had to contend with "Yankees" in the Northeast, and with "Columbians" and "sons of Columbia" generally for the favor of contemporary writers of song and story. One newspaper carrying Washington's farewell address headlined it "Columbia's Legacy."

Not even the Father of His Country could singlehandedly name that country or those countrymen. In a funeral eulogy read to Congress, Light-Horse Harry Lee, cousin of Richard Henry and father of Robert E., characterized Washington as "first in the hearts of his countrymen."

Couldn't Lee have said, "first in the hearts of all true Americans"? That would sound good today. But no such usage had grown up in the twelve years after Washington used the term. And it was not up to Lee the Virginian to say that about Washington the Virginian.

Perhaps someone in another eulogy called Washington the first true American. I have not come across it. Someone did refer to his countrymen in a different way. An anonymous set of verses got broad circulation in the press. It was titled "Mrs. Washington's Lamentation for the Death of Her Husband." It speaks of Washington's followers, and identifies them not as true Americans but as "Columbia's brave sons."

A generation goes by. The Massachusetts Historical Society decides to consider the lack of a national name, and appoints a committee of three. One of them is the son of John Adams, John Quincy Adams, who like his father had been president of the United States, the sixth under Constitution 2, from 1825 to 1829. I am going to let the Massachusetts Historical Society give in brief their opinion of the name "Columbia." "Before the close of the Revolutionary War," they write,

> the name of Columbia, was assumed by general consent, as significant of the whole Union, and has been familiarized to every mind, by two popular and patriotic songs, one written by Timothy Dwight, and the other by Joseph Hopkinson. . . . The same name was also given by the *act of Congress*, which organized the District ordained by the Constitution to be governed by the exclusive jurisdiction of the whole Union. We confess we perceive no adequate reason for discarding this name, nor wherein it should fail to answer all the purposes for which a national name is desirable. . . . We cannot imagine any other name more appropriate, or better suited to mark its distinctive character. The name of America, irretrievably stamped by uncompromising usage upon both continents of the new hemisphere, is a perpetual memorial of human injustice, by conferring upon one man [Amerigo Vespucci] a crown of glory justly due to another [Christopher Columbus]. This injustice will be in a great degree repaired by the universal adoption of the name of Columbia for this great and growing community.

"Ms. St. John?"

"Yes?"

"What country was George Washington father of, then?"

"Huggins, you're beginning to get the drift! Good question. Suppose you answer it."

"Well, Father of the United States doesn't sound right. And Father of America doesn't sound right, either."

"Right on both counts."

"What about Father of Columbia? Or Father Columbia? What about, first in the hearts of Columbia's brave sons? What do you think? Still not right, is it?"

"No. Won't do." She was gathering up her things.

Huggins tried to keep her longer. "You don't seem to like George Washington, do you?" he asked hurriedly.

St. John looked amused. "Do you think I'm cross that he had made so many toasts to King George and then didn't keep his oath?"

"No, that's not it. But, you know . . . a man who would ride or dance three hours straight . . . I like that about him."

"Oh, I see. You dance as well as ride, do you? I'm beginning to see new virtues all the time. 'Bye for now, Huggins." St. John scooted out the door with a wave.

"See you tomorrow," Huggins said, waving to her trim, disappearing back. Why was she always in such a hurry to leave?

5

THE COUNTRIES THAT SIGNED A CONTRACT TO BECOME A COUNTRY

FRIDAY

"Well, look at you!" Claire St. John's eyes swept Huggins's length from head to foot and back up without pause en route. "You look like something out of *The Great Gatsby*."

"I just finished playing two sets of tennis," said Huggins, panting a bit, grinning stupidly.

"Obviously." Fumbling with her papers, St. John started to sniff.

"Do I smell bad?" Anxiously.

"No, I was just trying to locate Constitution 2 among these sheets."

Huggins gave an appropriately fleeting smile. "I thought I'd have time to change, but the second set went over and I had to rush here like this. Do you play tennis, Ms. St. John?"

"Yes, doesn't everyone?"

"Oh, maybe we can—"

"Maybe we can what?"

Huggins sank into the nearest sofa. "Maybe I should put something on this knee."

"What happened to it?"

"Nothing. I just skidded on the court and skinned it."

St. John, the overworked, disgusted, emergency-room surgeon, bent over to examine Huggins's right knee, poked around it with a forefinger, and gave her prognosis. "It can wait."

Huggins caught a whiff of sun-heated brown hair. "It feels hot to me." Would she test it by laying her palm over his knee?

"Really? It will pass."

"Right," said Huggins, and to himself, Patient dismissed.

St. John straightened up and stretched, arching her back and pushing forth her belly. An old thought crossed Oliver's mind: flat belly under crepe de chine.

"Let me ask you this, Huggins. What's the motto of your country?"

"The motto of my country? Of America?" Huggins wavered.

"Well, say, of the United States of America."

"I still don't know."

"Haven't you ever seen the Great Seal of the United States?"

"Not really," replied Huggins, "except on television when they show it behind the president or Congress."

"Do you have a quarter on you? Or a nickel, or a dime, or a penny?"

"No, I'm sorry, I don't," answered a puzzled Huggins.

"I don't expect you would. Any loose change would fall out of those shorts. How about a dollar? No, wait, I have one."

St. John opened her case, extracted a small purse with some coins and bills. "Here we are, a dollar bill. On one side we have Washington, and on the other—" She fluttered the bill before Huggins's eyes and laid it out on the table. "You see the white-headed eagle with a ribbon in its beak, what does it say?"

"It says, *E pluribus unum.*"

"I'm sure you can understand that when the Declaration of Independence was proclaimed and the war joined, the Congress encouraged proposals for symbols of oneness out of severalness. They designed, for instance, thirteen stars and stripes on one flag. Now, as to this more explicit example, the laconic Latin motto: *E pluribus unum*, literally, 'Out of many, one,' what do you think they meant by that, Huggins? *What* one out of *what* many?"

"That's easy. They hoped that the many States would fight as one."

"A good answer and the committee report confirms it."

Huggins purred. Then brought himself around to asking, "What committee?"

————On the Fourth of July 1776, she answered, immediately after the Declaration of Independence was read, Congress appointed the Great Seal committee, a powerhouse composed of Dr. B. Franklin, Mr. J. Adams, and Mr. T. Jefferson. I'll try to avoid the technical language of heraldry with which these men though republicans seemed remarkably familiar. The shield lies within a circular border of thirteen escutcheons linked together by a chain with the initial letters "for each of the thirteen independent States of America" from N.H. to G. The designers described this much in their *second* paragraph. Their first paragraph had another "many" in mind. The shield itself divides into six spaces within the border: the first a rose for England, the second a thistle for Scotland, the third a harp for Ireland, the fourth a fleur-de-lis for France, the fifth the imperial eagle for Germany, the sixth the Belgic lion for Holland, "pointing out the countries," the committee said, "from which these States have been peopled." Directly underneath the shield the motto unfurls: E PLURIBUS UNUM.

I conclude that the designers of 1776 intended the Great Seal to represent the unity of purpose, first, of the immigrant populations composing the States, and second, of the thirteen independent States themselves. Noteworthy also was their reliance on the States.

Nowadays, about all that remains of that description—Congress went through many changes—is *E pluribus unum*.

The prevailing interpretation, dating from the Civil War, is that the motto has a single meaning: one nation out of many States with the implication that the one nation stands alone, supreme, having sprung from the loins of the many States who lie depleted after giving birth. Some have noted that these Latin words so popular with the federal mint were first tossed off by the poet Virgil in enumerating the many ingredients in a cake.

"The utility of the saying gains from its flexibility," pronounced St. John. "Out of many ingredients, one cake. It can apply to many things, states, peoples, regions, languages—and names. Take sports: from many tennis players with different names, one tennis club with its one name."

Huggins readjusted the collar of his knit shirt as she pursued the analogy.

————If we take the thirteen players by names (from Georgia to New Hampshire) we have thirteen different names. The club, however, has none. What club are we talking about? Is there one?

The *States* had names, the *countries* from which the States were peopled had names, the *many* had names, the *one* out of the many had none. This has been and still is the great advantage of the States—names. It was one thing for Washington in his farewell letter to say that the citizens of these States should consider their sentiment for their States to be but "local discriminations"; it was another to get them to reattach that sentiment to a sometime national thing.

While we're at it, we may as well consider other official markings, those that represent the government of the United States, or identify its property like weapons or other stores stamped with "U.S." or "USA." Constitution 2 grants Congress a monopoly in currency . . .

Huggins put in an oar. "Don't forget stamps."

"I haven't forgotten stamps," St. John denied. "Currency *and* postage: to reproduce them with intent to fob them off as the genuine article is the crime of counterfeiting." She pointed to the coins and bills on the table.

————Notice that these bear words or representations in addition to the title, United States of America. They insist on three mottoes:

In God We Trust, indicating that the United States of America trusts in God; *Liberty*, the United States is independent and provides people with liberty; and *E pluribus unum*, which we just talked about.

Also popular with the designers of coins and bank notes are engravings of busts of presidents. Or, in the cases of Hamilton and Franklin, of a statesman. The one-dollar bill features Washington, the penny Lincoln, the five-dollar bill Lincoln again, the twenty-dollar bill Jackson.

Once the penny and the nickel each carried the anonymous bust of a member of one of the tribes of North America, double-edged icons representing liberty (or freedom), or the loss thereof. These coins are now collectors' items.

Government parks and libraries, museums with their paintings and sculpture, monuments with their landscapes, federal prisons with their prisoners, military war memorials and cemeteries—the Vietnam memorial, Arlington Cemetery, Gettysburg—buildings, like the Supreme Court Building, with their interior and exterior furnishings and decoration, are all symbols of the United States of America, too. Federal engravers may re-represent these last on currency: on the penny and on the five-dollar bill, Lincoln's monument in Washington; on the ten-dollar bill, Hamilton and the treasury of which he was secretary. Or they may select private buildings associated with a president: Jefferson's home, Monticello, on the reverse of the nickel.

As for stamps, they may go beyond presidents and statesmen to represent other notables, for example, Philip Mazzei, Jefferson's friend who introduced Italian wine grapes to Virginia's soil. These all represent the United States government. People may call them national symbols, and such they may be if a nation does exist. But they name no nation.

This holds for the official seals of the House of Representatives and the Senate, the office of the president and the supreme court, based as they are on today's Great Seal of the United States. The obverse bears the American eagle (descendant of the Roman predator of the skies), a glory of thirteen stars above its head, a scroll of *E pluribus unum* clenched in its beak, an escutcheon of stars and stripes covering its breast. Its sinister talon clasps a sheaf of thirteen war arrows; the dexter holds the olive branch of peace. The fan of feathers at the eagle's tail might well have graced the bonnet of a Cheyenne chief.

Benjamin Franklin once proposed the wild turkey as a representative American bird. The suggestion met with little enthusiasm. Some thought that the eagle on the U.S. seal was taken from the crest of arms of the Washington family, but the Washington bird is a raven.

The reverse of the modern Great Seal carries other Virgilian mottoes: *Annuit coeptis*, to mean "God favors the enterprise," and the old refrain *novus ordo seclorum*, "a new order of the ages," to wit, the new political system of the United States of America. The first motto appears at the detached tip of a topless pyramid, a thirteen-layered stone structure resembling Peruvian masonry, out of which pops a huge eye in a triangular halo, symbolizing the eye of Providence; the second motto serves as text for a semicircular ribbon under the pyramid. The pyramid-and-eye, I've heard, comes from the iconography of the secret fraternal society of Freemasons, which to the Freemasonic Framers was no secret. The base of the pyramid bears in Roman numerals the date MDCCLXXVI.

So, in coins, bills and stamps, slogans, artifacts, structures and seals, to which we can add official uniforms, badges, ribbons, medals, and the like, *America* grammatically becomes object of the preposition, "*of* America," indicating the location North America, leaving us as before with the United States as the common noun title of a government or a political association and America as the proper noun name of a continent.

Besides these objects commissioned by the government are those persons holding government commission or office, in particular having to do with diplomacy—the president, secretary of state, ambassadors, envoys, members of Congress at times, and designated military officers. Their persons and their acts are often taken to represent the government. An important part of their official life falls under the heading of protocol or ceremony. A person's assigned position in a lineup or in other arrangements plays the part, you see, of representing not the government as a whole but rather a rank order within it or within the family of nations. That is, your place in relation to other persons in an officially set arrangement ranks your office or your country and its importance. Examples: seating a Senator, an Ambassador, a Supreme Court Justice at a state dinner; the order of precedence at a state funeral; the lineup waiting to greet a returning Ambassador.

A major concern of the Framers was that no matter what steps they might choreograph for the national ballet, people would not budge from the "love," "loyalty," "reverence," "allegiance" they had for their State. Some members claimed that their colleagues exaggerated the depth of this State patriotism. James Wilson, an erudite deputy from Pennsylvania, doubted that the States and their sovereignties were "so much the idols of the people" and that a "National Government" was "so obnoxious." He challenged, "Will a citizen of *Delaware* be degraded by becoming a citizen of the *United States?*" Others, however, saw in the States the greatest danger to their hope for a "national" government. In a contest of dual allegiance, they felt sure they would come out second best. They cut to the root of the matter by proposing to abolish States and State governments altogether. Tireless and tiresome on this topic was George Read representing Delaware. Attachment to the States must be extinguished, he repeated, and the States themselves swept away. They have no future. Hamilton of New York spoke for a plan that divided the States into election districts. His ally, the powerful John Jay, then secretary for foreign affairs in the Confederation Congress, preferred a more radical scheme that would have reduced the States to thirteen equally sized administrative districts.

He was no more radical than the New Jersey delegates. Judge David Brearley thought that "a map of the U. S. [might] be spread out, that all existing boundaries be erased, and that a new partition of the whole be made into 13 equal parts." His colleague William Paterson, before presenting the "Paterson" or "New Jersey Plan" as an alternative to Madison's "Virginia Plan," had made several drafts of which one put the idea formally:

> Whereas it is necessary in Order to form the People of the U. S.
> of America in to a Nation, that the States should be consoli-
> dated . . . it is therefore resolved, that all the Lands contained
> within the Limits of each state individually, and of the U. S. gen-
> erally be considered as constituting one Body or Mass, and be di-
> vided into thirteen or more integral parts.

Resolved, That such Divisions or integral Parts shall be styled Districts.

Under such systems the States would sooner or later have lost their history, the attachment of their people, and the names by which they were attached. Deprived of the old names of their States, to what could people attach their free-floating attachment? Administrative districts?

The deputies, you know, had signed their names opposite the State they represented. For example, South Carolina was written on one side, and alongside, bracketed, were listed

South Carolina
> (John Rutledge
> (Charles Colesworth Pinckney
> (Charles Pinckney
> (Pierre Butler.

Even that ardent nationalist Alexander Hamilton would not have liked his name standing alone alongside the words *District 2*.

"The Virginia deputies would have looked like this." St. John raised her hands before Huggins's face, shaping two brackets. Shaking first one, then the other, she said,

District 4
> (John Blair
> (James Madison, Junior

and George Washington would have had to sign 'George Washington, President and Deputy from District 4.' I doubt the idea would have thrilled him.

"What would have happened if the convention had inserted any such proposal in the constitution as it was submitted for ratifying? The death of Constitution 2 before its birth. The States would have aborted the fetus."

Huggins had been following closely. "If the several States had names and the 'one' has none, it makes you doubt a 'one' exists, doesn't it?"

"Decidedly," she answered. "So where do we stand now, Oliver? Would you like to draw the main battle lines?"

"I'm not sure I can."

"Let me help out." St. John's tone was friendly. "I'll make it simple. In the case of Moctezuma we found out that on these two continents everyone came from somewhere else, no one was new—the only natives had been the dinosaurs—and that the name of New Spain that the Spaniards had bestowed on the land was lost to the old one—Mexico. In the case of the Americas, we heard of Columbus, of Amerigo and the map-makers, of the situation of British colonies in North America, and of Thomas Jefferson's role in transforming them into independent countries. In the story of the name 'Columbia,' we heard of the different naming habits of the Spaniards, French, and British, of various names for the Atlantic seaboard States and peoples together and of how no title ever graced their official documents except as the United Colonies of North America and the United States of America. In the tale of George Washington . . ."

"I think I can take it from there," offered Huggins.

"Good, go ahead."

"In the tale of George Washington, the advantage of having a name for the whole had to be sacrificed to the free spirit of the States. They had just won a war and were so jealous of their independence that the drafters of the constitution, of Constitution 2 of course, had to resort to secret, illegal, and unconstitutional means to get it passed. If they had proposed a new name for one consolidated country, they would have given themselves away completely and lost the struggle."

"Excellent," said St. John.

Huggins added, "George Washington did make a try by calling people 'Americans,' without much luck."

"Good," said St. John. "Almost as good as I might have done. In some ways better."

Praise made Huggins bolder. "Now, where do we stand?"

"The way I look at it," replied St. John, "is this."

———Writing a constitution and designing symbols without a name to insert for the country seems curious and must have presented difficulties. What I propose to do now and over the next several days is to take a new perspective, to see how the Framers got around or thought they had got around those difficulties. A day or two ago, we saw that in some cases they simply skipped. Instead of "American" or some other adjective naming citizens, they just wrote "citizens." Sometimes, however, they had to work by indirection, as they did with slaves. The word *slaves* bothered many of them, as it did some of their predecessors in Congress who drafted the Declaration of Independence. In Constitution 2, they used a circumlocution. Article I, Section 2 refers to "free persons" and "all other persons." By all-other-persons they meant the slaves, the unfree. Section 9, at least until 1808, allows to the several States the "importation" of persons.

Concerning the naming of the country, "the United States" itself is the prime example of a circumlocution, a collective common noun juggled to get around the lack of a proper noun. Grammatically, the phrase requires special treatment. As in the first constitution, the second retained throughout the plural sense of the title "the United States." It escaped the singular by avoiding *the United States* as a subject, where the predicate, singular or plural, might give away the number intended. The phrase was almost always used as object of the preposition "of": "the Senate of the United States," "the judicial power of the United States," "the claims of the United States."

The only active clause appeared in Article IV, Section 4: "The United States shall guarantee to every state in this union a Republican form of government . . ." Now, which is it? "The United States guarantees" or "the United States guarantee"? Equivocal, yes, but I believe, unintentionally so. Lawyers often used *shall* to denote intending or obliging, to convey a promise of performance or an implicit condition: "*If* this draft of a constitution is ordained, the United States shall guarantee . . ." The plural would have been clear had not the "shall" made it ambiguous.

An unmistakable use of the plural occurs in Article III, Section 2, the treason clause. "Treason against the United States shall consist only in levying war against them, or in adhering to their enemies, giving them aid and comfort." Here, the collective common noun title, adapted as a name for government or country, causes confusion. Who is the "them" in the mixed pronouns: "against them" and "giving them"? Certainly the "their" is plural for the

United States. Whose treason is it, then, if some of these United States levy war against the others? Or if the government of the United States becomes the enemy of some of the United States? The Philadelphia delegates debated long over the clarity of this clause without success. As time went by, as threats of secession cropped up, this ambiguity became more dangerous. As we shall see.

Writers and speakers have interpreted this constitution in many ways, favorably or unfavorably, from one point of view or another, from one literary or legal theory or another, strictly or loosely, or according to the intent of the authors, of the ratifiers, or of different times and kinds of people. I'll keep using the different perspective I mentioned, of examining those circumlocutions that the Framers resorted to because of the lack of a name for country. We have briefly considered "the United States" in such a way. In the next few days we shall call before the bar two other critical phrases: "I do solemnly swear . . ." and the "supreme law of the land." But at this moment we must take a closer look at the opening words of Constitution 2: "We, the People of the United States." The first person plural purports to identify the authors of the text and of the action as well. The "We" are the ones who *do ordain and establish* this constitution for the United States of America.

I might note that the nearest usage in time and aim of We, the People appears in the 1780 Constitution of the State of Massachusetts, drafted largely by John Adams. I am going to cite this Massachusetts Constitution several times. Given our attention to Virginia and Philadelphia, we need some regard to New England. The Massachusetts Constitution described what it was doing as presenting a "Social Compact" and the opening—like that of Constitution 2—rings out in appropriately declamatory style. "We, therefore, the people of Massachusetts . . . do agree upon, ordain, and establish . . . the Constitution of the Commonwealth of Massachusetts."

The theory of a social compact or contract is as old as the hills. It holds that in their beginnings people live in a prepolitical stage, often referred to as the "state of nature," wherein they have rights that arise from nature's laws. Depending on the political philosopher advancing the theory, the state of nature may be a peaceful paradise that people long to regain, a violent hell from which they seek to escape, or some unstable gradient in between. To protect these natural rights they proceed to a political life, forming a government by contract. But they cannot in the process give away or sell these birthrights. God-endowed and nature-given, they are superior to government and set limits on political rule.

The contract does not have to be written: it may be grounded in custom as interpreted by common law. Some writers consider the understandings in feudal Europe between lord, vassal, and serf regarding land tenure and its obligations to have been unwritten social contracts.

The social contract we're interested in had its day in the seventeenth century for England and in the eighteenth century for the British colonies and the later thirteen independent States in North America. During these times the commercial contract was preempting an ever greater space in the courts and in the works of lawyers and jurists. In his final draft of Constitution 2, Gouverneur Morris could slip in a clause and be confident its meaning was firm. Article I, Section 10: No state shall pass any law "impairing the obligation of contracts." A related concept, the religious covenant, was extended to political situations by Protestant sects opposed to the Church of England. (*Covenant* is the word the King James translation of the Bible uses.) Meanwhile political philosophers discovered a new backdrop for the state of nature: the condition of "savages" in the wilderness of North America. You remember John Locke's saying that in the beginning all the world was America. The exotic world of the "woods of America" also impressed Thomas Hobbes and Jean-Jacques Rousseau, the other two great figures of social contract theory.

With or without benefit of aboriginal America and even before these great thinkers took the idea in hand, social contract phrases had ripened into a full-blown political vocabulary. Common law documents, speeches, and writings of the period left a paper trail strewn with *social compacts* and its better-known equivalent today, *social contracts*, along with such variants as pacts of society, original compacts, political covenants, charters, contracts or instruments of government; with supporting terms like state of nature, rights, reason, petition, agreement, convention, and consent of the people; and with modifiers to *rights* like inviolable and inalienable, and to *consent* like express, implied, and tacit.

The trail quickly branched off, in the Mayflower and Exeter compacts, to British North America where in the latter eighteenth century, after a hundred years or more of conflict with the Crown's representatives, it had broadened into a highway. The idea of government under contractual restraint, written or unwritten, dominated colonial and postcolonial thinking. Many colonists insisted that, beyond the royal charters creating them as colonies, there existed an implied political or social pact between them and England. Retaining their rights as Englishmen under the English constitution—rights of petition, assembly, representation, *habeas corpus*, jury trial, keeping arms, and so forth—was part of an obvious understanding between them and the king in exchange for their planting the flag among savages in the wilderness.

The first Congress, on October 14, 1774, declared and resolved:

> The inhabitants of the English colonies in North-America by the immutable laws of nature, the principles of the English constitution, and the several charters or compacts, have the following *RIGHTS*: . . . that our ancestors, who first settled these colonies, were at the time of emigration from the mother country, entitled to all the rights, liberties, and immunities of free natural-born subjects, within the realm of England . . . that by such immigration they by no means forfeited, surrendered, or lost any of those rights, but that they were, and their descendants now are, entitled to the exercise and enjoyment . . . of them.

And the Declaration of Taking up Arms of July 6, 1775, recalled forefathers who

> at the expense of their blood, at the hazard of their fortunes, without the least charge to the country from which they removed, by unceasing labour, and an unconquerable spirit . . . effected settlements in the distant and inhospitable wilds of America, then filled with numerous and warlike nations of barbarians.

Blindfolded, colonial lawyers could cite chapter and verse of written pacts in English constitutional history—the Magna Carta, the

Great Contract, Petition of Right, Habeas Corpus Act, and so forth.

The negative side of the social contract—breaking a pact—brings a threat to punish traitors or to depose, exile, or kill rulers who had become tyrants. By definition tyrants are rulers who do not keep to the faith and trust of their contract with the people. I'll illustrate the negative through a few names I've already mentioned. Juan de Mariana, an earlier social contract theorist, wrote in 1599 that desperate measures were sometimes called for to serve the welfare of the people against a king who violated his trust; he condoned killing the tyrant. You'll recall that Lord Baltimore had warned Charles I against naming the as yet unnamed Maryland *Mariana*, a variant of the name of his wife Henrietta Maria, fearing that people might associate it with the name of that Spanish Jesuit. In England, the writers, orators, and soldiers involved in the deposing and beheading of the same Charles I based their acts on the king's breach of contract. According to Oliver Cromwell (you *do* remember him), "the King is King by contract." And Patrick Henry's warning, "Charles the First [had] his Cromwell, and George the Third . . ." For John Locke the threat was not to behead the king but to dissolve the government. "But if a long train of abuses . . ." he wrote. Thomas Jefferson, in totally dissolving political ties to Great Britain, took the words from Locke's pen. "But when a long Train of Abuses . . ."

The positive side of the social contract deals with beginnings: peoples leaving the state of nature, proceeding to form a civil society or a new government by agreement or contract. Their political connections to Great Britain dissolved, the thirteen newly proclaimed States, suddenly out in the rain without the umbrella of the English constitution, had to shelter themselves with a new constitution, with fresh sets of rules for government. Did not the social contract philosophers foresee such an act, for men of reason to get together and come to agreement?

"I get it." Oliver had been following intently. "A constitution was the social contract put in writing."

"That's pretty much it," approved St. John. "The ex-British colonies had been immersed in social contract literature for so long that when they began to frame their own constitutions they thought of the task as putting the social contract to writing. The body politic, as the Massachusetts Constitution of 1780 instructed us, 'is a social compact . . .' "

————The words *the Article of Confederation* in the New England Confederation of 1643 and in the first constitution of the United States (that of 1777) borrowed the language of contracts: articles are binding contractual terms or stipulations. The first draft of Constitution 2, we know, was discussed under the title of "Articles of Union" and only toward the end of the convention did the Framers change the title to "constitution," dissociating it from the first constitution and following the States' example in putting their *social contract* in the formal frame of a *constitution*. Some may have remembered that *Articles of Union* was also the title of a contract of 1707, the twenty-five articles agreed to by the parliaments of England and Scotland.

When George Washington had the solemnly signed draft of this constitution transmitted to the united states in congress assembled in New York, he described its import in the familiar words of John Locke: "individuals entering society . . . ," the positive side of the social contract.

Claire St. John paused in her exertions, gulped some water, brushed her hair aside, took a few deep breaths. Her silk dress, a cool pale pink, with half sleeves and a rounded neck, bound at the waist with its own belt, clung to her loosely. Out of the corner of his eye, Huggins watched the rise and fall of her chest. Through the silk, the appearance and disappearance of twin pressure points . . . He thought wildly of Constitutions 1 and 2. Of equal prominence!

St. John was asking, "Do you know what I did this morning? I heard that Professor Wang Hegeu, the venerable scholar of American constitutional history, was visiting some friends in town."

"Chinese?"

"Yes. Anything wrong with that?"

Huggins shrugged. "No."

"Anyhow, I did a daring thing. I phoned to ask if he'd see me about some questions I had. I met him last year through the eminent student of China, my friend Fritz Mote. He would, with pleasure. So I went over, and to my surprise was greeted not by him but by his son. Who was very nice, said that his father was unexpectedly detained, was sorry he couldn't help me, his own specialty being contracts. I said, 'Oh, you could be of even greater help; you know that the present constitution of the United States is often thought of as a social contract . . . ?' "

St. John's look became wistful and a little far away. "He was sweet."

"Sweet," sneered Huggins.

"You know what I mean. Kind and helpful. He said he had studied under Malcolm Sharp. Wish I had, too. I was reading his book last night."

"How did you happen to pick that to read?"

"That's easy. Today's subject deals with contracts. I wanted to brush up."

Huggins took the plunge. "You should have asked me. I'm an expert on contracts."

"You?"

"Yes, me. My education hasn't been as neglected as you think. You must think I'm some kind of preppy jock."

"Well, your outfit today does nothing to deny it, except I admit white tennis shorts aren't as bad as hulking shoulder pads. Anyway, go on, what were you saying?"

"You know my father is a lawyer."

"I thought he was in international business."

"He is, as a lawyer. A lot of his work is in contracts. For two summers I worked in the office checking contracts. Man, was it boring! Every eight-hour day long. Took forever for the clock to creep around to four-thirty. But I learned a lot about contracts, or contract forms at least."

"Hmm. I guess I'll have to watch my step, won't I?"

"Maybe," said Huggins with relish, matching up and tapping together his fingertips, affecting to be a senior law partner. Not easy to carry off in bare legs and tennis shoes.

St. John said decisively, "Good! that ought to be a big help. Let's look at Constitution 2 as a contract, shall we? Maybe it'll show us what happened to these circumlocutions I spoke of. You be the expert. I'll ask the questions. Ready?"

"Ready."

St. John drew out her copy of the document in question. "What's the first thing a contract should have?"

"A date," Huggins replied like a shot. This wasn't going to be like her other quizzes. This time, *he* had the answers, or even better, he'd ask the questions.

"Okay," said St. John. "We've got a date here at the bottom. The seventeenth of September 1787."

"Good. Next, who is party to the contract? Who is the first party mentioned?"

"Here it is, right at the top. 'We, the People of the United States.' "

"What people?"

"What do you mean, 'what people'? The people of the United States."

"What is the United States?" asked Huggins, enjoying the game.

"The contract doesn't specify. According to a previous contract it was a confederation or union of thirteen States whenever their delegates assembled in a Congress."

"Was that previous contract related to this one and was it still in force?"

"Hmm," hummed St. John. "Yes, and legally, it was still in force."

"I see. Then at some point we'll have to take this up. There may have been restraints on the contracting parties. Do you have any other identification of these people?"

"I can give you the names of the member States of the United States. People lived in these various States along the Atlantic seaboard. Will that help?"

"It depends. Do you have the names of these people?"

"No. Is that necessary?"

"If you please, I'm asking the questions here." Huggins was stern.

"Hold on," objected St. John. "*I'm* supposed to ask the questions. You're supposed to have the answers."

"I know, but you were answering my question with another question."

"No, I wasn't."

"Shall we have the court stenographer read back the question?"

"No, not today," she muttered.

"If that's all you can tell me," continued Huggins, "I'd say that there is already an inadequate specification of the first party. What of the second party?"

"That party is even harder to find."

"Let me coach you," he suggested. This reversal of roles was fun. "Is anybody supposed to do anything, give anything, promise anything?"

"Oh yes, there is a Congress invested with the power to make laws. It doesn't *have* to make them but it has the power. There is a president. He doesn't preside over anything but has various duties. He takes care that the laws are faithfully executed. I suppose as commander in chief of the army and navy he may have to give commands—it depends on the circumstances; he has to give Congress information 'from time to time,' recommend laws, and receive ambassadors. Of course, if Congress makes no new laws, he has nothing new to execute; if Congress raises and funds no army, he has no armed forces to be commander in chief of; if he sees no treaties worth making, he has no treaties to make. He has no duty to address the people. And finally, there is a supreme court with judicial power that extends over a lot of things, but this constitution doesn't say that power *has* to be exercised," concluded St. John.

"Well, do they have to promise or swear to do any of this? Is there an oath?"

"Yes, there is an oath spelled out in the constitution itself. It's for the president."

"I see. What does it say?"

"Article II, Section I. 'I do solemnly swear (or affirm) that I will faithfully execute the office of president of the United States . . .' All other persons of the second party, too, according to Article VI have to swear an oath or affirmation 'to support this constitution.' "

"You mean those who agree to serve in Congress, the presidency, the court? Who are they? How do we identify them?"

"They must meet certain specifications of age, nationality, and so forth, and they must be chosen every so often by the people of the several States or by persons already so chosen."

"Are the people of the several States the same as 'We, the People of the United States'?"

St. John hesitated, then said, "I think you can grant that."

"Have you checked whether either of the parties had competing obligations or pledges? You know, like the banns in a marriage contract. How does it go? 'If any person know of any impediment or other just cause why this marriage should not take place, let him now come forth or forever hold his peace,' something like that."

"Yes, on both sides many persons had sworn oaths to the Crown, including George Washington, and to an existing constitution, the Articles of Confederation and Perpetual Union, including Gouverneur Morris."

"Did anyone stand up and object that these were impediments to the contract?"

"Yes, 'breach of the Articles' was often charged. A few of the delegates resigned and left the convention when their protests of impediments under the existing constitution went unheeded. Once the draft was made public, others protested that to subscribe to it would violate their pledge to the Articles of Confederation. In general, it might be said of all the delegates to the convention that they suspected or feared that they were acting with unresolved impediments."

"Was this challenged in court?"

"Not so far as I know," admitted St. John.

"Then I suppose we must hold our peace."

St. John gave limited assent. "Yes, for now."

Huggins squinted magisterially above imaginary spectacles. "So far, what you seem to have is something like a contract of agency or employment. The principal describes positions for qualified agents, makes a choice among those seeking the positions, and the contract is binding when the persons chosen take the oath."

"I see." St. John, all ears, moved to the edge of her chair.

"Oh, one moment. Is there a consideration, is the agent, the second party compensated for its services?"

"Yes, indeed. All components of the agent receive 'compensation' for their services from the principal."

"At least that's clear. Consideration or compensation is important. Otherwise it is not a contract out of which action arises but is a stark *nudum pactum*."

Huggins paused an instant, raising eyebrows, but seeing no change in St. John's attentive expression, went ahead. "Now to interpreting and construing the contract. Who do the parties turn to, to what independent tribunal, in case of a claimed breach of contract?"

"The supreme court of the United States, I suppose."

"No, I don't think so. The supreme court, you said, was created by the contract. It cannot claim to judge violations of the contract by which it exists and of which it is an integral part."

"Actually," offered St. John, "opponents did object that the supreme court for this very reason could not act as arbiter. And though nowadays the supreme court has arrogated to itself the right of interpreting and construing the contract, the Congress, the president, and the States have claimed that same right in the past and may in future claim it again."

"They can claim whatever they want. All of them are part of the second party of the agent. To be respected, judgment should be given by a tribunal standing outside and above the contract. Otherwise, interpretation devolves on the parties themselves. Which would make for uncertain authority and leave the enforcement of the contract up in the air, or to the *ultima ratio*."

"What's that?"

Huggins was above acknowledging irony. Sweetly he replied, "Force." Then frowning, "Tsk, Tsk. We have a serious problem here. No independent tribunal to warrant breach or to order enforcement of contract. Now, on to the date of expiration. What is the contract's duration?"

"I don't know that either, I'm afraid," she confessed with a grin. "I suppose it just keeps going."

"That cannot be." Huggins was firm.

"Judging from the date, two-hundred-odd years ago," ventured St. John, "the principals, the We, the People, all hundreds of thousands of them, are all dead by now. Still, the We, the People sentence of this constitution says that one of its purposes is to 'secure the blessings of liberty to ourselves and our posterity.' What about a contract lasting as long as posterity?"

"After a couple of centuries even posterity would be pronounced dead. Besides, the original contractors might have meant that posterity would be served by putting in place a contract to last no longer than their lifetime, a one-generation deal."

"Suppose the next generation of We, the People, liked the contract and wished to keep it going?" asked St. John.

"Then they should convene to provide an extension or to write a new contract."

"Yes, that must have been what Thomas Jefferson had in mind. Each new generation should write a new one, every nineteen years, he calculated. Still, what if people just kept on going through the same motions of elections, choosing and paying officers, et cetera, wouldn't that be an implied extension of contract?"

"Not necessarily. The people and the officials might be going through the motions for personal satisfaction, for the comfort of ritual, for gain, or advantage, or from simple laziness. There would have to be, I think, an awareness that a contract renewal was in question. If the principal is unaware of its contractual relation, the agent may let that relation wither on the vine. So there would be no contract but simply a governing going on by a government based not on voluntary consent but on allowing, encouraging people to a mere ritual performance, a simple 'going through the motions.' It looks like this social contract is falling to pieces."

"What is left for us to examine?" asked St. John.

"The signature. A sign or seal of the principal must be authenticated. But we're talking about the people and there must have been thousands, hundreds of thousands of them. They must have taken a yes or no vote, something like that. Was that it?"

"No, not exactly. We do have the signatures by States of the drafters of the instrument. Will that do?"

"Are the drafters 'We, the People'?" asked Huggins.

"No. John Adams once pointed out that the people were incapable of preparing such a document. You can add Madison's opinion that such a task was 'impossible for the people' and had to be proposed informally, irregularly, and without authorization by some patriotic and respectable citizens. We have the signatures of these men. They were a tiny minority."

"Stands to reason, doesn't it? Most of these men, you said, were lawyers. The parties don't draw up contracts; their lawyers do. Still a group of lawyers, no matter how patriotic, are not We, the People, are they?"

"Besides," added St. John, "as you know, lawyers when drawing up contracts customarily consult with their clients. Here there was no consultation. The contract they gave to We, the People was a yes-or-no proposition."

"Who signed for the people then?"

"The Ratifiers signed as agents or delegates for those people who had the vote in their respective State. In that sense *they* are 'We, the People.' Their names have been forgotten. I can retrieve them for you, all 1,644 of them."

"No need for that. I have two more questions. One, were they unanimous in their ratification?"

"Heavens, no," exclaimed St. John. "It was a fierce, close battle. In the three key States of Massachusetts, New York, and Virginia, the Yeas did not represent much more than one half of the small number of white adult males eligible to vote, but that was enough."

"Enough? That means that almost half of their Ratifiers voted Nay and so almost half of the people they represented voted Nay. Had they agreed on majority rule beforehand?"

"No, but that was the general rule in the State legislatures that chose the delegates to the ratifying conventions."

"I see. There was another set of agents in between the contract and the people. Why didn't the State legislators act directly as ratifying agents for the people? They had been chosen by We, the People of their State, hadn't they?"

"Yes," replied St. John. "You see, the Framers, the 'artful advocates'—another term used by their evidently artless opponents—had stipulated that ratification be determined by special single-issue conventions chosen by the people in each State. They trusted by this to improve their chances. Incumbent State legislators as a group were their fiercest opponents. In conventions the rules for choosing members would be different. State legislators as a class would be excluded, whereas other classes, for instance clergymen, ordinarily ineligible for State legislatures, could be elected to the State conventions. By bringing in different crews, the Framers hoped, the conventions would eliminate the voting power of legislators in one blow."

"Were these convention delegates, these Ratifiers, actually chosen by the people?"

"Not quite. They were almost exclusively nominated by the State
legislatures and then submitted in lists to the electorate. So the legislatures retained some influence."

Huggins was getting worn down. "How did We, the People
choose their State legislators then?" he asked wearily. "No, never
mind. Why didn't the Framers stipulate a simple yes-or-no referendum to the people?"

"Had they done so, their proposed constitution would have met
with sound defeat. Conventions were the more predictable model.
The States had already resorted to them in framing their constitutions. Moreover, the Framers knew they could influence a relatively
few convention delegates—through bribery, trickery, arm-twisting,
and sweet reason—more easily than they could a lot of people. No
doubt they were right. In South Carolina the legislature by a mar-
gin of a single Aye agreed to call a ratifying convention. The South
Carolina convention then voted to ratify by 149 Ayes to 73 Nays.
In Rhode Island, the one State in which a referendum was tried,
the score was roughly 300 Ayes to 3,000 Nays. That State was the
last to ratify and didn't do so until May of 1790 when economic
warfare against it by the new United States forced it into adopting
the convention delegate method. Which even then produced a bare
majority of Ayes, 34 to 32."

"If the referendum was not used to ratify, did We, the People
take part in choosing the State legislators who chose the convention delegates who ratified the contract? Sounds to me like, 'This
is the dog That worried the cat That killed the rat . . .' "

St. John chuckled. Huggins congratulated himself. Finally, he'd
got a laugh out of her.

"I'd estimate," she said, "that about one quarter of the electorate,
that is, of the adult male free population that had met State property and religious qualifications, voted for the legislators who voted
for the ratifiers."

Sadly Huggins shook his head. "Not good, not good. Here's the
last question. Did the ratifying delegates sign by individual states?"

"Yes, and that's what the Philadelphia convention and the Confederation Congress in New York asked for. The Framers' opinion,

given on September 17, 1787, was that 'Delegates [be] chosen in each State by the People thereof under the recommendation of its Legislature.' And in conformity the united states in congress assembled resolved unanimously on September 28, 1787, that the 'delegates [be] chosen in each State by the people thereof.' "

"So," determined Huggins, "We, the People, must have meant: We, the delegates respectively nominated in each State by the legislature thereof and chosen in each State by the voting people thereof. There was no sense of 'We, the one people of a single United States.' The Ratifiers all signed only as citizens and delegates of their respective States."

"I guess you'd have to say that, yes."

"I'm afraid I have to conclude that the signature does not correspond to the original identity of the principal, which was itself inadequate to begin with."

"What about the signatures of the agents, the representatives, and officials chosen?" St. John asked.

"There, there seems to be no problem. Once their taking of the oath is recorded, it is equivalent to a signature."

Suddenly, she leaned over, and startling Huggins, clapped him on the shoulder, hard. "Bravo, Oliver! You've raised some issues I didn't think of myself and gone deeper into the subject than I'd planned at this stage."

Huggins winced and rubbed his shoulder.

St. John smiled at his little act.

————What are we left with? she asked. Inadequate identification of both parties, contractual impediment in the agent, no specification of duration of contract, improper signature of principal, no independent tribunal. The main point I wanted to get across, you took care of admirably. If we take "We, the People of the United States" as the principal, it is inadequately identified and improperly signed, and for that alone the contract is null. I think you'll agree that the principal of the 1780 Massachusetts Constitution was better identified. We, the People were the people of the Commonwealth of Massachusetts, of a single State and a political unit with a centuries-old name.

The definite article *the* in the term "the commonwealth" brings me to a point about language. We have said that the title the *United States of America* was a common noun description, not a proper noun, with *America* referring to the location of North America and the *United States* to the States united. Would you like to know how to tell immediately whether you're dealing with the real name of a country or with a descriptive title? Answer: by the presence or absence of *the*. In English the noun has to be made definite by that definite article. *The* Commonwealth, *the* Union, *the* European Community, *the* League of Nations, *the* United States. The uniqueness of a proper noun, on the other hand, obviates the need for a *the*. The Commonwealth of Massachusetts is not a proper name; it designates the commonwealth or republican form of government of the State of Massachusetts. You have to put a *the* in front of it. When you speak of the State alone, you need no *the*. The name is Massachusetts. If the name of the country were Alleghania there would be no need for *the*. We would have, "We, the people of Alleghania." (*Alleghania* was what Washington Irving proposed in 1839 as a name for the country. A Maryland amateur historian wrote finish to this coinage, pointing out that the Alleghanian tribe had been a brutal, treacherous bunch, certainly unworthy of lending their name to this noble country.)

Noah Webster, the father of the American English dictionary, hearing that the "Constitution" had been ratified, exclaimed, "At last, we are a nation." He did not of course suggest that that document was an invalid contract. He thought of it as a signed agreement that created a nation. He believed in the omnipotence of written words. Today's edition of his dictionary defines *Founding Father* as "a member of the American Constitutional Convention of 1787."

The belief—such as Noah Webster's—that a state or country or nation springs out of contract or written agreement seems to have been endemic in those times.

All of a sudden the *H.M.S. Pinafore* came sailing into Oliver's musical memory. "*That's* why that line is so funny. 'It is greatly to his credit that he is an Englishman.' It's not to his credit, not to his parents' credit, not to anyone's credit, is it? He didn't sign a prenatal contract, did he, choosing to be born alive an Englishman?"

"Right." St. John's voice took on profundity. "It must have been a special kind of knowledge we had when we laughed at it. We knew the line was funny but didn't know or ask why. Now that we do know, is it still funny?"

"Sure. Funnier, maybe."

She looked doubtful. "Think so?"

————A cardinal assumption of the doctrine (St. John's voice sank deeper still) was that political community or organization is an artifact, a product of contract, of men's voluntary, deliberate, binding agreement. The idea has taken such hold on this side of the Atlantic that you may need to be reminded that there are other theories.

The main contrast is with Aristotle's view that man is born a political animal who at birth finds himself not in a state of nature but in a family, and proceeds from household to village to political community, which steps can be called natural since these institutions are universal and not due to human agency. Society and country exist everywhere, with or without social contract, as does government good and bad.

A contrast closer to the eighteenth century was James I of England's exposition of the theory of divine right. The people could not limit the Crown, kingship expressed the will of God, succession to the throne was by birth. The authority of the king came from God, not from the king's subject people. The king or queen was accountable not to them but to God who, of course, wanted all rulers to act for the public benefit.

Ironically, at about the time the *social contract* was stirring up the Colonies, changing them into States, and grouping them into the United States, the theory took several hard blows to the chin. At mid-century, the Scottish philosopher David Hume denied that the social contract had any basis in historical fact or personal experience. People might cheer the king on parade but that didn't mean they had consented to his rule. History informed Hume that "Scarce any man, till very lately, ever imagined that government was founded on compact. . . ." Traditionalists like the Savoyard Joseph-Marie de Maistre and the Dublin-born orator and member of Parliament Edmund Burke attacked the idea that a country, nation, government, or constitution originates by human agency.

Burke made the social contract so spiritual as to be unrecognizable as a contract, describing its parties as the dead, living, and unborn, and the visible and invisible worlds. Society is indeed a contract, he wrote. "It is a partnership in all science, a partnership in all art, a partnership in every virtue and in all perfection." Each contract of each particular state, he held, was but a clause "in a fixed contract holding all physical and all moral natures each in their appointed place." When he had finished, "contract" as a political term was useless even as an analogy.

The theory stood exposed. It had exploited the deceptive ease with which human relationships can be described as *quid pro quo*, as an exchange, something for something else, political life as a series of trade-offs. It had jumbled the words state, country, government, and especially, society, which it assimilated to contracts for tobacco or calico. It spawned countless variations, holding some terms steady and shifting others. It refused to budge from a belief, as one critic phrased it, in "imaginary pactions."

"And as you showed, Oliver, when applied to documents framed with social contract theory as a guide, it failed to qualify as a contract at law or a contract in law. The theory should be dead; yet it lives on, in no place more hardily than in the United States. No one is surprised to hear a president say, 'I have a four-year contract with the American people.' Or to see a group of Congressmen promise a particular legislative program and call it their 'Contract with America.'

"One thing social contract ideas did accomplish was to set We, the People firmly in the saddle of political theory for several centuries. No mean achievement. Whether the people showed as good a seat in the saddle of political practice is a horse of a different color."

Huggins liked this metaphor. "All this time you've been talking about an English saddle. Haven't you got a different saddle or horse to offer?"

"I'm speaking as a horsewoman, not as a horse breeder or saddler," retorted St. John. "There are plenty of other saddles and horses, and reins and boots and spurs if we wanted to ride off over the history of political philosophy on all continents. Since we've been focusing on names and country, let me describe one theory

that, like an English saddle on a Morgan horse, may suit you better for cross-country."

————In this theory a country is composed of an aggregation of
people living generally within a determinable space (which may expand or contract—witness the territory of nomads like the Great
Plains Indians who once they got horses abandoned bean crops and
rode out for bison meat), whose predecessors over generations had
recognized and acknowledged each other by a certain name, and
who show a powerful preferential sentiment toward those so recognized and toward the collective proper name. That name concentrates the group's history, customs, arts, topography, language
and literature, technology, mythology, political institutions, and religion; condenses its selfhood in a word. This view is sometimes
called the historical or organic theory of state or country. Or the
genetic, for to have got those people to recognize each other and
be recognized by the same name, a lengthy sequence of events in
time and space, facilitating intercourse and conceptions of kith and
kin, had to have taken place. You can look backward to see the
sequence, analyze the kind of events, isolate the factors and circumstances, identify the leaders, trace the spread of language and
population—but you cannot produce a country or nation overnight
by contract.

The deputies to the convention sometimes spoke of country.
"Confidential servants of their country," Madison called them. The
word was surely used to bolster those all-too-feeble sentiments of
patriotism Washington spoke of. Like Washington and Noah Webster, like all of us, the Framers were guided by what they believed
ought to be the case, hoped to be the case, and thought might make
others believe the same—that a country did and ought to exist.

They spoke of *the people* in general, as something out there, not
here in convention hall, heaven help us! They did not consider
themselves part of the people but special persons who thought
of the people as something to be taken into account mainly to lessen
the chance of popular protest, occasionally thinking aristocratically
of doing something for the good of the people—*noblesse oblige*—
considering them as those out there who most of the time could
not perceive that good as clearly as they, the creative minority,

could. What Morton White concluded about the '76 revolutionaries he concluded also about the Framers, that whatever the admirable features of their philosophical ideas of the Revolutionary era might have been, "a faith in all the people was not one of them."

They were wide awake, though, to the persuasiveness of *people* as a word. They knew the word's history from Runnymede to the present. State legislatures were falling victim to its power every day. The word bounced off their walls like a squash-court ball. The States called constitutional conventions in the name of the people; drafted bills of rights to protect the people; enlarged the suffrage to express the sovereignty of the people; enacted laws encroaching on property by the will of the people. Why should they, the deputies to a congressionally authorized constitutional convention, deny themselves the use of that rhetorical force?

"The engrosser of the '87 Constitution, whoever he was, knew his business. This is how he engrossed the heading."

St. John held out to Huggins a sheet of paper. At the top appeared:

We the People *of the United States*

"The printers, Dunlop and Claypole, limited by typefaces on hand, struck it off this way:

WE, the People of the United States

"What those patriotic and respectable citizens meant . . ."

Huggins mumbled to himself. "What they meant was the requisite bullshit, as Grandpapa would say."

St. John shot him a sidelong glance. "Did you say something?"

"Just clearing my throat."

"Oh. Well, what those good citizens knew was that this constitution was drawn up *For* the People, not *By* the People, but By Us.

"So, if the Founding Fathers didn't found a country, what *did* they do?"

————They framed a government. Which is why they are properly called the Framers. Actually the political term "constitution" had the fairly fixed meaning, almost a synonym, of the phrase "frame of government." The Massachusetts Constitution described itself as a frame of government; so did the Pennsylvania Constitution. The document the Framers fashioned bore no heading. When first printed for wide distribution it was generally captioned "A Frame of Government".

Now you cannot frame a government neutrally. The form you give it will fit, closely or loosely, one of the classifications that political philosophers have used through the ages to convey a rough idea of what they were talking about and to praise or condemn it. The heartiest of these clarifications divides governments or regimes into three forms: monarchy, aristocracy, and republic. If you remind me, I'll talk more about them tomorrow. For the moment, I'll note that Constitution 2 frames a government, a regime that—through its stipulation of citizens, elections, hostility to kings and hereditary institutions—constitutes a republic. When asked what the convention had accomplished, Benjamin Franklin answered correctly, "A republic, if you can keep it."

A form of government (as described in or enacted by a constitution) and a country are not the same thing. A country or nation is more durable than a constitution. A country can undergo conquest, be absorbed in an empire or commonwealth, change from monarchy to republic and back again, suffer tyranny, suffer conquest, and still remain a country, still retain its old name. The countries that have lost their name and disappeared from the face of the map are few compared to the shifts in forms of government that have taken place within them.

The thirteen Colonies were not in England but in British North America; yet, as we've seen, the colonists claimed the rights of subjects of that monarchy as framed by the English constitution. The Declaration of Independence transformed those imperial Colonies into independent States; the State constitutions changed their form of government from monarchy to republic. But Virginians were Virginians before and Virginians afterward.

Although at present most people may believe that the thirteen States signed an agreement to found one big country, or that We, the People signed it, whatever they signed, if ever they did sign, was an agreement to frame a republican government.

Huggins was turning this over in his mind and came up with, "Ms. St. John, this country could never have a king."

"Oh, Oliver, here we are, you and I, sacrificing tennis and dancing to meet day after day with what looks like a country with no name on our hands. As of today we don't even know whether we have a *country* on our hands. And here you are, wanting to talk about kings.

"Good-bye," she said disgustedly.

6

WE THE PEOPLE HAND OUT OATHS: YOU SWEAR, HE SWEARS, WE SWEAR NOT

SATURDAY

As Huggins barged into the room he caught a whiff of perfume. Chanel No. 5? Pretty conservative. Already seated was Claire St. John.

"Good afternoon, Oliver," she said brightly.

"Afternoon." He sat down and looked closely at the cheery creature in front of him. Hair was shorter and flatter, falling over her left cheek beyond the eye like a horse blinder; that eye could only see ahead or to the right. On the other cheek the hair was curved back to the ear. A string of pearls and a shorter gold chain with a pendant—a pale gem the size of a quarter, gold encircled—dangled down the long white-buttoned front of an ivory-colored lawn vest. Draped over this was an open peach jacket with half-sleeves slightly gathered at the shoulders. He watched her rise to reach over into her envelope of papers and sit down again. Pants! He had never seen her in pants before. Washed-out blue jeans. For the first time he saw that her long legs were joined to a rump. Compact *derrière*, he noted with appreciation.

Huggins got up and walked past the horse-blinder side to get her usual glass of water. Carrying it to the table he saw at the back of her jacket the suggestion of a bra. For some reason he felt relief. The jacket was so transparent that the vest underneath must have just covered her front like a dickie, or maybe—yes, that must be it—jacket and vest (without a back to it) were sewn together. He couldn't tell for sure.

He sat down and continued his furtive inspection while she took a few sips of water. Her semi-thick eyebrows a shade darker, her lips a shade brighter, her eyes darker too. She seemed taller but maybe that was part of the general effect of rings, necklaces, and perfumed mist. Was she wearing higher heels?

"I came in a little early," said this mysterious tutor, "because I have to leave a little early."

"Oh," said Oliver. He didn't at all like what he was hearing, seeing, smelling. What happened to that slightly sunbaked skin, that natural perfume he used to smell? Her fingernails unchanged, medium long, nicely trimmed and unpolished. Her toenails, he could see through the open shoes, were painted red. That must be different or he would have noticed before. Damn!

"Let's assume for the time being," she said, "that Constitution 2, this defective contract drawn up on the windy side of the law, is okay."

Down to business awfully fast, thought Huggins.

"And for a moment let's look at it as a literary effort. Quite a mess, you know. The first one-sentence paragraph, usually called the Preamble, written in the third person plural, active voice, present tense, identifies the author and the authority as 'We, the People.' "

"Why do you say 'usually called the Preamble'? Is it the Preamble or isn't it?" interrupted Huggins.

———The engrossed copy carried no such word or heading, as you saw yesterday, explained St. John patiently. The paragraph has since been referred to as "the Preamble" with a capital *P*, as though it

were something external to the document. Madison and other conventioneers referred to it as "the preamble" with a small *p*, and so
might we, to give it no more separateness than it deserves.

After that paragraph came the body of the text, the Articles, seven
in all. They shifted to the future tense and mainly passive voice. "All
legislative powers herein granted shall be vested . . . This constitution . . . shall be the supreme law of the land. . . . All executive and
judicial officers shall be bound by oath or affirmation. . . ."

The closing reads, "Done in Convention, by the unanimous consent of the States present," followed by the names of the States from
North to South, and the signatures of the delegates alongside the
names of their respective States as subscription to their State's consent, in the manner I described yesterday.

These are the signatures of the Framers, not of the Ratifiers, who
had signed in the ratifying conventions of their respective States and
whose names have almost been lost in the shuffle. In theory, they
gave the consent of We the People. To indicate this we should at
least capitalize the Ratifiers—as we do the Framers.

A number of powerful States, as they ratified the document, recommended in the strongest terms the immediate addition of a Bill
of Rights. Whether such a bill ought to be included as an integral
part of this constitution was debated in the new Congress, and the
decision made to leave the original as it was, not to open it up to
who-knows-what changes, and instead to add new articles as
amendments. Ten amendments (ratified 1791) are today generally
considered part of the 1787 Constitution (ratified 1788).

Huggins could show he was a quick learner. "You called them the
Bill of Rights. Shouldn't you call them 'the first ten amendments'
instead?"

"Either way," replied St. John earnestly. "The Framers, the Ratifiers, the new Congress (and Madison) referred to them as the Bill
of Rights, and both in language and structure they differ from the
'87 Constitution. They go back to the vocabulary of rights of
the Declaration of Independence and exhibit a style notable for
negative imperatives: 'shall make no law . . . shall not be in-
fringed . . . shall not be violated . . . no Warrants shall issue . . .' I'll
point up the significance of this next week.

"Now, Oliver, I'm about to discuss the final draft of Constitution 2, the one that with a few negligible errors was sent to the Constitution 1 Congress assembled (in New York), to the respective State legislatures and the newspapers, and then used by the State ratifying conventions to wrap the whole thing up. We can call it Draft B, and the previous one Draft A. Draft B worked a marked improvement on Draft A."

"I'm listening," said Huggins dryly.

"You seem a bit cranky today. Does your knee hurt?" St. John solicitously peered down in that general direction.

Huggins searched for something he could reasonably grouch about. "I can't get used to this Draft A and B and Constitution 1 and 2 business. It's like, 'in this corner we have Constitution 1 weighing in at 1,777 pounds; in this corner Constitution 2 at 1,787 pounds. Now shake hands, seconds out, go to your corners and come out fighting.' "

"Just be glad that so far there are no Constitutions 3 and 4," said St. John pleasantly. "Then you would have a free-for-all in the ring. But if it'll help, let's do this. From now on, we'll call Constitution number 1 'the '77 Constitution,' and number 2 'the '87 Constitution,' dating them from their drafting. As for the drafts of the '87 Constitution, let's have two. Draft A we'll call the first draft, and the final draft or B, we'll call Gouverneur's draft. Is that better? Now, answer me this: If you had to draft a constitution for a new country, how would you go about it?"

Intimidating pause.

Huggins panicked. "Well—"

"Come on, Oliver, think fast!"

"I'd divide it into three parts—the president, Congress, and supreme court."

"Hardly original," remarked St. John dryly. "I don't have to tell you what guided you to that triple-threat structure, do I? Think a bit. What did the Framers have in their memory or on the table before them as guides?" Without waiting for an answer she went on.

————Certainly the several State constitutions and Bills of Rights (which some of them had helped frame). They had Sir William Blackstone's *Commentaries on the Laws of England* also, the *vade mecum* of all lawyers; and the Articles of Confederation, the constitution they were busy supplanting, that they used mainly to remind them of which subjects to include. Furthermore they were familiar with seventeenth- and eighteenth-century English history, and their own history as colonies. The more scholarly delegates like Madison and Hamilton had a vaster library at their disposal. All of them seem to have left home a copy of the Declaration of Independence with its talk of unalienable Rights.

After a couple of months' debate, the convention appointed a Committee of Detail. Armed with notes and memory, it was to produce a draft. The committee took all the points already agreed on, however unsurely, the products of all the debates and the deals made "out-of-doors," as they used to say, and put them together in a twenty-three-article list, the first draft. The convention read it and handed it over for final drafting to a new committee, on "Stile and Arrangement," which we shall shorten to "Committee on Stile." Its drafter, Gouverneur Morris, got the job done within a week.

Remember him? Gouverneur Morris, this wealthy ladies' man, gave a performance at the convention no one was likely to forget—forever on the floor with remarks not always consistent with his previous ones but almost always worth thinking over, the only man reputed to have clapped George Washington on the shoulder in bonhomie, and (equally important) the probable author of Washington's phrase "true American."

Handed the first draft of the '87 Constitution, Gouverneur Morris immediately divided it into the three powers (Articles I, II, and III), a scheme then on the cutting edge of political philosophy—the legislative, the executive, and the judicial. Directly or indirectly, Gouverneur got the idea from Montesquieu. The colonials, you may recall, were familiar with the great French thinker.

The '77 Constitution did not use this triple scheme: it put all government in the hands of Congress. The Massachusetts 1780 Constitution did use Montesquieu's idea but did not divide the text into the three categories.

In one short chapter of his great work, *The Spirit of the Laws*, published in 1748 and read and quoted by clergymen, professors, and lawyers, including Jefferson, Madison, and John Marshall, Montesquieu divided the English constitution into these three powers—

legislative, executive, and judicial. Evidently the division impressed a number of our French-reading colonials, and continues to impress the world of political scientists to this day. One would think that heaven itself had divided the government of men into these three parts, whereas the most superficial reflection shows that any single act of government may be construed as consisting of any or all three functions. A "legislative" body like the Continental Congress can command an army, a king can hold trial, and a magistrate make law.

Montesquieu's faulty analysis of the English constitution provided a simple outline for grouping and trimming down the long miscellany that the Committee of Detail had passed along to Gouverneur Morris and his Committee on Stile. With more time and a free hand Morris would have done a better job. He would probably have put most of Article IV into I; VI into III; V and VII into a single amending and ratifying article, thus structuring the whole in four instead of seven articles. He could have rounded off more neatly the powers granted each branch, too, were it not for the particular interests and fears of some conventioneers and their respective States. The final draft was a committee's crazy-quilt, given some pattern by a man with style.

To Gouverneur we owe the opening one-sentence paragraph, the preamble, the We the People phrase, impressively engrossed and printed, and nowadays thunderously declaimed from platform, pulpit, and screen.

The Declaration and Resolves of the First Congress (1774) had read, "The good people of the several colonies of New-Hampshire . . ." listing the colonies North to South, down to South Carolina. The Articles of Confederation listed every State from New Hampshire to Georgia. The first draft of the '87 Constitution followed the pattern: "We, the People of the States of New-Hampshire, Massachusetts, Rhode-Island and Providence Plantations, Connecticut, New-York, New-Jersey, Pennsylvania, Delaware, Maryland, Virginia, North-Carolina, South-Carolina, and Georgia do ordain . . ." Some asked the Committee on Stile, why did they change this to We, the People of the United States? The answer was that the States couldn't be listed as before because now the approval of nine States had been specified as necessary to put this constitution in force, and no one knew for certain which the first nine would be. There was not much fuss over Gouverneur's change. In the new constitution, as in prior documents, the United States meant united states, plural. The convention looked Gouverneur's draft over, quickly approved, and scampered home.

Yet the substitution seemed to shift the meaning. When the States were asked to ratify, some opponents of the proposed constitution protested the unity it suggested. Patrick Henry, for one, demanded, "Who is this people of the United States?" They got the same answer, that no one knew which States would ratify. Of course, it would have been clearer to write, "We, the People of the signatory States," or "of the undersigned States." Much clearer but not dramatic enough for Gouverneur Morris.

Without much ado, the scratch of a pen had wrought a change worthy of the roll of drums and the blast of trumpets.

"Did you ever read Walt Whitman's poem . . . ?"

Huggins shook his head.

"Where he sings . . ."

Huggins shook his head again.

St. John tried another art form. "Haven't you ever seen those black-and-white movies where the hero or heroine at some point late in the melodrama shouts to an encircling public: 'Who are the people?' and then cries out, '*We* are the people, *you* are the people!' pointing to each one in turn, 'and *you*, and *you*, and *you*! You and me, *we* are the people!' Ta-rahhh!"

"No, I haven't." Huggins didn't feel like cooperating today.

"You're too young to remember."

This remark had Huggins fuming. Couldn't he think of something nasty to say? Yes!

"Didn't Benjamin Franklin write a letter or something in praise of older women?"

St. John stiffened. "Now, wait a minute. Benjamin Franklin's older women were—" She stopped, realized she'd been had, relaxed, burst into laughter.

Huggins, relieved, smiled weakly.

"If you can tear your mind away from age-grading," she said, laughter subsiding, "do push past the preamble along to the first sentence of the text."

————If we read this constitution, not in the order it was drafted with the opening paragraph composed last, but as it was read for approval by "the People" or by the Ratifiers, or as it is given to us today, we are in for a jolt. The nice phrase in the preamble about the People disappears and we are thrown into a swamp of future tense, passive voice legalese. To sustain the style of the preamble and its supposition that the people are the ultimate authority, the very ones who ordain and establish this constitution, the rest of the document should have taken the present, active voice of "do ordain and establish," and continued in the same vein. Article I, Section I, would have begun thus, "We the People vest all legislative powers in a Congress . . ."

In addition, after ratification, the new Congress should have rewritten this constitution. The future tense should have been changed to the present tense, and the document closed with the authorizing signatures of the ratifying rather than of the framing delegates, not only with a view to legalizing the contract, but to be in harmony with We the People. The consent of the people was more important than the creativeness of an aristocracy.

Such unity of style and presumed intent would have lent a much stronger people's cast to the document. Too popular a cast, no doubt. We heard Madison say that the Framers looked with alarm at such excess in the new State constitutions.

Massachusetts again provides a suggestive model. "We, therefore, the people of Massachusetts" not only "do agree upon, ordain, and establish the constitution," but throughout insist on the reminder that all power comes from the people, and that the people have rights. Although lapses occur, and after the opening paragraphs a shift is made to "the people" in the third person singular, the style is much more in the present tense, active voice: "and the people of this Commonwealth . . . do invest their legislature with authority . . ."

Getting back to the '87 Constitution, one of the things that We the People required of their representatives and officials was to take an oath of office. In contractual terms, as you remarked yesterday, this oath signifies acceptance of the post that We the People offer.

Compensation comes afterward, signifying that the agent's services have acceptably begun and that We the People are holding to our part of the contract. George Washington almost set a bad precedent by offering to serve without pay, asking only that his expenses be defrayed. Congress refused his generosity, whether because a republican contract required payment or for reasons of economy, I do not know. Washington had offered the same terms for his services as commander in chief of Continental forces in the War of Independence, and Congress had accepted. His bill for expenses in eight years of service came to $449,261.51—he was good at writing expense accounts. Had he accepted the regular salary offered of $6,000 a year, the total paid out by Congress would only have amounted to $48,000. As president, some of his expenditures were criticized. The earliest draft of his farewell letter, which he intended to publish after his first term, ended with a defense of his expenses while in office. "[M]y fortune, in a pecuniary point of view, had received no augmentation from my country, but the reverse. . . ." The cancellation is his. Holding that he had kept to his principle of "not to receive more from the public than my expenses" he was retiring "from the Chair of government no otherwise benefitted in this particular than what you have all experienced from the increased value of property." Bracketed alongside in the margin he noted: "This may, or not, be omitted."

Something out of the dim past came back to Huggins. "Didn't a rich presidential candidate not so long ago offer to serve as president without salary? Somebody from Texas?"

"Maybe so, I don't remember. In a republic, you see, salaries are paid not only to keep to the contractual pattern but also to enable a poor person to take a post if offered. Otherwise only those with sufficient financial resources could bear the loss in income over the years of service. A candidate's offer to serve without salary can be a demagogic ploy. It seems to say: I want to save the people money; and by not taking a salary, I show my independence of the influ-

ence of monied supporters. But it conveys also my independence of
We, the People, my disinclination to accept the role of paid public
servant.

"As you must know from the time you spent in Ethiopia, Huggins, ambassadors who are not career or service diplomats often get
posts where the salary they receive is not nearly enough to cover
expenses, largely unreimbursed, for the kind of life they must
lead."

"I was too young, of course, to notice who was paying for what,"
said Huggins slyly, but then allowed himself a recollection: "Embassy functions *were* lavish."

————The next point, she carried on, is that no man or woman
can accept public office or receive compensation for it without
swearing an oath. Article VI of the '87 Constitution stipulates, "The
senators and representatives beforementioned and the members of
the several state legislatures, and all executive and judicial officers
both of the United States and of the several States, shall be bound
by oath or affirmation to support this constitution. . . ."

Yesterday we tackled the phrase *the United States* as the first of
three circumlocutions. We come now to the second one, the need
for which occurred in the oath of office. The term the Framers used
to get around the lack of a name was *the constitution*.

One purpose of exacting an oath from a person is to bind that
person to a promised performance by more than just the usual coercion, to bind by a supernatural or supernaturally related religious
or moral force as well. A person so bound fears not only ordinary
punishment for violating a promise but also supernatural punishment—from God, if sworn before God, or from an ancestor, if
sworn on one's grandmother's grave. I'm sure you've come across
children making a sign of the cross over their heart and swearing,
"Cross my heart and hope to die," which if the promise isn't kept
beckons to supernatural intervention.

The words *oath* and *swear* in such contexts call on the Deity.
Which is why Quakers object to oath-taking and swearing, and why
in the '87 Constitution the words *affirm* and *affirmation* were substituted for *swear* and *oath*. Giving Quakers this choice, though, does
not take them off the hot seat. By long judicial practice "solemnly"

requires laying one's hand on the Gospels. To affirm *solemnly* calls up the dangers of self-imprecation, of violating conscience, of invoking God's displeasure.

The prospective "solemn" oath-breaker also fears the heat of moral indignation—the greater certainty and harshness of punishment. Think of the fury with which the colonial rebels regarded a loyalist who had broken the oath they forced him to take. Tar-and-feathering and riding the rail was too good for him. They would be looking around for a rope and a stout tree limb. Remember that those rebels—oath-breakers all—were subjects of the king of England. Out of twelve generals in the Continental army, eleven had held royal commissions. The members of Congress, the signers and good People of the Declaration of Independence, the signers and constituents of the Articles of Confederation, the signers and Ratifiers and peoples of the States, all had at one time or another sworn allegiance to the king and then, through the Declaration of Independence, openly "absolved [themselves] from all Allegiance to the British Crown." Martin Van Buren was the first president of the United States not born a subject of the Crown.

Evidently, the Declaration of Independence's abjuring of allegiance was not enough. Individual oaths had to be taken.

> I, Arnold Benedict, do acknowledge the United States of America to be free, independent and sovereign states, and declare that the people thereof owe no allegiance or obedience to George the 3d, King of Great Britain; and I renounce, refuse and abjure any allegiance or obedience to him; and I do swear that I will, to the utmost of my power, support, maintain, and defend the said United States against the said King George 3d and his heirs and successors, and his and their abettors, assistants and adherents, and I will serve the said United States as General of the Continental Army which commission I now hold, with fidelity, according to the best of my skill and understanding. So help me God.

Evidently individual oaths also were not enough. Benjamin Franklin, swearer of at least three opposing oaths, regarded all oaths "as the last resort of liars."

The Framers and the Congressmen in New York knew they were breaking their oath, sworn in perpetuity, to the '77

Constitution. Madison in *Federalist* XL of his newspaper articles urging ratification asserted "that the articles of confederation should be disregarded" for "the happiness of the people of America." He openly confessed, "The liberty of judging of that happiness was assumed irregularly by a *very few* deputies, from a *very few* states. . . ."

Bringing up the "very delicate" matter again in *Federalist* XLIII, Madison asked his readers, "On what principle the confederation, which stands in the solemn form of a compact among the States, can be suppressed without the unanimous consent of the States to it [as that constitution stipulated]?" And then answered: "The great principle of self-preservation, to the transcendent law of nature and of nature's God, which declares that the safety and happiness of society are the objects at which all political institutions aim, and to which all such institutions must be sacrificed." He was referring his readers to the revolutionary Declaration of Independence and insinuating that the existing constitution was tyrannical and therefore must be sacrificed. Neither in its preamble or anywhere else did the new constitution he was selling mention happiness as an aim, nor did it mention its subservience to the transcendent law of nature and of nature's God.

One supporter of the new constitution wrote to another triumphantly, "I answer we have all broken that Covenant & it is now prostrate in the Dust. . . ." They were not candid enough to abjure it officially, as the Declaration of Independence had done. They went through quite a few rough scuffles with supporters of the existing constitution, especially during the ratifying campaigns, but managed to escape tar-and-feathering.

"By the way, tar-and-feathering is no laughing matter. Descriptions are hard to find nowadays. There's one in Kenneth Roberts's *Oliver Wiswell*—"

"I knew it!" Huggins broke in. "I know it!"

"Knew what? Know what?"

"I know *that* book. The first day, no, the second day we met we couldn't think of a novel about the Revolution that told a story like your Tom and Becky's, of a man and woman in love, the one Tory, the other Rebel. I *knew* there was a book like that somewhere but

I couldn't place it. Now you've brought it up yourself: *Oliver Wiswell.*"

"I guess you're right. Wonder why I forgot it then." St. John fluttered her eyelashes in mock modesty. "Probably I have too high a literary threshold."

"It sold a lot of copies and went through a lot of reprints, and would make at least a Grade-B movie."

"Yes, and wouldn't you know . . ."

"Know what?"

"We must add another to our list of remarkable Olivers. Didn't he fight with the King's American Dragoons? I've forgot how the book ends. What happens?"

"A happy ending . . ."

"Yes, now I remember. Oliver didn't leave her pregnant, though, did he? That's an important difference from Tom and Becky. They didn't even bed together, did they? That takes a lot of tension out of the plot."

"No, they didn't. There's one thing they did do, though." Huggins tried hard to conceal his excitement.

"What was that?"

"Get up a second, I'll show you." His heart was pounding in his ears. "Stand here alongside me."

St. John looked at him quizzically but moved to his side.

"Now, about-face," he commanded, and as she complied, slipped his left hand into her right hand and twined fingers.

Huggins held her hand that way for a long moment, until she gently squirmed it loose. "At the end of the book," he quickly explained (as if explanation were necessary), "they locked fingers."

He kept his eyes on her face, but it gave away nothing.

"I see," she said, "and for that this little demonstration was necessary?"

Huggins gave a little smile and held his ground.

St. John resumed as if nothing had happened, when indeed, Huggins hoped, a lot did happen.

————Getting back to tar-and-feathering. It is not a judicial procedure. When the mob has done with stripping the man (I don't know whether women were ever tarred and feathered), pouring hot tar over his naked body and plastering chicken feathers to cover him, top to bottom—hair, eyes, ears, nostrils, genitals, toes—he looks like a monstrous bird with bits and patches of shiny black showing through. The encircling goons taunt and jab him with sticks to ruffle the feathers, sometimes setting fire to them, then thrust a sharp-edged, preferably green, fence rail between his legs, and hoist it up on their shoulders. The feathered monster hunches over unable to keep his groin from being torn and ripped by the rail, blood running down his legs, while the triumphant gang joggle it and jeering mates poke the prisoner with sticks, both to keep him off balance and to keep him from toppling off the rail, shouting, "Ride, Tory, ride!" To get tar and feathers off torn and burned skin is a long painful procedure with lard or grease, scissors and scrapers. For a serious case of being rail-split up the middle, you'd need a surgeon.

The history of oaths, their making, exacting, taking, and breaking, is a much neglected study. Oaths are contracts in miniature, political philosophies in a thimble, small but oh my! If ever you decide to write a thesis or book, there's an important subject for you. Let me whet your appetite by giving you a few pages from colonial and later State happenings.

An outbreak of oath-making in South Carolina in the early 1830s prefigured the beginnings of a secession crisis. To nullify tariff laws they held to be prejudicial, passed by northern majorities in Congress, South Carolina legislators proposed new oaths clarifying the relation of their State's oath to that of the United States. "Allegiance" to the State, they claimed, overrode any mere "support" of the '87 Constitution. According to Andrew Jackson, then president of the United States, under that constitution, the people had transferred its primary allegiance to the new government. The governor of South Carolina disagreed: "I recognize no allegiance as paramount to that which the citizens of South Carolina owe to the State." In reply to Jackson the legislature took the same stand, resolving that "the primary and paramount allegiance of the citizens of this state, native or adopted, is of right due to this state," and later ordaining that allegiance was due only to the State of South Carolina and all other allegiance was to be abjured.

★ ★

St. John stood up, raised her right arm, rested her left hand on an imaginary Bible, and declaimed:

" 'I, Athenea Bolingbroke, do solemnly swear that I will be faithful and true allegiance bear to the State of South Carolina . . . and that I will . . . preserve, protect, and defend the constitution of this State and of the United States; so help me God.' "

She sat down.

"Who is Athenea Bolingbroke?" puzzled Huggins.

"Me," she replied. "Uncle Gaspar says we may be distantly related to Henry St. John, Viscount Bolingbroke, a famous English orator who published a book in 1749 titled *The Idea of a Patriot King*. You have to shift the accent and pronounce his *St. John* with a lazy mouth—'*sin-jən*. His friend Montesquieu picked up from him the notion that the English constitution consisted of a happy balance of three powers—the 'monarchical, aristocratical, and democratical' or executive, judicial, and legislative."

"And where does Athenea comes in?"

"Oh, you know, in written oath-forms in the blank space reserved for a name, instead of 'I, John Doe' they usually print, 'I, A. B., do solemnly swear . . .' So I made up Athenea Bolingbroke. Pretty, don't you think?"

"Cool."

Thus justified, St. John reverted to her tutor voice.

———Some years later, with secession threats fresh in mind, the Massachusetts Historical Society, discussing the lack of a name for country, made no distinction between North and South. It laid the blame on men's stubborn allegiance to the States and to their singular names.

> That this name [Columbia] has not been so universally received and used, as might have been expected, may perhaps be accounted for from the political and personal emphatic importance attached to each of the separate communities of which the Union is composed, by its members. . . . [T]he social sentiment which binds men to their country is throughout the Union lavished almost entirely upon the State. . . . [T]he patriotism of which the whole

> Union is the object, has little hold upon the affections. . . . The patriotism of the heart, of the altar, and the fireside, is all absorbed by the State. . . . [A]nd there is no concentration of feeling from the circumference to the centre, inspiring the wish to be called a common name.

The notables of the day concurred, as I shall report to you after the weekend. We witness here how difficult it is for a descriptive title such as the United States of America to attract and bind popular sentiment, faith, loyalty, allegiance, or patriotism.

After fierce struggles over various forms of the new oaths, the fire of the early 1830s died down, to flare up a generation later, fanned by the antislavery wind blowing out of Pennsylvania and New England from the direction of Quakers, transcendentalists, and abolitionists, about whom also we'll hear more next week.

After the federal Fort Sumter fell to the South in April 1861, the North saw treason lurking everywhere. It became their turn to mount an oath-taking campaign, trying, as oaths in the Revolutionary War had tried, to separate the Loyalists or Tories (now the Unionists) from the Rebels (still the Rebels). In the border zone, a contested no-man's-land emerged between North and South, shifting about Maryland, Kentucky, Missouri, and Arkansas. Tar-and-feather parties revived with a vengeance, ending at times in lynchings.

Lincoln gave William Seward, his secretary of state, responsibility for an antidisloyalty program in the North. The secretary quickly demonstrated an aptitude for the job. In short order he had a web of police informants and private detectives covering the North and the shaky border States. The notorious Allan Pinkerton and his band of operators got their start from Seward, who boasted he could touch a bell and arrest a citizen of Ohio or imprison one in New York.

All government employees, from the head secretary to the lowest messenger, had to take the oath of allegiance anew. Why anew? Was there an expiration date on the original oath in Article VI exacted by the convention in 1787? No, but that model, pledging to support "this constitution" no longer sufficed. *Sentiment* had now to be sworn to. Congress began to compose new oaths, culminating in the "ironclad oath" of 1862. Oath-takers had to promise to support, protect, and defend the constitution *and* the federal government *and* swear "loyalty to the same, any ordinance, resolution, or law of any State Convention or Legislature to the contrary, notwithstanding." A number of northern states, reaching beyond government, required new swear-ins of all voters and in some cases of members of the professions of law, medicine, teaching, and the ministry. The northern keyword was *loyalty*, which I guess was supposed to lock out Carolina's *faith* and *true allegiance*.

"Sounds like *Catch-22*."

"I've heard of *Catch-22*," said St. John. "Was there something about oaths in it?"

"There certainly was." Huggins seized the chance to play tutor. "It's a great novel about World War II; there's a description of a Glorious Loyalty Oath Crusade at a wartime air base in the Mediterranean. I remember something called the Doctrine of Continual Reaffirmation, its aim being to keep the men pledging."

"Interesting. Isn't that what you said about social contracts and oaths? They avoid expiration dates."

"Right. The purpose of Continual Reaffirmation was to trap all those who had become disloyal since the last time they took the oath. The men had to re-swear or sign an oath form to get their pay, to get anything from the PX, to get food on their trays at mess, even to get their map cases and parachutes. To anyone who objected the reply was that people loyal to their country wouldn't object to signing the forms, that the more loyalty oaths a person signed, the more loyal he proved himself to be." Huggins waxed enthusiastic.

"A bit exaggerated," said St. John.

"It's supposed to be satire. You'd love the whole book."

"Hmmm. Sounds good. I'll look it up."

"I've got it somewhere. I'll find it and lend it to you."

"I doubt I'll have time to read it so soon. Thanks anyway."

Huggins sank into gloom. She wasn't giving an inch.

St. John, perhaps relenting, picked up the thread. "Who started the Glorious Loyalty Crusade?"

"A Captain Black," Huggins supplied, pretending indifference, but then looked up. "Hold on a sec."

"Yes?" The impatient anklet was bobbing again.

"I'm beginning to see the light."

"Yes?"

"When you read the southern oath, it went, 'I will be faithful and true allegiance bear to the State of South *Carolina*. Right?"

"Close enough."

"What did the *northerners* now have to swear to? The *loyalty* oath is new, as you said, but loyalty to what? Loyalty to the '87 Constitution and the federal government? They had to swear loyalty to things without a name!"

Claire St. John arose.

Now what?

She went around to his side of the round table and bowed in admiration before him.

In the scoop of her neckline he caught a glimpse of two small breasts down to their jutting nipples. Thank you, Ms. St. John! Glad to see you're not flat as a board. But I'm not made of wood, woman. Any more of this, all bets are off.

As if she'd read his mind, she quickly returned to her chair and went on in a monotone.

————In British North America, oaths served various purposes: keeping the bad elements out of New England's theocracies, distinguishing Rebels from Tories, deterring desertions from the Continental army, and so on. Washington, a prominent promoter of oaths, early in the war took a false step. As commander in chief, His Excellency issued a proclamation ordering all persons who had taken an oath to Great Britain to withdraw behind British lines or "take the oath of allegiance to the United States of America" or stay where they were and be "treated as common enemies of the American States." For this act Congress almost censured him officially. Civilians owed allegiance not to the United States but to the State of which they were already citizens. Their allegiance was the business of their respective States, not that of the United States. In the spring of 1778, Washington ran out of oath forms for the army. Time and again special messengers rushed in new stocks to keep up with demand. Washington dispatched special officers all along the line from Canada to Georgia to administer oaths.

Truth is, Washington did not put much trust in patriotism of any size. "Men," he wrote from camp in Valley Forge, "may talk of patriotism. . . . I do not mean to exclude altogether the idea of Patriotism. I know it exists, . . . but it will not endure unassisted by Interest."

In his farewell letter he emphasized for newspaper readers the need for religion, a part of the letter that historians have neglected. The strongest argument he marshaled is that belief in religion was necessary to keep men to their oaths: "where is the security for property, for reputation, for life, if the sense of religious obligation *desert* the oaths, which are the instruments of investigation in courts of justice?" By God, if the fear of hanging will not keep men loyal, the fear of God will!

St. John dropped an aside. "Niccolò said the republican Romans feared more to break their oath than to break the law; they were more in awe of the power of God than that of men. This kind of religion seems to be what Washington was counseling friends and fellow-citizens to cultivate."

For some things, Huggins had a short memory. "Who's Niccolò?"

"Niccolò Machiavelli."

"Gotcha."

————The State legislators, representatives of the people of their respective States, for years had been and were still hacking at property rights. The alarmed Framers in their proposed, more perfect union planned to stop that by binding members of State governments to the new rules. How did the Framers propose to bind them? Answer: By oath.

In this brief constitution they specified two oaths: one in full, for the president; another in sketch form, for all others.

Keep in mind that the Framers' purpose in exacting these oaths was to insure that members of State governments pledge "support" for the "national" government over and above that for their particular State. You remember that Washington in his farewell letter to friends and fellow-citizens put patriotism on the side of "national capacity" and called anything else "local discriminations," a lovely demeaning phrase for the faith, allegiance, and patriotism citizens felt for their own State. These citizens, one would assume, would have to swear allegiance to their new, big, consolidated country. Washington, in transmitting to Congress the draft of the '87 Constitution, mentioned "that country so dear to us all." He did not name it. As he (or Gouverneur Morris) had used the noun "American" in the same letter of transmittal, he might have written, "*America*, that country so dear to us all." Or, as others might have preferred, "Columbia."

Without a name for the *nation* of their "national government," to what oath did the Framers propose to bind each and every one with a hand in government and laws—senators, representatives, members of the several state legislatures, and all executive and judicial officers, both of the United States and of the several States? Answer: "to support this constitution." It appears in Article VI, Paragraph 3.

A more detailed answer appeared in Article II, at the end of Section 1, spelling out the oath the president had to take. It became the model for all oaths exacted of agents of the people. I quoted part of it yesterday. Let me give you the whole paragraph.

> Before he enter on the execution of his office, he shall take the following oath or affirmation:
> "I do solemnly swear (or affirm) that I will faithfully execute the office of president of the United States, and will to the best of my ability preserve, protect and defend the constitution of the United States."

Strange, don't you think? The '87 Constitution in the name of We the People dictates that the president swear to preserve, protect, and defend the '87 Constitution. If this is not going in circles, it means that the president swears he will perform his tasks according to contract and will also defend that contract.

Solemn as the '87 oath may be, all it exacts is that the oath-taker defend the existing regime. The elected president might have been asked to say, I do solemnly swear (or affirm) that I will preserve, protect, and defend America, or the American nation or union or people, or even the United States of America, descriptive title that it was. But no. All he has to do is to defend the 1787 Constitution of the United States with its amendments. Or if we wish to substitute other expressions for *constitution* in this context—he has only to defend the *general* or *federal* or *national government*, or the *regime*, or the *republican government*, as framed by the '87 Constitution.

The second part of the oath, moreover, presents a puzzle. If the president faithfully executes his office, what more is he supposed to do to preserve, protect, and defend the constitution? He is already doing all he is authorized to do.

The affirmation is unclear and seems unnecessary.

This second clause did not exist in the Framers' first draft. The Article read only, "I solemnly swear (or affirm) that I will faithfully execute the office of the president of the United States." George Mason and Madison moved successfully to add "and will to the best of my judgment and power protect and defend the constitution of the United States."

The records of the Philadelphia convention do not tell us what impelled these two men to add this clause. They were both Virginians. Mason had drafted much of the Virginia Constitution of 1776. That instrument also contains an oath for the chief executive, the governor. He promises and swears that he will "support, maintain, and defend the Commonwealth of *Virginia* and the Constitution of the same." Mere imitation of Virginia does not seem a sufficient explanation. Moreover, the Virginia oath asks much more of the governor. He will defend the Commonwealth "and protect the people" of Virginia in all their rights, so help him God. Mason and Madison did not propose to add such responsibility to the '87 Constitution.

No one elected or appointed by this instrument may rightly claim to speak for the country or the people or to have sworn to protect the country or defend the people.

Huggins couldn't contain himself. "That's a crock a' shit," he muttered under his breath.

"Sorry, what did you say?"

"I said," Huggins answered slowly, then with a gush of force, "That's a crock a' shit!"

The force stunned even him. What now? She going to walk out on him, a sad smile creasing her lips, a refined female martyr?

St. John looked at him blandly. "I've always admired that expression. Another one I like, almost as good, is . . ." Her voice trailed off inaudibly.

"Sorry, what did you say?"

"I said, 'The shit hit the fan'!"

The explosion rocked Huggins.

St. John lowered her voice to its normal level. "Now that we've got this republican machoism off our chests, maybe we can return to the more civilized discourse of a declining republic, which some say the country is turning into. And maybe now for a while," she added, "you'll kindly shut the fuck up."

Huggins was flattened!

"What was the point you wanted to make?" inquired Ms. Innocent. "What is it that's a crock?"

She's giving me a chance to recover, thought Huggins, pulling himself together. "Isn't the president elected by the people of America, by the whole people? So why doesn't he speak for the whole country?"

"Wrong, Huggins. The president is presumed to be the people's choice, voted by the whole electorate, yes. Whether or to what extent this is correct is debatable. The question here though is, once chosen, what's he supposed to do?" She answered her own question.

————Faithfully he executes laws of the United States, commands all armed forces, makes treaties, with advice and consent of the Senate, from time to time gives Congress information and recommendations regarding the state of the union, the union being that "more perfect union" framed by this constitution. No mandate to defend the whole country or the people. Presidents have keenly felt the constraint. Whenever they thought it necessary to exceed their constitutional authority, they asserted they had a direct mandate from the whole people and claimed a higher priority than the constitution, typically that of saving the country.

Most historians nominate Andrew Jackson as the first to vaunt himself as "the direct representative of the American people" and James K. Polk, four presidencies later, to be the second to declare that the president represents "the whole people of the United States, as each member of the legislative department represents portions of them." As for a higher priority of "country," most historians credit Andrew Jackson as the first to claim the mandate. They overlook Jefferson's justifying his purchase of Louisiana from France without written constitutional power. Written obligation "is not the *highest*," he stated. "The law of necessity, of self-preservation, of saving our country when in danger, are of higher obligation." To adhere to the constitution would amount to "absurdly sacrificing the end to the means." Presidents ever since, notably Jackson, Polk, and Lincoln, have similarly argued that they are uniquely entitled to speak for the people and to preserve, protect, and defend the country. Such a claim is based either on a presumption or a misreading of this constitution. We the People grant to no one the task, duty, or right to speak for or defend the country or nation or themselves.

Besides, mind you, in this same constitution We the People exact no oath from themselves. So any effort by their agents to exact oaths from them is not constitutionally protected. This raises a few difficulties with accepted practice. The case of naturalized citizens presents one hitherto neglected problem. Unlike born citizens, aliens, in order to become citizens, must swear an oath. Furthermore this oath is more spiritual or emotional than even that of the president's to support the constitution. They must swear, for example, to bear true faith and allegiance, and in addition that they have never been members of the Communist party or that they do not smoke or snort tobacco, nor advocate the overthrow of the government of the United States. Once they are citizens, however, the obligations of that oath should cease, whatever its exactions. Otherwise they would fall into a different class of citizens. Congress, which has the power to make uniform rules for naturalization, has not realized nor admitted that there is more than one class of citizen of the United States. As things stand, once a person becomes a United States citizen, he may, like any other United States citizen, consider himself free of national oaths.

We the People do not swear any oath, do not have an obligation to defend the constitution, or even to vote or obey the law. This exemption from the oath fits the political philosophy, the people-rule, sovereignty-of-the-people doctrine, prevailing then and now. We the People as the ultimate sovereign dictate the terms and can change our mind.

I'll tell you about a speech given a hundred years after the ratifying of this constitution.

A new president, Benjamin Harrison, the twenty-third in office since the '87 Constitution, approximately the thirtieth since the '77 Constitution, was about to give the customary inaugural address. He began: "There is no constitutional or legal requirement that the President shall take the oath of office in the presence of the people." Quite right, there is no such requirement.

He went on to say that "from the beginning of the Government the people, to whose service the official oath consecrates the officer [note the religious *consecrates*], have been called to witness the solemn ceremonial." There is no suggestion in this constitution that the people are to be witnesses. I don't know what he meant by that except perhaps that the event could in most cases be open in a limited way to the public. From that remark he took a leap. "The oath taken in the presence of the people becomes a mutual covenant. . . . My promise is spoken; yours unspoken, but not the less real and solemn." Perhaps the president had a sixth sense. "Surely I do not misinterpret the spirit of the occasion," he continued, "when I assume that the whole body of the people covenant with me and with each other to support and defend the Constitution. . . ."

President Harrison may well have assumed that to be the spirit of the occasion. But nowhere is it the letter of this constitution. That document does not say that We the People covenant with each other and with the president to defend the constitution. Defending the constitution is *his* job, not the people's.

The '87 Constitution is not the *Mayflower* contract, where people were supposed to have covenanted with each other. We, the People, already formed as "the people" in each of our several States (theoretically, if you wish, by an earlier contract) offer terms to would-be agents, and take on the obligation to pay chosen agents a salary only for so long as their performance, their following of the rules laid down by We the People is satisfactory. Their performance may include a limited laying down of laws and enforcing of penalties on the people themselves, but the rules lay no moral obligation or duty on the people to obey these laws. This constitution does not mention "duty." A sense of duty to obey the laws may grow on people—that is another matter—but obedience if left to anything is left to habit and self-interest, which include the avoidance of penalties and punishment.

Look for a moment at Article VI of this instrument where it states that all members, legislators, executive and judicial officers of the United States and the several States "shall be bound by oath or affirmation, to support this constitution." Close on its heels, separated only by a semicolon, a clause follows that, logically, seems misplaced: "but no religious test shall ever be required as a qualification to any office or public trust under the United States." What is a religious test and what does it have to do with an oath to this constitution?

In England "test-oaths" had flourished since the time of Henry VIII. That king, as everyone knows, broke the country off from the Church of Rome and established the Church of England. His rule devised test-oaths to weed out Catholic sympathizers. Subsequent Protestant separations from the Church of England provided a rich history of further test-oaths and violent struggles, all within the memory of British colonials in North America, some of the earliest of whom had left England and the continent to avoid taking one or another of these oaths. The term "religious test" in Article VI of the '87 Constitution followed British usage and meant *religious test-oath*.

The linking of oaths to religious tests leads to another observation. The '87 Constitution is held to be a written constitution; yet it requires a performance. The president has to swear before somebody. He cannot swear his oath alone, before the mirror. The written constitution requires an unwritten ceremony—the oath-rite. The first new Congress referred to it as a "ceremonial."

At a minimum an oath-rite involves the oath-taker, the oath-giver (a person or representative of authority), a sacred object, a gesture, and an oral text. To reveal such a rite in embryo, let's take the first investiture of the president under the '87 Constitution.

New York, April 30, 1789. A holiday is proclaimed, the streets of Manhattan Island around Federal Hall are jammed, the clocks strike noon. On the balcony of the building in front of the Senate Chamber, with Vice-President-to-be John Adams on his right, Chancellor of New York Robert Livingston on his left, and sundry others present, Washington appears. Dressed in brown with eagle-embossed buttons, white stockings, and the familiar sword at his side, he stands with hat removed, lays the left hand on a Masonic Bible, raises the right hand before the chancellor, also bare-headed. After the reciting of the written oath-text Washington bends to kiss the Bible lifted up to him by some ministering dignitary, straightens up, and pleads tremulously, "I swear. So help me God." The chancellor moves forward and offers his hand; Washington, who finds handshaking distasteful, clasps it. Handshaking all around. They move to the edge of the balcony. The chancellor cries out to the crowd below, "Long live George Washington, president of the United States!" Children shout for joy, women swoon, men weep.

The '87 Constitution specifies the time the oath must be given—"Before he enter on the execution of his office"—but says nothing of the site of the oath-rite (it has been performed in an aircraft); says nothing of the person who is to give the oath (it was administered once by the elected president's father, a justice of the peace); of the sacred object, the Bible (one president used two Bibles, another substituted his law book); of laying the left hand on it (bodily contact); of kissing it (a gesture known as "kissing the book"); of baring the head (expressing voluntary subservience and vulnerability); of raising the right hand open-palmed (placing it without menace in the service of authority and indicating the heavenward source of authority); of oath-taker and oath-giver clasping hands (signifying admission to the circle of authority); and of the oath-giver's unwritten text, beseeching the help of the Deity.

"There you have it, Huggins. What must be performed according to an *un*written text is the oath-rite. What must be spoken to an *un*written text is, So help me God."

This sounded to Huggins like a contradiction in terms. "An unwritten text?"

"Yes. The words are spelled out by the 1776 Virginia Constitution but not by the 1787 United States Constitution."

Huggins had his doubts. "If it's not spelled out, can't the words be omitted or changed?"

"I suppose you could mumble in your beard or make some small change like, May God so help me, but it would raise questions."

"Who says you have to say those words?"

"No one. All presidents have said them."

Huggins persisted. "Can't a future president omit them?"

St. John replied, "Maybe the future will offer a fresh constitution, while this unwritten old text, So help me God, remains. Who knows? I'm no prophet. For the present, I'll ask myself a question."

————I'll also answer it myself: Is uttering the unwritten phrase in the oath-rite subscribing to and passing an unwritten religious test? Yes, in simplest terms the president must affirm the existence of a single master-deity called God with whom he can communicate, with whom he *is* communicating in order to ask for help, and from whom he may hope for a favorable response.

I might also say, going back to the question of *swear* versus *affirm*, that Article VI, Paragraph 3 asks the impossible: first, it asks for a binding oath or affirmation, and second, it forbids any religious test. That you can't have the first without the second is clear: "So help me God" has become, not by law but by custom, an obligatory unwritten part of this constitution. Not even Quaker presidents have tried to exchange it for "This I do affirm under the pains and penalties of perjury."

To return to President Harrison, he of course passed the religious test by taking the oath with its unwritten attachment, "So help me God." In his address he went further to say that "we may reverently invoke and confidently expect the favor and help of Almighty God. . . ."

This oath-rite took place in 1889. A few years later there was a great hoopla, the four-hundredth anniversary celebration of 1492 and the ocean blue. The spirit of "Columbia" still sailed o'er the land. The president's speech marking the occasion called for patriotic exercises in school, and in October of that year of 1892 during a National School Celebration hundreds of thousands of public schoolchildren saluted the flag in a special pledge of allegiance. The staff of a magazine called *Youth's Companion* had prepared it for the event and mailed hundreds of thousands of copies in leaflet form to public schools.

Every school morning since, millions of children have recited this oath in a surrounding of flags, teachers, and appropriate gestures. In the original *Youth's Companion* form it read like this: "I pledge allegiance to my Flag and the Republic for which it stands; one nation indivisible, with liberty and justice for all." A "to" was quickly added in front of "the Republic." A national flag conference in 1923 struck out "my Flag" and substituted "the Flag of the United States," and a second conference in 1924 further added, "of America." In 1953, President Dwight Eisenhower, tuned in to Lincoln's Gettysburg remarks ("this nation, under God"), recommended that "under God" be added, and in 1954 the Eighty-third Congress in House Joint Resolution 241 made it Public Law 396.

Huggins regressed to infancy. "I remember reciting that pledge in school. I never knew what a republic was and I still don't know, really."

"I doubt you're in a minority," said tutor. "I'm glad you reminded me. And *because* you asked I'm going to bore you with a dry little lecture. It's good you know law Latin; it ought to help you a bit. Bear up."

————*Republic* is purely a Roman term, *Respublica, res + publica.* The form of government it applied to was born in Rome at the end of the sixth century B.C. after the expulsion of the kings. It lasted about four centuries.

Separately or together, there are problems with *res* and *publica*, problems of the many-sided splendor of all basic terms. Enough to mention two of the fundaments of *res*: 1) thing; 2) property. *Publica* offers fewer, but not many fewer, difficulties. The Romans in using two words *people* and *public* with almost identical political meaning found a usage to suggest that in Rome almost everybody had a hand in ruling, yet almost everybody was not quite everybody. Together, *res* and *publica* form the republic, the public's thing. The *res* is qualified by *publica*. The first complex signification of *public* is of a large group (from *populus*) of adults (perhaps from *pubes*, you know, *puberty*). Together they possess a thing or property (*res*). That varying thing or property we now call the government. The government is given form by the ones who own or possess it.

Typically, the rise of republics follows the fall of monarchies.

"Wake up, Huggins. Time for another quiz."

Damn! he thought, not again. "I thought we were through with quizzes."

"You'll like this one. It's easy. I'll give you a date and you tell me what monarchy collapsed on or about that date. Ready? Five hundred nine B.C. . . ."

"That must be the Roman kings you just mentioned."

"Good. I see you didn't doze off completely. Next, 1776 . . ."

"George III in the colonies."

"Seventeen ninety-two?"

"The French monarchy."

"Okay; 1918?"

Huggins slowed down. "What was happening in 1918? The end of World War I . . . Oh, I've got it: the kaisers in Germany."

"Yes, and that wasn't all—Turkey, Hungary, Austria . . ."

"What about Russia?" he prompted.

"I was about to say, the czars in Russia. There are still more. It was the twilight of monarchy. They all became republics."

"Not England." Huggins proved he was awake.

"No, not dear old England, but it did take to calling itself democratic, if not a democracy. Now, quiz over. Let's move on."

————The ancient Greek city or *polis* arose as an antimonarchical government, too. Its beginnings go back to the great poets Homer and Hesiod, when the old monarchies were on the way out. Where once there was one kingdom, as in Crete, fifty *poleis* appear. From *polis* we get the Greek word for citizen, *polites*, one who belongs to (and to whom belongs) the *polis*. In both *polis* and *respublica*, citizens dominate and, through the laws they authorize, stamp it with their character. They give this form of government the motif of political power ascending from the people rather than descending from a power outside and superior to the people. Properly speaking, a monarchy as distinct from a republic does not contain citizens. Its people are *subjects*, a word that has never lost the significance of deferring to someone politically superior or sovereign.

"Take me, for example." St. John arched her back and pointed to her chest. "I'm an English subject."

Huggins took her, for example.

"Whereas," she added, "the citizen of a republic has no political superior, in law or in person."

————A republic, we may say, is that type of government in which customary and legal rights to political participation are so openly and widely spread that formal rule by one or an exclusive few is barred.

We should also discuss democracies. Their similarity to republics may seem obvious, but the two forms are not identical. The main distinction is perhaps in quantity. How much of a population does the public consist of? Don't be led astray by a desire for precision. If you want, you can set a figure of anything over 50 percent to constitute the public's part of the population, particularly if one believes that the majority or "the most" has an ethical edge. This reasoning may not be wrong so much as extreme. Neither two nor ten persons suffice to constitute the public. In both republics and democracies, the *public* or the *people* has the sense of considerable numbers, of the greater part, but whereas republicans insist on rule by many, democrats seek rule by all. *All* can never be all, of course, not even in theory—what of children, criminals, the insane, foreigners, traitors?—but the idea of all-inclusiveness is there.

For elementary purposes, we can distinguish the various types of government by the number of those who rule:

monarchy = rule by one
aristocracy = rule by a few
republic   = rule by many (by more than a few, or by the
              greater part)
democracy = rule by all

Such classifications are not antiquarian. For instance, to this day, around the difference between republic and democracy and whether the convention of 1787 framed or looked forward to the one or the other, pivots a sharp contention in history and political philosophy.

But in both republics and democracies there is, don't you know, a special psychology or spirit of citizens. In democracies, including as they do a greater number of formal equals involved in political and military service, this spirit is more widespread, evident, and extreme. Both, however, rejecting one-person rule and hereditary principles, impress on citizens that the government is their creature. These citizens, the public, the people, composed of those whose voices can by law be heard, feel that the government is theirs and that they are therefore a free people. The sense of freedom releases energy all around.

The feeling of owning the state occurs in other forms of government, too, but in republics and democracies the feeling is common to many. The king himself is more or less free in his kingdom—"free as a king," goes the ingenuous expression—but in the political sense his subjects are not free. Citizens are free. No one grants them liberty. They frame their own liberty.

Also, the citizens' customary and legal rights, at their lowest possible denominator, give republics and democracies an air of egalitarianism. Citizens are peers. Their quantity and equality dispose them to complex electoral devices for choosing agents and making public choices. They count their own noses, and to demonstrate they belong to a community of equals in their fucking land of the fucking free, they often resort to vulgarity.

By now, Huggins was used to his tutor's vibrant speech.

"I'm sure," she was saying, "that such language is familiar to you, Huggins. You may be shocked to hear it from lips which up to now have only dripped pearls. I have lived long among barbarians," she explained demurely.

Huggins wasn't about to take this lying down. "*You* dripped a few fake pearls a minute ago, I do believe."

"Yes, that was the vanguard," she answered.

"I suppose you think aristocrats never swore," he challenged.

"Indeed they did. They punished others who swore: swearing was *their* prerogative. Aristocrats by definition, though, are few in numbers. When the rank and file adopt cursing, they do it to show that they, the band of equals, rule. And their escaping punishment confirms it.

"The game of politics takes on this language. Politicians show by their language that they know the vulgar world, that they are of vulgar origin, of the people themselves. I recall hearing about a judge's insisting that one political plum or another be granted a friend of his. The local political boss sent his aide over with a warning: Tell the judge that if that son-of-a-bitch friend of his turns out to be a cocksucking Communist, I'll have his ass."

That's my kind of talk, thought Huggins.

———Of course, that was in the days when communism was truly alarming, continued his tutor, but historians, clergymen, and foreign visitors have remarked on the prevalence of foul language or "oaths" on these shores from at least the early eighteenth century. Vulgarity enlivens the speech, if not the speeches, of the higher-grade politicians too. This petering-out century has had its share of presidential coarseness. One recent chief executive used it in foreign policy, threatening on television that if a certain foreign ruler did not behave, he the president would have to "kick ass." Another recent president was kind enough to tape himself, thereby giving historians the warm sound of White House intimacy.

Intriguing though it may be, let's not dabble in the mud too long. I have another trait of republicanism to point out.

Kingships and aristocracies put great store on blood-kinship and heredity, frequently adopting governing personnel and ruling policy on the basis of family history and succession. Such great care in the use of family names makes genealogy a favorite and important study. In contrast, republics and democracies depreciate the value of genetics. They rely more on environment and education to elicit qualities of intelligence and leadership. Instead of genealogy, they study population statistics, paying close attention to social or economic factors, at most admitting a vaguely biological ethnic category. Since blood-kinship and family relationship are rated low, family names become unimportant; social introductions are quickly and easily put on a first-name basis. First-name acquaintanceships are not a sure sign of intimacy or affection. As someone once observed, the employer may call his employee Jim, and Jim may call the boss Jack, but that does not keep Jack from firing Jim. Plainly, Jim's or Jack's surnames do not and ought not to matter.

"Ms? St. John, do you mind if I ask a personal question?"

"Ask away."

"Is it possible you're so interested in names because of your illustrious ancestors?"

"Of course. But I never claimed a real relation, did I? It's Uncle Gaspar who has these flights of genealogical fancy. You may be interested to know that the name of the first earl of Bolingbroke was Oliver St. John."

Titillated by this bit of news, Oliver forgot the question. Claire St. John went back on trail.

————It may take a while for the robust republican spirit to appear. Over the past century many self-titled republics have cropped up. They may so classify themselves as long as their constitutions do not specify one-person rule and hereditary succession. As opposites for *republic* (and for *democracy*) leading modern dictionaries most often nominate *monarchy*, and sometimes *tyranny*, *despotism*, *autocracy*, or *dictatorship*, all one-person forms of rule and misrule.

Today, as Aristotle remarked in the *Politics*, kings are out of fashion. Almost all states of the world are republican in name, and though many if not most of them may in fact violate basic republican principles, they keep to the nomenclature: citizens, elections, and no king.

"There, that ought to hold you for a while," St. John announced. "Now that you are acquainted with *populus*, *publica*, and *respublica*, you can better understand how rich and powerful the phrase We the People is."

————The substitution, she continued, of "the constitution" for the name of country or of people in the oath of office has produced surprising effects, among them a reverence for the constitution so remarkable that some writers have called it a civic or constitutional religion or faith or worship. Some have worried that it borders on idolatry. But what I sense is not worship or love for a paper document or for a group of laws. Patriotism, let us remind ourselves, means love of country, and throughout time and place the language and icons of patriotic and religious expression broadly overlap. Here, instead, we seem to have a confusion of country and constitution; a displacement of love, language, emotion, and behavior customarily reserved for country has been displaced onto the constitution, leading to a unique sentiment—constitutional patriotism.

The phenomenon, as far as I know, is foreign to the rest of the world.

To conclude, this circumlocution for a name for country has also generated a legal difficulty. It restricts the president to defending only the constitution. Actually We the People select many defenders, as many as swear by oath to defend this constitution. But We the People offer no position of "defender" or "tribune of the People," or of "defender of the Nation." Such constraint has compelled some presidents to expand their powers, typically by invoking a higher law than the '87 Constitution. But this is not a solution. For the same constitution describes itself as the supreme law.

"Huggins, do you want to know who is supposed to preserve, protect, and defend 'We the People'?"

"Yes!" hissed Huggins.

"Nobody. Themselves."

St. John turned on her heel. "I'm running late." She grabbed her papers and bag and swooped toward the door. "See you Monday."

"Wait, wait a sec! You haven't explained—" wailed Huggins, grasping at straws.

"No time today," her voice echoed. "Ta-ta."

7

JOHN MARSHALL

DEMONSTRATES THE POWER

OF LEGAL RAZZLE-DAZZLE

MONDAY

Huggins found himself alone in the room, awaiting Claire St. John. His mood was foul. All Saturday night and Sunday he had been brooding over the faithlessness of women.

In came St. John, wide awake and raring to go. "Huggins, you're early."

And you can kiss my ass, Huggins wanted to say. Instead he grunted.

"Oh-oh, not in the best of tempers today, I see. Sorry, but the show must go on."

————You know the tale of Marbury against Madison, don't you? It's the most famous case in the history of the '87 Constitution. If you decide to go to law school—heaven forfend!—and have to take your course in con law, don't think they'll say to you, "Get hold of a copy of the constitution and read it from top to bottom and side to side, see what sense you can make of it." No. The first thing they'll do is to throw at you *Marbury* v. *Madison* 5 U.S. 1 Cranch 137 (1803). In this landmark case, as lawyers love to call it, the chief justice was John Marshall, the last of the great Virginians I'll talk about.

Marshall was descended from the same immigrant stock more or less as the other Virginians—English, Welsh, Scotch, with a dab of Irish somewhere: he had deep, dark brown eyes. Virginians were riders; Marshall was a walker, covering miles each day. His favorite sport was not hunting to hounds but quoits, a game of disc-tossing. Another difference: his wife, unlike Washington's or Jefferson's, was not a rich widow.

For the rest he was like most land-rich Virginians, a gambler, tall, generous, chivalrous, indolent ("the most negligent man in the world," said one biographer; "he was always losing or misplacing important papers," said another), an indifferent reader, a tolerable speaker, a drinker (not quite as capacious as Washington or Jefferson). At the Virginia ratifying convention, to ratify or not the '87 Constitution, Marshall pitted against Patrick Henry made a fair show. In short, a man after one's own heart.

Coming from humbler origins, born in a log cabin near Germantown and raised in a hollow of the Blue Ridge Mountains, he did not have the taste of Thomas Jefferson, his third cousin once removed. A Monticello and a harpsichord or Cremonese violin would have been beyond Marshall's ken. The columned house he annexed to the paternal home in Fauquier County lacks elegant proportions.

"I know its proportions. I've slept there," St. John swung off to say.

"*Slept* there?" In her presence Huggins had difficulty understanding the word.

"Yes, a friend of mine owns it. Fair horse country."

"I'll bet you take your jumps with dash," said Huggins sourly.

"Don't know about that. Horse wiped me off a fence there."

★ ★

————The common touch came easily to Marshall, she said, getting back to business. Jefferson had to affect it, Marshall had only to keep it. Simplicity and shambling came to him naturally. Jefferson even in rags looked the gentleman. John Marshall in rags looked like some backwoodsman fallen on hard times. His portrait in the robes of chief justice shows him standing on shapely legs, a fine figure of a man, wearing a satisfied little smile.

"Like this." Claire St. John stood up and posed. She was wearing a black pongee man-styled jacket, unbuttoned, over a beige silk slip slit down the middle in front and back, dropping to the calf. ("Must have dressed for the occasion," mused Huggins.) She advanced her right foot slightly and pivoted toward the right to display a leg longer than John Marshall's and every bit as shapely. She pushed back the fold of the jacket with her left hand which she then rested on her hip with spread fingers. Her right hand she placed on the table with her fingers inserted in some papers. She stood motionless for a moment, a self-satisfied smile glued to her face, then relaxed and continued.

————In the portrait, although Marshall wears a gown and his best silk stockings and silver-buckled pumps, he reflects none of Washington's dandyism. Naturally, a portrait of a chief justice ought not to reflect a love of swords and uniforms. The affectation is in the small book in Marshall's hand which looks more like a book of poetry—Alexander Pope's, maybe—than a tome of law.

Marshall's eyes—set in a squarish face with a thin intelligent mouth—looked black under a mop of often matted black hair and heavy black eyebrows, lending him a devastating direct gaze.

"Of the great Virginians, he was to my taste the handsomest," said St. John with a personal touch. "When he lived in Paris as one of three ministers to France, he and one of his colleagues were particularly gallant to their landlady, Madame Villette, the adopted daughter of the philosopher Voltaire. She would have had no hesitation selecting John Marshall for her favors, though no one knows how far her favors went. I find it hard to believe that the woman we see in her portrait would not be amused to take a bumpkin *Américain* like John Marshall to bed."

————Marshall, St. John added in her tutorial voice, came from a solid family in which he held solid status as the first of fifteen children. He and his wife, Polly, were to have ten themselves. His father, Thomas, grew up with George Washington. The two later became fellow-surveyors of the huge Fairfax estate which, when broken up after the Revolution, netted our John about 100,000 acres. He was now a lawyer and ex-army officer under Washington. People called him "General." The profession of lawyer served him well. He joined the ranks of the hundreds of big patriotic land speculators, almost always engaged in their own legal disputes over landownership.

Marshall rarely mentioned his mother. He adored his father. "A far abler man than any of his sons," he recalled in his brief autobiography. Marshall Senior with foresight subscribed to Blackstone's four volumes of *Commentaries on the Laws of England*, a work that sold more copies on the Atlantic seaboard than in the British Isles. While John was in his teens, his father provided him with two Scottish tutors for a year each, one after the other, the second an Episcopalian and, it was claimed, a gentleman. During the Revolution, in a furlough granted his Virginia regiment, John attended William and Mary College for a course of law lectures given by George Wythe, the most illustrious jurist in the State and the law tutor of Thomas Jefferson. Jefferson stayed the course; Marshall stayed five or six weeks.

While at college the student-soldier's mind brimmed with a girl's lovely image. In his two hundred-page notebook the name Miss Maria Ambler, underlined, pops up on the inside cover along with other variants including "Miss M. Ambler—J. Marshall," written upside down, and on the facing page—"Miss Polly Am.," "John, Maria," "Molly Ambler." He was twenty-seven and she not yet seventeen when they married.

Mary Willis Ambler's family was respectable. The war had left her father in reduced circumstances but he now held public office as treasurer of Virginia. Her mother was related to the Randolphs.

★ ★

"Today, Oliver," said St. John, "keeping locks of hair may seem a silly fetish, but not to the Virginians." (Not to me, either, thought Huggins, exposed to a close-up of St. John's cap of brown, rough hair.)

"Remember Martha Jefferson's lock of hair kept in Tom's secret drawer?" she asked. "Well, when John Marshall, age twenty-five, proposed marriage, his Polly tossed by emotion said no. John rode off; Polly began to weep. A cousin present at the scene consoled her and surreptitiously snipping a lock of her hair, dashed after the rejected suitor. John turned back. He and Polly plighted their troth. She carried this lock of hair in a locket with chain; just before she died she placed it around her husband's neck. She had been ailing most of her married life; he always showed great concern for her. Three years after Polly died, Marshall died.

"Pitted against such stories of Virginian marital affection are the others," St. John remarked, "of miscellaneous philanderings, bedding with slaves, incests, and worse."

————One lurid case implicated Richard Randolph of a most notable Virginia family and his young sister-in-law Nancy in a rumored infanticide. A brushfire of scandal swept southern Virginia. To squelch rumors, Randolph presented himself at the Cumberland City Courthouse and insisted that he be charged with murder and tried for the crime. He asked his remote cousin John Marshall to defend him. He secured also, at a price, the services as co-counsel of Patrick Henry, master of forensic dramatics. The one's logic and the other's forensics did the trick. Richard Randolph was acquitted to the cheers of spectators. Cousin Thomas Jefferson told his daughter Martha that in spite of malignant tongues, she should continue her friendship with Nancy. Fifteen years later Nancy married . . . guess who? Our old friend Gouverneur Morris!

One day in 1809 Morris had written to his good friend Marshall, asking whether he might tax him to speak frankly of Nancy's reputation and standing in society. For himself he didn't give a fig about gossip: he just didn't want to hurt the Federalist cause for which he felt responsibility. Marshall obliged with a favorable judgment. The next day Gouverneur proposed, and the following day he and Nancy were married. Enough to add that the newlyweds were happy together and had a child. John Marshall had proved himself a good friend.

"You see, Huggins? Everyone who was someone knew everyone," said St. John.

————And now who should be involved in the famous controversy of *Marbury* v. *Madison*? Marbury and Madison? Hardly. They barely knew each other. The job at issue, a minor judgeship, was not worth Marbury's while; he had been pressured to bring suit. As for Madison, he never bothered to appear in court. Instead, the two antagonists were Chief Justice John Marshall and his cousin President Thomas Jefferson. The case well might be coded as *Marshall* v. *Jefferson*.

Between the two kinsmen no love was lost. Of course, contrasts in background and temperament grated on their sensibilities. In politics their mutual reserve and disengagement grew into something else—fear and hatred.

Marshall's idol was Washington. As his former commander in chief rode to the Philadelphia convention, thence to the presidency of the United States, his ideas continuously molded by the young Hamilton, the young Marshall marched alongside, distancing himself more and more from the views of his cousin. Jefferson saw Washington increasingly embroiled in big government, coercion, censorship, and favoritism toward England whereas he himself stood for the antimonarchism and equality of the Declaration of Independence, as the champion of farmers against merchants, and as the defender of the rights of the States against an engorging government of the union. The federal government, he believed, should manage the foreign affairs common to these united States, that is, diplomacy and war, and all else was the business of the States separately.

Marshall and Jefferson, two brilliant and attractive men, found themselves going down a maze of crosspaths without exit—the XYZ Affair, the Alien and Sedition Acts, the Kentucky and Virginia Resolutions, the lame-duck changes in the judiciary, and the case of *Marbury* v. *Madison* that we are about to review. After that came the impeaching of Justice Samuel Chase, the trial for treason of Aaron Burr, and other collisions that lay in wait for the two cousins to the end of their days. To discuss more than one or two of these battles would take us into next year.

The president's arrival at the president's house always seems happier than his departure therefrom. When inaugurated as president, George Washington was a hero standing tall; when he left office he had lost stature. Jefferson in his own inaugural speech, probably recalling this, remarked that he had "learnt to expect that it will rarely fall to the lot of imperfect man to retire from this station with the favor and reputation which brought him into it." Jefferson was now president number three under the '87 Constitution. Before him had reigned John Adams, president number two, and he too when leaving office was in the doghouse.

Discontent with the government, much of it still part of the strong anticonstitutional resistance that led to the Bill of Rights amendments, had resurged with passage of the Alien and Sedition Acts. Through these laws John Adams's followers in Congress had tried to weaken the opposition mounted by Jefferson's followers. Zealous federal judges handed out harsh punishment for publishing "malicious or defamatory" material about Congress or the president. They paid scant heed to the First Amendment's protection of free speech. The acts, wrote Jefferson to Madison, are "palpably in the teeth of the Constitution." Counterattacking together, these two men composed the Kentucky and Virginia Resolutions reelaborating the theory that there were no countries except the named States, that the United States was simply the title of the government apparatus of the limited federal union of these States, that every State within its own borders had the inviolable right to judge what was lawful for a congressional majority to decide.

As we shall see, this theory was to serve as the basis for every major attack to come against the unitary sovereignty of the federal government. It lies in readiness even today for those who sense the oppressiveness of that government.

Speaking of the partisan fever that gripped the 1790s, Jefferson wrote, "Men who have been intimate all their lives cross the street to avoid meeting, and turn their heads another way, lest they should be obliged to touch their hats. . . ." He called the two contending factions "parties." His followers became known as Republicans, and Adams's (and Washington's) as Federalists.

Jefferson enjoyed at least one item of this rivalry, a Republican campaign song that went like this:

> *Rejoice, Columbia's sons rejoice*
> *To tyrants never bend the knee*
> *But join with heart and soul and voice*
> *For Jefferson and Liberty.*

He pasted a copy in his scrapbook.

In November of 1800 after a bitter campaign, Thomas Jefferson is elected president of the United States, to take office on March 4, 1801. John Adams, incumbent president, is aghast: not only the presidency but also the majorities in Congress have fallen to the Republicans. To prepare against the future, he and his outgoing congressional majority decide that before leaving office they must enlarge the federal judiciary and stuff it with Federalists. At least the courts will be left to oppose Jefferson and the new government.

In December, Chief Justice Oliver Ellsworth, old and afflicted with gout and gravel, resigns. Rather than give the incoming president the courtesy of appointing a new chief justice, Adams asks John Jay to serve. Jay had served under both Washington and Adams, indeed, you may remember, was the first ever to fill the post of chief justice. Jay declines, remarking that the supreme court lacked energy, weight, and dignity. Adams turns to his secretary of state, John Marshall: "I believe I must nominate you." With surprise and joy, and without resigning as secretary of state, Marshall accepts and is confirmed in January of 1801.

With little more than two months left of their tenure in office, he and Adams set to work on judiciary legislation and appointments. They have to move fast. Congress passes one judiciary act on February 13, the Circuit Court Act. (While secretary of state, John Marshall had worked on it with the congressional judiciary committee.) It creates sixteen federal judgeships with life tenure and assigns them territorial circuits, thus relieving the supreme court from going out

circuit-riding itself and allowing it to stay in Washington. It also en-
larges access to federal courts generally.

Jefferson's antagonistic position on the judiciary is well-known.
He aims to reduce access to federal courts and to keep the supreme
court out of Washington. He is as opposed to a standing judiciary
as he is to a standing army.

The act further provides that the next vacancy in the supreme
court (Justice William Cushing was along in years) should not be
filled, thereby reducing the size of the supreme court from six to
five justices and taking a second appointment to the court away from
Jefferson. Along with the judgeships, the act calls for a legion of
marshals, sheriffs, constables, attorneys, and clerks. Of course, there
is no thought of allowing the newly elected president the pleasure
of making these appointments. Within two weeks Adams makes
them all.

At the same time—we are now at February 27, 1801, one week
before Jefferson is to take office—Congress passes another act further increasing the federal judiciary by authorizing the president to
appoint justices of the peace for the District of Columbia. Within
three days Adams submits forty-two nominations. The Senate
quickly approves them all: Adams has only to sign the commissions.

The deadline is upon him. It is March 3, the day before the
inauguration. Adams works by candlelight until nine o'clock that
night, affixing his large signature to what will soon be called the
"midnight appointments." Among others he appointed Marshall's
nephew William Cranch (whom we have to thank as court reporter
for *Marbury* v. *Madison* and other early supreme court cases) and
Marshall's younger brother James. Having signed every piece of paper in sight, Adams has the bundle carried over to the Department
of State for sealing, recording, and delivery of the commissions by
the secretary of state.

The next morning, March 4, 1801, Jefferson, in a show of cordiality, has cousin Chief Justice Marshall swear him in office, and
makes his inaugural speech, holding out an olive branch to the outgoing Federalist party. Later in the day, however, apprised of the
midnight appointments, he is furious. He takes Adams's "outrage on
decency" personally. Years later he will write that "that one act of
Mr. Adams' life, and one only, gave me a moment's personal dis-

pleasure. I did consider his last appointments to office as personally unkind." By hook or by crook, Adams's party has hung on to the federal judiciary and turned it into a federal fortress. Jefferson drops the olive branch and draws the sword.

His opening agenda had called for reducing the army by about one half, the navy by two thirds, and for pardoning those persons still in prison under the Alien and Sedition Acts. He now gives priority status to judicial reform. His Republican Congress repeals the Circuit Court Act, putting the supreme court on horseback again, revising its schedule, and postponing its next session for a year so as to delay any court challenge to the reform.

As it happened, four of the midnight appointments—William Marbury among them—did not receive their commissions, the pieces of paper signed by President Adams, notifying them of their appointments as justices of the peace. These men, getting no satisfaction from the new secretary of state nor from Congress, together bring suit, asking the supreme court for a ruling: should not the court, by means of what is known as a writ of mandamus, command the new secretary of state, James Madison, to deliver their commissions or to explain why not? The court puts the case on the docket.

Such temerity enrages the Republicans. The court had no impelling reason to accept the case. It is an obvious Federalist plant to embarrass the Republican president.

So we arrive at *Marbury* v. *Madison*. The case attracts us not so much for its authority in the teaching and practice of constitutional law as for being the first to assert that the supreme court may declare laws of Congress unconstitutional and null and void. What interests us is that this assertion was facilitated by an indeterminate word in the '87 Constitution. The Framers had inserted the term "land" in place of a name for a whole country. It occurs in a phrase of Article VI where presumably the object is to say "the supreme law of X," intending by X the country of whatever name, of which the United States was the government. Instead, the phrase reads "the supreme law of the *land*."

"I must give you the full clause, for constitutional lawyers (many years after 'the landmark' of *Marbury* v. *Madison*) took to calling it 'the supremacy clause' and 'the linch-pin of the Constitution.' If this were a big class, Huggins, I'd have a slide and a pointer, and I'd put the whole text on the screen. But as you realize by now"—St. John flicked a conspiratorial smile—"the only true education is face to face, isn't it? So I've copied the paragraph on this slip of paper. Here you are."

She handed it to Huggins. Their fingers touched. The edges of the slip curled with the heat of contact.

"Read it aloud, please," asked St. John breathily breaking touch.

With the slip in his hand Huggins stood up and read the text in a voice that managed to be surly and flat, the voice of a schoolboy called on to recite.

> This constitution, and the laws of the United States which shall be made in pursuance thereof; and all treaties made, or which shall be made, under the authority of the United States, shall be the supreme law of the land; and the judges in every state shall be bound thereby, any thing in the constitution or laws of any state to the contrary notwithstanding.

"Hold on to it to come back to," she instructed. "We have a landmark, a linchpin, and a supremacy clause to examine. A run-through of the first moves in the case might help."

———When the case is called, Madison does not appear nor appoint counsel. Marbury's counsel, the able Charles Lee, Esquire, former attorney general (under Adams) and a member of the Lees of Virginia, a family as numerous and nameworthy as the Adamses of Massachusetts, presents supporting affidavits and witnesses and begins to argue his clients' case. Before he is finished, the new attorney general, acting as secretary of state, whom the court had summoned in the absence of Madison, appears and makes clear that Madison will not appear; he is not sure he should be there either. He pleads the delicacy of his situation, says he knows next to nothing about the commissions, and furthermore does not care to incriminate himself. The court excuses him, and Charles Lee finishes with his affidavits, witnesses, and argument for Marbury and the others.

Chief Justice Marshall then delivers the opinion of the court (in truth his own opinion, for he writes the opinions and convinces his brethren to vote with him as a court without dissent). It is an ingenious, sophistical, brazen, largely irrelevant, largely question-begging opinion, flecked with bad history, bad political theory, bad law.

"Ha!" exhaled Huggins in disdain.

St. John shot him a glance with one raised eyebrow, and went on.

————Probably Marshall underestimated the will and power of Republican reprisal. He had encouraged the Marbury plea; he wished to show the Republicans that they could not revenge themselves with impunity on Federalist individuals still in office, that the supreme court, Federalist to the core, was not a force to scorn. But as soon as the Republicans began to flex muscle, his fellow-Federalists began to desert him. In vain did he try to convince them to join him in declaring the new Circuit Court Act unconstitutional. Not one of the circuit court judges whose posts had been abolished would bring trial. In vain did he try to persuade his associates on the bench that the act's requirement that they and he had to get back on horse and ride out to hold circuit courts was unconstitutional. They replied that by the time the case came to trial the requirement would be seen merely as a return to the old arrangement—which it was—and was sure to be held prescriptive, to have been settled by usage.

His colleagues were getting more cautious, more fearful of Congress' demonstrated ability to legislate against the court and impeach its members. Clearly the Republicans were going to be in power for a long time. Just as clearly they had forgotten neither the midnight appointments nor the excesses of federal judges under the Alien and Sedition Acts. They had already impeached a lower court judge and were muttering threats against the high court, against Justice Chase and Marshall himself. Hell, they could impeach anyone!

Marshall was on the defensive. He had to take and make do with *Marbury* v. *Madison.*

He had a year to study a strategy, moved by some murky motives about which he was not exactly clear. He would have loved to sink cousin Jefferson deep in the nearest latrine. Also, there was something of the southern preacher in Marshall. He wanted to expound the political philosophy of the '87 Constitution, to sermonize the public at large and to lecture the president and the Republicans. This urge he could satisfy—and he did in his opinion—by page upon page of irrelevant excursions, technically known as *obiter dicta*, whereas all he had to do, granted he were right (and as Jefferson pointed out), was to say, "Sorry, but this court is without jurisdiction in the matter."

His one clear-headed objective was to raise a shield against the president's and Congress' powers over the supreme court, while skirting two pitfalls: first, a showdown with the president, and second, a challenge to the laws of the present Congress.

He would have to avoid giving a court order requiring the president to hand Marbury the commission. Jefferson would simply ignore it—he had already said as much—or would *nolle prosses* it, tell his officers not to enforce it, as he had already done with the Alien and Sedition Acts of the previous Congress. The president's refusal to act would leave the court powerless and humiliated. But if Marshall dare not order the president to remedy a legal wrong, he could without much danger charge him with a moral wrong. Marshall is at his most amusing when he scolds the president for "sport[ing] away the vested rights of others"—while he, the chief justice in this very case, commits serious breaches in argument and procedure, as I intend to show.

The task of protecting the court from Congress' anger, of ensuring that Congress would not diminish the supreme court's power and jurisdiction, was more difficult. With little hope of cooperation from the incumbent Congress, much less from the incumbent president, Marshall had to try to secure the court through the court itself. This was too bad. He would have liked judges and the court to have authority independent of a constitution, and sometimes argued as if they did. The only authority they had, however, was derived from the '87 Constitution: so a constitutional issue had to be found. Counsel for the petitioners, alas, did not raise one.

The chief justice had to find an issue himself. Petitioners were seeking a writ of mandamus, were they not? The ground-laying Federal Judiciary Act of 1789, enacted soon after the '87 Constitution was ratified, had legislated on the subject, permitting the court to issue such a writ. Conveniently, that law had been made by the previous Congress. A decision against this law would not be a direct challenge to the new Congress. Marshall had found his opening! He would hold that Section 13 of that act was in conflict with a clause in the constitution. (I'll explain in a minute.)

It would mean leaving Marbury and the other petitioners out in the cold, denying them the writ they were pleading for. That didn't bother the chief justice; they had brought suit to oblige their fellow-Federalists. He would shed a few tears over the "injured" individuals, crocodile tears, for the material issue was paltry, the post of justice of the peace next to worthless, its five-year term already half-expired.

Still, it was an uneasy solution, requiring him, as we shall see, to close his eyes to an important phrase. At best, argument would be moot. There was another hitch, a big one: he himself was involved in the facts of the case. Opposing counsel, if present, would certainly implicate him. Marshall decided to take the risk, counting on the executive branch not to appear in court.

Luck was on his side. Just at this time Jefferson was beginning negotiations for the Louisiana Purchase. Wisps of dreams—ridding the continent sea-to-sea of the French, expanding the empire of liberty—seeped along government halls and into the smoking and drinking rooms of the great houses and taverns. The decision on *Marbury* v. *Madison* came and went, the president grumbled about personal animus and a moot opinion of little importance; the House of Representatives did not impeach the chief justice.

Huggins asked, "Whatever happened to Marbury? I'm sure he didn't like the decision."

"As far as we know," answered St. John, "he raised a family, became president of a Georgetown bank, and died about the same year as Marshall and Madison, still bereft of his commission. And you won't believe this. Today in the John Marshall Dining Room of the Supreme Court Building, above the sideboard, hangs a portrait of William Marbury. Side by side is James Madison in a smaller portrait!

"Let's see now. I was about to say something about Marshall's rhetorical sallies. A few examples may impart their flavor."

★ ★

————The chief justice makes much of the '87 Constitution's having been committed to writing. He rhapsodizes that it represents
"the greatest improvement on political institutions, a written constitution," and as such it entitles him to claim that a written
constitution is "a paramount law." This of course does not follow.
Written-ness does not imply paramountcy.

Jurists classify the English constitution as unwritten: while some
parts are set to writing, other parts are not—common law, parliamentary custom, protocol, oaths, ceremony. Some argue that this
sort of constitution is more flexible than a wholly written one,
which like a written contract is supposed to set down all its terms
in writing. The Framers and courts had not worked out, however,
what the relation of their written constitution was to unwritten or
extra-textual considerations such as natural law or justice, first principles, common law, or reason. Early supreme court decisions took
varying positions.

In *Marbury* v. *Madison* Marshall lays such stress on the importance
of the written limits of a written constitution that he commits himself to these limits. Simultaneously, willy-nilly, he overpasses them.
He seeks help from foreign legal authorities like Lord Mansfield and
Blackstone, and from foreign laws like "the laws of England." He
appeals 1) to common law (English) in determining that Marbury
had a right to his commission, 2) to natural law in claiming that
Marbury had on his side the "very essence of civic liberty" and "the
first object of government," and 3) to natural rights in claiming that
the case can be decided simply by recognizing "certain principles"
of the people's original right to establish government "for their own
happiness."

For greater support he ushers in the lessons of history. "Certainly," he claims, "all those who have framed written constitutions
contemplate [*sic*] them as forming the fundamental and paramount
law. . . ." This is not faulty history, it is not history at all. Who were
these other Framers and who confided to him what they contemplate? Are they still alive?

Perhaps he had in mind the '77 Constitution or the constitutions
of the several states of North America: "in America where written
constitutions have been viewed with such reverence." Perhaps this

is why he cites no examples and why he uses "contemplate" in the
present tense. Yet he would be the first to deny that the '77 Constitution and the State constitutions were fundamental and paramount law. Anyway, what difference does it make what other
Framers may have contemplated? *This* supreme court is empowered
by *this* constitution.

Marshall resorts to slogans too. "The government of the United
States has been emphatically termed a government of laws, and not
of men." John Adams, the ex-president, had inserted this laws-not-
men phrase in the Massachusetts Constitution. He said he had taken
it from James Harrington, the English republican of the previous
century whose book, *The Commonwealth of Oceana*, a number of
Federalists had taken to heart. Harrington had written not "government of laws," but "empire of laws."

If slogans of this sort are needed, I can propose a better one: The
government of the United States then and now can be emphatically
termed "a government of lawyers, and not of men."

Another example: "Between these alternatives, there is no middle ground. The constitution is either a superior paramount law, un-
changeable by ordinary means, or it is on a level with ordinary
legislative acts. . . ." There is no middle ground, to be sure, because
these two propositions are not opposite poles. Marshall plays a game
with the word "ordinary," using it to apply to statutory law-making
and transferring it to apply also to amendment law-making. But
there is ordinary law-making and ordinary amendment-making
(not to mention ordinary treaty-making). All three kinds of law—
constitutional, legislative, and treaty—are changeable by their own
ordinary means, and one is not necessarily more difficult to change
than another, and even if it were, that in itself would not make it
superior paramount law. It may just as easily make it inferior law,
as champions of the flexibility of unwritten constitutions might
sustain.

In exalting the written constitution, Marshall dabbles with the
words *fundamental* and *superior* and *paramount*—all three characteriz-
ing this constitution as law. (He got the undigested notion of the
'87 Constitution as fundamental law not from this constitution itself but from one of Hamilton's *Federalist* articles. He read and lis-

tened to Hamilton devotedly.) But when speaking of "certain principles" he calls them "fundamental" too. In the uncertain usage of the times "principles" may constitute fundamental law, but they are unwritten. They form no legal part of a written constitution. As he sustains that a constitution issues from these fundamental principles, it would seem that a constitution is almost but not quite fundamental: it lies on top of the bottom where fundamental principles rest. And if it is at the same time "superior paramount law," well . . . Truth is, Marshall would wish this constitution to be both at the fundamental bottom and at the paramount top, poised to crunch any law unlucky enough to fall in its jaws.

"Huggins, are you awake?"

Huggins sat up a little straighter, stifled a yawn, and nodded.

"Sorry about this hair-splitting, but it seems necessary if we're to penetrate Marshall's word-tossing. I'm glad you have background in law. We may have to get a wee bit technical."

————We have just shown Marshall reading words and phrases into the '87 Constitution. We come now to more obvious tactics, his omitting and changing words. The '87 Constitution when talking about itself says "this constitution." And for good reason. Marshall invariably changes *this* to *the* as in "arising under *the* [instead of *this*] constitution."

As for omissions, the most obvious is the one permitting Marshall to claim that a given law of Congress is unconstitutional. Marbury's case, originating in the District of Columbia rather than in a State, was filed directly in the supreme court without having to come up from a lower court appellately (that is, on appeal) and so can be classified as a case of *original* jurisdiction. The '87 Constitution does assign the court original jurisdiction in some instances, but as the chief justice quotes from that document: "In all other cases the supreme court shall have appellate jurisdiction." But he chops the sentence off. It does not end with the word "jurisdiction" and a period. Instead, there is a comma and the following words: "both as to law and fact" and then the important pertinent phrase, *with such exceptions and under such regulations as the Congress shall make.*

The clause Marshall left out gives Congress explicit power to make changes regarding the supreme court's jurisdiction whether the words are construed as applying to original or to appellate jurisdiction. And evidently the Congress does not have to pass through the president to enact such exceptions into law. This clause destroys the ground for the court's finding of unconstitutionality (assuming that it had the right to make any such finding in the first place).

In his opinion in the case, the chief justice laid great emphasis on the importance of the court's being permitted to read a written constitution. Quite rightly. What is the point of a written constitution, he asked, if it is to be not looked into? So, can it be that the chief justice was reading from an abridged copy?

"Ha!"

St. John stared at him coldly. "This is the second time today you've blown a 'Ha!' Would you mind explaining?"

"Look, John Marshall is the greatest justice the supreme court has ever known," Huggins blurted. "Who do you think you are to toss him on the junk heap?"

Claire St. John stayed calm. "Never fear. I'm not going to argue anything a reasonable person wouldn't argue. Besides, I'm not alone in my conclusions. I could quote Thomas Jefferson and others who have made similar criticisms."

"Similar criticisms maybe, but not the same, or if you haven't made them yet, you soon will." The dogged Huggins was hanging on. "You've got points of your own."

"Well, thank you, I'm glad you noticed," St. John said smoothly. "Now let's see what *you* can do. I'll take the role of rebutter and you take the side of John Marshall."

"Oh no you don't. I'd just as soon let you do it all. You're the tutor."

"You're not entering into the spirit, Huggins. But never mind. To save time I'll just say, 'He says' and 'She says.' 'He' will be Marshall and 'She' will be . . . Who will 'She' be?"

"I already know who the 'She' is," said Huggins.

"You do? Who?"

"Portia."

"Portia?" St. John stood up, gazing at her tutee. The seconds ticked away a small eternity. Then, "It shall be as you wish. Theater, tales, and courtroom trials are of a piece. John Marshall from the bench and Portia at the bar. The tale of *Marshall v. Portia*. I'll have to practice lowering my voice if I'm going to play Marshall, too. Where is my wig and gown?"

"Wait a minute," popped Huggins. "How can you appear in court? There was no opposing counsel, you said."

"I'll go as a friend-of-the-court, *amicus curiae*, they call it."

"But you won't have heard the Court's opinion. And who will you represent?"

"You're a stickler for detail all of a sudden, Huggins. How come?"

"I learned it from you," said Huggins not without spite.

"Well, unlearn it. Quit being a grump." Annoyance clouded her brow, but in a flash good cheer cleared it away. "Let yourself go. The play's the thing!"

Huggins jumped to his feet. "All right! Here we go." He turned his back to her, motioned with both arms in the air as if to open the curtain, made an about-face, and took a step forward to announce, "Ladies and gentlemen.

"The case of *Marshall v. Portia* (Cranch 180a–b 1803), a play in one act, conceived, written, produced, directed, choreographed, and performed, and sets and costumes designed by the distinguished Claire St. John. With the participation of Oliver Huggins."

The time: Winter, 24 February 1803, mid-morning.

The place: a small, badly heated basement make-do courtroom in the office of the clerk of the Senate.

Onstage: four men (dummies) gowned and seated at the bench: Justices Samuel Chase, William Paterson, Bushrod Washington (the late president's nephew), and Chief Justice John Marshall presiding.

Offstage: Portia wraps her black gown tightly around her.

st. john: Brr! It's cold in this damp, dark, dingy room. My! You look fetching in your wig and gown.

HUGGINS (*nastily*): Wish I could say the same for you. Why do
    we have to wear these wigs anyway? *They're* not wearing
    them.

ST. JOHN: As a bow to English tradition. And I thought a wig would
    become you, and it does.

HUGGINS: *You* look like a mouse peeping out of a bag of rags.

(*St. John laughs and snatches at the hem of Huggins's gown, trying to lift
it. Huggins jumps back in alarm.*)

ST. JOHN: What have you got on underneath, your tennis shorts?

(*Huggins recovers and poises for a retaliatory leap at St. John's gown when
the bang of the gavel sounds.*)

A VOICE (*announcing*): The Supreme Court of the United States is
    now in session.

(*Enter a woman, Portia—alias Balthazar—a sheaf of paper in hand; and
a man, Nerissa, a companion. They take seats at the bar.*)

ST. JOHN (*aside to Huggins*): Look at him, Oliver. Didn't I tell you?
    Isn't he good-looking?

MARSHALL (*to associates on the bench*): What have we here? An un-
    lesson'd girl, unschool'd, unpractic'd. (*Adds with a broad
    wink*): Ah well, I could have used another week's schooling
    meself.

    (*To Portia*): We are in possession of your credentials.

    (*Spotting Huggins*): How did you get here?

    (*To Portia*): Who is that at the bar with you?

PORTIA: That, Your Honor, is Mr. Nerissa, my law clerk.

MARSHALL: Nerissa. That's an odd name for a young man, isn't it?

PORTIA: Quite so, if Your Honor pleases.

MARSHALL: What's that there under his gown, dragging on the floor?

PORTIA: Those are trousers, m'lord, a garment favored by our pres-
    ident, I'm told.

MARSHALL: Favored by the Jacobins too, I'm told.

PORTIA: Quite so, sir.

(*Nerissa starts to rise to protest something or other, but Portia puts a re-
straining hand on his shoulder.*)

NERISSA (*aside*): Seems to be a helluva lot of interest in what I've got
    on underneath.

MARSHALL: We have approved your most unusual request, madam,
    in the absence of opposing counsel, to present an oral brief

as *amicus curiae*, or I should say (*half-turning to his associates*) *amica curiae*. We understand that the Confederalist Society of the District of Columbia takes interest in your brief, but that is neither here nor there. You have read the testimony of petitioners' counsel and the opinion of this court as well. This court will hear you before handing down its decision. If you will take your place you may now address the court.

PORTIA (*clears her throat, pauses, and begins*): May it please Your Honors. In the case before the honorable court, counsel for the petitioners nowhere raised the question of unconstitutionality or, as the court calls it in colorful Cokean language, of repugnancy to the constitution.

Nor did the secretary of state raise it. He did not deign to appear. So no conflict of laws appears in the case as presented. Yet the honorable court has treated the case as a conflict of laws, indeed of highest laws. If I may quote the honorable court . . .

MARSHALL: I know what I said. Allow me to repeat it for your benefit: If two laws conflict with each other, the courts must decide on the operation of each. So if a law be in opposition to the constitution . . .

PORTIA: Thank you, Your Honor. The court's position is that it itself is to decide whether a law of the United States lying before it is repugnant to this constitution. If so, the court will pronounce it null and void.

I do not believe this position will hold. The principal caution I have to offer the honorable court is to beware of begging the question. Before one asserts that a given Act of Congress may be unconstitutional, one must determine not only who may decide it to be so—something this court has not done—but, before that, determine whether such a thing is constitutionally possible, and this question, too, the honorable court has not examined.

Now, in simple language, a *bill* refers to a legislative proposal by one or other chamber of Congress. Once such a bill has been duly enacted, it is an act of Congress, a *law* of the United States pursuant to this constitution.

JUSTICE PATERSON: We are with you, Counselor.

PORTIA: Thank you, Your Honor. I hope you will stay with me. I shall state my main argument in one sentence: This constitution does not contemplate a repugnance of laws between itself and laws (and treaties) of the United States.

By this constitution a bill originating in one house of Congress must receive the concurrence of the other house, and obtain the approval of the president. If there is disagreement over constitutionality or anything else, it is at this time, before the bill becomes law, that it will be weeded out. This constitution invests legislative review in the two-chambered Congress and a limited legislative veto in the president of the United States.

While a bill is in deliberation they may reject it for whatever reason they wish, within the range of their oath of office, including the grounds of constitutionality. This constitution does not limit the grounds Congressmen or the president may choose in their deliberations.

Most Congressmen are lawyers: conflict of laws is no stranger to them. Oliver Ellsworth, a most able lawyer, we all agree, a delegate to the Philadelphia convention, a member of the first drafting committee, of Detail, and your predecessor, Your Honor, as chief justice of this honorable court, drew up the Judiciary Act of 1789, with its Section 13, whose harmony with this constitution the honorable court now denies. In the Congress at that time were many other able lawyers, many of whom had been delegates to the Philadelphia convention. Moreover, five years later, in 1794, this supreme court acted upon Section 13 without demurrer. On the bench then were three justices who had been delegates to the convention: John Blair, James Wilson who had done most of the drafting work in the Committee of Detail, and William Paterson, whom I am pleased to see sitting as justice today. The president of the United States at the time, Mr. John Adams, himself a lawyer of no small ability as the court well knows, found no repugnance to this constitution in the bill. Nor did any other of these men. How much lawyerly review do we need?

Your Honors, the proper answer to a challenge to the constitutionality of a law of the United States is that the question has already been decided in the negative, by both houses of Congress and by the president. At the time a law of the United States reaches the supreme court, if ever, its constitutionality has already been assured, end of story. A bill may be unconstitutional, a law of the United States never.

It may seem to some observers that the honorable court is trying to encroach upon the law-making power that this constitution vested in Congress and the presidency. Your Honor has declared, "It is, emphatically, the province and duty of the judicial department, to say what the law is." Where in this constitution are we to locate such judicial pre-eminence? The source of the remark, as Your Honor knows, is an old Latin legal saying, ambiguously translated and even so, not to be found in this constitution.

JUSTICE WASHINGTON: Counselor, you keep referring to the constitution as *this* constitution. If you don't mind my asking, is there any reason for this unusual usage?

PORTIA: Yes, Your Honor, for the same reason this constitution refers to itself not as *the* constitution but almost invariably as *this* constitution. One must recall that this constitution was written only six years after the first constitution of the United States was ratified. In its brief life, although titled the "Articles of Confederation and Perpetual Union," this earlier document was commonly referred to as the constitution. Before and during the Philadelphia convention, Your Honors and others had spoken and written of it as "the Constitution."

This first constitution was never abrogated. The men at Philadelphia would not have referred to it at all, except that under it laws had been enacted and treaties negotiated; some of these they wished to keep, some not. They most surely wanted to keep alive all debts and contracts, and they managed to do that in the first paragraph of Article VI. "All debts contracted and engagements entered into, before the adoption of this constitution, shall be as valid against the United States under this constitution, as under the confederation."

You can see here an example of using *this* instead of *the*. You see here also the one time the Philadelphia drafters felt they could not avoid mention of the *confederation*, that is, of the government formed by the first constitution, the Articles of Confederation. The debts referred to included those that this previous United States' government owed its bondholders, its large creditors, many of whom were members of the Philadelphia convention and their friends.

As the drafters wished to avoid any other mention of the confederation, they had always to spell out "*this*" constitution, and also at times to switch tenses around. Having to keep valid those treaties negotiated in pursuance of the first constitution—specially the Treaty of Paris of 1783—they had to phrase the case as follows.

(Portia turns to Nerissa.)

PORTIA *(out loud)*: Mr. Nerissa, would you please read out the second paragraph of Article VI?

(Nerissa, caught by surprise, stands up, fumbles hastily under his gown for the slip of paper handed him before, finds it, and reads pompously but with appropriate emphases.)

NERISSA: "*This* constitution, and the laws of the United States, which shall be made in pursuance thereof; and all treaties *made, or which shall be made* under the authority of the United States, shall be the supreme law of the land."

(Nerissa sits down. Portia gives him a nod and a smile, and resumes.)

PORTIA: Your Honors will have noticed that the meaning of the phrase "which shall be made in pursuance thereof" now becomes clearer. At that moment there coexisted among the laws of the United States those laws made under the first constitution (the Articles of Confederation) and those future laws (existing as yet only in the minds of the drafters) "which shall be made" under the new, second constitution. The drafters thus made sure that, except for treaties and the payment of debts, the laws made in pursuance of the first constitution were of no account.

The little word *this* confesses that the drafters aimed at supplanting the legitimate constitution with *this* one.

(Giving her words a chance of sinking in, Portia pauses, motions to Nerissa to pass her the glass of water, takes a sip, and continues.)

To return to my main argument, it is this constitution that says what the law of the United States is. Article I, Section 7, Paragraph 2 declares, ". . . and if approved by two-thirds of that house, [the bill] shall become a law." The bill is now a law according to the constitution itself and is not merely what the honorable court has demeaned to be an "ordinary act of the legislature," conceivably in conflict with the constitution and vulnerable to repeal or veto by the court. Your Honors can recall, I am confident, that particular part of the Latin saying that was left out. "It is the province of a court to declare the law *and not to make it.*"

This constitution has no place for a judicial veto either before a bill becomes law or afterward. The court cannot reject a law by saying it is not a law, which is what the honorable court seems to insist on when it presumes to pronounce a constitutionally enacted law null and void and thus in effect to legislate going back to the prior state of things.

The power to veto a bill that this constitution gives the president reads in no uncertain terms (Article 1, Section 7): "Every bill . . . shall, before it become a law, be presented to the president of the United States; if he approve he shall sign it, but if not he shall return it." Where do we find like words for the powers of the court? Yet this court's opinion claims a veto power not over mere bills but over constitutionally enacted laws of the United States—without a whisper of such power in this constitution.

(Silence. Portia composes herself, drawing a cambric handkerchief from her sleeve and dabbing her brow. The chief justice says nothing. He and his associates look at the friend-of-the-court impassively, like so many lizards basking in the sun. Somebody in the courtroom drops a pin, several others cough.)

MARSHALL (*finally*): What you say is interesting but unconvincing.

We as judges must stand on our solemn oath to discharge our duties agreeably to the constitution.

PORTIA: Yes. Your Honor has said that his oath requires him to read
the constitution. I have said, with all respect, that the learned
court is not reading that part of this constitution that defines
what a law of the United States is. The court now switches
direction to remind me that a judge should not only read
the words of this constitution with his eyes; he must also
listen to the words of the oath with his ears.

The oath that Your Honors take, like this constitution itself, brooks no conflict of laws. The court in giving its opinion neglected the last few but important words of that oath.
Judges swear to discharge their duties agreeably "to the constitution *and laws of the United States.*" The judicial oath is
so contrived that if you array one part against the other, you
are in violation of both. If Your Honors pronounce a law
of the United States null and void, as you may be about to
do in this case, you are acting against the written constitution and your sworn oath. You are refusing to support the
laws of the United States for a reason that finds no confirmation in either this constitution or your oath. To use the
chief justice's forceful words, this is worse than solemn
mockery, it is equally a crime. It is subverting this constitution of the United States.

The president of the United States, too, solemnly swears
to support the constitution. In it he reads what a law of the
United States is and that he is to "take care that the laws be
faithfully executed." By his oath he is to take not Your
Honors' but *this* constitution's definition of what a law is,
and so must faithfully execute the Acts of Congress as laws
of the United States, any opinion of the supreme court to
the contrary notwithstanding.

Like this constitution itself, the oath which Your Honors
have sworn does not contemplate that a constitutionally enacted law, a law of the United States, might be in conflict
with this constitution. That oath, enjoining equal conformity to this constitution *and* to the laws of the United States,
precludes a judicial conception or finding of unconstitutionality.

You may not like that oath, but as you lay one hand on the Bible and raised the other to swear, no one was holding you at sword's point. You took the oath freely.

MARSHALL: Madam, are you intimating that this court does not honor its oath?

PORTIA: No sir, of course not. Surely my remarks are not made to reflect discredit on the eminent court. If ever this court dishonors its oath, I am certain it will have done so unintentionally.

In the present case, as friend-of-the-court, I venture to say that the honorable chief justice was led astray by a smooth but misleading clause in this constitution itself. Your Honor used it to ask whether an act (that is, a law of the United States) repugnant to the constitution (that is, somehow, known to be unconstitutional) can become the "law of the land."

A swift glance at the history of the phrase *law of the land* will repay—

JUSTICE CHASE: Begging your pardon, will there be any charge for your lecture on the law of the land?

PORTIA: I appreciate your concern, sir. I trust it will be less of a lecture than a tale, a tale from this constitution.

JUSTICE CHASE: Go ahead then, whatever you mean by that.

PORTIA: It may at once sound less like a lecture were I permitted to ask the honorable justices a question, a rhetorical question, to be sure.

NERISSA (*aside*): Oh God! I feel another quiz coming on!

PORTIA: Were I to ask the honorable justices what "land" is referred to in the phrase "law of the land," what would their answer be? . . . They could give no other reply, I believe, than "the United States."

The answer seems justifiable. After all, the phrase occurs in a document that contains its own description—"this Constitution for the United States of America." The United States of America is the common noun title, picked up from the Declaration of Independence and the first, the '77 Constitution, of a government of a confederation or union of the several States. In this constitution of '87, the title always intends the plural sense of the several States, united in a specified way. The clearest example occurs in the first sentence of Article III, Section 3 (the second sentence of which the court has already quoted). "Treason against the United States, shall consist only in levying war against *them.* . . ."

These United States have their own names, as Your Honors know, and *United States* is not the name of a consolidated land or a single country or nation. Although the honorable court in its opinion speaks of *country*—of "this country" or "the courts of the country" or "the laws of [Mr. Marbury's] country"—the word has no constitutional status. The court does not name the country intended and in the text of this or of the previous constitution would be unable to find the name written anywhere.

Still, instead of "land" why not at least say the "United States"? Unfortunately, Paragraph 2 of Article VI, where the word *land* appears, has already used *the United States* in the phrase "laws of the United States," so that the substitution would come out thus: "This constitution, and the laws of the United States . . . shall be the supreme law of the United States."

The substitution does not quite succeed. It sounds like an echo. Moreover, it would admit another and, I should suppose, undesirable meaning: that as the law of the United States government it applies supremely to the confederation or *union* of the states but not to the states individually. And the rest of the paragraph could be similarly construed. *Land*, it seems, was meant to substitute for something else.

Perhaps in the language of the courts *law of the land* does have a fixed meaning. The phrase's grand debut appears to us in the Latin of the Magna Carta of England, the pact often cited as the signal fire of the rights of Englishmen. Though it appears there in Latin as *lex terrae* (more properly *lex terrenae*, or "law of the terrain") and thus also on the Continent (where it arose out of feudalism) it has an earlier usage in England, too, as the more rhythmical *law of the land*. In those times, it indicated the custom and common law of the counties and shires of England with its protection, particularly through habeas corpus and jury trial, and typically against the king's justice, of individual and property rights. It boasted of a connection to the Saxon folkright and excluded by implication the foreign, civil, or Roman law in which nonetheless it had a relative in the *ius commune*.

ST. JOHN (*aside to Huggins*): Psst, Oliver, note that we'll talk more about the common law, at home later.

HUGGINS (*whispering too*): Home? What home?

ST. JOHN: Shhh! What home? What are you talking about? I said common *law*.

PORTIA (*continuing*): The phrase presents itself in the 1628 Petition of Right and in the 1689 Habeas Corpus Act in more or less the same guise. Like the equally rhythmical "lay of the land," the law of the land conveys local knowledge; intimacy; a long familiarity with towns, counties, and shires and baronial holdings, predating written law.

MARSHALL (*with a smile*): I must remark, Counselor, you are certainly learned at law. Do you spend all your time with the law books?

PORTIA (*adjusting her wig a bit*): No, Your Honor, I may be bookish, true, but not a bookworm. I like to ride, and to pitch horseshoes, and to . . .

MARSHALL: Horseshoes? What about quoits?

PORTIA: Quoits? Yes indeed. Almost the same thing. . . .

MARSHALL: Do you know who the champion is in these parts? I suppose you would use the lighter brass rings. I use iron. Well, never mind that. What are you doing Saturday morning around eleven o'clock? Would you care to meet at the house for tea and then come to the club for a toss or two?

PORTIA (*pondering her busy schedule*): Would Sunday . . .

MARSHALL (*with a furtive glance at his associates*): Hmmpf. I beg your pardon. Go on, Counselor.

HUGGINS (*aside*): Damn! Why didn't I take on the role of John
      Marshall? That old pussy! *(To St. John)* He's just a dummy,
      a lecherous old dummy.
ST. JOHN (*to Huggins*): Come on, Huggins. He can't be more than
      forty. Did you see that charming smile? I think he likes me.
(She winks at Huggins, and continues.)

PORTIA: The honorable court will please recall that *the land*, these
      terrains—these counties, shires, and towns—"the town of
      London"—and even the whole country—"the people of
      England"—all have names. And, I ask again, what name do
      Your Honors have for the *land* found in this constitution?
          If we substitute for the *law of the land* an equivalent us-
      age like *custom and common law*, we still have to ask, law of
      where? Of England? And ask also, how can a written con-
      stitution, and treaties and statutes enacted as the laws of
      Congress, be the equivalent of customary or common law
      which is in origin and for long thereafter and sometimes for-
      ever, unwritten?
          On this side of the Atlantic, in the Virginia Declaration
      of Rights of June 1776, or better, but a few years ago, the
      phrase the *law of the land* reappears, more or less as in the
      Magna Carta. The Massachusetts Constitution of 1780, Ar-
      ticle XII, proclaims that no subject shall be arrested or de-
      prived of his life, liberty, or estate but "by the judgment of
      his peers, or the law of the land." Here, at least, "the land"
      bore a name—Massachusetts—a name so old it predates the
      arrival of the palefaces. Excuse me, I mean of the Pilgrims.
      Also here the *law of the land* as *habeas corpus* and jury trial
      or as due process within a named locality fits common and
      legal usage.
          We see that to translate this constitution's *supreme law of
      the land* as the supreme law of the United States is repeti-
      tive and confusing; to translate it as the supreme law of a
      country or nation leaves that country or nation without a
      name; and to translate it as supreme customary or common
      law makes no sense, like saying that this tripartite written
      law (constitution, laws of the United States, and treaties)

shall be the supreme unwritten (common or customary) law.

Well, might *supreme law of the land* mean supreme over the laws of the several States? Say, over the laws of the State of Massachusetts or of Virginia?

(The justices stir in their bench chairs and seem to want to confer with each other, but hesitate. Portia pushes on.)

I see I had better tell the story of how this flawed clause was framed, just to refresh the memory. I know the honorable justices are familiar with parts of the story. One of Your Honors was present at that convention in Philadelphia, and others of Your Honors have friends like Mr. Hamilton and Mr. Gouverneur Morris who may have vouched details. I do not mention the various papers Your Honors may have read, like the *Federalist* or the *Federal Farmer* printed in favor of or against ratifying this constitution: they are unreliable sources, rhetorical pieces designed to persuade voters to one side or the other.

Friends of mine who were delegates to the Philadelphia convention have told me how the second paragraph of Article VI evolved. The principal architects were struggling to frame a provision that would *seem* weak, and yet be strong enough "to negative all laws passed by the several states," and they thought to put the nay-saying power in the hands of "the national legislature" (which they later thought prudent to call, as before, "the Congress"). To this phrasing Mr. John Rutledge, delegate from South Carolina, objected. My friends remembered his stinging words. "If nothing else, this alone would damn, and ought to damn, the constitution," he exclaimed. "Will any State ever agree to be bound hand and foot in this manner?"

After debating the question on the floor, the delegates hit upon the ingenious idea of coercing the states by binding all officers and judges in the several states with an oath to support this constitution and by setting up a law supreme over the respective states. The first resolution on the clause in the convention does not mention a supreme law *of the land* but *of the respective states.*

Here, Your Honors, is the equivalent of *the land*—"the respective states."

The delegates then turned the resolution over to the Committee of Detail which let the wording stand. The *supreme law of the respective states* was still there.

As of that date, July 26, 1787, the word *constitution* does not yet appear. Its precursor in the convention was "the Articles of Union," and even this phrase is not mentioned first in the clause, nor as law. There were then only two parts to the law—"the legislative acts of the United States" and "all treaties." Mind that it is these two, not three, that the drafters first said "shall be the supreme law of the respective states."

Reported out of committee, the resolution went back to the floor. Late in the summer, Mr. Rutledge moved to amend it to begin with, "This constitution . . ." and gave it the horizontal, triple form it keeps today.

The title, "Articles of Union," by which from the beginning the developing document had been designated, dropped out: it smacked of the "Articles of Confederation and Perpetual Union," seeming like an abbreviation. The new title, "constitution," was an improvement but, as I noted, had to be prefaced with "this" to avoid confusion with the previous constitution, the aforesaid by now doomed "Articles of Confederation." It might have been better to call the new instrument simply and unromantically *a* "Frame of Government for the United States."

To declare that "this constitution" was law too, as Article VI does, was not strictly necessary: the first sentence of the document had already reported that "We, the People" had enacted it—

JUSTICE PATTERSON: If I may interrupt, madam, your clerk seems to have dozed off.

PORTIA (*looks down at Nerissa*): Your Honor, he has been serving me as devil's advocate. Though appearing to nod, he is intent on finding holes in my argument. He is a good clerk, often working into the small hours. (*Aside to Nerissa, kicking his ankle*) Psst, Nerissa. Bestir thyself.

(Portia returns to the story.)

Approved without objection the resolution was sent to the Committee on Stile and Arrangement for the final draft. Here it got into the hands of the esteemed Mr. Gouverneur Morris. He has since remarked that he spent more time on the judiciary passages than on any others and that the passages, as they had come to the committee, were alarming. He had said earlier that the negativing power as expressed would disgust all the States. The most momentous change he and the committee made was to take out the words *respective states* and substitute *the land.*

What did Mr. Morris stand to gain by this change? He avoided the direct threat of subordinating the *respective states* to the United States government. And he replaced the plural *states* with a singular *land*. He might furthermore have guessed that the familiar *law of the land* when prefixed by the exalted *supreme* (which word he kept) might grow in meaning, might recast the government of these *United States* into the mold of a single country or nation.

In the Massachusetts Constitution *law of the land* was not modified by *supreme*. By squeezing this latter term into the old legal phrase colored by localism, the Framers blurred the meaning even more, making it fit for grandiose settings. *Supreme* we may take it means "highest," as in *supreme court.*

Was there any disadvantage to this change made in the penultimate day of the Philadelphia convention? Most certainly. It threw the entire passage into confusion. Once you remove *the respective states*, the word *supreme* is left suspended over a void. If supreme means highest in a rank, where was the rest of the rank? The word *land* is an intrinsic part of a fixed term—law of the land. To modify it with *supreme* takes the emphasis from *land* and puts it on *law*. The new phrase invites inferior comparisons, invites a ranking with other inferior forms of law. The law of the land is supreme over what? This opens up Pandora's box.

(She sighs heavily and goes on.)

Supreme, I say, over what other law? Over common law

as derived from the beliefs and customs of the people? Over fundamental principles, written and unwritten, of the people? Over natural law, natural rights, or the laws of nature? Over the law of conscience, or of reason? Over the law of nations when dealing with one another? Hardly. Neither this constitution nor any other has power over these unenacted forms of law.

The implications are serious. If the supreme law of the land cannot be superior to these other forms of law, it may be judged inferior. My fear is that the indeterminacy wrought in this last-minute clause will create problems for posterity.

In defense of that esteemed gentleman, Mr. Gouverneur Morris, we must allow that for reasons already mentioned he could not solve the problems of Article VI, Paragraph 2 by repeating "the United States." Likewise, he could not use "the supreme law of the union": it would be argued that supreme law applied only to the union and not to the States. Nor could he write "the supreme law of the nation," or as the French would have it, the law of the "supreme nation." *What* nation?

The word *nation* itself was (and I daresay still is) ominous. So was "national" as in "national government." As you know, the drafters shunned even the term "general government" as too suggestive of a central government over the States.

Though this constitution would have been the appropriate place in which to record the name of the country, Mr. Morris could bestow no proper noun, such as Atlanta or Atlantica, America or Columbia.

His last-minute choice of phrase passed muster. *Law of the land* was a familiar term to lawyers trained in the English tradition. Besides, time was running out. It was late, autumn a-coming in, the conventioneers impatient to get back to comfortable homes in their home states. They toasted the good ship "Land" with champagne, and left the vessel on shore patrol. Its orders were to circumnavigate the country, a country with no name or a country that as yet did not exist or whose existence was not certain enough to warrant a name or on whose plain existence there was still no agreement.

I fear now that this eminent court may find *the supreme law of the land*, for its very ambiguity and the possibility that it may come to signify the supreme law of "the country" or "the nation," too alluring. The phrase will give too optimistic an impression of the depth of national sentiment in the several States and will destroy the harmony of law this constitution harbors.

What the court has done is to set this constitution to fighting itself. To quibbling about conflict of laws and unconstitutionality, and who's boss around here?

Suppose we take the liberty of defining the supreme law of the land as this constitution does: 1) this constitution, plus 2) the laws of the United States, plus 3) all treaties of the same. The court looks at these constituent parts and asks, Which of them is King of the Hill?

Then it gives the answer: number 1. And how does it know this? By observing that "in declaring what shall be the supreme law of the land, the constitution is first mentioned." The drafters, we are to believe, meant thereby to rank this constitution-as-law supreme over the other two kinds of supreme law they specified—laws of the United States and treaties.

The argument is trivial. It is something like a child's finishing prayers at night with, "And God bless . . ." and stopping to ask, "Who comes first, Mummy or Daddy or Grandma?" Much less trivial indeed would it be to argue that the drafters ranked Article I, Congress first; Article II, president second; Article III, supreme court last, or that they capitalized the Congress and left the president and the supreme court in lower case.

Without question the three constituents of supreme law are different: this constitution is the empowering document, laws are the laws, and treaties are the treaties, and this constitution graces each with a legal supremacy equal to itself. To use your own forceful expression, Mr. Chief Justice, either the word *supreme* means what it means or it does not. This written constitution for the United States of North America is one unrolling document, consisting of itself with amendments, the laws of the United States, and treaties—all on a horizontal plane, equal and supreme as law.

One may seek and yet not find in this constitution words that rank its three constituents of law by supremacy—one, two, three. An assertion—that one part is super-supreme and trumps the others, and a second part supreme and trumps the third, leaving the third supreme and trumping nothing— illustrates the kind of loose thinking that this vague phrase, *the supreme law of the land,* encourages. What is being expounded here, the laws of whist?

MARSHALL (*breaking in, black eyes glowering*): We have heard enough, madam. You forget that you are here at our pleasure and—

PORTIA (*uncowed*): If Your Honor please, I have but one observation more.

(*Portia places her notes down on the table. Nerissa, fearing the worst, tugs at her sleeve.*)

NERISSA (*to Portia*): Psst, let's get out of here before they tar and feather us.

PORTIA (*to Nerissa, urgently, pulling her sleeve away*): Stay with me, baby.

(*She smooths out her gown, leans on the table, and looks up at the bench.*)

PORTIA: One thing about this case has nagged me all along—I come now to my most grievous ground—the main facts are murky. Did the former president sign an appointment for Mr. Marbury, and if so, in whose presence? Was it sealed and by whom? Was it recorded and by whom? Was the commission not delivered and if not, whose responsibility was it? The principal in all these events, the *whom* and the *whose,* is you, sir.

(*The chief justice, scowling, muttering, half arises from the bench. The associate justices sit agape and immobile. Portia picks up speed, allowing no interruption. The chief justice sits back down.*)

PORTIA: In all sincerity, Your Honors, and as friend-of-the-court, I believe that the chief justice should excuse himself from this case.

MARSHALL (*aside to his associates*): I *knew* we should come to this. Here we go again with that red-headed son-of-a-bitch.

(*To Portia*): What is the reason for this outrage? The possible involvement of the president of the United States, Mr. Jefferson, who happens to be a distant relative? If you rule out Virginia cousins, madam, you would decimate the United States government (*laughter in the courtroom*) although the effect today would not be entirely without merit.

(*Again, laughter.*)

PORTIA: No, Your Honor. Rather, it is this: In the present case the incumbent secretary of state deigned not to appoint opposing counsel on grounds, I presume, that the judiciary was not authorized to intrude, as you so nicely put it, Your Honor, "to intermeddle with the prerogatives of the executive."

Assuredly, opposing counsel, had it existed, would have recused you on at least three grounds. First, your brother James is involved; his testimony for the petitioners has been admitted. Second, Your Honor at the time of the events of this case was holding two positions, that of secretary of state and of chief justice, in violation, you must admit, of the doctrine you yourself sustain to be constitutional, of the separation of powers, in this instance, executive and judicial. Third, as secretary of state, you neglected to deliver the petitioners' commission to them, with the result that now as chief justice you sit on the bench, free of questioning and in judgment on yourself. Surely, opposing counsel would have asked you to step down from the bench and called you as witness to the circumstances of nondelivery and before that, to testify to the very existence of the various commissions in this case, for the existence of all of them has not been proved beyond doubt, testimony being especially inconclusive regarding the particular commission of Mr. Marbury.

I should have thought that petitioners' counsel himself might have joined in asking you—the person most directly implicated in the facts of the case—to leave the bench, at least in order to testify. (I shall not speculate about why petitioners chose not to do so.) Indeed, had it not been for your apparent carelessness as secretary of state this case would never have existed.

This court is all too aware, I am sure, of today's political climate, that Congress is carefully scrutinizing the judiciary's conduct and that it has power of impeachment. You may well have been derelict in duty while secretary of state, a fault reflecting on your behavior as chief justice, a fault committed while you were already chief justice.

As friend-of-the-court I believe that you would show yourself to be a jealous guardian of the reputation of this eminent court by stepping down from the bench for the present case. One cannot at the same time be party and judge.

(Marshall arises abruptly, bristling, hammers fiercely on the bench with his gavel.)

MARSHALL *(to Portia)*: Madam, the only protection you have against commitment for contempt is your sex.

(He hammers twice with the gavel.)

(To the courtroom): Having heard *amicus curiae*, the last matter before the court, our opinion stands: The ruling requested by petitioners requires the application of an act of the legislature repugnant to the constitution and thereby null and void, and inapplicable by this court. The rule must be discharged.

Court is adjourned.

(The gavel hammers a final blow.)

VOICE *(booming)*: Be upstanding!

(The justices in file exeunt. Portia sits down, exhausted.)

PORTIA: There you see Authority. The gavel has the last word.

(Slowly she stands up, slumping, turns around and softly speaks.)

My little body is a-weary of this great world.

(She steps up close to Huggins. Her breath steaming with cold bathes his

face like a tropical breeze. She lays her hands on his shoulders and kisses him on both cheeks, pensively.)

Bassanio, your Portia bids you *addio.*

(She shakes the wig out of her hair, shrugs the gown off to the floor, and steps out of it, svelte once more. She takes a lazy stretch.)

st. john: Thanks, Oliver. *(Exits.)*

huggins *(thunderstruck)*: Damn! I'm left to live upon the rack!

Curtain

8

JOHN CALHOUN ZEROES IN
ON THE FATAL FLAW AND
ONE MILLION MEN FALL

TUESDAY

When Huggins entered the room St. John was already there pinning on the wall a big sheet of paper—the kind kindergarten teachers paste things on and artists sketch on with charcoal. She got it fastened just as he came in view, and turned around.

"Greetings, Huggins. Did you get a good night's sleep?"

"Big deal," peevishly ignoring the question. "You think you've beaten John Marshall with your feminine wiles and putting me in skirts . . ."

St. John was unsympathetic. "Oh, my Hercules, did this little hand steal your club and lion-skin?"

". . . exploiting your femininity . . ." Huggins was still muttering in indignation.

"Didn't get me very far, did it?" St. John was smiling.

"That's right. What you said doesn't change a thing. The court still has the judicial veto."

"We do what we can in our little way. Some change is clear already. You said judicial 'veto,' not judicial 'review.' Let's take a look at what you claim, though."

————The fuss over *Madison* v. *Marbury* left Chief Justice Marshall shaken. He was saved—and he must have known it—by President Jefferson's excitement over the Louisiana Purchase. In a private letter the chief justice expressed the view that if the court believed a law unconstitutional, it might refer it back to Congress for reconsideration and clarification, an opinion far from his claim in *Madison* v. *Marbury* that only the court could declare a law of the United States a nonlaw.

In 1809 the court declared another section of the Federal Judiciary Act unconstitutional, with negligible consequences. Not until 1860, a half century later, did the court again attempt to foil the laws of the United States and not until the North won the War of Secession, also known as the Civil War, did *Madison* v. *Marbury* begin to be a celebrated case. In the meantime, in a series of decisions, the Marshall court became instead the instrument for expanding the central government's judicial power over the States. The supreme-law-of-the-land clause was soon having difficulties.

To refractory States the law of the land seemed something less than supreme. Early in the nineteenth century the Cherokee agricultural land within western Georgia covered 26 million acres but within two decades had shrunk to 9 million. Outside this territory, land for cotton was already selling at a premium, and then in 1829 gold was discovered within Cherokee borders. Georgia wanted that acreage and the Cherokees out of the State. The Cherokees, a special kind of "nation," had long had their own courts and tried all cases, civil and criminal, themselves. In defiance of existing treaties between the United States and the Cherokee Nation, Georgia now passed a law extending its jurisdiction over Cherokee territory and appropriating their land. President Jackson, far from preparing to defend the Cherokees, ordered federal troops withdrawn from the State and let it be known that he would take no steps to enforce Cherokee claims.

In this excited period, one Corn Tassels, a Cherokee, committed a murder in Cherokee territory, was arrested, brought before a Georgia court, and found guilty. At trial he argued that he could be tried only by his own nation according to its solemn treaties with the United States. The Georgia court rejected his defense; he applied to the supreme court for a writ of error; Marshall granted the writ, notifying Georgia to appear and show cause why there was no error in its proceedings. Georgia refused to send counsel to the supreme court, maintained that that court had no jurisdiction in the case, and summarily hanged Corn Tassels. All the king's horses and all the king's men . . .

Shortly thereafter, Marshall had a chance to face down President Jackson and to save the Cherokees from massive expulsion, but failed. Under a new Georgia law requiring a license for any white man residing in Cherokee territory, a New England missionary working there was arrested, tried, and condemned to four years at hard labor. The United States supreme court ruled that Georgia's law was repugnant to the constitution, and that judgment on the missionary ought to be reversed and annulled. Georgia did not release the man, and the president stuck his tongue out at the supreme court. "John Marshall has made his decision, now let him enforce it."

A few years later, the Georgia militia moved the Cherokees with some of their slaves out of the State, starting them and other tribes on a march to what was to be Oklahoma. Thousands died on the "Trail of Tears." Jackson wrote a friend exulting that the supreme court decision had "fell still born."

This is where John C. Calhoun comes in . . .

Huggins raised his hand and asked with a tinge of sarcasm, "Permission to speak?"

"Yes?"

"I have some questions before we leave John Marshall."

"The floor is yours."

"What happened to the commissions of Marbury and the others?"

"When Jefferson arrived in Washington he found them on Marshall's old desk and tossed them in the wastebasket. Next question?"

Huggins shook his head.

St. John said, "There's something important I neglected to tell you about John Marshall. Did you know he recited 'Now I lay me down to sleep' every night of his life?"

"So do I," said Huggins.

"So do I," said St. John. "Who taught you to say it?"

"My mother. Who taught *you?*"

"My father." She smiled, cleared her throat, and asked, "Permission to get back to Calhoun?"

————Calhoun had an advantage over those early anti-Federalist writers who attacked the '87 Constitution as it came off the press. Had they been privy to the debates that took place behind closed doors in Philadelphia, they would have been loaded for bear. But the minutes had been put under lock and key, the key safe in Washington's pocket. Decades later, Madison's incredibly painstaking, conscientious notes surfaced. Calhoun read them.

There wasn't much Calhoun didn't read. As a young man he showed a scholarly bent. When he was eighteen a neighbor caught him in the field with a book tied to the plow. In a spurt of community spirit, neighbors sent for his two older brothers working elsewhere, recommending that they put John to better use. The family council met and decided to pool resources to give the boy a good education.

A solid Scotch-Irish family. The immigrating grandparents had come from Donegal, Ireland. With them was their five-year-old son, Patrick, the future father of our John. They landed in Philadelphia like many others of their countrymen, made their way southwest to the mountains of South Carolina, and settled in frontier country where, in the Long Canes Massacre of 1760, the Cherokees killed Patrick's mother and took two young nieces captive.

"Damn!" exclaimed Huggins. "Travel all that way to be killed by Indians."

His tutor peered at him, then proceeded without comment.

————Patrick grew up to be an Indian fighter and one of the Regulators, a kind of anti-Cherokee posse or militia which, given the lack of State police and courts in the area, patrolled on the frontier and took over many law-and-order functions. He became leader of his small town, organizing the first church, building the first frame house, bringing in the first slaves. He rose to the South Carolina legislature by leading a band of his neighbors two hundred miles to the edge of Charleston where they seized a polling place at gun point and elected him. In politics these men breathed a rough Jeffersonianism—small government, small taxes, God helps those who help themselves. Patrick was fifty-four when his young wife, Martha Caldwell, also of Scottish origin, gave birth to their third son, John Caldwell Calhoun. The boy was a little too young to understand what was going on when his father, a few years later, thundered against the '87 Constitution for allowing the United States to tax South Carolina.

With this wild and woolly background, young John attended a nearby "log college" where, for two years, he grappled with Greek and Latin. The family then sent him to New England to study law at Federalist Yale, where his intelligence and ambition were appreciated. Timothy Dwight, president of the school and, you may remember, author of the song with the "encrimsoned name" Columbia, is supposed to have predicted that the young scholar would one day become president. For advanced study John went next to a prestigious law school in Litchfield, Connecticut. On holidays he stayed with cousins in Newport, Rhode Island.

Back to South Carolina Calhoun completed his law studies in Charleston, hung out a shingle in Abbeville, and began a rapid political ascent. In 1807, at age twenty-five, elected without opposition, he took his father's seat in the South Carolina general assembly. We find him in Washington a few years later aligned with other young frontier freshmen in Congress, the so-called War Hawks, hot for renewed battle with England. The former mother country had been impressing United States seamen and sinking United States ships with cargoes thought to be headed for her arch-enemy Napoleon Bonaparte. Outraged, Calhoun drew up a report to Congress calling for fifty thousand volunteers and the arming of ships for war. He even pushed hard for military conscription, but Congress turned a deaf ear. During his years in Congress he advocated a national bank to restrain the paper money floating everywhere and backed the building of interstate roads and canals. As secretary of war under President James Monroe, in the space of a year he modernized the army and strengthened the United States military academy of West Point, appointing among other promising cadets Robert E. Lee and Jefferson Davis, about whom more another day.

At forty Calhoun was ready to bid for the presidency. So far his position differed little from those of his Federalist associates at Yale. At the same time, nothing in his public statements opposed the independent policy of South Carolina. He settled in a plantation residence in Pendleton, South Carolina, renaming it "Fort Hill." He threw his hat in the presidential ring and promptly drew it out again: the odds were against him. He settled for the vice-presidency under John Quincy Adams. Growing uncomfortable with that president's slippery politics, he began shifting his support to Andrew Jackson as possible successor, although earlier while secretary of war he had voted in a cabinet meeting to censure General Jackson for exceeding orders in a campaign against the Seminole Indians. The debate that day was considered an internal cabinet matter and not noised about.

When Jackson in 1828 was elected president, Calhoun, for the second time, was elected vice-president. All he had to do now to become the next president of the United States was to stay in Jackson's good graces.

Calhoun stayed on good behavior, but his wife did not. Rather, her behavior was too good. And thereby hangs a tale.

Floride Bonneau Calhoun was Calhoun's second cousin, daughter of a rich Charleston family. John was upland, Floride was lowland, he was dirt-soil, she plantation. He had won her hand and they had married soon after the South Carolina general assembly elected him to Congress.

By the time of Jackson's administration, "the Palace," the president's residence, had already begun to be called the "White House." (After the British burned it in 1814 the gray exterior was painted white.) The city of Washington, District of Columbia, was that stretch of Pennsylvania Avenue running from the Capitol to the White House; the White House stood in a pasture traversed by a sewage ditch for a mall.

The president's wife was the first lady of society, but Jackson's wife Rachel died a few weeks after her husband won the election. Against Jackson President Adams had unleashed the foulest election campaign since that of his father against Jefferson, worse for being directed in no small part against Rachel. She had married Jackson after receiving news of divorce from her abusive first husband. The news was premature by two years. During those two years she lived with Jackson as man and wife. Technically she was an adulteress and a bigamist. On such grounds was the husband's divorce finally granted. Jackson blamed her death on the vicious campaign of slander against an innocent woman. He had once killed a man in a duel who had bandied her name in taverns. He hung Rachel's portrait in their bedroom so that he gazed on it last before sleeping and first on awakening.

Upon Rachel's death, the crown of Washington society fell to Floride Bonneau Calhoun, wife of the vice-president.

President Jackson had an old Tennessee friend, Senator John Eaton, whom he wanted to appoint secretary of war. Before accepting the post Eaton confessed to Jackson that for about ten years he had a mistress, a tavern owner's daughter who, as her husband had recently departed this world, wished to be made an honest woman. She had had, evil tongues wagged, a checkered past, including a miscarriage a year after her late spouse had sailed with the fleet. I don't know how much of this Eaton brought to the president's attention but he did say he feared to stain the president's cabinet with gossip. Jackson and Eaton had once boarded at the O'Neill tavern in Washington. Jackson knew the woman and had liked her. The president's reply fulfilling the senator's innermost hope, could have been predicted. Damn the gossip, full-speed ahead, marry her!

The whip-wielding, slave-holding Jackson treated her not only with the courtesy due the wife of a member of his cabinet, but as though she were somehow the embodiment of his beloved, slandered, gentle, dead Rachel. He staggered his cabinet one day by asserting that Peggy Eaton was "as chaste as a virgin." Contrast this with the news announced by another senator: "Eaton has just married his mistress—and the mistress of eleven dozen others!"

To Floride Calhoun, Peggy O'Neill Eaton was nothing but a

slept-around, rough-tongued barmaid. By the way, Floride's portrait—unless prejudice misleads me—leaves her looking rather prissy.
The Eatons, after their honeymoon, called on the Calhouns: Floride
did receive them, in cool propriety. The next day she announced:
"I have determined, Mr. Calhoun, not to return Mrs. Eaton's visit."
Someone had to uphold the standard of gentility if society were not
to be overrun by the rabble now infesting the city, and who better
than a Bonneau of Charleston.

At Jackson's inaugural ball Peggy Eaton made a grand entrance
with all the poise of a lady. The president greeted her with southern gallantry. The cabinet wives to a man turned their backs on her.
In succeeding weeks the Eatons made calls on cabinet members who
duly returned the calls, leaving their wives and their wives' cards at
home. The Eatons gave parties; nobody who counted came. The
international diplomatic community looked on highly amused, as if
such jockeying for the rail was unknown in Europe.

Jackson had a handsome niece-by-marriage, Emily, the wife of
his secretary. Since Rachel's death Emily had been serving in the
White House as his hostess. She considered Peggy incurably vulgar
and told her uncle so. Humiliation and spite throwing him back on
his heels, he demanded that she continue to receive Peggy Eaton as
a lady. No more daunted by the president than were the other ladies,
Emily packed her bags and returned to Tennessee. Jackson became
a lonely, enraged man. Rumor of a cabinet conspiracy swept the
capital. Jackson called in the attorney general, the secretary of the
navy, and of the treasury and ordered them to lay off Mrs. Eaton.
They promised, but what could they do? Their wives followed
Floride's head held high.

"If you ask me," Huggins broke in sourly, "that cabinet was pussy-
whipped."

"What?" exclaimed a startled St. John.

"Pussy-whipped, you know, whipped by pussy-willows," improvised Huggins.

St. John seemed not at all convinced by this derivation of the
term.

"If you think they were pussy-whipped," she demanded, "what

about Calhoun? Jackson by now knew that Floride led the wives to battle, and Calhoun knew that Jackson knew. Why didn't this cast-iron man shut his wife up? Was he a man of putty?"

"I'm listening," said Huggins.

"If you listen closely," said St. John, "you'll hear the molting of a toad in the leaves, the slithering of a snake in the grass."

————The only unattached male in the cabinet was a widower, a plump, suave little man, name of Martin Van Buren. He saw Opportunity and before she slipped by, seized her by the hair. He fawned on the Eatons. He murmured in Peggy's ear that she shouldn't tell Jackson he said so, but that the president was "the greatest man who ever lived." Peggy tripped off right away to tell the president, who with tears rolling down his face sobbed, "That man loves me."

Soon the cabinet was split, 3 to 3, a Calhoun side and a Van Buren side, with Jackson beginning to look on Calhoun with suspicion. Van Buren and a couple of other ill-wishers gave the president an eyewitness account of Calhoun's censure of the Seminole foray. Jackson sent Calhoun a brusque note asking for an explanation. There wasn't much Calhoun could say in reply: he reiterated that he had believed Jackson had overstepped his powers. Foreseeing now what was coming, he had a pamphlet published setting forth the reasons for his earlier censure and recording the craftiness of Peggy O'Neill Eaton.

Calhoun fell from grace. Jackson would never support him for the presidency. The next president of the United States was to be toady Van Buren. Calhoun had lost the Petticoat War.

"I could have told you that," said Huggins. "What I want to know is what happened to Peggy O'Neill? Don't do what you did with the Randolph affair yesterday, don't abbreviate the story."

"Oh, Huggins," lilted St. John. "You're getting so masterful in your old age."

Huggins lapsed into silence.

"When Eaton was appointed ambassador to Spain, his wife became the toast of Madrid. Back in Washington, after her second husband died, Peggy, still attractive in her sixties and by no means poor, married a handsome Italian dancing master in his twenties. He left with her money and a partner more his own age—Peggy's granddaughter. Last heard of, Grandma was angrily writing her memoirs."

"Come on," Huggins said. "Is that true?"

"Cross my heart. Can we get back to Calhoun now?"

Huggins gave a grouchy nod.

"I must admit," began St. John, "that John Calhoun for all his honor, courage, and courtesy, kindness and intelligence, had one unlovable trait—he had little sense of humor, even less than Washington, if that were possible. Tall, thin, and dressed in black, he had, it might be argued, none at all. What more to say about such a man?"

Huggins leaned back.

"You know what a political philosopher is, don't you, Huggins?"

"Of course. Plato and Aristotle were political philosophers."

"Yes, Plato and Aristotle *are* political philosophers, Huggins, *are*. And they are the greatest, like Bach and Mozart, and in that order. Calhoun is not in their league, but he was the greatest political philosopher the United States had ever produced. In comparison, before him there were but talented phrase-makers, journalists, amateur political scientists and economists . . . You think I'm exaggerating, don't you?"

"Well . . ."

————Not so, said tutor firmly. He was the greatest, and we owe it all to Peggy O'Neill. Had that desirable woman not provoked the rebellion of the wives, John Calhoun may well have stayed next in line for the presidency. Instead, he resigned as vice-president, was immediately elected senator from South Carolina, and ran up the flag of the South. His thinking became more and more theoretical, more concentrated on the nature of the union called the United States. In his mid-forties Calhoun set to writing his two short but major works: *A Disquisition on Government* and *A Discourse on the Constitution and Government of the United States*.

During his years in the federal government, as secretary of war and as vice-president, Calhoun had advocated an active military, interstate, and international policy, all the while, as I hinted, keeping an eye on the welfare of South Carolina. What bothered him most was the union's tariff policy. As vice-president in the Adams government, his vote broke a tie in the Senate and defeated a bill to raise the tariff. A year later, his reservations gave way; he denounced federal tariffs as a whole. At the time, vice-presidents were not expected to be the yes-men they are today. Even so, Calhoun took pains to put his denunciation in the form of an anonymous pamphlet, "The South Carolina Exposition and Protest." The South Carolina Legislature later made it the basis of an Ordinance of Nullification.

"I'll let you judge for yourself how good Calhoun is," said St. John, branching off. "In the political treatise *A Disquisition on Government*, he sets out not as a pamphleteer like the Federalist and anti-Federalist writers. He starts out like an Aristotle to lay a solid foundation for political science." St. John reached into her case, brought out a small fistful of papers, and began to read:

> I assume as an incontestable fact that man is so constituted as to be a social being. His inclinations and wants, physical and moral, irresistibly impel him to associate with his kind; and he has, accordingly, never been found, in any age or country, in any state other than the social. In no other, indeed, could he exist. . . .

"Neat, think you not so?"

> I next assume [he writes], . . . on universal experience [that] in no age or country has any society or community ever been found, whether enlightened or savage, without government of some description.

"So, with or without a woodsy state of nature or a so-called social contract," interposed St. John, "men will have government. Why should this be? he asks, and finds the answer in the twofold nature of all animals, foremost among them humans, with one part of that nature stronger than the other."

> . . . while man is created for the social state and is accordingly so formed as to feel what affects others as well as what affects himself, he is, at the same time, so constituted as to feel more in-

tensely what affects him directly than what affects him indirectly through others, or, to express it differently, he is so constituted that his direct or individual affections are stronger than his sympathetic or social feelings. . . .

"The result is inevitable."

Each, in consequence, has a greater regard for his own safety or happiness than for the safety or happiness of others, and, where these come in opposition, is ready to sacrifice the interests of others to his own. And hence the tendency to a universal state of conflict between individual and individual, accompanied by the connected passions of suspicion, jealousy, anger, and revenge— followed by insolence, fraud, and cruelty—and, if not prevented by some controlling power, ending in a state of universal discord and confusion destructive of the social state and the ends for which it is ordained. This controlling power, wherever vested or by whomsoever exercised, is *Government*.

———The *Disquisition*, St. John continued, expounds Calhoun's theory in a different political vocabulary from the Declaration of Independence. He will have no truck with natural rights and the proposition that all men are created free and equal. In one of his Senate speeches, he brought Adam and Eve to the fore. The Bible, he reminded colleagues, reports that only two human beings were *created*. All others thereafter were born. Moreover, you cannot say, all men are born equal; you must say, all men are born infants, and you cannot say that all infants are born equal because all infants differ in a thousand ways; and you cannot say all infants are born free, for they all are born subject to parents, guardians, or elders without whose care they would quickly expire. He concluded there was "not a word of truth in the whole proposition as expressed and generally understood."

Nor does Calhoun indulge in the language of rights. Rights are what can be won by power. Only power can counter power, not necessarily power in the sense of force, but particularly in the meaning the '87 Constitution uses as it vests power in Congress or the president.

As for men's predominantly selfish nature, there are exceptions, to wit, women. A mother's care for her infant shows the strength of social nature, and under certain circumstances, so may education and habit. But, Calhoun qualifies, these instances are few and always regarded as something extraordinary.

Personally, I don't see mother–infant relations as few and extraordinary, but he does at least manage to mention women. Anyway, the sweet, social side of man's nature invites him into society, while the stronger self-centered individualist side impels him into government, the latter being necessary to preserve and prosper the former.

Of course Calhoun's portrait of human nature is simple, and I've made it even simpler by skipping around. All political philosophers make a similarly simple assessment of human nature, and they are usually ingenious in working out what follows.

This nature wherein man loves himself rather more than his neighbor is a gift of God—the Infinite Being, the Creator of all—who has assigned to man a social and political state best adapted "to develop the great capacities and faculties, intellectual and moral, with which he has endowed him and has, accordingly, constituted him so as not only to impel him into the social state, but to make government necessary for his preservation and well-being."

But, and this is a big But, government calls for governing or administering which, if it is to be done at all, has to be done by men who like all men are subject to suspicion, jealousy, anger, revenge, insolence, fraud, and cruelty issuing from the self-centered part of their nature. Thus government will fall into abuse and disorder.

Government is God-contrived: like breathing, one cannot will to avoid it. However, to make and keep government good, something else, man-contrived, is needed. That something is a constitution whose primary principle is to keep rulers obedient to the community they govern. A constitution will manage to do that through the ballot which represents "the right on the part of the ruled to choose their rulers at proper intervals and to hold them responsible for their conduct" and thus to convert them from "rulers into agents." From this description, it is clear, Calhoun's constitution will be republican.

But we must *but* with another *but*: the ruled like the rulers, or the people like the government, are men too, alas. They all will have their private interests and will try somehow to twist government and laws to their purposes at the expense of the common interest. To control the government a struggle to form a majority will take place among the various interests. These interests will congeal into two great parties. The major party will gather to itself the great advantages of wealth, honors, and command that inevitably gravitate to those in big government; it will sooner or later control all three branches of government, and execute its laws at will.

We've arrived at a roadblock. Men cannot keep putting another government atop the electorate to channel and restrain individualistic natures: that other government will need another constitution to control itself, and that constitution will need another electorate to elect another government, and so on to infinity. A power of some kind is lacking in constitutions (and that is why most of them are short-lived), the power to offset the power of the majority's selfish aims.

That counterpower—and, again, only power can counter power— will have to be lodged with the side of majority-rule government that is typically oppressed: the minority.

One might bring up at this point one or two objections. Calhoun cannot be thinking of the worldwide application of the majority-minority clash. He knows that most governments in the world do not have written constitutions, nor try to restrain rulers by ballot, nor believe in the fairness, dispatch, or wisdom of majority rule. Second, when Calhoun speaks of a minority he doesn't mean the leftover of a majority victory at the polls, a statistical minority that has no consciousness of itself and can be divided by statisticians into a hundred categories of height, weight, sex, political preference, eye color, and oh yes, socioeconomic status. Calhoun intends a "long-standing minority," a self-conscious one with a history. The minority par excellence is the southern section of a group of States, the South, distinct in its way of life from the northern section.

A divide between the northern and southern States had always existed. The Congress, you may recall, made George Washington commander in chief, not just because of the military experience testified by his wearing a sword to meetings, but also because the New Englanders hoped that by choosing a southerner to captain all forces, they might hurry the lagging South into the battle against England. When Washington mentioned to Jefferson that he was thinking of retiring after his first term, Jefferson begged him to stay: "North and

South will hang together," he wrote in May of 1792, "if they have you to hang on."

Long before the '87 Constitution was ratified, the two areas recognized ethnic, economic, and religious differences between themselves. Richard Henry Lee's letter of October 1, 1787, to another southerner, George Mason, already saw majority discrimination in the proposed '87 Constitution: "the greatness of the powers given and the multitude of Places to be created produces a coalition of Monarchy men, Military Men, Aristocrats and Drones whose noise, impudence and zeal exceeds all belief—Whilst the Commercial plunder of the South stimulates the rapacious Trader." In a letter of 1785, Thomas Jefferson once penned for a foreign friend a description in parallel columns of the cultures:

In the North they are	In the South they are
cool	fiery
sober	voluptuary
laborious	indolent
persevering	unsteady
independent	independent
jealous of their own liberties, and just to those of others	zealous for their own liberties, but trampling on those of others
interested	generous
chicaning	candid
superstitious and hypocritical in their religion	without attachment of pretentions to any religion but that of the heart.

Huggins brightened. "Maybe there were two countries rather than one, two countries with no name."

"Good point, but not quite. They were neither two countries nor two sectors of one country. The 'South,' like the 'North,' is a common noun. Each referred to a geographical cluster of culturally allied States, restive members of a union or association of States that included both of them. It's getting harder and harder to find a single country to name."

★ ★

————Calhoun's solution, you see, does not have to apply to a country. The case in hand for him is the government of an association or union entitled the United States. The remedy he offers is to give the well-defined, long-standing minority the basis for a power that it doesn't have in ordinary majority-rule constitutions— the power of vetoing any laws of the majority that oppress it. Such a countervailing power was the tribunate in the ancient Roman constitution. A tribune had the power to veto laws harmful to the interest of the Roman people or plebs. Calhoun gives other historical examples, but the Roman one is perhaps the most familiar. No, correction, the more familiar example is the jury of twelve jurors tried and true. "So say we one, so say we all." If but one disagrees, the majority verdict is blocked. With a written veto power grounded in a constitution, the majority will be forced to negotiate with the minority and come to a deal. They will then reach an agreement far more just and secure than a mere, ordinary *numerical* majority. That new agreement which has thus taken the minority into account Calhoun calls the sense of a *concurrent* majority.

Such a resolution of conflict offers greater security: it removes the grievance the minority has, a grievance that may lead it to resistance. And it is more just: it gives tongue to hitherto silenced voices. As a result a government, a union, an association, or a country will be more harmonious, the social part of men's nature will express itself more easily, and the constitution has a chance at long life.

The solution could resolve or stave off many crises but not all. It was not failproof. Calhoun never claimed it was. Even so, he suffered from the collective delusion: faith in the power of written documents. A written document enacting a minority-veto law might indeed have the conciliatory effect he hoped for, but it would not suffice to counter the power of moneyed interests claiming to be fighting with the angels against the forces of evil. The North could cripple or even repeal a minority-veto amendment or encourage the courts to an opportune construction.

A majority could not be expected to give up power voluntarily. Calhoun's own description of the joys and benefits of running big government portrays them as an irresistible temptation to men's selfish instincts.

★ ★

Huggins jumped in excitedly. "But isn't that just what the Framers provided for? From what I heard, they didn't think men were angels. That's why their constitution is full of checks and balances. If it wants to, the minority can block the majority by Congress's overriding the president, or by the Senate's blocking the House, or by the supreme court's blocking Congress, as we saw yesterday in *Marbury v. Madison*. By the time a bill goes through all those blocks, a minority would have a chance to get a wedge in somewhere and reach, what did he call it, a concurrent majority?"

"Oliver," said St. John, "I'm going to propose you for a scholarship. Name the university of your choice. Your observation is very good. Calhoun, that canny Scot, took it into account."

Huggins had stopped listening. "The university of his choice," she'd said? He already knew what that was: the same university *she* attended—much as he disliked her. He forced his mind back on track.

"You can have as many checks and balances as the Venetian Republic," she was saying. "What matters is the '87 Constitution wherein every one of these checkers and balancers—the president, Congress, even the appointed supreme court—are where they are because of majority rule, they owe what they are to majority or at least to plurality tallies.

"As you yourself indicated, Oliver, when clarifying the '87 Constitution as a contract: the president, Congress, and the court all make up the one party of the agent. Do you remember?"

"Right," said Huggins back on cue.

———A government, Calhoun insisted, could not be the judge of last resort in questions between itself and its principal. He condemned the idea of one great nation "with the right to construe finally and conclusively, the extent of its own powers and to enforce them at the point of the bayonet." The government of this union has become "as absolute as that of the Autocrat of Russia."

The tax power of the government provides a good example of how the majority oppresses the minority. The government collects taxes from its citizens and then spends the revenue received. A percentage of that money will go to its own personnel expenses or overhead like salaries, wages, and buildings, the ordinary costs of government. What happens to the rest of it? The rest goes back to the taxpayers. How?

The government cannot give it back to them in the same percentage they contributed in taxes. It must distribute the money differently. Otherwise taxes might just as well be handed back to the taxpayers in the amount they paid less expenses. What would be the point of that?

"None at all," replied Huggins automatically, pulling out of reverie just in time. He had been crossing Harvard Square, idling in Sproul Plaza, strolling along the Midway, and cutting past Nassau Hall—with Claire. She, obviously not given to reverie, still pursued taxes and tariffs.

————The government may collect taxes from all equally but must distribute taxes (or whatever goods and services they purchase with the taxes) unequally. This unequal and unavoidable fiscal action of the government will "divide the country into two great classes—tax-payers and tax-consumers." A tariff on imported goods is a form of indirect tax, levied on whoever must purchase the goods at a price increased by the tariff. Given the nature of men, the majority in control of law-making will use the taxing or tariff power not for the common benefit but to feather its nest, plucking the minority bare to leave it shivering in goose pimples.

When writing the *Disquisition*, Calhoun did not cite the South as an example, though to everyone who knew of his career in the Senate, it was obvious that the analysis applied to the growing tension between North and South. In the question of taxpayers versus tax-consumers, between those who bore the burden and those who received the bounty, he was placing the problem, then and for decades agitating the South, in its proper theoretical setting—a problem of all governments that rely on a numerical majority.

At first the southern States and Calhoun had not objected to a moderate tariff, but as it increased and seemed never to be lifted, they pointed out that the South was paying higher and higher prices for whatever they had to buy—and they had to buy everything except cotton, sugarcane, tobacco, and moonshine. Many southerners like Governor Robert Y. Hayne of South Carolina wore rough homespun cloth to protest the costly tariff-rigged British broadcloth. The government got revenue from the tariff; northern States got a higher price for their manufactured goods; the southern States—producers of agricultural goods largely for export to foreign countries—paid the bill. Fifty years of this had depleted the South's capital.

"What about slavery?" Huggins asked brusquely.

"The 'agitation about slavery,' Calhoun believed, was spawned by extremist groups in the Northeast, which, if not stopped, would endanger the union. I plan to talk more about this tomorrow."

————Underneath the slavery and tariff issues, she went on, crouched a constitutional crisis. Calhoun said with a sense of doom, "Equilibrium . . . between the two sections . . . has been destroyed."

To feel the foreboding in this statement, think for a moment of the written constitution as an attempt to stop history. Of course those who craft it, generally the rich and well-born, wish to keep themselves and those like them and their posterity in a position to make the important rules, perpetually. To do this they will have to throw opponents a sop or two, such as a difficult revision or amendment procedure. Having reached agreement or equilibrium among themselves, they write up an instrument and get it authorized according to prevailing standards. Later, if conditions change so that one or more of the parties become convinced that the initial equilibrium has broken down and that they are trapped, a constitutional crisis arises. History is on the move again.

The '87 Constitution, balancing the number of States, their population and economic strength, achieved an equilibrium of sorts between North and South. This simple though uneasy partnership fast gave way to an economically dominant North and a subordinate South saddled with heavy burdens. The influx of immigrants into northern parts and the Westward ho! trudging of populations created new States—more than doubling the original thirteen—whose ties and sympathies led mainly to the North.

Article IV, Section 3, of the '87 Constitution stipulated that "New states may be admitted by the Congress into this union." In Calhoun's day the clause was on everyone's tongue. With thousands of miles of western and (especially after the Mexican War) southwestern lands now occupied and coming of an age to seek admission to the union of the United States, slavery within their borders became an explosive issue. The struggle raged over Senate seats (two to each State) and, somewhat less, over House seats (according to the State's population).

Meanwhile, the South felt, the North was trying to discourage population from moving to the South and Southwest, was allowing Quakers and abolitionists to use the pulpit, newspapers, printing presses, and government mail to attack its southern sister States, to denounce agrarian slave labor as an abomination (when in truth compared to industrial wage-slavery it was a benefaction), and to paint a conflict between two economic systems as the eternal struggle of Good and Evil.

So, the greater growth in technology and immigration in the North and the westward dispersal of population upset the apple cart. The South lost law-making power while the North gained congressional dominance and aimed to keep it. It had the power to pass tariff laws protecting its industries and holding the South captive as a market for its tariff-rigged prices. The South wanted the old equilibrium back where it was one of two more or less equal partners and could try to defend itself against exploitation.

Such was the constitutional crisis. One side or the other had to give way. The South couldn't move: its economic, cultural, and political life was at stake. The North was not vitally threatened, Calhoun thought. It could repeal harmful laws, dampen abolitionist vituperation, help make a fairer North/South balance of voting power out of the new populations and States and, to prevent future constitutional crises, sponsor an amendment for a minority veto. Calhoun begged Congress to propose such an amendment. Congress wouldn't hear of it, though warned that without it, the constitution, relying on a *numerical* majority, would prove to have a short life.

Back of the *Disquisition*, then, one feels the pressure of this ongoing, bitter struggle of North versus South.

★ ★

"Do you remember, Oliver, the day last week when you arrived late, out of breath, in your tennis shorts?"

Huggins smiled.

"I'm sure you do," said St. John with a smile to equal his. "I mentioned then that the idea of voluntary consent of the people was an inseparable part of the ideas of contract and written constitutions."

————Here, she continued, is where Calhoun's fight against the numerical majority as the sense or consent of the community takes on value. For, if consent is given by acclamation which presumes a comparatively small and assembled people, or if by 100 percent vote, Calhoun would not object. Such occurrences are rare, unless faked—ballot boxes stuffed to 102 percent, acclamation staged by mass rallies in squares and arenas. Consent by majority rule, however, always leaves a minority that has not given consent. Calhoun wants to enable that minority to count for something.

The grievous error, writes Calhoun in the *Disquisition*, is to mistake the numerical majority for all the people, and this so completely as to regard them as identical: to believe that if a majority consents, the whole people is consenting. The defense is often made that all the people agree implicitly before voting to acquiesce in the majority decision. This argument works only so long as issues are not bitter. If they are fiercely contested, the question of nonconsent arises. The counterargument is that there was no implicit agreement or that not everyone voted or that the tallies omit minority consent. Then—as between North and South—neither side gives in. With or without a constitutional power of nullification, with a concurrent majority or with a mere numerical majority, it doesn't matter, a clash follows. The next phase is the splitting of unity, the dissolution in part or in whole of the union.

The idea of the consent of the people is as old as the hills. Political philosophers have used it in ways that evidently made some sense in their respective times. More recently, after the social contract webs spun by Hobbes, Locke, and Rousseau (don't worry about these names—you'll get an earful of them at school), after the massive growth in the voting body and the spread of the idea that the ballot expresses consent, their notions begin to seem vague. It is Calhoun who halts them and orders about-face, march! Do 100 percent of you consent? If not, what are the proportions of consenters to dissenters? Those in the majority will have their representatives and their laws. Who is to represent the minority? Who to enact *its* laws, to guarantee *its* freedom?

The predicament was prefigured at the 1830 annual Jeffersonian celebration dinner. In a famous exchange of toasts, President Jackson stood up and raised his glass, and glaring at the vice-president proposed, "Our Union. It must be preserved!" Vice-President Calhoun, no more cowed by the president than Floride was, arose, and glaring back at Jackson, lifted his glass in challenge. "The Union, next to our Liberty, most dear!"

If looks could kill, two Scotch-Irish would have fallen over the table dead, still glowering.

A couple of years later, South Carolina in a special convention at Columbia proclaimed that within its boundaries the Tariff Acts of 1828 and 1832 were null and void, and began requiring the oaths of allegiance I described last Friday. Jackson alerted federal troops and forts in South Carolina. In anticipation of trouble, Charleston became a city in arms. After recommending a scaling down of the tariff, Jackson on December 10, 1832, addressed the South Carolinians in a Proclamation: "Fellow citizens of my native state, to say that any state may secede . . . is to say that the United States is not a nation." He warned: "Disunion by force is treason." Privately he threatened that if one drop of blood was shed in defiance of the laws of the United States, he would hang the first of the nullifiers he could lay his hands on. If that happened to be John C. Calhoun, so much the better.

The president asked Congress for a bill allowing him to enforce the tariff laws militarily. Congress obliged with what became known as the Bloody Bill. To the South this was the writing on the wall.

For the present, the South elected to save face, but it was learning a sequence of steps, a sequence that Calhoun had laid out with remorseless logic.

Step 1: Nullify oppressive United States laws as they operate in your own State.

If the United States government threatens military force against

State judges and officers, or to collect revenues, take Step 2: Separate from the union of States, withdraw, secede.

If the government and other States threaten to use force to keep you from seceding, you've arrived at Step 3: Cave in or fight.

The second time around, in 1860, with Abraham Lincoln in place of Andrew Jackson, the South at Step 3 elected to fight.

Huggins demonstrated scholarly curiosity. "Where did these ideas of nullifying and seceding come from?"

"You know, Oliver," obliged his tutor, "just as you may be an expert on contracts, I'm an expert on secessions. The idea of a State's nullifying laws of the United States and seceding from that association did not first show up in the 1830s with Calhoun and South Carolina. We may speak of nullification and secession, real or threatened, as a tradition of the United States. I'll sketch for you a short series of threats."

————When Congress in 1798 passed the Alien and Sedition Acts, no less a figure than Jefferson wrote opposing resolutions approved by the Kentucky legislature (while Madison wrote similar ones approved by Virginia) declaring that "by compact under the style and title of a constitution for the United States" the several States composed "a general government for special purposes" and "that the government created by this compact was not made the exclusive or final judge of the powers delegated to itself . . . but that as in all other cases of compact among parties having no common judge . . ."

"Here, Oliver, he made the same point you made about the lack of an independent tribunal."

"Thomas Jefferson did?" Huggins puffed up. "So . . . maybe I'm not the preppy jock you think."

"Hmm," hummed St. John, and picked up the loose end of her topic.

————And, Jefferson underlined, ". . . *each party has an equal right to judge for itself, as well of infractions as of the mode and measure of redress.*" He concluded that therefore the Sedition Act "which does abridge the freedom of the press, is not law but is altogether void and of no effect."

The last sentence exemplifies State nullification of a law of the United States. Jefferson's earlier phrase about a State's right to judge "the mode and measure of redress" it will take, does not exclude secession or war. Calhoun acknowledged that his position was corroborated by the Kentucky Resolutions.

Yesterday I spoke of Federalist apprehension upon Jefferson's election, the so-called Revolution of 1800. The strength of Jefferson's party continued to grow in the by-elections to Congress in 1802, the year Calhoun entered Yale as a junior. In the following year, the Louisiana Purchase threw leading New England Federalists into a tizzy. When they thought of this new vast territory they foresaw their influence on the wane. Ohio, admitted as a state in the same year, had soon fallen in Virginia's sphere.

Little did they expect that eventually most new States would change direction and align with them. Their view was that the Louisiana domain would soon upset the original North/South equilibrium and give too much power to the South. This eventuality, they reasoned, absolved the thirteen States from their adherence to the '87 Constitution. The Revolution of 1776, a Massachusetts senator said, "pointed to the remedy—a separation." Well-connected men in Massachusetts and Connecticut secretly laid plans for a northern confederacy of New England and New York, to free themselves from the corrupting influence and oppression of the South. If Vice-President Aaron Burr's candidacy for governor of New York proved successful, he was to bring that State into the confederacy. Burr lost the election; the northern confederacy foundered.

The enterprising Burr then contrived an even more likely secession conspiracy. The plot went through different stages. The plan in 1805 was to detach Louisiana territory from the United States with the help of the British, and invade and annex Mexico, whereupon the Mississippi Territory would fall voluntarily into the projected new empire. The governor of the Louisiana Territory, a marvel of duplicity, already in the pay of Spain, decided to betray his old friend Aaron Burr. He wrote to Jefferson of the conspiracy, keeping his own skirts clean, of course. Jefferson ordered Burr arrested and brought to trial for treason. The Marshall court acquitted him. As this secession plot was unrolling, Calhoun was attending law school in Litchfield, Connecticut.

The next separation move, during James Madison's presidency, again took place in New England, incensed this time over the blocking of shipping trade during the War of 1812–1814 with England. New England States furious with "Mr. Madison's War," the doings of "that little man in the Palace," refused to call up their militias, claimed the right to nullify federal law in their respective States and threatened secession as their right and duty, basing their reasoning on the Kentucky and Virginia Resolutions. Gouverneur Morris, our hero of the '87 Constitution, condemned the war and came out for secession from that "more perfect union" he worked so gloriously to frame.

Massachusetts, having batted about for a year or two the idea of a convention to revise the '87 Constitution, summoned Rhode Island, Connecticut, New Hampshire, and Vermont to a meeting. A secret convention took place at Hartford, Connecticut, on December 15, 1814. The extreme wing of the Federalists wished to draft a new constitution, present it to the original thirteen States alone, leaving out the new western States. If they were accepted, there would be a new, an 1815 Constitution; if not, New England was prepared to negotiate a separate peace with Old England.

The convention proposed a few constitutional amendments which went nowhere; delegates were proceeding to Congress with them when news came of Jackson's resounding victory over the British in the Battle of New Orleans. The Federalist party, after toying with secession twice in one decade, never recovered its reputation as the patriotic advocate for a single great country.

One of the Hartford convention's aims was to cut off the "Virginian Dynasty" of presidents. Virginia denounced the convention as treasonable. Whatever news got around of the Hartford scheme would have come immediately to Calhoun's attention. He was then a new Congressman.

So we may speak of a tradition of secession and conclude also that Calhoun was well acquainted with it. But he goes further than earlier theorists. He attacks the advocates of one big country at their underbelly. He—

★ ★

Huggins broke in. "You've been talking for a long time, and all this is fascinating, but I don't see you doing what you said: that you'd concentrate on those points in the '87 Constitution where no name for country forced the Framers to circumnavigate—I think you said circumnavigate—points like "the supreme law of the land," "We, the People of the United States," and the oath "to preserve the constitution." Huggins finished with folded arms and a so-there look on his face. He had planned this little outburst and thought he had done rather well.

"Huggins, you are too much. I've just been running with the ball around left end, a clear fifteen yards for a touchdown ahead of me. Didn't you hear what I just quoted President Jackson as saying? That a State could not secede because *the United States* was a nation?

"Now look at what I wrote on the wall." St. John stretched out an arm to point to the big sheet she had pinned up earlier. "It was hanging in front of you when you came in but you ignored it. Please read it," she said, nodding at the makeshift screen, "and tell me who said that."

Huggins looked up with a this-is-baby-stuff attitude. He screwed his eyes, pretending to make out with difficulty St. John's oversized script, then proceeded to read it aloud:

THERE IS, INDEED, NO SUCH COMMUNITY, *POLITI-CALLY* SPEAKING, AS THE PEOPLE OF THE UNITED STATES, REGARDED IN THE LIGHT OF, AND AS CON-STITUTING ONE PEOPLE OR NATION.

"Who said that?" insisted St. John.

"Damn," muttered Huggins under his breath. One of these days he was going to catch her off base. One of these days? He didn't have many days left. St. John crossed and recrossed her legs, distracting him even more. She wasn't wearing stockings today; her skin . . .

Finally he quipped: "*You* said it."

"Very funny," ironized St. John. "Of course, at the time I *might* have said it and for some years thereafter too. It was written about 1845, over a half-century after the '87 Constitution. As you must have guessed by now, the one who wrote those lines, who denies that the United States are a nation, that a We the People of the United States ever existed, is John C. Calhoun.

"*You* said more or less the same thing," she added.

"I did?" Huggins was really surprised.

"Yes. Look again at what I've written on the board."

"Okay, I'm looking."

"Can you recall again your expert interrogation concerning the '87 Constitution as a contract?"

"Ye-es," said Huggins warily.

"What was the conclusion concerning the principal in the contract?"

Huggins snapped to. "The principal was inadequately identified and confusingly signed, and the contract therefore null, without legal force."

"And what was that principal called?"

The dawning sun shone through the clouds. " 'We, the People of the United States.' I get it."

"Correct. Calhoun is telling you now why those sharp lawyers at the Philadelphia convention seem so incompetent. That principal did not exist. You can cross that identity—one people united in a political community—off the list of possibilities. How can a nonexistent thing, a nothing, sign a document?

"You see, Calhoun answers the question we posed yesterday. Is the United States a country with no name or a country that as yet does not exist or whose existence is not certain enough to warrant a name or on whose existence there is still no agreement? His answer is, the United States as a country does not exist."

"President Jackson said that it does exist; the United States is a nation, *is*, singular."

"Sharp ear, there, Oliver. Jackson's is one of the earliest official uses of the singular. Maybe he used 'is' because he wasn't so good at grammar. But maybe also because he wanted to make 'the union' out to be a block of granite, one 'nation,' made up of one people alone, with himself the one legitimate leader, his head at the column's top, carved and polished unto marble. 'King Andrew the First' his detractors called him."

★ ★

————Calhoun won't have any of this rubbish. The term "national" is applied commonly to "the federal government of these States," he observed, while the term "federal" has almost entirely fallen into disuse. Even those who knew that the word "national" was repudiated by the Framers and "how falsely it is applied—have now slid into its use without reflection." The press "make me say, 'this Nation' instead of 'this Union,' " he complained. "I never use the word Nation. We are not a nation, but a Union, a confederacy of equal and sovereign States. England is a nation, but the United States are not a nation."

The term "nation" was and is one of those words that can mean opposites. Nation signifies a small country when applied to the Cherokees and a big one when applied to England. In the phrase "an infant nation," sometimes applied to the United States by Federalists, it meant a small country destined to get big. Yankee Doodle uses it to signify a huge measure. "It made a noise like father's gun, only a nation louder." To the northerners who had begun to use it, it was serviceable: it signified a country large enough to border on empire. And it was singular: a nation was a unity, it had no constituent parts such as the States held themselves to be. But *nation* denotes other things. It comes from the Latin "to be born," from which it takes the meaning of a place or community where over time a group of persons were born together and so blood-related, however thinly. The supposed blood tie may be stressed or downplayed but rarely excluded. We shall see Abraham Lincoln resorting to this meaning as the War of Secession reaches climax.

If you read *A Discourse on the Constitution*, you will find Calhoun following our thinking with fidelity.

"Following our thinking! He died before we were born!"

"For goodness' sake, Huggins, do you have to be so chronological, so linear? You're like an old railroad schedule."

Huggins sulked in his tent.

————Let me run back over some of Calhoun's positions, St. John proposed. Government issues from the God-contrived nature of man and needs no contract for its establishment. Constitutional government is a man-contrived contractlike attempt to better control that government. This particular constitution of the United States was written and signed by delegates of the several States, and ratified by other delegates of the several States. In composing the preamble, the convention delegates used the term "United States" (instead of listing the several States by name) because, they said they did not know then which of the several States would ratify the proposal. We covered this last week.

So, "We, the People of the United States" = "We, the People of the signatory States."

But there is a more important flaw. Calhoun hones the phrase down. Why did they write the word *People* in the singular? Each State, whether Pennsylvania or Georgia, had its people, didn't it? If the ratifiers were to be delegates from at least nine different States, each with its own people, why didn't the Framers write, We, the People*s* of the United States?

Because, remarks Calhoun, "the term 'people' has, in the English language, no plural, and is necessarily used in the singular number, even when applied to many communities or states confederated in a common union—as is the case with the United States."

"That sounds a bit fishy to me," objected Huggins.

"It did to me, too," St. John admitted. "But an earlier political thinker, John Taylor of Virginia, attacking John Marshall's assertion of a single people of the United States had also insisted that 'the people' meant the several peoples of the individual states. Thinking about this led me to realize that today, too, *peoples* is rarely used except to refer to nameless hordes, as in 'the migrations of peoples.' My curiosity piqued, I resorted to the *O.E.D.*" Oliver raised uncomprehending eyebrows. "The *Oxford English Dictionary*. And you know what? Calhoun was right! Here"—she handed him a slip— "I copied it down. Read," she ordered.

Huggins read out loud:

> *plural* **peoples**. This plural form was avoided in 16th century Bible versions, and by many 17th and 18th century writers. It was thought to require defence or explanation even in 1817 and 1830.

"Read further down, the example at *d*, the quotation from Thomas Jefferson."

1793 Jefferson. It will prove that the agents of the two people [the U.S. and France] are either great bunglers or great rascals.

Huggins was gaining a new respect for the power of research. "I'll be damned. So, if Gouverneur Morris were drafting today, he would have to write 'We, the Peoples of the United States.' How different that sounds."

St. John pursued her advantage. "Good stylist that he was, that's what Gouverneur Morris would have to write. But more correctly, 'We, the Peoples of the signatory States.' If he had had then to compose the phrase in the French he spoke so well, it would have been crystal-clear; he would not have been able to hide the plural for 'people' and for 'United States': *Nous, les peuples des États-Unis.*"

"That would have put the people back in the States."

"Where they belonged," added St. John smugly. She paused and then made a pronouncement.

"Calhoun's *s*, this is the fatal flaw."

————In two small books, she went on, Calhoun bound earlier expressions of separation-from-union into a comprehensive theory with scholarship, logic, and clarity, based on history, law, and a textual sounding of the '87 Constitution.

When our political philosopher was in his prime he drove his speeches with inexorable logic, his style concise, periods short, voice steady, delivery staccato. As he spoke he stood immobile, rooted in stone, eyes alone moving to target his words. In his last speech to the Senate on March 4, 1850, read by his colleague, he sat there, wrapped in a cloak, too weak to deliver it himself. Later that same month he died.

This constitution of the United States, with all its imperfections, John Calhoun regarded with admiration. The union it set up, he treasured and tried to preserve with all his might. South Carolina was the "dear and honored State" that has "never mistrusted nor forsaken me." He regarded her as his mother.

Patriotism, or in this instance, matriotism, does not take shape in the South Carolinian's political philosophy, which is too bad. Had he bent his keen mind to it, he would have realized that the sorts of analysis he applied to power, tariffs, and taxes might not work so well if applied elsewhere in political life, that here at least was a phenomenon that did not readily respond to whether one was a taxpayer or a tax-consumer, a phenomenon that went almost equally across the board—the South Carolinian's love of South Carolina.

"We have talked now and then about a country with no name, haven't we, Oliver?"

"We sure have," Huggins concurred. "We've become name freaks."

St. John ignored the sarcasm, but Huggins had learned the diversionary ploy of asking a question. "What was the situation in Calhoun's time?" he asked. "About names, I mean."

"I'll tell you a tale," decided tutor.

————In March 1845, the New-York Historical Society appointed a committee to report upon the subject of the "irrelevant appellation, at present used for this country." That appellation is "the United States"; *irrelevant*, it becomes clear, because it is a multiple term used for a single country. The Committee on a National Name, so it was called, was to seek a name that was "both single and distinctive." Its passionate report repays quotation.

> What we want is a sign of our identity. We want utterance for our nationality. We want a watchword more national than that of states, more powerful than that of party. We want the means of proclaiming by one word our union into one nation. We desire to see written on the pages of the world's history, one name. . . . Our condition is altogether anomalous. There never before has been a nation, of any consequence in the world, without its own appropriate distinctive name. . . . [T]he names [of the great nations] themselves re-acted as a spell upon their people, prompting them to heroic deeds, heightening and concentrating their love and pride of country.

Apparently, the committee disclosed, this was a subject "that from time to time, since the commencement of our national existence, has engaged the attention of some of our most eminent and patriotic citizens."

"Do you hear that, Oliver? You should be gratified: we have been working on a problem that has exercised some of our most eminent and patriotic citizens."

"That's news to me," Oliver acknowledged.

————Unfortunately, at the end the committee endorsed Washington Irving's suggestion to name the country "Alleghania." The society as a whole quite rightly felt that this was not the right name and rejected the choice. Meanwhile the report had been sent by circular letter to various historical societies (there were hardly any in the South and West) and "to eminent gentlemen throughout the country."

The Domestic Correspondence Secretary of the society, John Jay, whom I mentioned last week, the grandson of Washington's chief justice, seems to have taken a personal interest in the committee's work. His covering letter to the various societies and gentlemen made its own proposal, not for a geographical name but for a hero's name—"the Republic of Washington"—a name which "might be adopted by acclamation, and which if adopted, would be instantly recognized and identified in distant lands, and command the approval of the whole world."

This initiative by the New-York Historical Society was unique. At last a group of persons openly acknowledged the lack of a national name and considered steps to provide one. That John Jay's grandson played a leading role revealed that the initiative was Federalist or Whig in inspiration, taken by men who desired to see a consolidated or single country rather than a confederation of States.

By now they seemed to have realized that the absence of a proper noun name for country was favoring the doctrine of States' rights. One respondent candidly remarked that the effect of the lack of a name was "greatly to increase the value of our individual state names in our fancies, and we are more apt, wanting a pleasing general appellation, to call ourselves New Englanders, New Yorkers, Kentuckians and Carolinians, than Americans. . . . I have no doubt that the want of a general national name contributes much to our sectional individuality."

Doesn't this recall Washington's complaint in his farewell letter fifty years earlier about the strength of "local discriminations"?

Of great interest are the replies of some of the other eminent gentlemen. Martin Van Buren, ex-president and arch-foe of Calhoun, bitterly disappointed in 1844 at not being nominated again for president, doesn't say much; he had mislaid the report, replied late, doesn't see the necessity or expediency of a national name, probably hadn't read it through. William H. Seward, former governor of New York, writes back that "every man would wish that the fathers had established the name of the 'Republic of Washington,' " but that adoption now would be unpracticable. Joseph Story, supreme court justice and exponent of the one-people, one-nation view of the constitution's preamble, also regrets that the chance for naming had passed. Nonetheless he proposes another name, "Vesperia," to indicate the Western world, but has no hope for it nor for "Alleghania," and "I shall have preferred Columbia if it had not become the distinctive title of another nation." He too laments that the Framers had let occasion fly by. "I have long, in common with many of my countrymen, felt the inconvenience of my country not possessing a distinctive national name, and have regretted that when the convention framed the national constitution it had not affixed thereto a national name. If it had so done, by this time the novelty would have disappeared, and we should have acquired throughout the world the appellation thus assumed."

Senator Henry Clay, known as the Great Compromiser for his valiant efforts to legislate for both North and South, writes in reply of the difficulties in adopting a name now. "I am not sure that it would not excite with some, the frightful apprehension of a consolidation." He above all respondents puts the question explicitly in the context of secession: "If the great calamity of a dissolution of the Union should befall us, no common name that we might adopt would, in that direful contingency, be applicable to any of the dissevered parts." Events, we shall learn, proved him right. The separation of parts is approaching fast.

Replies come in also from a southernly direction. The Maryland Historical Society is firmly opposed to the adoption of a national name. These two simple words, the *United States*, the Society wrote, "express, in a single phrase, the character of our government, our perfect *State Sovereignty*, and still our perfect *National Union*."

There seem to be no kindred societies farther south except for the Georgia Historical Society in Savannah. It observes that the term the "United States" is acceptable because "*descriptive* of our federative character as a nation." The only other southern reply is also from Savannah, from one of the various gentlemen addressed. "States' rights men," he writes, "might say that we are satisfied to be Georgians or New Yorkers, and let the confederation retain the appellation of United States."

In sum, the southern reply stresses States' rights, State sovereignty, the federative nature of the union, the appropriateness of the "United States" as the title of that union, and contentment with their own proper names as sovereign States.

In this report of the Committee on a National Name we detect important changes: the naming of the country is openly identified as a problem; and North and South take opposing stands—the one worried about the lack of a name and hoping against hope for a consolidated nation to apply it to, the other seeing nothing wrong with the existing common noun description of the union government, resting comfortable and happy in the bosom of their old names.

Calhoun, too, is content with the "United States" so long as one keeps in mind that it's a plural description of an association. Having determined that no people or nation or country of the United States exists, he goes on to deny that one such people ever did exist. So there cannot be one country or nation called the United States or Columbia or anything else. It was not that there was a country with no name. There was no country to name.

No one people, no one country, no one name.

If there was no country, what was there?

This leaves a government framed by a group of States united for limited purposes, in whose separate peoples rests the sovereignties of free and independent States. At present, this government backed by a majority of these States, located geographically in the North and West, takes steps to keep the States in the South from their wish to "part in peace," coercive steps destroying any notion that the association is voluntary and based on consent.

Calhoun foresaw that an attempt by the government to compel his State by arms would "be resisted at every hazard . . . even that of death. . . . It is madness to suppose that the Union can be preserved by force."

The Union was on its way to dissolution. For lack of an *s*, a war was fought. In the next generation the corpses would pile up.

Huggins asked, "What do you think would have happened if Calhoun had wanted and been able to control his wife? Could he have stayed on Jackson's good side and become president?"

"I suppose so, if he had also been able to cage the cagey Van Buren."

"If he'd been elected president, do you think there would have been a war?"

"These *ifs* end up in guesswork. My guess is that he would have tried much harder to strike a bargain. But let's not get ahead of ourselves. We'll understand the possibilities better once we see how Lincoln played them."

Huggins was loath to let the session end. "You said you need 100 percent for consent. What if only 1 percent dissents? What if the minority is one man alone?"

"Oliver, you amaze me! Sometimes I wonder how you do it. That's the very thing I plan to talk about tomorrow."

Huggins hung in. "You seem to admire Calhoun. I notice you didn't criticize him much."

"I notice that *you* introduced some criticisms."

"Yes, but if you had to make just one, right now, what would it be?"

St. John thought this over. "I do wish he'd had a sense of humor."

9

THOREAU PITS CONSCIENCE
AGAINST CONSTITUTION

WEDNESDAY

"Did you ever see a portrait of Thoreau?" asked Claire St. John.

"No, I don't think so," answered Huggins.

"If you had I would have asked you to describe it. I must take you to Washington some day and lead you by the hand through the halls of the National Gallery."

Take him by the hand? thought Huggins. A little school-class outing, not a bad idea. He replied sweetly, "Be nice if we didn't have to stick to looking at portraits."

"Yes indeed," said St. John blandly. "I doubt we'd find Thoreau anyway, but we could shift to still lifes. For today pull up your chair. I've got a whale of a tale, of an individualist male. Oh, by the way, speaking of males, I've been thinking of inviting a friend of mine in my place tomorrow to talk about Lincoln. She's here for the day."

"Is she Chinese by any chance?" asked Huggins maliciously.

"No, she's from south of the border, and beautiful."

"No, thank you," said Huggins firmly. "I've got enough to handle as it is. You're supposed to be my tutor. Let's leave it at that."

"The subject of her thesis is Lincoln's peace efforts." St. John went on as if she hadn't heard him. "You'd like her. Every bit as beautiful as Peggy O'Neill."

Huggins was not thinking of more or less beauty. What relation was this female to his tutor? He recognized the pangs of jealousy. Can you believe it? He, jealous of another woman.

"If I were a man, I'd be tailing her, chasing her down the street," persisted St. John.

What was *that* supposed to mean? The unhappy Huggins looked at her closely. She wasn't teasing, she was determined.

"Thank you, no," said Huggins with equal determination.

"So be it. You'll have to be satisfied with the portrait of Peggy O'Neill. Now for this tale. I'm going to give it a name—'The Beard of Stubborn Refusal.' "

———It is 1830. The man is forty-two years old, of sturdy Yankee stock, and of various intellectual and literary interests. When he left his nearby farm and came to live in town, he had grown a beard. Now if you'll conjure up the portraits of Washington, Jefferson, Madison, and Hamilton, and I'll throw in Marshall and Calhoun for good measure, you'll note that most of them carry a fair crop of hair on the head but not one whisker on the face. Not one of the signers of the Declaration of Independence and of the '77 and '87 Constitutions sprouted a beard. Uncle Sam, by this time a standard cartoon figure, was long and lanky with a tall crowned hat, much as he is today, except that he smoked a cheroot and shaved clean as a whistle. No one could recall a bewhiskered great-grandfather. The last person anyone remembered to have worn a beard was Captain John Smith.

Along comes this man, then, with his flowing beard. He may have been preparing himself for a life of civil resistance: he was asking for trouble. Soon boys threw stones at him, calling him "Old Jew." Grown men jeered, women sniffed and huffed away, clutching their skirts. Some ruffians shattered the windows of his house. The old local doctor told him to his face he should be prosecuted for growing such a monstrosity.

But when the local minister gave him a bawling out, he turned on the man with a slew of Biblical praises of the beard—he knew them all. One communion Sunday as he knelt at the altar, the minister offering the bread and wine passed him by. The enraged would-be communicant jumped up to the altar, took a hearty swig of the cup, and shouted, "I love my Jesus as well and better than any of you!"

A few days later in Merrie Olde New England four men mugged him, threw him down, and held him on the ground. The town's verdict, they claimed, was that the beard had to go. Flourishing scissors, soap, brush, and razor, they tried to shear him. Our hero, however, pulled out a jackknife and laid about like a whirling dervish, cutting two of the amateur barbers in the leg and setting all four to scampering. He pulled himself upright, the cuts on his face dribbling blood down his whiskers.

For daring to defend the beard—unprovoked assault the judge called it—he was arrested and fined. He refused to pay the fine and stayed in the county jail for a year, at first in solitary confinement. Even in jail he had to defend his beard's chastity, beating off would-be violators, whether jailers or prisoners, it was all the same to him. Meanwhile he managed to smuggle letters out to a newspaper. The citizens of Massachusetts, always ready to fight or persecute for a moral issue, began to take his side. Research proved that nothing in the Massachusetts or federal constitution or in local ordinances forbade bewhiskered facial adornment.

Caught in the shifting tides of moral indignation, the sheriff, to get rid of him, suggested he move out and forget it ever happened. Nothing doing. "I won't walk a single step toward freedom," he shouted at the throng outside the prison bars. The judge and jailers had put him in there, they would have to put him out. Which they did. The sheriff and jailers, to his cries of "Heathens!" lifted him, chair and all, and set him down in the street.

Thereafter no one came along with scissors and razor to shear his facial locks. No minister refused him communion. Having beaten off the shavers, antislavery became his cause. He was a celebrity. Emerson came to see him, Thoreau, too, and sat down with him to baked beans and bread and butter.

Huggins was confused. "Whoa! Which Thoreau? His brother? Does he have a brother? How many Thoreaus are there?"

"Thoreau? Who said anything about Thoreau?" said St. John. "I've been telling you about that unrenowned New England individualist, Joseph Palmer. His marble headstone—he died in 1875—bears his name and dates, a medallion depicting the prophet's head and beard, and the legend: 'Persecuted for Wearing the Beard.' "

Huggins didn't like to be taken in. "What has this got to do with Thoreau?" he demanded. "Just that he had a beard, too?"

"Did he? Are you sure he did? Maybe we just think he did. Anyway, something about Joseph Palmer reminds me of Thoreau. For one thing, they lived about the same time in the same country of Massachusetts. You see, as I promised, we are moving away from Virginia and South Carolina. From the horsey South, we are traveling to that other cradle of great men—preachy New England."

——From this part of the seaboard in the second quarter of the 1800s emerged a countercurrent of religion and politics. A number of Protestant ministers felt that their creeds laced them up too tightly. They also were repelled by the party politics of Andrew Jackson, with its pandering to the common man—the farmers and mechanics, the wage earners and small producers—and by the mushrooming in the cities of New England and New York of banks, mills, factories, and trading companies. Added to these were everyday scenes of Irish Catholic immigrants swarming into the cities, turning them into sprawling, filthy hovels, polluting Anglo-Saxon culture and Protestant religion. Far away in the West new territories and States were cropping up. People were rushing to California and Oregon. Everyone could feel the center slipping. America the continent was moving westward. From the West, too, these clerics felt excluded.

They were not uneducated. At Harvard, turning away from the British empiricism and French materialism that relied on the tangible world, they picked up a nodding acquaintance with the German idealism and transcendentalism of Johann Fichte and the great Immanuel Kant and more accessibly in the writers Goethe and Novalis. They were better acquainted with the primitivism (the noble savage) and naturalism (the state of nature) of the Geneva-born Rousseau, and the English romantic poets—the great Coleridge and Wordsworth.

"Again, don't fret about these names, Oliver. You'll hear of them at whatever university you may go. It doesn't have to be Harvard nowadays. And likewise, you'll hear of the Hindus, the Buddhists, and the Confucians, whose world views our clergymen and their sons were dabbling in."

"What a hodgepodge," Huggins remarked.

"True, too true. All these foreign imports were wrapped in a hand-me-down cloak of puritan morality which they could not shed, try as they might. They called it transcendentalism, but we'd better think of it as New England transcendentalism to mark it off from Kant's, with which it had little similarity.

"Out of this mixed-up period comes a literary bent, sometimes called exaggeratedly the American Renaissance, its strength found in the great prose writers Nathaniel Hawthorne and Herman Melville. You've probably heard of *Moby Dick* . . ."

Huggins was not going to let that remark slip by. "And I've read *The Scarlet Letter*, and heard of *The Marble Faun*, too, in case you're interested."

"I *am* interested," St. John lifted her eyebrows, rounding her eyes, then lowering them, "and ankle-deep in admiration."

————In truth, she continued, one can debate whether Melville and Hawthorne were transcendentalists, though they exhibit some of the trademarks. The weaker literary group, the more definitely New England transcendental, consisted of the preacher-writers reacting with gentility, invidious manners, concern for the select individual about to be engulfed by urban masses. They railed against stultifying employment, greedy commercialism, short-sighted practicality, republican vulgarity, and stink-hole cities—and bully for them! They were among the first to attack these diseases. Too bad they were so moralistic and blown up with defensive superiority. Jefferson recognized the type early. "The noisy pretenders to exclusive humanity," he called them in an 1820 letter to La Fayette. These writers pictured themselves as a high caste, a happy few, an elite: We with our refined tastes and quivering morality, breathing and soaring above institutionalized things like churches and states, we know better.

If New England theology, Jacksonian party politics, and the material world of commerce, industry, and machines were bad, what was good? What did the transcendentalists have to offer? Immerging oneself in things of the spirit. Freedom, Nature, the stars, friendship, music—sent them into rhapsodies.

God spoke in metaphors of Nature, in whispering blades of grass, in time-packed droplets dripping down icicles, the swirl of leaves, the sound of birds swooping from trees, streaks of sunlight and shadow, shimmering pools, clouds dancing to winds. God was always talking, even in silence. Not necessarily the God of Jesus Christ but the Over-soul of which everything and everybody was part and parcel, the melange-God of all universal religions. Yet a chatty God, chattering through the buzzing of the bees and—

". . . and the cigarette trees and the soda water fountain," Huggins piped up.

"What's that?" St. John was puzzled.

"It's a folk song hoboes used to sing." Huggins glanced at the other side of the room, in the general direction of the small grand piano. "It's the opening line of 'The Big Rock Candy Mountain.' "

"Really? Do you know other songs like that?"

"Quite a few."

"Good! That gives you an edge in American history. The transcendentalists didn't go in much for that sort of song. They sang hymns and went in for middle names."

———Their leading light was Ralph Waldo Emerson, descended from a long line of clergymen, and himself until age thirty or so the pastor of the Second Church of Boston, his father's church before him. The titles of his essays give an inkling of his concerns: self-reliance, spiritual leaves, the Over-soul, intellect, manners, nature, politics. Nature, he wrote in *Nature*, his first book, published in 1836, "refers to essences unchanged by man; space, the air, the river, the leaf."

In the usage current among New England commercial and educated classes Emerson occasionally used the terms "American" and "the nation" (typically with the western domains in mind) much as "Columbia" had been used in an earlier generation. An influential lecture and essay of his titled "The American Scholar" urged writers to choose American themes, to distinguish their writings from foreign literature, to Write American. Though no longer a youth, Emerson arose from his chair to follow Horace Greeley's urging "Go West, young man" and his own map "America begins with the Alleghenies," taking long and frequent journeys westward on the lyceum circuits.

"What about James Fenimore Cooper?" asked the knowledgeable Huggins. "What about the Mohicans and Natty Bumppo?"

"I was about to mention them. Emerson traveled farther west than the Mohicans and had more than Indians in mind."

————To write American was not particularly a sign of patriotism. The Northeast was stuffed to the gills with the culture and literature of England. Emerson wanted to clear the cobwebs from his head with whooshes of fresh air. His journals cover the farms and mines and towns, the wagons, sleds, and trains of the Ohio, and peek as far west as the Rockies, places spiritually far removed from that disreputable entity, the state. "Every actual state is corrupt. Good men must not obey the law too well." So, the fewer laws and "the less government we have the better."

The solution to bad government would be "the appearance of the wise man; of whom the existing government is, it must be owned, but a shabby imitation." Emerson's enthusiasm for the wise man flows over into mysticism. "His relation to men is angelic; his memory is myrrh to them; his presence, frankincense and flowers." Among the closing sentences of his essay on "Politics" are these words: "I do not call to mind a single human being who has steadily denied the authority of the laws, on the simple ground of his own moral nature."

In his coterie was a remarkable woman, Sarah Margaret Fuller. "One of my luminaries," patriarch Emerson described her in a letter of introduction. She had graceful carriage; a long, pliant neck; and stringy, reddish blond hair that could have withstood more frequent washing. She wore homemade outlandish dresses of a vaguely mystery-of-the-Orient style, spoke in nasal tones, and blinked nervously. Quarrelsome in manner, she was ready to spit in the eye of any man. Fuller was a writer. Times were tough for women writers who had to work for a living and simultaneously argue that every barrier be thrown down, every path be laid open "to Woman as freely as to Man."

Emerson who, a contemporary charged, persisted in regarding her "as the glory of Columbia," gave her the job of editing *The Dial*, a literary journal he started. In its four years of life it became the chief literary vehicle of the transcendentalists, and in its first two years Margaret ran it. Theodore Parker, a well-known Unitarian minister, singled out the trouble with the magazine: it needed a beard. Emerson himself admitted that Margaret had "a mountainous ME," but the transcendentalists if lined up would have made up a long parade of swelled heads.

Though dubbed "the high priestess of Transcendentalism," Fuller was too red-blooded to remain a transcendentalist. She came to believe that the city no less than the country was part of nature and that romantic friendship was not the same as romantic love. The brother-sister relationship the transcendentalists aspired to was a fine and noble thing, but not enough for her. She continued her literary career in New York (once out of range of Boston you were no longer considered a transcendentalist), went abroad as a news correspondent, got married, and bore a child. Hadn't she once told a shocked Emerson, "I know all the people worth knowing in America [that is, New England] and I find no intellect comparable to my own."

In the Emerson circle, or rather, tangent to the circle, stood Henry David or David Henry or just plain Henry Thoreau. The name is French; the family had shifted the accent to the first syllable, English-wise, like "Thorough," as people sometimes spelled it, along with "Thoro," or "Thorow" as Hawthorne spelled it.

"What's in a name?" mumbled Huggins.

"A good deal, evidently," said St. John.

————The Thoreau we are interested in was baptized David Henry. When he was twelve, he signed a school essay Henry David. At home they called him Henry. Townsfolk knew him as David. After college he insisted that his name be listed on official documents as Henry David. Perhaps the Henry came from an uncle or other relation.

Certainly in France and England, and perhaps generally, *Henry* is more kingly than religious. Maybe David was too Biblical a name. He was better acquainted, he once wrote, with the scriptures "of the Hindoos, the Chinese, and the Persians, than of the Hebrews," though this is doubtful: his allusions to the Bible far outnumber those to all other great religions put together. His brother had a New Testament name—John—as did his father and his father's father, whose "Jean" easily became "John."

Thoreau died in 1862 of tuberculosis, a disease that had killed others of his family. He was buried in New Burying Ground in the Dunbar family plots of his mother's family. Several years later his remains were transferred to Sleepy Hollow Cemetery in a Thoreau group of plots. What's in a name, right, Oliver? A headstone there bears in Roman capitals the single name HENRY. That settles that.

Henry was the only one of the transcendentalists to be born and bred in Concord. But this was not enough to rank him high in Concord society. The first Thoreau crossed the Atlantic in the late 1680s, but he was a Frenchman after all, a Huguenot fleeing Catholic domination. *Thoreau* was not a local name. One grandfather and the female branch were of Scottish extraction. Of Anglo-Saxon blood there was little.

Yet our Thoreau preferred a Saxon lineage. A line of his verse celebrated "manly Saxon, leading all the race." His speculations on genealogy concluded that "from one branch of the family were descended the kings of England, and from another myself." He wanted to be taken for a Yankee, that is, a New Englander, and wrote of himself as one. Emerson in his funeral eulogy said "no truer American existed," thus situating him in Emerson's own Write American camp, and remarked that the Frenchness of his blood appeared "in singular combination with a very strong Saxon genius," all of which need not have been mentioned had there been no doubts on the subject. Lucky for us, his French ancestry deprived him of a family tree laden with the clergy that other transcendentalists boasted of and suffered from.

His father, John, appears to have been a quiet, good-looking man, a reader, fond of music, an amateur flautist. Also a reader, his mother, Cynthia Dunbar, daughter of a Massachusetts clergyman turned lawyer, Scottish in descent, comes across more as a talker and as a forceful woman. She dedicated herself to nature and the abolition of slavery. From his father, Henry inherited his quiet, contemplative side; from his mother, the agitated, do-good side.

Henry David's appearance was not prepossessing. He was five feet seven inches tall, of compact, medium build, with abundant fine dark hair, overhanging heavy eyebrows, large gray-blue eyes, a big, bony hooked nose, pursed full lips, a receding chin, sloping shoulders, a narrow chest, and a long, hirsute body balanced on short, strong legs. He had the habit of clenching a fist at his side, tensely. He spoke with a slight accent or burr, more Scottish than French.

His father John, after a few fruitless attempts at small business, had little capital left. He settled for a home industry and became a pioneer of the lead pencil. At last, at the end of his life, he was doing moderately well. The lead pencil, an object not to be found in nature, took final shape in France at the end of the 1700s after several centuries of experiment. Once perfected, it lightened the pen-and-ink load of the writer, especially the traveling writer, the keeper, like Thoreau, of journals and notebooks. Henry always kept in pocket, and sometimes under pillow, his diary and pencil. Seemingly simple, the pencil's manufacture required considerable equipment—settling tanks, grinding mills, heating crucible, hydraulic presses; the raw materials of graphite, clay, and selected woods; a series of processing steps; and a workplace at least as large as a big shed.

Given his parents' financial ups and downs, their strain to make both ends meet, Henry spent his early life in ten or more houses, always in Massachusetts—Concord, Chelmsford, and Boston.

His mother worried often about where the next dollar was coming from and sometimes that her son, who seemed loath to pursue an occupation, might become a loafer like her simpatico brother, Uncle Charles. One day—Henry was in his late teens—she threatened to push him from the nest. Henry, weeping, begged not to be thrown out in the cold. His sister Helen sprang to his defense, held on to him, wailing that she would never let Mother do that.

"My mother . . ." Huggins began.

St. John pricked up ears. "Your mother, what?"

Huggins smiled knowingly, sauntered over to the piano, and still standing, with his left hand began vamping the first and third beats of a bouncy three-eighths rhythm. To Claire's look of surprise, he began singing in an exaggeratedly tenor voice:

> *My mother thought that I would be*
> *a man of some renown*
> *but I am just a stumble-bum*
> *as I go ramblin' 'round, boys,*
> *as I go ramblin' 'round.*

St. John was pleased, he could tell. "What's that, another hobo song?"

"Yep."

"Can you play with two hands, too?"

"Yep."

"You must have had a piano tutor."

"I forgot to mention it," said Oliver.

"Henry played the flute, you know, but as he doesn't mention lessons, he must have taught himself, or sister Helen or Father taught him, maybe gave him the instrument he played on."

————His father worked with his hands at pencil-making and taught his son to use his hands, too. Emerson tells us that Henry could reach into a bushelful of pencils and pick up in quick handfuls an even dozen at a time. Father and Henry (at age twenty-seven) with the aid of a carpenter built a house for the family on the outskirts of Concord. Out of a couple of shanties that Father had bought from departing, unemployed Irish laborers (part of the growing, mobile labor force) they also put together a big shed for the pencil factory. So Henry was no stranger to manual work.

In reply to his Harvard class secretary's letter he described himself: "I am a Schoolmaster—a private Tutor, a Surveyor—a Gardener, a Farmer—a Painter, I mean a House Painter, a Carpenter, a Mason, a Day-Laborer, a Pencil-Maker, a Glass-paper Maker, a Writer, and sometimes a Poetaster."

I suspect that Henry's reputation as a jack-of-all-trades was built up by other transcendentalists who couldn't tell a good from a bad job of whitewashing or stone-masonry. Henry who didn't descend from a long line of all-thumbs, smooth-handed clergymen must have seemed the perfect all-around odd-jobs-man.

Making a virtue of necessity, he lorded the independence that his odd-jobs-manship afforded him: *he* was not bound to an employer and a daily job. Yes, but he depended on his own labor, and on several patron-employers who sometimes out of friendship or charity invented work for him to do in their house or on the property. When Emerson went to Europe he left his wife and children behind, and arranged for Thoreau to dwell and board in the house. In return, as Emerson described the contract: "He is to board &c for what labor he chooses to do" in the house and garden.

Truly, Henry had solved the problem of every hard-up writer and thinker—the wherewithal. For a few hours' work a week he was master of the rest of his time. It was as close as he could get to the life of leisure he needed, and gave him the freedom to read, to take small trips, to scribble, scribble, scribble. None of this would have been possible without something he never acknowledged—the parental roof and table.

Henry never left his parents' household. He was born there; he was still living there when his father died; three years later he died there himself. His mother outlived him.

The women in the house—mother, sisters, aunts, boarding spinsters—always outnumbered the men—father, an uncle, and every so often a boarding widower. Small wonder that in that squawk-box Henry dreamed of a house of his own. For years he had kept his eyes peeled for a place. He liked the site of a pond called Walden. Then, marvel of marvels! Emerson bought Wyman Field, fourteen acres of land right there on the shore of the pond, and offered to let him make use of it if he would do a bit of clearing. He would indeed.

On a rise about two hundred feet from the water, Henry built a house—entirely with his own hands, as he said and as the plaque now on site records—and took occupancy on July 4, 1845. The date, a commemoration of 1776, was also a personal declaration of independence.

Henry knew just what to do: he had done it with his father and the carpenter hardly a year before. Rails had been laid for the Fitchburg Railroad passing through Concord. Many of the Irish immigrants who had labored on it and built their houses nearby were now being laid off. One of these, a James Collins, had put his house up for sale. Henry inspected it under the eyes of the wife, chickens scuttering at his feet—peaked roof, wall and floorboards and a window, all sound. He judged it uncommonly fine, a bargain at $4.25 and showed up the next morning at 6:00 A.M. with a cart to dismantle it. His *Journal* reports, "I passed him [James Collins] and his family on the road. One large bundle held their all,—bed, [their new] coffee-mill, looking-glass, hens. . . ."

That's it and no more for them. Where were they going? What were they going to do? Where were they going to sleep? 'Tweren't no business of Henry's.

"I took down this dwelling the same morning, drawing the nails," he wrote, "and removed it to the pond by small cartloads. . . . One early thrush gave me a note or two as I drove along the woodland path."

"Wait a minute," protested Huggins. "I thought he built the house all by himself, maybe a log cabin with that young timber Emerson wanted him to clear. He *bought* a house, a *prefabricated* house! All he had to do was *reassemble* it!"

"At least he had to set the walls and roof, didn't he?"

"Naturally. Did he do that by himself?"

"Come to think of it, he had a raising party composed of literary lights."

"I can't see literary lights raising the roof. That must have been a scene out of the Keystone Kops."

St. John smiled recognition. "Agreed. Henry's description did not exploit the humor. Instead, he wrote of the honor bestowed by the presence of his guest-workers. Oh, I should add that a local farmer with three sturdy sons also participated in raising the frame and roof."

"Just what I thought," smirked Huggins.

"He bought a lot of other materials, too—more boards, glass windows, nails that he proved unable to drive in straight, his claims of one-at-a-blow notwithstanding, a thousand secondhand bricks . . ."

"More prefabricated materials," snorted Oliver. "So much for Robinson Crusoe."

"The bricks were for the fireplace. The next year he bought a stove."

"Hmpf."

"Our squatter was now ready to—"

"He wasn't a squatter," corrected Huggins severely. "He was on Emerson's field by permission, you said. He was a settler."

"Our settler," conceded St. John, "was now ready to read, write, and contemplate nature."

"Contemplate his navel," chimed the uncharitable Huggins.

"Commune with nature," compromised St. John. "On moonlit nights he would push out with his little boat and play the flute in the middle of the pond."

"I wouldn't call that going native," badgered Huggins. "I never heard of an Indian doing that."

"Let's say he was cozy in his little shanty and small domain. Nearer to God and heaven in this life he could not come. Walden became his state, his realm, a utopia, no one to nag him, no ruler but himself, a king, lord of all he surveyed. A delirium lasting all of two years. Do you know how old he was when he went to live in the woods? . . . Twenty-eight."

"Twenty-eight? *That* old?"

"I should have called that young. He was not long out of college, could walk all day long, and more than hold his own at running, swimming, skating, and boating."

"Hmpf," uttered Huggins. "Where were these woods he lived in?"

"About a mile and a half from Concord."

"You call that *woods*? Didn't you say it was a 'field'? A hop, skip, and a jump from town. Any bears, any wolves, anything bigger than a raccoon? A man-eating deer? Maybe a scared, poisonous snake or two. And in the pond, no sharks or piranha? Maybe a snapping turtle. Oh, oh, careful there, Henry."

St. John began to laugh. "He hated snakes and eels."

Encouraged, Huggins went on. "I'll bet he took his laundry and mending home to mother . . . ?"

"Yes he did."

"And did his sisters come out to bring him choice morsels of food, and did he go into town for a dinner of steaks and butter every now and then?"

"Yes, but did he ever claim to be a hermit? Oops, yes, he did, I remember now."

"He said he lived a life in the woods, didn't he? How long did you say he lived in this home from home?"

"A little over two years."

"How many times did he go into town? How many nights did he spend there? How many days without visitors, without gawking good-for-nothings?"

"Now that you ask, I don't know exactly. Let's see, he went into town every other day for a gossip. The shortcut to the parents' house was along the railroad tracks, and that's the path he took."

"Did he go off on any excursions, in company? Did he have guests bunk in with him?"

"Yes to both questions." St. John waited patiently for Huggins to run out of steam. "Is the quiz over?"

Huggins nodded, smugly.

"The thing is, Oliver, he wrote about this house-building and bean-planting in nice, clear language, as if for a do-it-yourself manual—"

"Or a Boy Scout Handbook." Huggins couldn't resist.

". . . with interpolations—observations of nature, personal reflections, pepperings of romantic poetry and European, Hindu, and Confucian classics."

————Harvard had given him a classical education, St. John continued, skewed by rather much theology and many notions of romantic nature, "the indescribable innocence and beneficence of Nature." As soon as he left college he started to keep a journal, as did almost the whole New England literary class in those days, and in it began talking to himself. " 'What are you doing now? Do you keep a journal?' So I made my first entry today."

Settled in the shanty he wrote a piece on the Scotch Romantic writer Thomas Carlyle. Then he wrote about a two-week rowboat trip he had once taken with his brother John, to whom he had been deeply attached, now dead some three years. He had boned up on all the maps, charts, and travel narratives he could lay hands on. The result, *A Week on the Concord and Merrimack Rivers*, was a chatty travel book, crammed with personal opinions and classical and poetic irrelevancies.

His second book in great part was written at Walden, too. In true transcendental style he referred to it in lectures as "The History of My Life." He later changed it to *Walden or Life in the Woods*, a title whose accuracy you've already appreciated. At the end of his days he struck the subtitle altogether, not wishing perhaps to magnify the do-it-yourself part of the book at the expense of autobiography and the-cosmos-through-my-eyes philosophy.

Travel books had arrived on the scene long before and Thoreau read hundreds of them. You can imagine how interested Britons were in North America and the Caribbean Islands, while New Englanders and other Easterners were eager to hear more about the woods, the wilderness, the fabulous West. St. John de Crèvecoeur, the man you like to think of as my ancestor, wrote three volumes in French about his voyages in upper Pennsylvania and the State of New York, trips up the Hudson and to Niagara and a winter among the Mohawks. Washington Irving wrote in English about *Travels in New York*. Others wrote of travel on the Missouri River, and so forth. Margaret Fuller, Thoreau's blue-penciling editor at *The Dial*, wrote *Summer on the Lakes*, a work that may well have suggested to him larding travel descriptions with thoughts on life and classical literature.

"Want to bet he made them sound like the Lewis and Clark expedition to the Northwest?" challenged Huggins.

"No bet, thank you," declined St. John. "You know your little song makes me wonder: if a railroad network had existed then, would Henry have taken to the road?"

"Henry the Hobo?" derided Huggins. "Not him, not adventurous enough to stray far from home."

"I suppose you're right."

————Toward the end of his life, accompanied by a male friend, he traveled to Minnesota, seeking a healthier climate, but soon discovered that it was the wrong air for bronchitis or tuberculosis. He got worse. His book *A Yankee in Canada* was based on a trip with William Ellery Channing to Montreal and Quebec a decade before, a $7, ten-day excursion, along with 1,500 other tourists. Channing, who lived in a house near Emerson and was the nephew of a well-known Unitarian with the same threefold name, had married Margaret Fuller's pretty sister and, seizing any excuse to escape the house, became Henry David's best friend and traveling comrade.

Thoreau went several times to Maine—he had cousins in Bangor—the first time to look for a job. The second time he had a bad experience: he saw the dark face of Nature and it terrified him. He had climbed the summit of Mount Katahdin alone. There he met not with sweet and gentle Mother Nature, but with Stepmother Nature, vast, titanic, inhuman, who spoke to him in those words: "I cannot pity nor fondle thee here. . . . Why seek me where I have not called thee, and then complain because you find me but a stepmother? Shouldst thou freeze or starve, or shudder thy life away, here is no shrine, nor altar, nor any access to my ear." For your own good, go back to the plains and valleys, she advised. So he did, back to Walden whence he'd strayed and to Mother Nature sweet and pure.

Thoreau applied for teaching or tutoring positions in various faraway places like Michigan. Luckily, nothing ever came of these efforts. "I am engaged to Concord and my own private pursuits by 10,000 ties," he wrote to a friend. He did go to Staten Island, New York, as tutor to the children of William Emerson, brother of Ralph Waldo. From there he wrote to his mother that he would be content "to sit at the backdoor in Concord, under the poplar-tree, henceforth forever." Ill and homesick most of the time, at half term he went back to Concord. Emerson said his one-time protégé wanted to go not to London but to Oregon, which was a nice "Write American" thing to say. He went to neither place. He had nothing to learn in Paris he couldn't learn in Concord. That too was never put to the test. "I have a real genius for staying at home," he wrote to the same friend. Concord was "home, home, home," it was the old familiar coat he wore.

He rationalized his attachment to a two-mile radius on the theory that he could travel just as well or better in his imagination. No need to go to Canada or Maine or even Cape Cod. A little walk facing southwest from town was enough.

"Sounds like Concord kept him on a pretty short leash. Or maybe"—Huggins was surprised at the sound of compassion in his own voice—"his poor health worried him more than he realized or admitted. But as far as the woods go, he would have made a good scoutmaster."

St. John seemed surprised at Huggins's tone, too. "I'm not so sure about that. There's the story of a campfire that didn't go so well."

———He was twenty-seven and back in Concord after his unhappy stay in Staten Island. One spring day he and a young friend went fishing on the Sudbury River. The two built a fire to cook their catch. In a rising wind the fire blew out of hand and set the Concord woods ablaze. The friend, by boat, raced back to town for help; Henry, on foot, started to do the same, but then decided to climb the highest rock to watch three hundred acres burn.

This was bad, this was like absconding with church funds. If anything was needed to confirm the strangeness of David Henry, this was it. For years, townsfolk raged, shouted after him, "damn rascal" and "burnt the woods." He mentions in his *Journal* that the very stable boys damned him. The town might have summoned him to court, had it not been for the prominence of his companion's family, who may have paid damages to soften the local fury. Much later Henry confided to his *Journal* that he had "set fire to the forest. . . . It was a glorious spectacle, and I was the only one there to enjoy it."

Here you see one of the flaws in Thoreau's and the transcendentalists' notion of Nature. Nature was something undefiled by human presence. The river as it rolled along, he discovered in *A Week*, did not (in those days) pollute Nature. It was man's eyes (the white man's eyes, particularly) that violated her. Even worse, if man wrote about the Nature he penetrated, his writing would bring other eyes. Henry admits, "I myself have profaned Walden." He was in ecstasy when his virgin eye pierced virgin Nature. He would want nothing more than for her to stay as she was in that moment of consummation and defilement.

"What a woodsman," scorned Huggins. "Good thing he didn't range far and wide, he might have set half the States afire." Then the word *virgin* came tumbling back to his ear.

"Did you say he was a virgin?"

"No, I didn't, but yes, he never knew a woman. And so missed Nature at her most pressing and pleasurable," replied St. John. "The end of the Thoreauvians. And don't think to find any bastard descendants."

"Poor guy," said Huggins, compassionate again. "But with his fix on nature lore he must have seen sex in the woods everywhere. Even in the backyards of Concord town he could see turtles mounting turtles?"

"Ah yes, Oliver, good point."

————Thoreau and the transcendentalists didn't like to see the animalistic part of nature, even less of man. This side of man was "reptile," he wrote in *Walden*, and perhaps cannot be wholly expelled; like the worms which, even in life and health, occupy our bodies. Man was or should be all spirit. He would scold his pal Channing for telling dirty jokes. "I lose my respect for the man who can make the mystery of sex the subject of a coarse jest," he explained to himself in his *Journal*. "I would preserve purity in act and thought as I would cherish the memory of my mother." (Mother, however, was still alive and kicking.)

The transcendentalists saw nature as sweet and pure and man in nature as the noble savage; they were blind to nature red-in-tooth-and-claw. The struggle-for-existence, dog-eat-dog, survival-of-the-fittest variety is just around the corner and will dominate nature-thinking for a century or more. Thoreau read Darwin late in life, but views similar to the great naturalist's had long been current. Take another observer of nature, the irrepressible Crèvecoeur. His travels led him to conclude that "the might of the strongest rules the world always, high in the air as well as on the earth and under the water." In one of his *Letters*, he describes *d'après nature* a hundred years before Thoreau, a primal battle between two hummingbirds. I brought an excerpt.

St. John reached into her case, took out a note, and read:

> Sometimes, I don't know why, the humming bird will tear and lacerate flowers into a hundred pieces; for, strange to tell, they are the most irascible of the feathered tribe. Where do passions find room in so small a body? They often fight with the fury of lions, until one of the combatants falls a sacrifice and dies.

"We got onto this track of nature," she recalled, "because of the nature boy whose eye pierced the woods and set them ablaze. I may as well tell you of another crazy episode, crazy, you understand, by the standards of his neighbors. It happened when Henry David was about our age, I mean, your age."

Ah ha! There's a slip of the tongue for you. Huggins congratulated himself and got set for another tale.

————Thoreau had been teaching at a Concord school for two weeks when a deacon, a member of the school committee, dropped in. Observing the class to be disorderly, he asked Thoreau to come out in the corridor and there told him that he must punish recalcitrant pupils, that he must not spare the rod and spoil the school. Henry took offense. He returned to the classroom. Like some Roman general decimating the legion, he drew out from the class six of his pupils and, don't ask me why, whipped them one by one. Among them was a young maid in his mother's household. That evening, commendably, Thoreau resigned. But those who survived to tell the tale remember being shocked and then bitter about being whipped for doing nothing.

"Don't you think it curious, Oliver? Why not just resign? Why flog six young persons picked at random? Why birch an innocent girl? To make a livid statement?"

Huggins said nothing. The guy's a weirdo, he thought.

"It was several years later that he tutored Emerson's brother's three children on Staten Island. They seemed to have liked him. His contract called for $100 a year plus board and room."

Out of the blue, trying to look like he knew something he wasn't supposed to know, Huggins said, "I'd think twice before asking you what your contract calls for."

St. John flushed, stared stonily in his eyes for a full moment, and said, slowly and distinctly, "That was an asinine remark."

The oxygen in the room went thin. Huggins went blank. What was wrong?

A moment passed. St. John, more relaxed, added, "Would you rather have had Thoreau as tutor?"

Huggins, taken aback again, his mind jostled by a melee of fears and competing fantasies, made no sound.

"Well?" insistently. "Do I do for you?"

"I'm perfectly satisfied." Huggins had recovered somewhat. "I've had other tutors before, you know, when we lived abroad, mainly for languages."

"I see," mused St. John. "Male?"

"All male," Huggins retorted dryly. He wasn't sure whether he was barefoot on a slope of heather or tiptoeing through a minefield.

"What about your piano teacher?"

Two can play this game of self-contradiction, thought Huggins. "I didn't have any piano teacher. I taught myself, the way Thoreau taught himself the flute."

"I'd guess you had a better instrument than his. I don't think he could coax out of that flute more than a few improvised notes."

———No one ever said he played well, she went on. At his sister Helen's death, it was told, he brought in a music box with an odd sound. He sang in the choir on special occasions but probably couldn't read music. Still he imagined himself as Apollo, Orpheus, and the Great God Pan. When he first met Margaret Fuller he took her out boating, and I like to think that at the pond he played the flute for her. Sounds like pretty serious courtship, doesn't it? But it never went anywhere. Surely he, the brother-sister transcendentalist, never intended it to go as far as the smoldering Margaret was dreaming of. She described the boatings in a letter to her younger brother Richard.

St. John pulled another slip of paper from her seemingly inexhaustible supply.

> Mr. Emerson has a friend with him of the name of Henry Thoreau who has come to live with him and be his working man this year. H. T. is three and twenty . . . has a boat which he made himself, and rows me out on the pond. Last night I went out quite late and staid till the moon was almost gone, heard the whip-poor-will for the first time this year. There was a sweet breeze full of apple-blossom fragrance which made the pond swell almost into waves. I had great pleasure. I think of you in these scenes. . . .

Thoreau made her think of her brother! Later she arranged for Richard to be Henry's tutee, although Henry and herself became, in the opinion of contemporaries, fast enemies.

"We'd better return to his writing. Maybe you can explain why his writings had become popular by the twentieth century."

Huggins cursed under his breath. Damn! Another quiz? He thought a moment. "Maybe they appealed to whoever secretly wanted to get away from it all, to throw off duties and responsibilities, to leave the job, and wife, and children."

"That's possible, especially if you—"

"I've got a song to fit."

"Oh? Good." The merest tinge of sarcasm. "Are you going to play with both hands this time?"

"Don't need to. It has a simple tune but can be run off without it, like a fast recitative, in talking-union or rap style."

"I'm all ears."

Huggins stood up, staged a to-do of clearing his throat, and chanted rapidly:

> *Oh, what was your name in the States?*
> *Was it Johnson or Thompson or Bates?*
> *Did you murder your wife*
> *And flee for your life?*
> *Oh, what was your name in the States?*

St. John's face struggled not to grin. "I like it."

"Bill Roth, one of *my* friends," said Huggins, "thinks that it comes from the early Far West, perhaps from the '49 Gold Rush, before California became a State."

"Sounds like it, all right. More broadly, it fits all newcomers. After all, who came to these shores but people wanting to get away from parents, naggers, creditors, tormentors, jailers, from themselves, from everything? From old names! Your chant would make a good introduction to the subject of the fluidity of names on this continent. But we've had enough excursions for today, I'm afraid."

"Right." Huggins felt half-encouraged, half-squelched. "Why are we wasting so much time on Thoreau anyway?" he complained. "What's he got to do with this constitution?"

"Grist for the mill, Oliver, all grist for the mill. Let's pass over the topic of names which your charming ditty introduced, and zero in on an essay that, like a moving battleship, stirred up giant waves, reaching into Russia, sweeping down over India—the land of the Hindu philosophy Thoreau was enamored of—to wash over the shores of California in the late 1950s and '60s and drench universities across to the Atlantic."

————Leo Tolstoy, the great Russian writer, author of *War and Peace* (St. John was back in academic stride) read Thoreau's essay on "Civil Disobedience," and asked why people here ignored this man while tipping their hat to money and the military. The Fabians in England and the early Labour party had discovered the essay, along with *Walden*. They even formed Walden clubs. In the Great Depression the labor unions in the United States also discovered Thoreau's piece. Mohandas Gandhi learned about it as a law student in England. When he became an Indian newspaper publisher in South Africa, he printed and distributed it in pamphlet form, and later, as leader of the groundswell that ultimately moved the British out of India, stated that he took from Thoreau the name of his great movement—Satyagraha or nonviolent resistance. In the United States, the Reverend Martin Luther King, Jr., and the civil rights movement considered themselves heir to Thoreau's "legacy of creative protest," and not-so-poor university students protesting many wrongs and rebelling specifically against being drafted to fight a

mean war in Asia took the essay as a program for resistance to the
United States government.

"This was in the sixties. Before your time, Mr. Huggins."

Huggins, quick on the draw: "Before your time too, Ms. St.
John."

St. John, inscrutable: "Point well taken."

————In due time this little work of about a dozen pages, she kept
on, stirred interest in Thoreau's other writings and set his reputation beyond that of Emerson, his mentor and sponsor. Today the
amount written about him (much of it of a psychological, ecologi-
cal, mystical, or idealistic drift) rivals that written about Washington or Lincoln.

When not long out of college Henry David and his brother John
had debated the subject "Is it ever proper to offer forcible resistance?" against the transcendentalist Amos Bronson Alcott. The
locale was the Concord Lyceum. The Thoreau boys took the affirmative. The memory must have lingered. Whether he thought of
the idea anew or someone or the more and more heated antislavery mood about him suggested it, he agreed to give a political talk
at the Lyceum on "The Relation of the Individual to the State."

Bored with his lordship of the Pond and tempted by the offer to
live for a year or more in Emerson's house, he had left Walden. In
the fall and winter of 1841 while he drafted the speech, recruits for
the Mexico-Texas conflict were drilling in the square. But the pre-
cipitating event may have been his going to jail the summer of the
year before.

While still living at Walden he had wandered into town one
evening to get a shoe repaired, he wrote. (Curious, that he couldn't
repair his own shoes.) The jailer Sam Staples, his neighbor and
sometime surveying assistant, recalling that he had not paid his voting or poll tax for six years, put him in jail. Nothing better could
have happened to him. He does not say whether he didn't pay the
tax on principle or whether he just forgot. Anyway he went to jail;
enjoyed his cellmate's story of smoking a pipe in a barn while drunk,
of falling asleep and setting the barn on fire; had a breakfast of a
pint of chocolate and brown bread, and then was turned out—over

his protest! He was "as mad as the devil," reminisced Sam Staples, who had told him that if he would not go, he would have to put him out.

One night in a comfy jail hardly counts as political protest. Our protester did the best he could, reporting it in imaginative detail over four pages of the essay on civil disobedience.

"Why only one night in jail?" Oliver asked.

"Evidently, his aunt Maria had intervened and paid the tax. Removed from jail, he got his shoe mended, put it on, and—listen to this—he said a huckleberry party was ready and waiting for his leadership. He led them to one of the highest hills where 'the State was nowhere to be seen.' "

"I told you he would have made a good scoutmaster."

"You did," said St. John, "but for him the episode illustrates that 'They only can force me who obey a higher law than I.' We'll meet this higher law again, soon."

————He gave the speech in January 1848 and repeated it in February. The opening sentence reads, "I heartily accept the motto,— 'that government is best which governs least.' " This more or less was the motto appearing on cover and title page of the *United States Magazine and Democratic Review*, probably devised by Emerson, editor of the magazine, who had said a similar thing in his "Politics" and probably also a hand-me-down from our old friend, Tom Paine. What we learn from this first sentence is that Thoreau endorses the motto. He begins with "I." No doubt that is enough to give it special significance.

"It may amuse you to hear, Oliver, that there were so many instances of the first person singular in *Walden* (about eight per page) that the compositor ran out of I's in setting type for it. On the first page Thoreau explains that he will retain the "I" throughout in 'respect to egotism.' "

"Were the transcendentalists all such egotists?"

"Yes. For instance Amos Bronson Alcott, the debater I just mentioned, was, according to Emerson, 'the majestic egotist.' As for Thoreau, he wrote as if everything, perhaps excepting South and

North America, was his own discovery, from the dancing of a flower to the squirreling of nuts, from constructing an outhouse to moonlighting on the pond. But I think he was less egotistical than he sounds. Self-touted superiority was a bad habit of the transcendentalists. He wanted to be considered one of them and early picked up the habit."

————The beginning of Thoreau's talk recalls Margaret Fuller's well-known utterance, "I accept the universe," which wouldn't have become so well-known hadn't two more famous writers commented: one to warn, "Egad, she'd better!" and the other to warn further, "Gad, she'd better not!"

Thoreau's next paragraph holds that this American government (meaning by this the government of the United States)—"what is it but a tradition, though a recent one . . . ? It has not the vitality and force of a single living man; for a single living man can bend it to his will."

Huggins didn't like the sound of this. "What is he talking about? What single living man? The president of the United States or any single living man? If the president, ho-hum. If *any* man, why doesn't he save us the trouble and bend the government to *his* will?"

St. John looked amused. "You get eloquent when you're excited," she said. "Still, you can't always ask a man to practice what he preaches. He may be like a lamppost, able to light up the way, unable to follow the illumined path. Thoreau the lamppost tried to walk the path, and after toppling over, had to transcribe his few halting steps into derring-do. He reassembles a prefabricated house—'built entirely by myself.' He spends one comfortable night in the local jail—he is the 'enemy of the state.' He goes on one excursion—it becomes an expedition to Patagonia.

"You'll find in him exaggerations, half-truths, contradictions, rhetorical bits, muddy waters that he claimed to be clearing up. If as Emerson said, a foolish consistency is the hobgoblin of little minds, Thoreau on that score never suffered nightmares. Of everything I say he says, you can find the reverse. Suppose I say he does not believe in corporal punishment and quote from *Walden* . . ."

St. John lifted a sheet from her little pile of papers and began to read.

————"I am convinced, that if all men were to live as simply as I then did [at Walden] thieving and robbery would be unknown. These take place only in communities where some have got more than is sufficient while others have not enough." *He* never bolts his door night or day, and concludes with Confucius: "You who govern public affairs, what need have you to employ punishments? Love virtue, and the people will be virtuous." Then in his *Journal* you read that two young women once came to the door of his shanty asking for a drink of water. He lent them his dipper. What did they do faced with such shining virtue? They made off with the dipper. "I had a right to suppose they came to steal," fumed Thoreau. "They were a disgrace to their sex and to humanity. Pariahs of the moral world. Evil spirits that thirsted not for water. . . . Such as Dante saw. What was the lake to them but liquid fire and brimstone." On and on he rants. Eluding him, they will not elude Hell, Thoreau consoles himself with a vengeance.

I could make up parallel columns of opposing quotations, but what would that suggest? The author's opportunism, uncertainty, confusion?

Thoreau is a master of the disjointed phrase, memorable and quotable. "Most men live lives of quiet desperation." He badgered that thought nearly to death before it got its final expression. Given more time still, he might have changed "quiet" to *mute* and "desperation" to *despair*.

Nothing wrong with this; lots of writers do the same, beat their brains out for the right two words, Flaubert, for example. Except that Thoreau likes to think of the writer as one whose words, smelling of the fields and the woods, flow onto the page without dotted *i*'s and crossed *t*'s, perfectly expressive of the inner being, not one who labors them long and hard, drawing phrases and paragraphs from notes and journals and calculating where they might ring up highest profit. His manuscripts are chockful of pencilled insertions and corrections. Henry would not have liked to be told that his writings smelled of the lamp and the library. His buddy Ellery Channing who wrote poetry never revised a word for fear of spoiling the freshness of lines.

Take this famous essay, "Civil Disobedience," a repository of jots and tittles, some not only catching but powerful. We owe a few of them to oratory: remember that he gave this piece first as a speech. He was a fair speaker, with a sense of humor that sometimes appears in his writings. Emerson vouches that his protégé's lectures on his first book, *The Week*, had the public rolling in the aisles. Maybe Thoreau ad-libbed a lot, for that laughter does not come through the available texts, and the book never achieved much of a readership. You can be sure, though, that he had lots more humor than Washington or Calhoun.

There is so much nonsense in Thoreau that it doesn't usually pay to try to figure out what he had in mind. Reading any passage, one can't help thinking that he might just have been looking for a place to paste a scrap from his *Journal*. Some admirers of his prose find in it schemes of complex design, but his forte was patchwork composition. Often he put in order by days, by seasons, or by single subjects those scrapings from his mind that he had laid to treasure in his notebooks. All said, however, he wrote excellent modern nonfiction, less academic than Emerson, less gothic than Melville and Hawthorne. At age thirty-two, no longer the jack-of-all-trades, he underlined in a letter to the president of Harvard, "I have chosen letters for my profession."

"But with so much patchwork and self-contradicting, how can you discuss his ideas?" Huggins's tone was querulous.

"It ain't easy, let me tell you. I'll try to group some of his sentences, particularly those in 'Civil Disobedience.' It will have to be a ragged, not a careful, effort."

————I've mentioned that Emerson attacked the majesty of the law. In Thoreau's refrain, "Unjust laws exist . . . then, I say break the law."

Breaking the law is not so terrible a thing. One should not have that "undue respect for law" that affects soldiers, along with militiamen, jailers, sheriffs, and politicians. Thoreau is hard on the

United States Marines. "Behold a marine," he chirps, "such a man as an American government can make, or such as it can make a man with its black arts, a mere shadow and reminiscence of humanity, a man laid out alive and standing, and already, as one may say, buried under arms with funeral accompaniments. . . ."

Thoreau goes further: he details various ways of disobeying the laws. Pay no taxes, refuse military service, break particular laws, and—always ready to suffer the consequences—incur fines, forfeit your property, go to prison.

"Civil Disobedience" suggests still another step: using the weight and volume of one's body not to harm but to block or obstruct the enforcers of law. "Let your life be a counter friction to stop the machine," he urges, for "a minority is irresistible when it clogs by its whole weight." The sit-down strikes of labor unions, the building take-overs, the body barricades, the traffic tie-ups of bodies prostrate or self-cuffed to pillar and post—on streets and in front of entrances—all these tactics intending to clog with human bodies (and in the twentieth century they were broadcast and televised) came from Thoreau.

Those in public office like judges or mailmen or tax collectors can take another step: Resign your post in protest. This does not require breaking the law. Neither does another tactic of protest that Thoreau recommends in a later article: laying on an embargo, refraining from buying articles that directly or indirectly support the unjust law or government. So, he instructs "the free men of . . . New England" not to buy a newspaper that criticizes John Brown (about whom more in a moment). They have "only to withhold their cents, to kill a score [of these sheets] at once." The people who read them are like "the dog that returns to his vomit."

The heated journalism of William Lloyd Garrison's *The Liberator* had for years been agitating for the secession of New England or at least of Massachusetts from the United States. But Thoreau demands, why wait? Secession from a state by the individual can be done as easily or even more easily than secession by a State from the Union. "Some are petitioning the State [of Massachusetts] to dissolve the Union," he reports. "Why do they not dissolve it themselves— the Union between themselves and the State . . . ?" Secession by individuals will force a State, Massachusetts, to secede from the union. "This people [of the United States] must cease to hold slaves, and to make war on Mexico, though it cost them their existence as a people."

John C. Calhoun, senator from South Carolina, might object that they never had an existence as one people. Clearly he and the South Carolinians are not the only ones disaffected and contemplating secession from the United States. These abolitionists threaten, as emotionally as the South Carolinians (even *more* emotionally, Calhoun would say), to secede from the union if the United States government does not comply with their demands. "No Union with slaveholders!" they cry.

It becomes clear that breaking the law has special meaning. It signifies the individual's withdrawal of allegiance from the government, his secession from the State, the State of Massachusetts or the United States.

When Thoreau gave this major political piece as a lecture to the Concord Lyceum, he entitled it "The Relation of the Individual to the State." It appeared a year later with his permission in a short-lived magazine, *Aesthetic Papers*, under the title "Resistance to Civil Government." After his death, it appeared in the volume of his writings entitled *A Yankee in Canada, with Anti-Slavery and Reform Papers*, headlining a new and not inappropriate title by which it is known today, "Civil Disobedience." His devoted sister and dear friend Channing had edited the volume. The author may have made the change earlier himself.

Our Thoreau knows that he cannot advocate law-breaking and secession, individual or collective, without offering some justification. He mounts an attack on obedience to law along three main fronts: the oath, which he treats as a contract between the individual and the government; voting and majority rule as the basis of lawmaking; and a constitution as supreme law.

A just government must have the consent of the governed, he writes; it cannot have a right over his person or property except "what I concede to it." He can at will unilaterally break off all connection with the government. Has he sworn an oath giving his consent and promising his support to the State or the United States? Evidently not. But for those who will have sworn allegiance he provides an escape. Once, he tells, when refusing to pay an assessment for the church (we are still in theocratic Massachusetts) he put in writing a declaration for the government's guidance: "Know all men by these presents, that I, Henry Thoreau, do not wish to be regarded as a member of any incorporated society which I have not joined." Yet he still refers to himself in this same article as citizen and subject, indiscriminately. Perhaps like the poet Coleridge he can proclaim: "I am a member of that great and universal religion of which I am the only member."

Huggins had a question. "What happened to Thoreau's middle name?"

"Oliver, the things you notice! I don't know why he left out his middle name here. Sorry. I can only add that on his deathbed he summoned a friend and presented him with a copy of *A Week*. Inscribed was a verse, "Where'er thou sail'st who sailed with me." Below the verse a lock of hair was attached with the identification, "From a lock of John Thoreau's hair." The book carried the autograph, "Henry D. Thoreau/Concord."

————Whichever name the "I" refers to in his declaration doesn't matter much. As he never signed on to the government or the state (two terms he uses interchangeably), he needn't ever sign off. Signings off and on seem less individualistic or ridiculous taken in the Massachusetts setting where in the battle of denominations, persons signed off one church and signed on another. One of Thoreau's aunts, for instance, signed off Congregationalism and signed on Unitarianism.

The oath or social contract, then, is of no fixed duration. The citizen or subject or individual may at any time revoke it unilaterally.

As for the ballot and majority rule, people vote and count their votes and to the majority goes the power of lawmaking, because the majority all together is physically stronger than the minority. Thus they avoid a test of force. Thoreau protests, though, that the majority is not more *right* than the minority. The mass of people serve the state with their bodies. "They have the same sort of worth only as horses and dogs."

Further, while a government to be strictly just must have the consent of the governed, voting is not necessarily a true expression of that consent. Calhoun had attacked majority rule on the ground that it could not take fair account of the minority. Thoreau attacks the ballot itself, making a point that political scientists tend to overlook, that a count of the votes does not reflect wholeheartedness of the consent given or intensity of the opinion or belief that voters hold. A nicely turned sentence expresses the matter: Thousands *"in opinion"* are opposed to slavery and to the war. "At most, they give only a cheap vote, and a feeble countenance and God-speed to the right, as it goes by them." The ballot is only a strip of paper. Might as well count pebbles.

Politicians and lawmakers are elected by the ballot and majority vote: how does that qualify them to make good law? In matters of convenience or expediency, as Thoreau calls it, like traffic ordinances in Concord, there would be little harm in letting majority vote decide . . . were it not "that our whole life is startlingly moral" and "there is never an instant's truce between virtue and vice." In issues of right and wrong, of good and evil, then *cost what it may* there must be justice.

Now for Thoreau's third front of attack, against the constitution. The "men of '87," he calls them, drafted the document. Ratified and made into law by majority vote, it cannot be a source of truth. Thoreau advocates violating both the constitution of the State of Massachusetts and this constitution of the United States. At any given moment it may be a bit of a puzzle which of the two constitutions he is attacking. In the pure sense, to use his language, they are both evil, the one for subordinating itself to the federal government and providing no remedy for the federal Fugitive Slave Act (requiring the return of runaways), the other for sanctioning slavery from the very beginning.

Did Thoreau's bulging book-bag ever hold a little pamphlet entitled "A Constitution for the United States of America"? He mentions it as something familiar and passes judgment on it, yet he never speaks of it in the slightest detail. He has heard on all sides that it defends slavery and claims to be the supreme law of the land. Had he read it he would surely have pointed out the irony of one of its great achievements: to make slavery constitutional without mentioning the word (Article I, Section 2, Paragraph 3), a fine illustration of the Framers' skill in lawyerly circumlocution.

We're pursuing today another circumlocution, the one contained in the so-called supremacy clause, the phrase "the supreme law of the land." Almost as soon as the '87 Constitution appeared in print, the question of a "higher law"—whether natural or divine—began to disturb the sleep of judges, lawyers, and ministers.

The issue goes back a long way. Manmade or secular law, if it conflicts with natural or divine law, is not law, and in consequence cannot ask for obedience. The early Puritan immigrants often cited divine or God's law as "higher law," comparing it condescendingly to manmade law.

The Declaration of Independence grounded itself in divine law and natural right by calling on the laws of Nature and of Nature's God and on Creator-endowed rights. The '87 Constitution, however, drafted later by other people in another mood, avoided speaking of natural rights or divine law. It proclaimed only the supreme law of the land. You remember we scolded Chief Justice Marshall for boasting that he confined himself to a written constitution while bringing to bear on his decision ideas and conceptions from outside the written text.

"*We* scolded?" Oliver broke in teasingly.

"Yes," Claire said, "you and me, Nerissa, my little law clerk."

"I remember: *Marshall* v. *Portia.* Marshall talked about certain principles of the people's original right."

"Exactly. Their original right to establish government for their happiness. This is the language of the Declaration of Independence and of his not too beloved cousin, Tom Jefferson. The Declaration of Independence, however, was never enacted into constitution or law."

————When the issue of slavery put New England in turmoil, the question of higher law appeared with greater intensity. Abolitionists contrasted it not to manmade law in general but to this constitution in particular. Politically the problem looked like this: The '87 Constitution supports slavery; to amend the document will require a vote at the ballot box or in the Congress, a vote that because of the opposition of southern senators will never succeed. But to obey the law issuing from this constitution would be to violate a law higher than the so-called supreme law of the land.

Had the men of '87 retained the wording of their original draft of the supremacy phrase, had the final draft left unchanged "the supreme law of the respective states," the *higher law* of the Puritans, of the transcendentalists, of Thoreau and the abolitionists would not have seemed to be in open conflict. The phrase would clearly have identified the '87 Constitution's "supreme" law as supreme *man-made* law over the respective states. The Framers altered the phrase, however, to weasel out of a dilemma: how to put states with strong names in subordination to a hoped-for, consolidated, big state as yet impossible to name. At the time the difficulty (as I pointed out to Chief Justice Marshall) could only be dimly foreseen—that the pedestrian "supreme law of the respective states" would become the glorious "supreme law of the land," and so would challenge those who believed that above it ruled a superhuman or transcendent law. If the abolitionists were part of the "land," how could they regard this constitution as the supreme law? Divine law, the word of God, was supremest.

William Lloyd Garrison, with whom Thoreau had long been in correspondence, whose paper *The Liberator* had published some of Thoreau's writings, who had been demanding the immediate, un-conditional emancipation of slaves since 1831 and who was calling upon the North to secede from the compact, denounced this con-stitution as a "covenant with death and an agreement with hell." William Henry Seward, now senator from New York and future secretary of state under Lincoln, disputing that United States terri-tories should permit slaveholding, asserted that "there is a higher law than the Constitution." Our own Thoreau in a talk at an antislav-ery convention in Framingham, Massachusetts, in 1854 protesting the arrest and extraditing of escaped slaves by that State, called for men "who recognize a higher law than the Constitution, or the de-cision of the majority." He also handed down his legal opinion on whether Massachusetts may secede from the federal Union. "She [Massachusetts] may wriggle and hesitate, and ask leave to read the Constitution once more; but she can find no respectable law or precedent which sanctions the continuance of such an union for an instant."

Thoreau agrees with the South Carolinians that under this constitution a State may secede unilaterally. A central theme of the
"Civil Disobedience" piece follows: "Let each inhabitant of the
State of Massachusetts dissolve his union, as long as she delays to do
her duty." Her duty is to secede.

As usual he composes this talk largely of passages culled and re-
furbished from his *Journal*. He is now wholly caught up in New
England's anguish over slavery, the invasion of Mexico, and the an-
nexation of Texas as a slaveholding state. His language grows viru-
lent. In "Civil Disobedience" he had written, "I quietly declare war
with the State, after my fashion. . . ." In "Slavery in Massachusetts,"
the talk he gives at the Framingham convention, he rages, "My
thoughts are murder to the State and involuntarily go plotting
against her."

To cap this same convention, Garrison in a public demonstration
burns the '87 Constitution, shouting, "So perish all compromises
with tyranny!" Thoreau is present, no doubt nodding his approval.

"As you said earlier, Huggins, fires always excited him."

Huggins's face, he hoped, showed nothing but a becoming
modesty.

————So emotionally involved in politics is Thoreau toward the
end of his life that the failure of government and men to live up to
his standard destroys his contemplative life and enjoyment of nature.
He pens lines of sadness: "I walk toward one of our ponds; but what
signifies the beauty of nature when men are base? . . . Who can be
serene in a country where both the rulers and the ruled are without principle? The remembrance of my country spoils my walk."
And later he writes of his surprise at finding nature so indifferent,
at finding "the routine of the natural world surviving still."

Poor Thoreau. He had believed that his State and "this American government" were hardly worth considering, so little did they
enter his life, so little did they touch his simple pleasures. Now, because of them, he has lost Nature and "my country."

"Country" is not a term he has used in a political context
before. He has talked of the State, meaning the government of Massachusetts or a state government generally. He speaks of the Amer-

ican government, the nation, and the Union, meaning by them the federal government or United States of America. He speaks of seceding from all of them, presumably as a Massachusetts man or a New Englander or Yankee. He speaks of America as the whole continent. He never speaks of seceding from or disowning his country. *Country* for Henry Thoreau seems to refer not to a sign-on/sign-off contract but rather to an emotional attachment, like that of Nathan Hale to Connecticut or New England.

The last of Thoreau's predominantly political talks and writings consist of a series of three speeches in praise of John Brown. This gloomy, religious man, of Congregationalist background, sire of a score of children, otherwise bankrupt, a ne'er-do-well, turned his hand and that of his sons to antislavery violence in Kansas. In the so-called Pottawatomie massacre, in retaliation for the murder of five free-state settlers, he ordered five pro-slavery settlers killed in cold blood. Convinced that he had a divine mandate to destroy slavery by the sword, he planned to set up a free state in the mountains of Virginia and spread a slave insurrection southward. While in Canada, he and somewhat less than fifty white and black men adopted a "Provisional Constitution and Ordinance for the People of the United States" with Brown as commander in chief. On a money-raising tour of the Northeast he found churchly donors, including Theodore Parker, almost all in Boston, not wide-awake to his plans for insurrection but fully aware of his violent history. Heavily armed with weapons thus paid for, Brown and sons together with five black and five white men assaulted and captured a section of the United States arsenal at Harpers Ferry, Virginia, holding about sixty leading citizens of the town as hostages. The next morning a small force under a Colonel Robert E. Lee cornered the rebels and after a sharp shoot-out took Brown and the survivors prisoner. Tried for treason, conspiracy, and murder in the first degree, he and four of those with him were hanged.

The force that captured John Brown and his followers was a company of United States Marines. A dozen years earlier the marines had crossed into Mexico in what Thoreau, writing "Civil Disobedience" at the time, called an invasion. The marines under General Winfield Scott, fighting their country's battles, had just taken Mexico City and were strolling the halls of Montezuma. You can see why Thoreau was so fond of the marines.

Many in New England held John Brown to be a martyr; the South considered him a monster, the forerunner of insurrectionary invasions of their countries.

Brown had met Thoreau through various Concord and Boston acquaintances. He had nothing but scorn for milk-toast abolitionists such as he might privately classify Henry David. Thoreau, trying oh-so-hard all his life to prove that he not only could think and write but also be a man with backbone—could build a house, live in the wilds, explore rivers and mountains, pay no taxes, go to prison—fell in love. He called John Brown peerless, a Cromwell, the crucified Christ, the most American among us—and above all a transcendentalist!

Was Thoreau, the individualist, ready to take up arms and follow Brown wherever he might lead, had he been younger and feeling stronger? (He was forty-two, Brown was fifty-eight.) Might we have seen Thoreau hanged, twisting in the wind? Probably not. Kansas and Virginia were far from Concord. His fellow-transcendentalists coughed up money; they did not enlist. Anyway, Brown may not have wanted such namby-pambies as comrades-in-arms.

Thoreau defended Brown against those who called him crazy. He repeated the antislavery and break-the-law arguments of his previous political writings—"Civil Disobedience" and "Slavery in Massachusetts." The rifles and revolvers procured with Boston money were "employed in a righteous cause," the tools "in the hands of one who could use them." As for Massachusetts, still a slave of the United States, she, he underlines, will have *to pay the penalty of her sin.*

Himself, though, remains on the bench, never to run onto the field strapping on a helmet. He wishes neither to kill nor to be killed. He "can foresee," however, circumstances in which "both these things will be by me unavoidable." Can foresee? What more does he need? John Brown is about to be or is already hanged by the neck.

Most of the thousands in the twentieth century who swore by

Thoreau's "Civil Disobedience" thought of it as hostile to government yet nonviolent in its program. They failed to see that Thoreau does sanction violence. The fiery Garrison stuck to his plugged-up guns, nonviolent to the end. But Thoreau insists, "It is not too soon for honest men to rebel and revolutionize."

Nor for honest women either. In that same year, a group of feminists convenes in Seneca Falls, New York, the home of Elizabeth Cady Stanton, a brilliant speaker and organizer, and draws up a Declaration of Sentiments and Resolutions: "We hold these truths to be self-evident: that all men and women are created equal. . . ." In the Declaration of Independence, George III played the role of tyrant; in the Seneca Falls Declaration, the tyrant is Man. "He has usurped the prerogative of Jehovah himself, claiming it as his right to assign [Woman] a sphere of action when that belongs to her conscience and to her God."

The year is 1848. Revolutions everywhere are sweeping Europe, in back rooms, cellars, conspiratorial clubs. Men and women are dying for nationalism, socialism, anarchism. The *New York Tribune* sends Margaret Fuller to Europe to cover the revolts, making her the first woman foreign correspondent. Heinrich Karl Marx is writing *The Communist Manifesto*'s ominous line: "A specter is haunting Europe—the specter of Communism." A specter is stalking New England, too—the specter of slavery.

"But even if blood should flow," the revolutionary Thoreau demands, "is there not a sort of blood shed when the conscience is wounded?" And in foreboding (once more like Calhoun), "I see this blood flowing now." Does he mean the conscience "sort of blood" or dark, arterial blood?

He does admit rebellion and revolution both as a right and as a duty, but does not spell them out programmatically, as he does with the strategy and tactics of civil disobedience.

You are threatened with arrest for breaking an unjust law. What does he advise you to do? Go to prison. He does not say, Gather round you some stout like-minded souls and plot to overthrow the government, as did the outlaws who founded the Han Dynasty, or for that matter, the British American colonials who formed Committees of Correspondence. Nor does he advise what would be more in keeping with his individualist temper: Grab your gun, like Massai the Apache, and take to the hills.

Thoreau's program stops at civil disobedience, "a sort of blood."

Nor does he clarify his own role in violence. Emerson said Thoreau "seemed born for great enterprise and for command" and regretted that "instead of engineering for all America, he was the captain of a huckleberry party."

Thoreau's thoughts, not his arms, are murder to the state. Perhaps his written words were murderous, too. In his piece on "The Last Days of John Brown" he provided a new simile for writing: "The art of composition is as simple as the discharge of a bullet from a rifle. . . ."

So much for Thoreau's program of disobedience to an unjust, a tyrannical government. We have yet to consider how he and we, having overthrown the ballot and majority rule, the law and this constitution, did manage to know that the government was unjust and tyrannical. The majority of persons, he admits, do not think so: they obey the government like zombies. They follow "the Supreme Court of the land" which recognizes "no authority but the Constitution."

What authority should we recognize if not this constitution? What has Thoreau to pit against the supreme law of the land? If we are to disobey it, what should we obey? He and many others have talked about a higher law. What is this higher law and how does one become privy to it? In answer, Thoreau brings forth a concept seldom mentioned in his nonpolitical writings.

The supreme law of the land, of any land, is conscience. Your only obligation, Thoreau insists, is to do at any time what you think right. You the citizen must not even for a moment or in the least degree resign your conscience to the legislator. Nor to a constitutional delegate, one may assume, who drafts a law of the land supreme over conscience.

The notion of conscience is far from clear in Thoreau's essay on civil disobedience, and his other writings do little to clarify it. Every individual has it, an encapsulated thing affected neither by law nor by the subtle and gross influences of wealth, love, nepotism, or ambition. It was not given to us as a hindrance or without purpose.

Given to us, so be it, but by whom or what? The transcendental-ists went outside Christianity to other religions in their search for truth. But whatever religion or combination of religions, or what-ever great, silly superstitions Thoreau may have explored, the buck stops with the universal God.

Conscience goes back to the earliest possible New England lineage: the Puritan preacher's conscience as the imparted or implanted Word of God, as his line of communication with God. Without this conscience, without this divine command higher than state and fed-eral constitutions and the duly enacted laws of legislatures, Thoreau could not advocate unseating the government by disobedience or by force of arms.

In the history of common law, appeals to conscience are as fre-quent and important as arguments from reason. With God on his flank Thoreau diverts conscience from its customary use in law—as an accompaniment to reason—opposes it to law, sets law and rea-son beneath it, and challenges the constitutions and laws of the States and the United States, or of any government in the world past and present, including ancient Thebes.

In his first published book, *A Week on the Concord and Merrimack River*, he had already identified conscience with divine or God's law. "Does not his law reach as far as high light?" he asked, and narrated the well-known case of Antigone in Sophocles' play. Antigone de-cides to give her dead brother a ritual burial even though he has been judged an enemy of his country and his burial is forbidden by law on pain of death. Creon the King demands to know whether she dares to transgress these laws. As Thoreau quoted her, she re-plies that "it was not Zeus who proclaimed these [laws] to me, nor Justice who dwells with the gods below: it was not they who es-tablished these laws among men. Nor did I think that your procla-mations [of the law] were so strong, as, being a mortal, to be able to transcend the unwritten and immovable laws of the gods. For not something now and yesterday, but forever these [laws of the gods] live, and no one knows from what time they appeared." It is mor-tal presumption to believe that a constitution enacted by men can reign supreme over the unwritten, unmovable, immemorial divine law embodied in the individual's conscience, in this case Antigone's.

The talk on "Slavery in Massachusetts" brings the lesson closer to home. "The question is, not whether you or your grandfather, seventy years ago, did not enter into an agreement to serve the devil . . . but whether you will not now, for once and at last, serve God,—in spite of your own past recreancy, or that of your ancestor,—by obeying that eternal and only just CONSTITUTION, which He, and not any Jefferson or Adams, has written in your being."

Indifferent to the eternal constitution, the '87 Constitution works by counting ballots and tallying pluralities and majorities. In an uncharacteristically weak sentence Thoreau asks, "Can there not be a government in which majorities do not virtually decide right and wrong, but Conscience?" As there is no way of counting consciences, is there a form of government other than a republic or democracy that could avoid this fate of individual secession and breaking of the law? Cannot conscience reach the government peaceably?

Thoreau has no clear answer except to plead that the elect, what he and Emerson both call the wise minority, be allowed to turn on government the rays of its conscience. "Why does [the government] not cherish its wise minority?" he pleads.

A government that would cherish its wise individuals, it seems, would be something other than a democracy. "Is a democracy, such as we know it, the last improvement possible in government?" he asks at the end of "Civil Disobedience." There is "a still more perfect and glorious State, which also I have imagined, but not yet anywhere seen." Nor yet entrusted to written words, one might add. From what he has so far hinted, though, we can say that in this state, every moral act or law follows the conscience of a wise minority, a select group, an aristocracy, government by the virtuous.

"Question," said Huggins waving his hand frenetically, annoyingly.

He succeeded. St. John was annoyed. "I know what you're going to ask, but go ahead, ask it," she said.

"Did Thoreau have a beard or didn't he?"

"Oh," said St. John, eyebrows lifted. "What reminded you of that?"

"I don't know exactly. Because Thoreau is so stubborn in his righteousness, I guess, or is it, so righteous in his stubbornness?

Whatever his conscience tells him is right is absolutely right, and the consciences of other men don't count, they are wrong—unless they're on his side, like what's-his-name with the beard, the Beard of Stubborn Refusal you called it—and then God is on their side. What makes him think the ear of *his* conscience is closer to God than his neighbor's?"

"Your second question is harder than the first, and it's a good one. Thoreau didn't give a direct answer—maybe because he had no Oliver Huggins to ask the direct question."

————God, it seems, gave everyone a conscience containing His law, but somehow the various consciences turn out not to be equal. Thoreau describes some of them "as irritable as spoilt children" and scorns the "sickly conscience" while poetizing a "conscience wise and steady," or a "conscience exercised about large things," not about "every pimple." For one thing his neighbors don't have easy access to their conscience whereas he seems to possess an inner compass, its needle always pointing North to the absolute right. On that compass there are only two markings—N and S, where $S =$ the Mexican War and Slavery.

Sometimes it seems that an act of will is necessary to consult the compass. Most people must lack a prompting conscience or else lack the will to get in touch with it. Thoreau's seems to reside in him as a solitary individual—in both the spiritual and the social sense. A childless bachelor, he does not belong to any family, although he is surrounded by female relations, nor to any incorporated society, thus excluding state and church generally, the United States of America, the State of Massachusetts, and the town of Concord, in particular. He admits social feelings only toward "neighbors." Still, neighbors are only found in human aggregates, however small, like Concord. Is Henry David a member of the Concord Lyceum? For a time he was its official secretary.

The only unincorporated society he belongs to seems to be the wise minority, a group whose conscience-needles all point North. Thoreau writes about finding the way to wisdom and preaches it to those yet stumbling in the dark. This may be a clue. A certain group of persons have a purer conscience than the majority and a greater will to tune into it, a group composed probably of several Massachusetts men whose consciences are always in session, plus a woman or two, possibly Quaker. Surely among the Seneca Falls women one would find likely candidates: they declared their sphere of action to be assigned by their conscience and their God. The wise minority would not serve in the military, not hold public office, not work at stultifying jobs, yet would not need to trouble about the wherewithal, about keeping a roof overhead and the wolf from the door. It begins to smell like a priesthood.

Let's look for a moment at our newly ordained political philosopher's proposal. If supreme law issues from conscience, if conscience issues from God's word as the wise minority receives it, or as God has written it in their separate being, if the government cherishes the wise minority, then God's word (or divine law) rules. In spite of all the wind and waves of Eastern religions, we find ourselves moored to the old Puritan theocracy. Isn't this the kind of state that commands Henry David to pay his tithe?

Moreover, for the proposal of a wise minority to work, the government must cherish it and follow its lead. That government, whether republican, democratic, or theocratic, whether exacting taxes or tithes, will be an incorporated society, all forms of which Henry Thoreau has sworn off.

Recalling what he wrote about the neighbor who was a good neighbor until he turned into a marine or an officeholder or a tax collector, I gather that he supposes men to be born with a good, pure conscience. Over all, that which prevents them from getting in touch with it, corrupts them, and turns them from Dr. Jekyll into Mr. Hyde is the American government with its voting and majority rule, its meaningless oaths, its false laws and presumptuous constitution, "its black arts."

Not just the American government, *any* government in the world does this to men. We saw that Thoreau opens this essay of his with the motto "that government is best which governs least." His insistence on the corrupting influence of government on humankind leads Thoreau toward the camp of the anarchists.

"Do you know what anarchism is, Oliver?"

"I think so," replied Huggins. "Isn't it the complete breakdown of law and order brought about by violence?"

"Hmm," pondered St. John. "That resembles a legal definition of anarchy, the kind Gouverneur Morris and Alexander Hamilton threatened would occur if delegates refused to sign the draft of the '87 Constitution. Incidentally, natural calamities like earthquakes, famines, or disruptions in public utilities can lead to anarchy in the sense of no effective government. But I'm speaking of anarch*ism*, the political doctrine. It has a nice musical sound, don't you think, made up of two Greek words: *an* or 'no' and *arche* or 'overarching rulership.' No rulership."

————Coined in France shortly before, the term was barely available to Thoreau. The then-current expression for anarchists was "no-government men," a phrase stemming from an extension of Jeffersonian principles. No standing army: no standing government. Anarchists believe that people are by nature good, that the state or government makes them bad, that the only solution is to create a country or world without government, where all collective activity is performed piecemeal by individual or group consent, by voluntary cooperation.

Some of them insist that such a world can only be attained by violence, that the property, institutionalized greed, and ambition that prop up and are propped up by the state will give in only to guns and bombs, never to moral persuasion. Others say that no matter what happens, their goal must be reached without violence on their part, for spiritually he who takes up the sword dies by it: violence brutalizes the violent. Some anarchists accuse religion of concealing or distracting mankind from the coercive reality of the state and property. Others view the state as the instrument of the devil, as the Antichrist, the manufacturer, depository, and enforcer of evil in the sight of God.

Part of the ideas of the seventeenth-century Levellers and Diggers in Oliver Cromwell's army were both Puritan and anarchistic, and may have seeped into New England via emigration and the works of the English writer William Godwin at the turn of the eighteenth century. Most native anarchist thinkers, beginning with its philosophical founder, the Bostonian Josiah Warren (1798–1874), came from Massachusetts. You remember, too, don't you, that the first constitution, the Articles of Confederation, made no provision for a central or standing government. Once the "united states in congress assembled" disassembled, there was no United States government; about the only thing left was a committee to forward the mail.

When men are prepared for it, Thoreau writes, a government that "governs not at all" will be the kind of government they will have. Until that day Thoreau will distinguish himself from the anarchists, the "no-government men," because they want no government at once, whereas he will be satisfied with mere better government at once. Not surprisingly, his ideas of better government are murky. The "wise minority" theocracy may be the kind of better government he would have "at once." In the long run he would prefer a government that governs not at all. Thus, Thoreau may be a no-government man or anarchist compromising for the time being with a wise-minority notion of government. The just and happy world of the anarchist treats the individual with respect as a neighbor but holds no place for Thoreau's elite, the wise minority, another variety of standing government, however ethereal. The anarchist creed is, Be neither subject nor king, master nor slave.

In the first chapter of *Walden* on the "Economy," Henry David discourses at length on employment and labor, wondering why "we can be so frivolous" as to pay attention "to the gross but somewhat foreign form of servitude called Negro Slavery." "Somewhat foreign form of servitude": a curious turn of phrase. Did he say "foreign" because slaves come from Africa? Africa had slaves before the Portuguese came to buy them. Some freed slaves in the several States held slaves. Was it because slavery was foreign to this continent? The Tabascans made Malinche a slave. Cortés freed her, with the name Doña Marina, making him technically the first liberator. The Cherokees had no taboo preventing them from owning slaves. The Kwatkiutl of the Pacific Northwest Coast took slaves, gave them away as gifts, and to display wealth, sometimes burned them at the stake during festivities. Slavery was alien neither to palefaces nor to blacks nor redskins. And what is *"somewhat* foreign" supposed to tell us? The whole expression is unclear, but coming from Thoreau ambiguity should be no surprise.

The transcendentalists in their condemnation of industrial labor as slavery unwittingly allied themselves with a lasting argument of the South, that wage slavery, not plantation slavery, was the Evil. It is hard to have a southern overseer, Thoreau continues, worse to have a northern one, worst of all to enslave yourself like the young men who inherit farms only to become serfs to the soil. Government is the archdevil, under whose umbrella hide many lesser devils like money and property, and degrading work on farms, in bureaucracy, in commerce, in the dirty coercion of law and the military, in any employment in which the worker finds no joy, in which, one imagines, a face like that of Melville's girl in a New England paper mill, "pale with work, and blue with cold; an eye supernatural with unrelated misery," a poor being who cannot at any time lift her head and see, hear, breathe, and dance in the glories of Nature, nor listen to her conscience, which according to the Seneca Falls Declaration is what she should be doing.

We return full circle to Henry David, nature-boy. It cost him only 27 cents a week to live, he calculates (exclusive of a few things like furniture, microscope, surveying instruments, books, his "tailoress," and Mother's warm house to go home to at any time). Should we open the gates of the factories of nearby Lowell, and offer the inmates the Thoreauvian economy? They may not know how to ship, swim, or survey—for surveying you need geometry—but they can do odd jobs, chop wood, repair a rowboat, mend a fence, plaster a chimney. Let the workers, male and female, stream out of the factories and gather their children and their book-bags, and walk a mile and a half to a dismantled shanty and a piece of land lent them gratis by their well-off friends the Emersons. Maybe they can lose their pallor by the time they realize that they have to go back to Lowell, that there are not enough odd jobs to go around to feed those pinched faces.

Walden won't work out for poor workers. But Thoreau has another use for it. For the politically persecuted it may be salvation. In this guise Thoreau presents it in "Civil Disobedience." For most of his life he had been trying to teach you that the good life is the simple life, that a bigger farm or a bigger property or a bigger bankroll is a snare, that "absolutely speaking, the more money, the less virtue." Now in politics, he urges you to secede from the State, to break the law. What do you do when the State comes to arrest you?

Go along to jail, he says, as I did in Concord. What about wife and children? They must follow you. What if the State takes or lays waste my property, leaving me without house or home? Go live as I did at Walden.

"You must live or squat somewhere, and raise but a small crop, and eat that soon. You must live within yourself and depend upon yourself. . . ."

The simple life is the heroic life and the hero is that model man who went to live in the woods.

His 27-cents-a-week way of life lasted him just two years, though seasoned with smuggled butter and steaks and dinners in town among candle-lit company. There's always a place at table for a bachelor, even a crotchety one like Henry David, even one—as Oliver Wendell Holmes (another middle-named) tells us—who insisted on nibbling his asparagus at the wrong end.

Somehow one has the impression that Thoreau was always old. He never reached old age. He died before he was forty-five. A sketch of him in full-length profile made when he was thirty-seven shows him in town in cold weather, a clean-shaven, slight man, standing with legs together, still and straight, the figure topped by the huge fedora of the day, trimly wrapped in a shortish, double-breasted overcoat with fur collar, holding in his left hand a small satchel or large purse and in his right hand a large folded umbrella. A few years later according to Emerson—brace yourself for this—his face was covered "with a becoming beard." His fellow-traveler Channing thought it "terrible to behold."

Sometime before the beard, Thoreau visited what's-his-name, Joseph Palmer, possibly in Worcester, or met him in Boston perhaps at an antislavery or antiliquor meeting. Anyway, he took to wearing hair on his face just when the wearing of the beard was taking root. That Emerson in his eulogy mentions it as becoming indicates that sporting a beard still occasions comment. Beards, more than signs of stubborn nonconformity, may announce the dandy as shown in *Harper's Illustrated Weekly*, may possibly be signs of

prophetic vision, like that of John Brown, or of Romantic poetry, like that of Wordsworth. And then, isn't it more in keeping with Nature to let a beard grow than to shave it off with regularity?

To let it grow wild, yes, but not to trim it in different styles. Thoreau first grew a beard known as Galway whiskers, a scraggly black ruff around his neck. He claimed he grew it to prevent head colds. B. E. Maxham took an excellent daguerreotype of him at that time. From it Leonard Baskin made a fine stamp portrait. In his last year of life Thoreau switched to the full beard which Emerson remembers, and an ambrotype portrays it as covering his face, actually as dropping below the nose and over his bow tie. This massive model, a contemporary remarked, did wonders for his weak chin.

A new day for whiskers was dawning. Beards will become manly, military, smart. Sam Staples, the village jailer, will appear with a prophet's beard. We are entering a period in which a kiss without a beard is like soup without salt.

Claire St. John arose from the creaking chair she favored, took a deep breath, put her right hand over her left breast, and looking down seriously at Huggins, declaimed:

—"God and my conscience tells me I am right, says the man from Massachusetts. Amen, says God."

She put her hand down for a second, then raised it to her breast again.

—"God and conscience tells me what is right, says the South Carolinian. Amen, says God."

Huggins jumped in protest. "They can't *both* be right!"

St. John smiled at him calmly, knowingly. She went through the little hand-to-heart ritual a third time, and declaimed:

—"They can't *both* be right, says Oliver Huggins. Amen, says God.

"With that cliff-hanger I leave you." St. John headed for the door.

"Wait, wait a minute." Something more important was troubling Huggins, but all he managed to say was, "Do you know what day today is?"

"Of course. It's Wednesday and tomorrow's Thursday. Time flies, Oliver."

10

LINCOLN WANTS A NATION OF BLOOD BROTHERS

THURSDAY

A Nation of
Readers
USA 20c

The north windows overlooked St. John's approach, up the walkway to the porch. Huggins stood before one of the windows facing south. Through it wafted a misty afternoon breeze. A damp day. He felt as dreary as the weather. A small growl of thunder, far away, registered faintly on his ears. Every now and then the sun broke out, throwing long shadows through the trees. Fall was coming in. He'd forgotten about his tennis game. Helen was rightly pissed off about it. He hadn't seen or even thought about her over the last week, much less gone to bed with her. His head, body, and soul was crowded with Claire St. John. He wondered what he had done with himself before he had met her. He wondered what he did *now*. Life was one hour a day, six days a week. He spent most of the time sleeping and daydreaming, reading and writing up anything that might interest her. Before meeting her, was he alive? Tennis and swimming—he'd outgrown them. Why was she doing this tutoring bit? Obviously she didn't need the money. How much was she getting paid anyway? Not enough to buy her soft leather shoes. Could it be . . . ? No, it couldn't be. Supposing that . . .

All guesswork ceased. St. John was making her entrance, jaunty as ever.

"Good afternoon, Oliver."

The day sparkled. "Good afternoon, Claire."

At the sound of her first name St. John's long eyelashes blinked once. She half-turned and gave him a look, not disapproving nor approving, just a look, calculating, as if she were coming to a decision.

"Damp day, what? No tennis today, Oliver."

"No, no dancing under the stars either."

"Yes, and 'tis a pity. Make the best of it. Sit down and hearken to my tale."

He sat down. She stood before him, uncoiling a long silk scarf from a long neck in seductive slow motions over her head, letting it fall to her waist where her other arm waited to catch it in one unbroken cascade of coils. Like the peel of a Spanish orange, he thought. Her silk blouse rustled pleasure, confiding how delighted it was to wrap around her skin. He couldn't imagine her wearing cotton underpants. Now she was fingering the top of her blouse. She unbuttoned one button. Her fingers dropped to the next. Oliver drew in breath. No, she stopped there and sat down. He knocked his head with the heel of his hand. Man, you've got to douse these fantasies.

"What's the matter?" asked tutor. "Been swimming? Got water in your ear?"

Huggins ignored the sarcasm. "Why must we always stay indoors? We could at least go sit on the porch."

"Because if we go outside we'll be distracted by bees and flowers. We're at a critical point in our course of tales."

————One fall day in 1865 a straight-backed man, fifty-five years old, clad in gray, dismounted, tied up a white stallion to the rail, climbed slowly up the wide steps to a long wide porch, removed

his hat, and peeling off his gloves entered the office of the notary
public of Rockbridge County, Virginia. His beard too had once
been gray. Over the war years it had grown white.

The notary public had had word he was coming and rose to greet
him. An exchange of amenities. Then: "Sir, if you will raise your
right hand and swear after me." The gray man raised his right hand
and repeated the words. "I . . . do solemnly swear in the presence
of Almighty God, that I will henceforth faithfully support, protect,
and defend the Constitution of the United States, and the Union of
the States thereunder, and that I will, in like manner, abide by and
faithfully support all laws and proclamations which have been made
during the existing rebellion with reference to the emancipation of
slaves, so help me God." The notary indicated the chair on the other
side of his desk. "Please sit down, sir."

He sat down; the notary picked up a sheet of printed paper from
the desk, a form for the amnesty oath on which he had already filled
in the blanks for date, name, and place of residence. He handed the
sheet across, pointing to its bottom right-hand corner. "If you will
please sign here." His visitor nodded thanks, fumbled for his glasses
attached by a cord to his coat, found them, adjusted them to his
nose, and glanced at the words he had just sworn. Wearily he mumbled to himself, "Sign it, sign it . . ." How many of these had he
sworn to and signed in his lifetime! Oaths to the Constitution of
the United States, oaths to the State of Virginia, to the Constitution of the Confederate States, oaths to the Union . . . Life was a
succession of false allegiances: if not false, broken.

The gray man thought: Love of country and countrymen led me
down this lane. Five years ago had I only said, "Sir, I accept with
a deep sense of responsibility the honor you have conferred on me,"
I would now be on the other side of the fence, a triumphant general, and the next president.

And what had the war amounted to? Butchery. The Civil War,
they call it. The *Un*civil War was the way they fought it. Burning
the houses of women and children, burning food and fields, stealing, looting, shooting horses, killing prisoners of war . . . A war to
free the slaves, they said. In the end both sides were looking to slaves
to support their gaping infantry lines and promising them freedom
in exchange.

Would he have given the president the same reply, knowing what he knew today? "I'm sorry, sir. I cannot fight against Virginia." Probably. Nothing had really changed that.

Today was the day he was to begin as president of Washington College of Lexington. He was little more than a figurehead, eking out his days, *cum dignitate*. A very good thing he did not have to teach. What had he to teach students, that life was a series of empty oaths? No. Straighten up, young men. Silence and patience, and trust in God.

Truly, what qualifications did he have for a college president? He had been superintendent of an important school once—the United States Military Academy at West Point. But that was like comparing a peach to a peanut. His eyes half closed, his mouth relaxed. Absently he ran his fingers through his once black hair. He thumbed the ends of his mustache, once a thick black mustachio. Who ever thought those days would end? He held the sigh of nostalgia within his chest. His coat felt tight. At his age he should take to wearing loose, sloppy shirts, like Grant. What a world! Beaten by a president who couldn't ride a horse, who rose to heaven on a mule, by a general who couldn't hold his whiskey, by a madman who razed cities and countryside closer to the ground than the stubble on his chin.

Then that other one who touched off the fire—that lunatic, John Brown. The idea! To seize a federal arsenal and start a slave uprising against white people! He had double-marched to surround and capture the madman. Virginia had quickly hanged him. That raid struck more terror in the South than the uprisings of Haiti and Nat Turner put together. To every southerner it was the opening shot of the war, the call to arms.

The blurred figure of the notary intruded upon his thoughts, offered him a pen already dipped in ink. He took it, murmured a thank you, and at the end of a long printed line wrote the brief, tall signature, "R. E. Lee."

Claire St. John paused, swigged her water, glanced at the person across from her, gave a dangle or two to her braceleted ankle, and said, "How's Polly?"

"Who's Polly?" puzzled Huggins. "A horse?"

"A horse, ha!" She snorted. "Your *partner*. Isn't that her name?"

"What partner?"

"Your *tennis* partner. I don't know about other partners who might have toyed and kissed."

"You mean Helen. She's okay, I guess. What's this toyed and kissed stuff? Is it part of the course? Aren't you getting into privileged communication?"

"Right. Sorry. Put it down to the moist weather."

————The moment R. E. Lee told Lincoln that his heart belonged to Virginia, the moment 187 other West Point graduates, officers of the United States Army, and numerous nonmilitary government officials said more or less the same thing, the jig was up. Lincoln, in his message to the special Congress of 1861, reviled them as "treacherous officers," men "who have been favored with offices, have resigned, and proved false to the hand which had pampered them."

Before secession there were thirty-three States in the union. First South Carolina, then ten other states had proclaimed that they were withdrawing from the government of the United States. Thirty-three States minus eleven equals twenty-two: the '87 Constitution required only nine for its ratification. The Union could lose thirteen more States and still meet this constitution's requirement. But if thirty-three was the magic number for the "U.S.A.," then the United States were dead. These thirty-three States were now the "D.S.A.," the Disunited States of America.

Northern orators in the previous decade had been scrambling for a new name for the one big consolidated country that didn't exist—the Republic, the Nation, the Union, all common nouns. "Columbia," the up-to-then leading contender, had been snatched up by others. In South America in 1819 appeared Simón Bolívar's Republic of Colombia, later the United States of Colombia. In 1858, "British Columbia" officially became a British colony. Worst of all, since 1786, Columbia was the official name of the capital of South Carolina.

The southern secessionist States, not at all interested in consolidation, chose for themselves an emphatically severalist title going back to the Articles of Confederation—"The Confederate States of America."

On both sides the war waged without noteworthy use of the United States or of America as the name of a country. The initials U.S. continued to be stamped routinely on federal land deeds or rifle butts. In everyday language, instead of the United States or American army there was the Union army. The war was of the Union versus the Confederacy, the North versus the South, the Blues versus the Grays, the Yankees versus the Rebels.

America still referred to a location, as in "the Confederate States of America." When so much of Mexico had been appropriated after the Mexican War and the hemisphere almost cleared of Spanish-language claimants, northern expansionists with gleams of glory and of land speculation in their eyes embraced the whole English-speaking continent with the adjective "American." Facing the buildup of heavy Union forces, the Canadians, worried about United States aggressiveness, began deploying troops in border provinces. They might be next in line after the Mexicans, they feared. Victory left northern military forces with 1 million veterans under arms.

Lincoln's first choice of a name for country was "the Union." Andrew Jackson had made the same choice. During the '87 Philadelphia convention the Framers had initially referred to what they ultimately termed "this Constitution" as the "Articles of Union." In the final version of the document the word appears in the preamble: "a more perfect union," and in Sections 3 and 4 of Article IV, "New States may be admitted by the Congress into this union," and "The United States shall guarantee to every state in this union a Republican form of government." Section 3 of Article II states that the president shall from time to time give to the Congress information of the state of the union.

In terms of the '87 Constitution, "Union" now becomes the new circumlocution for name of country.

In a way "the Union" was a good choice: it was singular and less awkward than the United States. Unfortunately, it did not lend itself to the adjective form either. Unioner? Unionist? Unionian? It still suffered from common-noun status.

★ ★

Abraham Lincoln, the man who made the choice, said that his mother, Nancy Hanks, came from a well-bred Virginia family. She died when he was nine, but not before she had taught him to read. His father, Thomas, also from Virginia, was sometimes a carpenter, sometimes a farmer, illiterate, not very ambitious, a sociable man. The first Lincoln ancestor, apprentice to a weaver, had emigrated from Higham, Norfolk, to Higham, Massachusetts, in 1637. Nancy and Thomas named their only son Abraham after a grandfather killed by Kentucky Indians. Growing up in States with western customs and manners of rough equality, he saw the light of day in Kentucky, moved at age seven with the family to Indiana, removed at age twenty to southern Illinois, and remained there until his election as president of the United States.

He reached six feet four, was thin, angular, strong, dark, with bushy black hair, a high broad forehead, and deep-set gray eyes above large cheekbones. Witty, tender-hearted, patient, and cheerful, simple and direct on the surface, he loved easy talk, stories, and jokes. Yet, wrote William Henry Herndon, his law partner and biographer, melancholy dripped from him as he walked. He had a lot to be sad about—his hard early life, his difficulties with women, a misunderstood and misunderstanding pretentious wife, her problems that caused *him* problems, a son dying while the war went badly, his heading into a conflict that tolled a million and more in casualties. You can't count a million men. The war, he knew, was partly his own doing. Presidents James Buchanan and Franklin Pierce before him had averted the call to arms; he could have done so, too. Nightmares stalked his sleep.

Nightmares and premonitions, I am sure, would have stalked him no matter what. He once marveled that Negroes could suffer what they suffered and yet laugh and sing and dance as if without a care in the world. The Lord, he moralized, shears the sheep to the wind. The Lord did not shear him likewise. He was sad to the very genes. His genes also brought intelligence; his training in law, logic, and rhetoric sharpened it into a precise mind, cold, confident, standoffish.

"You're pretty cold and confident, too," put in Huggins, amazing himself.

"Think so?" St. John rebutted. "How do you know it's not a

cover for a natural shyness? Or that I'm not just acting like my super-professor models, trying to impress you with my authority and knowledge? I've never had a tutee before, you know. Maybe with my next one I can afford to act with less obvious authority."

"Are you going to tutor others?" Horrified.

"Why not? I'm sure some Ruling Prince or Brahmin family must be looking for a tutor. I could place an advert in the paper: 'Let Claire St. John, tutor *extraordinaire*, take you through pre-American history.' Want to sign up now?"

"Damn right I do."

"Why, thank you, Oliver. May I use you as a reference? Truly I don't know whether I shall continue or not. I doubt it."

Huggins chewed his lip. St. John plowed on.

———During the reign of "King Andrew," politicians had felt the legislative impact of the office of the presidency when backed by a congressional majority. Parties with programs that could attract voters across the States took on a shape calculated to secure this power. The Democrats, descended from Thomas Jefferson, still favored the theory that government was the creature of the several States. The Federalists of New England, ever aiming at solidifying these States into a whole, now more openly referred to the government as "national," less and less as "federal." To find a program that would appeal to voters to the west they had become the "Whigs," and over the tariff and slavery issues they had turned into the "Republican" party, all the while pressuring for consolidation and expansion.

In and out of Illinois politics for years Lincoln now aimed at Washington, D.C. He had been a Whig state legislator, fought hard campaigns for the Senate and lost; the next time around he ran as the Republican candidate for president of the United States and won. Early in his political career he had found he could play to his audience and win it over with well-chosen phrases. A stock of homespun stories and fables served him well. He had the gift of the backcountry southern politician: almost any ticklish question put to him reminded him of a story. Like as not, the joke was on him. This precious stock gave the sad, superior man a reputation for homespun humility and wit.

People thought of him as an Illinois lawyer. Instead, they were dealing with an eel as slippery as a Philadelphia lawyer. True to type was his answer to an opponent's charge of religious infidelity in his younger, skeptical years of running for Congress. He had, he replied, "never denied the truth of the Scriptures" and would not like to support any man for office whom he knew "to be an open enemy of, and scoffer at, religion." Since he could quote Scripture as well as if not better than his opponent, a Methodist preacher, it was difficult to catch him off-base.

Notice that today we are looking at no mind-straying nature boy, no woolly-minded backwoodsman, but at a clever lawyer and perennial politician. His law partner colorfully described his ambition as "a little engine which knew no rest."

The North's arming and spiritual support of John Brown seemed to southerners a taste of things to come. Though the United States Marines had quickly disposed of Brown, his plan to arm the slaves against their masters forewarned the South. Southerners had better prepare for northern-led slave uprisings, for a barrage of abolitionist literature pouring through the United States mail, for a president and a Republican party who hated the South and held it a holy duty to stamp out slavery. Faced with a hostile northern press, a declaredly antisecessionist new president, and the possibility of military action, the southern States decided to reclaim and occupy federal military installations on their territory, including Fort Sumter, South Carolina.

As Lincoln took office, seven southern States had already seceded from the organization known as the United States, declaring that their people for various serious reasons no longer consented to be a party to that association. James Buchanan, the previous president, had not tried to prevent them forcibly from seceding. Constitutionally, he had no authority to do so. Neither the president, "a mere executive officer," nor Congress, he affirmed in his last annual message, could "coerce a State into submission which is attempting to withdraw or has actually withdrawn from the [Union] Confederacy." The constitution does not delegate "to Congress or to any other department of the Federal Government" the power "to declare and make war against a State." He concluded: "Congress possesses many means of preserving [the Union] by conciliation, but the sword was not placed in their hand to preserve it by force."

Let us imagine how a reasonable man if elected president might decide his course. He picks up and rereads the '87 Constitution. He finds nothing there to prevent States from withdrawing. This constitution neither contemplates nor prohibits secession. Moreover, if a State claims secession as a right or power not enumerated by this constitution nor delegated by it to the United States, it is according to the Bill of Rights a right "retained by the people" or "reserved to the States respectively or to the people," Amendments IX and X. (We'll tiptoe later around one of these two sleeping dogs.) Of course the president does have to take care that United States laws be faithfully executed, but this duty does not extend to a State or country outside the federal frame of government. To apply these laws under such circumstances would constitute intervention in the domestic affairs of a foreign country.

But, he recalls, the southerners have appropriated federal property. Property is property, even in international law. This calls for negotiation. He confers with his cabinet, with House and Senate leaders, and sends the following message in appropriate form to the seceded States: We don't want a State in the federal government that doesn't want to be there. Besides, we don't approve of slavery. So secede if you wish, but pay us for the investments we have made in that fort and in other property of the United States within your States, less of course your own investments in that property. Once you do that, goodbye and good luck. One proviso regarding the territories of the United States: the United States Congress and I shall undertake to pass a law for the establishment of a joint commission consisting of five Congressmen from your side and five from ours, to administer these territories until they wish to apply for admission as republics. They may then apply for statehood to your side or ours as they choose. It won't be easy, but with goodwill on both sides, we can do it. We remind you that we do not wish to have any States in our union who do not remain there of their own free consent. As our much-admired Artemus Ward advises us, "Let them secesh."

Clever as he may be, President Lincoln does not choose this

course. He immediately trumpets for 75,000 volunteers for Fort Sumter. This action he justifies with the strained political theories descended from the Federalists, the torch passing from James Wilson of the Philadelphia convention to Justice Story and his three volumes of *Commentaries on the Constitution of the United States* (1833), thence relayed to Andrew Jackson as president, who was as determined as Lincoln to prevent nullification and secession by strong-armed methods if necessary. Lincoln added to their arguments phrases from latter-day Federalists and Whigs, and from congressional orators, in particular Daniel Webster; drew in for good measure transcendentalist writers like the historian George Bancroft and the preacher Theodore Parker; and mashed them up for dollops to his First Inaugural and other speeches.

Subsequent generations across the North and West have wildly praised these speeches. In part they are very good speeches. Their reception in the North at the time, though not extravagant, was favorable. Of all presidents to this day, as writers of speeches and letters, including those sparked by batteries of ghost-writers, Lincoln has no equal.

But he does take some outlandish positions. In that First Inaugural of March 4, 1861, he makes two bizarre claims: first, that the existing union is older than the constitution and the States; second, that it is perpetual. He cites two grounds, the legal and the historical, and goes on to expound them principally in several subsequent addresses: the message to the special Congress of July 4, 1861, the Dedicatory Remarks at Gettysburg, and the Second Inaugural.

"I hold," he declares in the first of these orations, "that in contemplation of universal law, and of the Constitution, the Union of these States is perpetual." The '87 Constitution does not contain the word *perpetual*. As for universal law, what is that? And what would perpetual mean in universal law—forever and ever and ever until time stops? Lincoln's next sentence tries to clarify his meaning: "Perpetuity is implied, if not expressed in the fundamental law of all national governments." This is not a *universal law* but Abraham Lincoln's private, muddled observation. Is he thinking of the Roman or Chinese empire? No national government in history has been perpetual. As for *national* governments, is the United States a national or a federal government? And if by *fundamental law* he means constitutional law, the '87 Constitution must be an exception to the rule: perpetuity is neither expressed nor implied. If he means something outside the written constitution, it is none of his business.

The legal proposition of perpetuity, continues the president, is "confirmed by the history of the Union itself. The Union is much older than the Constitution. It was formed, in fact, by the Articles of Association in 1774." Ridiculous. He refers to the first meeting of Congress of the British Colonies in North America and the articles of association they drew up and even by his count the Union is only thirteen years older than the Constitution (1787 − 1774 = 13). Is this supposed to confirm that the Union is "much older" and "perpetual"? Rather it illustrates that constitutions claiming to be perpetual may last as long as thirteen years. The Articles of Confederation of the United Colonies of New England (Massachusetts, Plymouth, Connecticut, and New Haven) did better than that, lasting forty-one years (1643 to 1684). It too claimed to be perpetual.

Except that it did not suit his purpose, Lincoln should have said that the several Colonies formed that union. These Colonies were much older than any Congress or association of colonies. All of them had proper-noun names and a history of a hundred years and more before 1774, the year Rhode Island declared itself an independent State. These historical reminders make even more peculiar Lincoln's further contention (in the speech to the special Congress) that the Union is older than the States, "and in fact created them as States."

Lincoln moves on: "The Union was matured and continued by the Declaration of Independence in 1776."

This document did not mature "the Union." It declared the common desire of the Colonies to unite in revolt in order to become free and independent States, a desire fulfilled through military might in alliance with a foreign power and through a new status confirmed by peace treaties (in 1783) that listed each of the States as a separate treaty-signing country.

Lincoln continues his historical survey: "The Union was further matured and the faith of all the then thirteen States expressly plighted and engaged that it should be perpetual, by the Articles of Confederation in 1778."

Note how, by using the passive voice here and throughout his legal and historical survey, Lincoln avoids mentioning the actors, those who drew up and individually subscribed to the various documents, that is, the Colonies and the States.

Put in the active voice, the event might read something like this: "No longer Colonies, and most of them now with their own separate constitutions, the free and independent States met and composed their first joint constitution, the Articles of Confederation and Perpetual Union." Evidently, having too long matured, this tomato got overripe, dropped to the ground, and started to rot. So had concluded the artful trio—Washington, Madison, and Hamilton—eight years later, as they pushed through the second constitution.

Here is Lincoln's version: "And finally, in 1787, one of the declared objects for ordaining and establishing the Constitution was to *'form a more perfect union.'* " But, he persists, if one or more States can lawfully get out of the Union, "the Union is less perfect than before the Constitution, having lost the vital element of perpetuity." Lincoln overlooks that the Framers purposely avoided the word *perpetual;* they were busy destroying unconstitutionally the still existing "Perpetual Union," thereby allotting it the outside life-span of a decade.

A more perfect union need not be a more perpetual one; it may be a less perpetual one, as Thomas Jefferson would have it, or more perfect in ten different senses, like being better organized financially, assigning treaty powers more practically, arranging greater facility of amendment, or containing fewer but more compatible States. If Gouverneur Morris wanted to say that they wished to specify perpetuity, he could easily have written, "to form a more perpetual union." Were you to ask Gouverneur Morris what he meant by this superior superlative phrase—to form a more perfect union—he might reply with some irritation, "Isn't it obvious? To form a new and better union." Better than which union? you might stupidly insist. "Better than the previous one, of course. *C'est très clair. Qu'est-ce que vous voulez de plus, monsieur?* Good-bye. Nice to have met you."

"Actually," St. John recalled, "the colonial 'Declaration of Taking Up Arms' of July 6, 1775, had already stated, 'Our union is perfect.' "

"What would Gouverneur have done," asked Huggins, "if you'd mentioned *that* to him? Laughed?"

"Good guess. He'd have laughed and said, 'Perfect is *always* good.' "

———Like Presidents Jackson and James K. Polk before him, she proceeded, Lincoln claimed to represent the whole people. The argument puts Congress in an inferior position: its members individually represent only statewide sections of the "Union." The fact is that under this constitution originally and as amended (by Article XII in 1804) voters did not vote directly for a presidential candidate but for State electors in an electoral college whose votes were reported and tallied State by State. This peculiar college elected the president.

The '87 Constitution established only one legal class of representatives, the House of Representatives. The word *representative* is not used for the Senate, not even after the Seventeenth Amendment (of 1913) which provided for the direct election of two senators by each State's people. The supreme court is a court, its members are judges, not representatives. The president is vested with the executive power. He presides over nothing, neither over Congress nor over the supreme court. He executes laws. He does not represent any people or peoples or the people. The House of Representatives as a whole represents the peoples of all the States together.

Lincoln in his First Inaugural boasted that the American people were "my masters." As Calhoun insisted, there was no American people, nor had there ever been one. Threats of secession currently proved this. Actually, not a single elector from a southern State voted for Lincoln. Who was to represent the southern minority?

Lincoln sets forth the thesis, legally and historically, that the author of the Union, of this train of documents, was and is "We, the People," and that for this great struggle "these free people" had confided to him, their only national servant, a vast and sacred trust. Actually because of a split in the Democratic party, he was elected by less than 40 percent of the votes cast, by a mere plurality. For this he was called the "minority president." He had no mandate from his "masters."

But he had good reason for raising the banner of the people. To prosecute the war he would need more people than he had first thought. His party had criticized the outgoing president for doing nothing except appease the South. Lincoln gave notice in his farewell to Springfield, the capital city of Illinois, that he had decided to act. "A duty devolves upon me which is, perhaps, greater than that which had devolved upon any other man since the days of Washington."

Shortly after this farewell, in his First Inaugural (a speech made somewhat conciliatory on the advice of Seward), he called for an army of volunteers to suppress what he defined as an insurrection, and summoned Congress to special session. He soon discovered, and so did the South, that this was not the United States cavalry chasing and being chased by Indians. This was a war of massed infantry. Both sides had reckoned without the other side's will to resist and without the huge cost in men of a modern war. In his Second Inaugural, Lincoln said: "Neither party expected for the war, the magnitude, or the duration, which it has already attained. . . . Each looked for an easier triumph. . . ."

Calhoun had not foreseen an easy triumph. Nor had Lincoln's nowadays much-maligned predecessor, Buchanan. Even if we had the constitutional authority to war against a State, that president told Congress, war could not only destroy the union but would banish "all hope of its peaceable reconstruction. Besides, in the fraternal conflict a vast amount of blood and treasure would be expended, rendering future reconciliation between the States impossible. In the meantime, who can foretell what would be the sufferings and privations of the people during its existence? The fact is that our Union rests upon public opinion, and can never be cemented by the blood of its citizens shed in civil war. If it cannot live in the affections of the people, it must one day perish."

Increased firepower called for increased cannon fodder. Men had to man the guns and charge the breastworks. Manpower needs outraced the supply of militia and volunteers. Lincoln called for conscripts in the face of constitutional doubts and draft riots.

The search for manpower went abroad, at first for officers—so many southern officers had left the army of the United States for that of their State. After the Union rout at Bull Run in July of 1861, Seward offered the highest commission in the president's power to grant, a major generalship in the army of the United States, to the "Soldier of Freedom," General Giuseppe Garibaldi, then resting on his laurels after triumphs in Italy and Latin America. The general answered that to accept he would have to be commander in chief of Union forces with authority to emancipate the slaves. Negotiations lapsed. Imagine what would have happened to the morale of the Army of the Potomac with an Italian general at its head. Far safer to make do with the popular general George B. McClellan, slowpoke that the president held him to be.

Then came the search for men. The North sought foreign mercenaries directly with pay and indirectly through grants of citizenship to immigrants—Irish and German by the thousands—who would serve in the armed forces. A number of Garibaldi's ex-soldiers crossed the ocean to join northern forces and receive immediate citizenship. Still the jaws of war yawned for men. Before long Lincoln had to lay a "strong hand on the colored elements" in border states by granting emancipation to slaves who enlisted in the Union armies, thus achieving "a gain of quite a hundred and thirty thousand soldiers, seamen, and laborers" to "our white military force."

Toward the end of the war, the South with its smaller population needed military manpower even more. It, too, was ready to offer emancipation to slaves who enlisted.

In the Second Inaugural, the president said that colored slaves localized in the South "constituted a peculiar [read, particular] and powerful interest. All knew that this interest was, somehow, the cause of the war." Yet the war ended with both sides proposing freedom to slaves.

"This is essentially a People's contest," he had proclaimed earlier, in his Fourth of July message to Congress. He might have said, "a Manpower contest." Small armies may fight for hire without sharing the limited interests of those who hire them. Slaves may fight for freedom, immigrants for citizenship and pay, but if they are to fight, die, or be crippled in a general slaughter, the masses in mass armies must always be given a noble objective, a great cause to share—to die for country. Here, to die for "the Union."

With this term, "the Union," Lincoln gets himself deeply involved. The passion and mysticism in his use of it struck writers of both North and South. He could turn this common, cold noun into a warm name for country only because he believed that's what it was, and that's what he was saving. In his well-known letter of the summer of 1862, responding to a critical editorial by Horace Greeley (whom we have met as the *New York Tribune* employer of Margaret Fuller), he denied that saving or destroying slavery was his policy. "My paramount object in this struggle *is* to save the Union, and is *not* to save or destroy slavery."

We begin to see why Lincoln spent so much time in his First Inaugural on the perpetuity and hoary age of the Union. He wishes to line it up with the '87 Constitution so that he can swing on a flying trapeze from one to the other. "The Constitution itself expressly enjoins upon me, that the laws of the Union be faithfully executed in all the States." He translates the presidential oath into preserving "the Union."

This constitution itself expressly enjoins upon him no such thing. The oath enjoins upon him that he "will faithfully execute the office of president of the United States, and will to the best of [his] ability, preserve, protect and defend the constitution of the United States" (Article II, Section 1, last paragraph). The passage he is specifically referring to (Article II, Section 3) states that "he shall take care that the laws be faithfully executed." Under this constitution there are no laws to execute except the constitution itself, treaties, and "the laws of the United States" (Article VI). No mention of "laws of the Union," no mention of executing them "in all the States."

From the start Lincoln was determined to run up the North-South conflict into something grandiose, an epic world struggle. Years before he became president he had prophesied: "We shall not only have saved the Union . . . millions of free happy people the world over, shall rise up and call us blessed to the latest generations." This was his purple vision, redemption through the Union. Coming to believe that he had been entrusted with the global mission of saving an imperiled country—"the Union," the last hope of an unfree world—he assumed the mantle of savior.

"Do you remember, Oliver, his diagnosis of John Brown?" Oliver shook his head. "I meant to quote it when we discussed Thoreau but maybe I forgot. Here it is, from his speech at Cooper Union on February 17, 1860: 'An enthusiast broods over the oppression of a people till he fancies himself commissioned by Heaven to liberate them.' "

————Upon the fall of Fort Sumter, the president spoke at that special session of Congress he called on the Fourth of July, just four months after his inauguration. "And this issue embraces more than the fate of these [*sic*] United States. It presents to the whole family of man, whether a constitutional republic, or a democracy . . . can, or cannot, maintain its territorial integrity, against its own domestic foes. It presents the question whether discontented individuals . . . can . . . break up their government, and thus practically put an end to free government upon the earth." The war will be a life-and-death contest to keep the one example of free government from being wiped from the face of the globe.

Had they not led toward such tragic consequences, these remarks would be comical. For one, as we have seen, a republic and a democracy are not the same thing. For another, the government of these United States was not the only free government upon the earth. Take England. A constitutional monarchy, to be sure, but not a free government? Weren't Englishmen free? From where had the ideas of a constitution, a bill of rights, of representation and *habeas corpus* sprung?

By his legal and historical survey Lincoln hoped also to destroy the seceding States' claim to sovereignty, to independence. By citing the Revolution of '76's temporary union (announced in the Declaration of Independence), he thought to destroy the later doctrine of dual sovereignty expounded by Thomas Jefferson, whereby each of the States and the federal government is independent in its own sphere, as laid out in the '87 Constitution. This constitution is for him not the federal but, as he repeats, "the National Constitution."

Why did not at least one southern senator stand up and say, "Sir, do you not mean to say 'our *federal* constitution'?" No southern senator stood up, no group of southern Congressmen hooted and howled, or got up and walked out as a body, because they had already walked out. Having left the United States, they had no business sitting in the United States Congress. Lincoln was addressing a Congress devoid of the South, loaded with the "patriotic hearts" of the North thumping like military drums. The Thirty-sixth Congress (1859–1861) counted sixty-six senators; the Thirty-seventh (1861–1863) counted forty-nine. A rump Congress.

In no legislation by the United States Congress for over a decade was the South represented. Neither was it represented in the reelection of Lincoln and his party. Nor in the subsequent Amendments, XIII to XV, when its membership in Congress was uneven, coerced, and pro forma.

From the time the Quakers and abolitionists defined slavery as an evil, the press and then Congress began to discuss the matter not as just a question of moneyed interests or of property or of tariffs and markets, but as a moral issue. The Framers had not been so convinced of the evil of slavery—although voices were raised against it—that they had voted its exclusion. They put off the problem as lawyers often do—as we have seen them do with the problem of naming the country—with circumlocutions. They slipped it under the rug. Lincoln was aware of this; he said they hid it away.

Namelessness and slavery, two problems that the '87 Constitution camouflaged, emerge together in this murderous war. How could a hellish issue like slavery be resolved by a majority government of a country that didn't exist or, that was at best just beginning to exist, nameless itself and facing powerful opponents bearing definite, evocative old names?

Lincoln's remarks as a young man cast him as a religious skeptic, an eighteenth-century rationalist. At first he resisted the abolitionists with their threats of hell-fire, their damnation of the '87 Constitution, their advocacy of a secession of their own. Had they taken steps to secede, he would, as president, have fought against them just as fiercely. In that case, West Point and Washington, D.C., would not have witnessed a wholesale resignation of southern officers and federal employees. But before long the transcendentalists, abolitionists, and evangelists all conspired to bring him into the nineteenth century, and prepared him to regard his destiny as a religious mission.

The eleven southern States harbored many varying views but knew that the great divide was horizontal, between South and North. Lincoln tried to slight the cultural gap. "You say we are sectional," he said to the southern people in his Cooper Union speech.

"We deny it." In his Second Inaugural, five years later, he scraped the bottom of the barrel. "Both [sections] read the same Bible." The same Bible, to be sure, but read differently by Anglicans, Congregationalists, Lutherans, Unitarians, Presbyterians, Methodists, and Baptists. And since the Revolution, John Calhoun argued, differences had grown wider; religion in particular had split into even fiercer factions along South-North lines. There were other differences as well. New England and the upper Middle West was three quarters English by descent, the white South was three quarters Scottish, Irish, Scotch-Irish, Welsh, and Cornish, a grouping at times called Celtic in opposition to Anglo-Saxon. Confederate armies displayed a marked preference for Saint Andrew's cross and other emblems of Scottish provenance.

Did these northerners and southerners drink their tea the same way? Their liquor? Did they laugh at the same jokes, at the same dialects and accents? Had they the same ideas about family, love, children, manliness, trade, femininity, philandering, jealousy, literature, honor, duels, cleanliness, animals, employees, slaves, servants, music, the value of life and of death?

When Lincoln spoke of the United States as a house divided, he was wrong. There were two houses. The trouble was, he wanted to keep both houses under one roof and play father to two batches of children, the twenty-two nice ones and those eleven brats. George III had the same wish for his thirteen naughty children who ran out from under the parental roof and started to raise roofs of their own. Lincoln went further, claiming that if the obstreperous children left, the roof would collapse. He denounced them for trying to destroy the family. If the North had opted for peace and the southern States had remained seceded, I wonder whether the president would have had the spirit to say what the king had blurted out, what Artemus Ward had suggested, and what the Unitarian minister Theodore Parker was in effect saying all along: "Good riddance." Or what Horace Greeley wanted: to let "erring sisters go in peace."

Something clicked. "By the way, wasn't Parker the one who said that what Margaret Fuller's magazine needed was a beard?" Huggins asked.

"Yes," confirmed St. John. "Speaking of beards, when Lincoln was president he decided to grow one. I would give more weight to the president's decision were it not that by then everyone of note wore them."

"Not women," pointed out Huggins.

"No, there were women nurses, Dorothea Dix, women hymnists and abolitionists, women writers—*Uncle Tom's Cabin* and Mary Chesnut—but no women generals or women soldiers, bewhiskered, be-mustachioed or not.

"The president's black beard gave him a paternal and even graver look. Lincoln, once the young, lean rail-splitter from Illinois, became Father Abraham blessed with good children but unutterably sad for having to send them to fight and kill those brothers who wanted to topple their house down and destroy the good it stood for."

————None of this "go in peace" stuff for Lincoln. He acted as if secession meant mutilation leading to death by gangrene. He claimed—without constitutional grounds—that it was his duty to leave the Union as he found it, that is, containing the same number of States. In speech after speech Lincoln cries out that either the wayward eleven be forced back in or the Union is destroyed.

All or nothing. This argument was more than a lawyer's either-or trickery. It was that, too, of course, and one can see it put to use in almost all of Lincoln speeches. With him, though, especially on the larger issues, it was a reflex. Either the president has war powers or he does not (He shares them with Congress). Either peace or war (What about negotiation?). Either war or unconditional surrender (What about a truce?).

Even before he occupied the White House, Lincoln was saying that "this government cannot endure, permanently half-*slave* and half-*free*. . . . It will either become *all* one thing, or *all* the other." Perhaps not a government but something Lincoln called the Union had already lived that way for nearly a century. And what was the South saying (and the transcendentalists too) about northern wage-slaves? About the North's labor-marts outside of factories where men, women, and children clamored in foreign tongues for a chance to sell their body by day and return to their rat-holes by night, were they not half-slave, half-free? To take up *their* cause, one couldn't count on Lincoln. One had to wait a few years up the road, for other martyrs, for the anarchists, for Albert R. Parsons, the Alabama boy who became a northern worker, who knew both chattel and wage-slavery at close hand, who thought the latter as bad if not worse, whose last words were as he stood on the trapdoor, noose around his neck, "Will you let me speak, Sheriff Matson! Let the voice of the people be heard! Oh—"

From Lincoln's idea of half-freedom we now turn to Lincoln's equally primitive idea of equality.

"I ask you, Oliver, where in Lincoln's trail of Union documents is the word *equality* to be found?"

"Well, in the Declaration of Independence, for one: 'all Men are created equal.' Then . . . I don't know."

"What about the '87 Constitution?"

"I don't remember its being there."

"Memory fails you not. It isn't there. Though most people think it is, and that's his doing. 'Let us readopt the Declaration of Independence,' he cried."

————Lincoln took the '87 Constitution down a peg by affirming the *Union* to be older and perpetual. He downgraded it further in 1854 by substituting for silver the gold of the readopted Declaration of Independence. In 1860 in the speech at Cooper Union in Manhattan, he changed back, rediscovering "our thirty-nine fathers," in the signers of the '87 Constitution. But in the most famous of all his speeches, the brief remarks at the dedication of the Union cemetery at Gettysburg in November 1863—mindlessly recited and memorized ever since by generations of northern and western schoolchildren—he once again supplanted the Framers of the '87 Constitution, this time for good, with the men of eighty-seven years ago. He began with a Biblical phrase: "Fourscore and seven years ago our fathers . . ." Take eighty-seven years away from 1863, and you get 1776. Our fathers, now, are Thomas Jefferson and the signatory members of the 1776 Congress and their constituent "good People" of the Declaration of Independence. Repeating "fathers" and "forefathers," identifying the men of '76 as the true fathers, Lincoln sets up ancestor worship as a basis for patriotism and the Declaration as the ancestral constitution. Evidently, these fathers of yours "brought forth on this continent [that is, North America] a new nation . . ."

If Jefferson and company set out to bring forth a new nation, they didn't happen to mention it. Independence was uppermost. In the zigzagging next-to-last sentence of that document, in which the signers consider themselves representatives both of States and of Colonies, individual and united, they declared in capital letters to all mankind that what they wanted to do, were doing, and indeed had done was to bring forth FREE AND INDEPENDENT STATES. If we hold independence to signify liberty, as they did, then Lincoln's next phrase "conceived in liberty" is correct, except what was conceived in liberty, out of subject colonies, was FREE AND INDEPENDENT STATES.

As for the next phrase "dedicated to the proposition," the Declaration, of course, says nothing about the birth of a new nation dedicated to a proposition. That "all Men are created equal" is not a proposition therein, nor a Right, but one of a number of self-evident Truths. It wasn't self-evident to Calhoun. The document dedicated itself to one proposition, that Men have certain Creator-endowed, inalienable Rights, and if government doesn't allow them these rights, "it is their Right, it is their Duty, to throw off such Government, and to provide new Guards for their future Security."

This is what the southerners claimed was their Right and Duty now and precisely what they claimed to be doing: throwing off a despotic Government by separating from that Government and providing new Guards for their future Security in the Confederate States of America.

Both sides, picking and choosing their path through the word-jungle, claimed the blessing of the Declaration of Independence.

Many of the speakers in the 1850s and into the '60s—including those two exemplars of the art of oratory, Senators Daniel Webster and John Calhoun—spoke of the bonds that bind us; or of the bonds that no longer bind us, bonds that are or will be broken asunder or cords that are snapped. *Cords* was also spelled *chords*. James Madison in one of his newspaper articles had written of the people (of ex-

British North America) who were "knit together by so many chords of affection." Lincoln at the close of the First Inaugural, with the help of his secretary of state, Seward, turned out a memorable phrase "the mystic chords of memory," stretching from every battlefield and patriot grave to every living heart. Mysterious chords of music to "swell the chorus of the Union." The other day as I was refreshing my recollection of the president's speeches, I came across an earlier, 1858, Fourth of July speech. He brought up then the Declaration's principle that "all Men are created equal," but with a different metaphor. That principle "is the electric cord" linking the hearts of patriotic and liberty-loving men together. A more up-to-date and forward-looking metaphor certainly, but nowadays it has lost currency.

She paused. Huggins was listening with interest.

"Well, which is it?" he asked. "Were the chords of the Union musical or electrical?"

"One of each."

————The remarkable thing, she added, is that Lincoln used that electric cord metaphor in a nationality theory, to explain how the new flows of immigrants to the United States—the German, Irish Catholic, Scandinavian, and Chinese—though not related by blood to the men who wrote the Declaration of Independence might nonetheless "feel that they are part of us." I confess I don't see by what genealogical scheme he himself and about half our people, as he said, got to be "descended by blood" from the closed, sometimes incestuous, circle of "the fathers."

Their minds overshadowed by social contract theory, the fathers, whether of the Declaration or of the '87 Constitution, gave little play to the blood theory of nationality. Here and there, though, it cropped up. The Declaration manuscript refers to "our Brittish [sic] brethren." John Jay, writing one of those newspapers pieces collected in 1788 as The Federalist, claimed that Providence had been pleased to give this country to "a people descended from the same ancestors." Madison in the same set of papers wrote of "the kindred blood which flows in the veins of [ex-British] American citizens." Such occasional droplets, and others about "one people," meaning one English or at most British people, kept the blood theory from dying of thirst. Lincoln, however, groping toward an ancestral constitution, had to think his way through a problem. An ancestral constitution, confronted by increasingly diverse populations, has to devise a way of relating them to ancestral fathers. He tried to provide a solution.

All these newcomers have to do, Lincoln instructed, is "look through that old Declaration of Independence" where they will find in that equality phrase "the father of all moral principle in them [the Founding Fathers], and they have a right to claim [that principle] as though they were blood of the blood, and flesh of the flesh, of the men who wrote that Declaration, and so they are."

So they are, blood of the blood. It seems to me he is selling British blood cheap—for a line of type or two. Anyway, assuming that these newcomers know how to read, suppose that their eyes light instead on that other moral principle of Lincoln's fathers several lines below, that "it is their Right, it is their Duty to throw off such Government." Are they still equally "blood of the blood"?

Lincoln overdid the equality phrase. In all States except those of the South the Declaration of Independence is confused with the '87 Constitution. Mind that he doesn't recommend that immigrants read this constitution or any of its clauses. Yet the very thing the Bureau of Immigration and Naturalization concentrates on is to make these newcomers, seeking to become "part of us" citizens, swear that they will preserve the constitution. They are not asked whether it is self-evident that all Men are created equal or whether they believe they have a Right and a Duty to throw off this or any other Government if . . . Nor are they asked whether the president can break the rules of the constitution in order to protect the country.

"Which reminds me of the story of the Logician and the Faulty Constitution."

"How does it go? asked Huggins.

"One day the physicist Albert Einstein and an economist friend, as witnesses, accompanied the mathematical logician Kurt Gödel to Trenton, New Jersey, where he was to be examined on his citizenship application. The mischievous Einstein had advised Gödel to learn American history thoroughly, neglecting to tell him that the examiner typically asked elementary questions about American government, like how many States there were in the union, how many senators, who was the president, where was the capital, and so on. Gödel took Einstein's advice seriously, going so far as to study the texts of basic documents. As he was being examined he started to mention a concern he had, that there was a fault in the constitution that would make it easy for a dictator to come to power. Einstein quickly shushed him up, to the mystification of the examiner. Luckily, Gödel's English was still so heavily accented that the official did not get the drift. He impatiently stamped the papers, pushed them over to Gödel, turned around, and said, 'Next!' "

————Looking at Lincoln's early Fourth of July speech some writers have remarked how very transcendental it was: the vital thing was not the material fact but the moral idea or principle, in this case, equality. But there's something else. The principle of equality, inscribed in the Declaration of Independence, felt or held in common, a good and powerful thing in itself, transforms its holders into something better and stronger, common flesh and blood, a kindred people, a nation of blood brothers. Lincoln effects a transubstantiation: from the reading of a principle to a change in flesh and blood.

Congress was already moving in the direction of a blood theory of nationality, the *jus sanguinis* of Roman law. In 1855, it voted that any child born in a foreign country was automatically a United States citizen if at least one of his parents was a citizen. In 1866 the Rump Congress, in order to make former slaves citizens, relied on the birthplace theory (*jus solis*). "All persons born . . . in the United States," but this did not affect the 1855 provision for relying on blood to transmit nationality to a citizen's foreign-born issue.

The transforming of principle into blood was not the only time Lincoln used blood imagery. "Let us wash ourselves in the spirit if not the blood of the Revolution," he once said in an antebellum speech. Elsewhere he spoke of "the cardinal duty of obedience to law—let every man remember that to violate the law is to trample on the blood of his father. . . ." Now the daily butchery of young men on the battlefield left the taste of blood on everyone's lips. On God's lips too.

Over several years Lincoln worked on a huge mural depicting

war, death, complicity in sin, God, blood payment, purification and redemption—a new birth. It was at the Gettysburg cemetery that Lincoln abruptly abandoned "the Union" for "the Nation," and there that he exchanged northern lives for the life of this Nation which, "under God, shall have a new birth of freedom." It was in the following year in his remarks to a group of Kentuckians, disturbed about using blacks as soldiers, that he brought out northern as well as southern guilt for the war: ". . . God now wills the removal of a great wrong, and wills also that we of the North as well as you of the South, shall pay fairly for our complicity in that wrong . . ." Here also he attaches God's purpose to history: "impartial history will find therein [in the payment for complicity] new cause to attest and revere the justice and goodness of God." God was exacting payment in blood-soaked ground.

South and North had both sinned, the president said, the South for supporting slavery and the North (as the transcendentalists would have it) for allowing slavery to exist all these years, and North and South together for the sins of their fathers, the Framers of the '87 Constitution who had known slavery was evil, yet slipped it in and hid it in the mealymouthed phrase: persons held to service or labor.

The short, sincere Second Inaugural makes a graduated payment explicit. God now wills to remove the offense, striking both North and South with the woe they deserve. God may continue "this mighty scourge of war until every drop of blood drawn with the lash, shall be paid by another drawn with the sword." God was weighing spilled blood on the scales of sin.

Lincoln, the word-painter redeemer, kneels before a God who, like the God of the Mexica, demands blood sacrifice. He asks whether this drop-for-a-drop demand is not "one of the divine attributes which believers in a Living God always ascribe to him," and replies, "as was said three thousand years ago, so still must it be said. 'The judgments of the Lord are true and righteous altogether.' "

The North didn't think it had offended God, nor did the South. Although the Unitarians, Congregationalists, Quakers, transcendentalists, and abolitionists may have believed that the offense came also from themselves, they had been most active in blaming it on others and probably held themselves if not guiltless at least less guilty. The freeing of the slaves freed them to go on to other good causes held in abeyance—lips-that-touch-wine-shall-never-touch-mine and equal rights for women—where one found them and their descendants until recently . . .

While talking, St. John reached into her purse to draw out a small silver case, clicked it open, selected a cigarette, and began tapping it on the case. Slipping the case back she sat with elbows on the table, expectantly, cigarette in hand. Huggins hastily looked around for a match and an ashtray. Old habits never die. She handed him a lighter and leaned forward. He lit the cigarette for her. What kind of cigarette was it? From the fragrance and bright color, he'd guess Virginia. She took two lazy puffs like an Indian chief and laid the cigarette on the plate. Was she a smoker or was this one of her dramatic underscorings?

———. . . where one found them and their descendants until recently, she resumed, gathered around abortion clinics, driving over the country saving the environment in belching cars and, like thousands of Torquemadistas, condemning drinkers and smokers to the stake—stoking the smoldering fire, impatient as Thoreau for the wind of another big blaze. All this in the tones, compassionate and condemning, of rectory morality.

Like the Indians, our southern fathers of four score and seven years ago gathered and smoked tobacco. George Washington raised tobacco, distilled, sold, and drank whiskey, bought, bartered, and sold slaves. Lincoln, a westerner who neither smoked nor drank, advocated the "cold water pledge" and looked forward to a utopia where there would be "neither a slave nor a drunkard on the earth."

What of Lincoln, was he guilty of sin, too? I mentioned his premonitions. In his days in Springfield he would tell his partner Herndon, "Billy, I fear that I shall meet with some terrible end." After each of his two elections, he told of hallucinations that he would be elected to a second term but would not live to complete it. A few days before his assassination he dreamt he had seen a crowd running to the East Room of the White House. Following it he saw his own body laid out and heard voices saying, "Lincoln is dead."

The events of history had tossed him onto the fire like a straw dog. "I claim not to have controlled events but confess plainly that events have controlled me," he said a year before his assassination. He who was innocent, who led the nation to the sacrifice, was to give his own life-blood, too. He was sure, almost to the day, that death was coming.

"No historian today proposes sin as the cause of the war. Nowhere to go with it. But who says the historian is the one to know? What do *you* say, Oliver?"

"You mean, instead of the tariff or slavery as the cause? Didn't the South's agitation over the tariff come before the North's agitation over slavery?"

"That's hard to answer. Over time, these issues had ups and downs in intensity."

————Suppose we take a broader view, she suggested, and ask whether something else related, as yet unrecognized, was going on elsewhere in the world, in this case a trend toward larger countries or nations. This would make tariffs and slavery but parts of a larger movement. R. R. Palmer has observed from a world perspective that an impulse to get bigger with the aid of technology was then consolidating Italy, Germany, Hungary, Austria, and the Russian Empire.

In the United States new inventions were springing onto the market every year. Many came to the eastern seaboard from Europe, especially from England—textile mills, steamboat and railway construction. Important ones came to fruition here—agricultural implements (the cotton gin, iron and steel plow), textiles (the sewing machine), the telegraph (and the telegraphic line), transport (sailing and steamships, the railroads); the Colt revolver made with interchangeable parts; ether for surgery; almost all taking root just in time for the "irrepressible conflict." The future secretary of state W. H. Seward, senator from New York, coined that phrase in a speech in which he sustained that advances in transport were continually pushing the two antagonistic hostile systems into grating contact and ultimate collision.

Forces can be multiple, of course. The War of 1861 reminds us that technology as well as any other force, artifact, or idea may be shunted onto the political arena. One may look on any one or other of them as contributing to constitutional crisis. The '87 Constitution, having originally drafted a balance of political power between North and South, by double-dealing with slavery and independent, named States, could not absorb later shocks without terrible violence.

The marching of millions of men to battle, men from all walks of life, hundreds of thousands of whom were to be shot with assembly-line guns, die in factory-cut uniforms, placed in uniform boxes, and buried in thousands of rows of uniform cemetery plots at $1.59 each—gave proof that all men were equal at least when marching to death and glory.

Think of a field outside a town of 2,500, the site of a battle costing 50,000 dead, wounded, and missing. Think of tens of thousands of contorted bodies—horses, mules, men and boys—rotting in the late summer heat. There you have the new Union cemetery at Gettysburg. There the president helped dedicate the field to Union fatalities.

One could not expect a politician to say that men died and were dying by the hundreds of thousands to keep eleven States from seceding. Or that many poor northern soldiers were not against slavery so much as they feared that if the South won, slaves might swarm into the North, whereas a defeated South would have to keep them.

Lincoln has his say. The men who died on that battlefield (excluding Southerners) died so that "that nation" born in 1776 "might live." (A few Confederate corpses there did slip into burial slots accidentally.) Perhaps Lincoln did believe that eleven southern States were shivering to fragments the united hulk of the other States and that if the South won the war, cotton would be grown on Boston Commons. Still it's hard to credit our wily lawyer with that much naïveté.

It is tempting to think of Lincoln's new birth of freedom to mean the freeing of slaves and their equal inclusion in the life of this born-again nation. Yet his view of equality was not so straightforward as the North later made it out to be. He reminded Horace Greeley that his "oft-expressed personal wish was that men everywhere could be free." In 1864 in his remarks to a small meeting of Kentuckians published in a Kentucky newspaper, he started with a similar sentiment. "I am naturally anti-slavery. If slavery is not wrong, nothing is wrong."

So far, so good, Henry David Thoreau might have said. Your conscience is telling you what is wrong. Go out to fight that wrong. Give up your public office, pay no taxes, go to jail. Not Lincoln. He had fought for the office of president and won, and took the oath.

St. John looked up at Huggins.

"What might Thoreau have said to that, Oliver?"

Unhesitatingly Oliver replied, "He would have said, 'Why take office? Why would you want it in the first place?' "

"Right. Lincoln denied he intended to cheat. It was not 'my view,' he said, 'that I might take an oath to get power, and break the oath in using the power. . . . And I aver that, to this day, I have done no official act in mere deference to my abstract judgement and feeling on slavery.' "

"In other words," Huggins sneered, "he claims he stripped his conscience bare and did nothing to help the cause against slavery. Even so, Thoreau would have turned his back on him. 'No hope for him,' he would have said. 'He's in the grip of ambition. He trades conscience for power.' " Huggins was warming to his thesis. "What about other presidents seeking and winning office when they know they'll have to execute laws that go against their conscience? Do they check their conscience with the guards at the White House gates? Thoreau had a point."

"I'm glad you think so."

―――――The freedom Lincoln intended to give slaves, tutor continued, was to return them to the state in which they were created. Men are born equal, no doubt. What more did Lincoln mean? Surely, that they were to be free of their masters and no longer to be bought and sold. He also insisted that they should be free to eat the bread they had earned by their labor, a point few slaveholders would deny.

Lincoln thought that once slaves were free, they would crouch

at the starting line ready to push off—to use a phrase he repeated—
in "the race for life." His own racing success proved that working as a laborer was better than as a slave. "Twenty-five years ago,
I was a hired laborer." His running-a-race metaphor illuminates only
the start of the race when all are equal, not the end when all are
unequal. "The hired laborer of yesterday," Lincoln continued,
"labors on his own account today; and will hire others to labor for
him tomorrow. Advancement . . . is the order of things in a society
of equals." But the race over, aren't runners now unequal, and
isn't the winner living off the bread earned by the sweat of the
losers?

He had few kind words for the losers. In another speech he
pointed out that "if any continue through life in the condition of
hired laborer, it is not the fault of the system, but because of either
a despondent nature which prefers it, or improvidence, folly or singular misfortune." Lincoln narrated this bit of personal work history
as a hired laborer before he became president. Afterward his success
story got to be grander—Look at me now! Toward the end of the
war, he told assembled troops that the nation, "an inestimable
jewel," was "worth fighting for," for it insured them "equal privileges in the race of life." The present occupant of "this big White
House" could testify to this. "I am a living witness that any of your
children may look to come here as my father's child has."

Is that all? No, there is another side. Not even at the start of
the race for life are all equal. People of color run with a handicap.
Lincoln had expanded on equality for Negroes in a speech at
Charleston, Illinois, as he was campaigning for the Senate. Here is
an excerpt:

> I will say then that I am not nor ever have been in favor of bring-
> ing about in any way the social and political equality of the white
> and black races—that I am not nor ever have been in favor of
> making voters or jurors of negroes nor of qualifying them to hold
> office, nor of intermarrying with white people; and I will say, in
> addition to this, that there is a physical difference between the
> white and black races which I believe will for ever forbid the two
> races living together on terms of political and social equality. And
> inasmuch as they cannot so live, while they do remain together

there must be the position of superior and inferior, and I as much as any other man am in favor of having the superior position assigned to the white race.

Can this be the new birth of freedom the Union dead died for?

"Sure!" Huggins broke in sarcastically. " 'As much as any other man' means the Negroes were not men. The slaves have their life, Lincoln aimed to exchange it for a liberty, planted in the middle of a superior race, and to let them run for their happiness."

St. John looked at him silently for a moment, then said, "You didn't raise your hand."

"What?"

"You forgot you're supposed to raise your hand when you want to comment or ask a question."

Where was she, back in Mexico with Cortés and Moctezuma? Huggins had been anticipating some such put-down. "I've made comments before without raising my hand. You made no objections; I assumed we had progressed to something more like a tutorial and less like a class."

"You assumed, did you?" St. John did not seem cross. "You assumed correctly. Think of the proverb 'Look before you leap.' How do you know Lincoln didn't have a change of heart and mind about racial superiority once he became president?"

"That's possible."

"Of course," she went on, "proverbs often have their contraries, as you will learn when you read *Don Quixote*. Have you read it yet?"

"Not yet," admitted Huggins. "What's the reverse proverb here?"

"That's easy. 'He who hesitates is lost.' "

Which to me, thought Huggins, means, "Faint heart never won fair lady."

————There was nothing new to offer the world, Claire resumed, if by this new birth of freedom Lincoln meant simply the outlawing of chattel slavery. In 1838, slavery was abolished in the Bahamas. By the first half of the century, slavery and the slave trade had been banned in England and Europe, in South America, Mexico, and Canada. In 1861, Russia emancipated the serfs.

Some say that by "a new birth of freedom" the president meant the extending of democracy. Extended to where? The North and West almost everywhere had universal male suffrage. Lincoln was not thinking of extending it to women. Maybe he was thinking of giving slaves the right to vote. Many believe that to be the case, that democracy for him meant a government run by people who were equal in that they had the vote, and "all" or "the people" were to have the vote. This ideal had found current expression in Theodore Parker, Daniel Webster, and other orators who in phrases evocative of the French Revolution defined democracy as a government of all, by all, and for all. "By democracy," preached Parker, "I mean government over all the people, by all the people, and for the sake of all."

Yet the ideal is far from clear. Who does "all" or "the people" include? Lincoln's Gettysburg remarks are vague and rhetorical. They do not revise his Charleston, Illinois, speech. They propose a further reason why these soldiers of the North fought and died and a further resolve for "us," the living persons present at the northern ceremony—"that government of the people, by the people, for the people shall not perish from the earth." That government is the Union or the Nation, and, mind, not just an ideal; according to Lincoln, it is an accomplished fact: that government already exists and must be kept from extinction, with or without slavery. So the question of extending the suffrage further to blacks or whites need not arise.

Possibly the president himself didn't know what he meant by the people in triplicate. His eye and ear had picked it up and his pen polished it on the train ride to Gettysburg.

If we apply the ancient Roman standard of degrees of freedom, the three *c*'s of *commercium, commensalium, connubium,* the freedom to trade with free persons, to eat at table together, to intermarry, Lincoln seems opposed to all three. You have just heard him say that he never dreamed of mingling with "them" in terms of political and social equality.

Only a few blacks could ever be part of *the* people, people in the political sense. He did barely suggest early in 1864 for the "private

consideration" of a newly elected Louisiana governor, "whether
some of the colored people may not be let in [to vote] as, for instance, the very intelligent, and especially those who have fought
gallantly in our ranks." But this, he made clear, is "only a suggestion, not to the public, but to you alone." Lincoln was making
progress. The most intelligent and brave of the blacks evidently
would be on a par with the least of the whites.

To die in defense of democracy (whether it is a government of
all or just of most people) is sweet. Did Lincoln truly believe that
the United States was the only example of such government that
ever existed, that it was threatened by the bad men of the South
with destruction, and might perish from the face of the earth, presumably never to appear again, a one-shot thing? This is either
naïveté or rhetoric. Take your pick. I prefer to think it was naïveté,
a variety of the "New World motif"—wholesome and clean, virgin and pious, the New Jerusalem, the city on a hill, God's model
for the putrefying Old World.

Yesterday I shaped the form this conceit took with the transcendentalists. They at least were widely read in history and languages.
So were the Framers. *The Federalist* mentions among other republics,
great and small, ancient and modern, those of Athens, Sparta, Rome,
Venice, Switzerland, and the Provinces of Holland. Unlike "the fathers" of the Declaration of Independence, of the Stamp Congress,
or of the '87 Constitution, the president knew little of the tall tales
of history. What he knew were his law books, the Bible, whatever
his partner Herndon put in his hands, the notable speeches of Congressmen and presidents, and the sermons of prominent clergymen.
Lincoln was a great writer of speeches and letters, not an original
thinker.

With all the people more firmly ensconced in the authority of
"We, the People," with presidents declaring themselves the rightful
leaders of the chosen whole people, leaders empowered not only by
the '87 Constitution but more broadly and strongly by "the Union"
or "the Nation" and by the military necessity to "save" it, the elements for a theory of dictatorship are at hand.

Lincoln's magnified sense of the presidential oath, to preserve
"the Union" and later "the Nation" rather than the Constitution,
added to the presidency an unwritten power. In times of crisis, the

president could, as Lincoln did, claim the right to violate the constitution to preserve the nation. "Was it possible," he asked in his lecture to Kentuckians on the ethics of recruiting and freeing 130,000 slaves, "to lose the Nation and yet preserve the constitution?" Right or wrong, he claimed, "measures, otherwise unconstitutional, might become lawful, by becoming indispensable to the preservation of the nation."

He may have acted justifiably, but not legally. A decree violating this constitution to save the Constitution or the Nation is not one of its three classes of law. It is, however, the sort of unconstitutional claim on which dictatorship or tyranny builds. What Lincoln did was to form a precedent for crisis dictatorship and create a higher law than the Constitution of the United States, the unwritten law of *the Nation*.

This is not the place to scrutinize Lincoln's violations of the '87 Constitution. "Treason against the United States," reads Article III, Section 3, "shall consist only in levying war against them." Article II, Section 4 reads that the president "shall be removed from office on impeachment for, and conviction of, treason, bribery, or other crimes and misdemeanors." Had he had a Democratic instead of a Republican Congress, particularly had there been a southern Senate, he might have been impeached, tried, and convicted for his unconstitutional role in raising armies, providing for a navy, and calling forth the militia; further, for conscripting citizens of the several States, suspending *habeas corpus*, suppressing free speech, not executing the laws of the United States according to the supreme court, depriving persons of their property in slaves without due process of law, acting according to the rules of war when Congress had not declared a war, warring against States of the United States, permitting the formation of a new State (West Virginia) within the jurisdiction of another (Virginia), and forswearing his oath to preserve the constitution of the United States.

Pretty heavy stuff, thought Huggins. "Where was the supreme court while all this was going on?"

"Firmly opposed, to no avail," replied St. John.

★ ★

————The supreme court was the one branch of the government where southerners had a majority, six out of nine justices. Chief Justice Roger B. Taney, appointed by President Jackson at John Marshall's death, was no pushover. In the famous case of *ex parte Merryman*, Taney denounced the president roundly for violating the constitution by suspending *habeas corpus*. You know as well as I that the privilege of the writ of *habeas corpus*, the most important safeguard of personal liberty known to English law, entitles a person taken in custody to obtain immediate inquiry by a court to determine whether the cause of restraint is good and if not, to be set free. Commander in chief Lincoln arrested 13,000 suspected subversives without allowing *habeas corpus*.

His tactics were to take necessary action and, afterward, as an expert constitutional lawyer, to justify himself to the Rump Congress which then, as in the case I just mentioned, took measures to legitimize the action.

Lincoln demoted the '87 Constitution by declaring that before it ever existed the Union had already been founded; moreover, it had compromised with slavery. He demoted Congress by sustaining that the president was the unique representative of all the people. He also demoted the supreme court. He followed Jefferson and Jackson's argument that each branch of the government has the right and ability to interpret the constitution, and added new conditions under which a court decision was not to be considered "irrevocably fixed." If the court's opinion was not unanimous, if it might reverse itself or be reversed by Congress or by clear "public" disapproval, he would not consider the constitutional question "fully settled." The people should not resign the government, he stated in his First Inaugural, "into the hands of that eminent tribunal," the supreme court.

Huggins stirred, about to raise a question again. St. John forestalled him. "I'm sure, Oliver, you'd like to delve more deeply into some of these matters. Lincoln justified his actions on almost each point with fervor and sophistry, but he fails to convince me. I'd prefer to move on to—"

Huggins was not to be sidetracked. "Ms. St. John, I think that you're prejudiced in favor of the South and of the States' rights position, you know, that Jefferson was in favor of."

"Obviously. I'm trying to redress the balance. In these northern parts that position has not been well presented. But more than that and more than just an English point of view, I'm trying to give you a more cosmopolitan perspective. I move on now to—"

Huggins was not in the mood to brook suppression of speech. "On another point, if I remember the Gettysburg Address right (and I should, I once knew it by heart), Lincoln doesn't mention the Union; instead, he talks about the Nation. You said that, didn't you?"

"So he does, so he does, Oliver, referring to it five times in less than three minutes."

————At Gettysburg, the president drops the emphasis on "the Union" and instead holds up as the supreme good "this Nation." "The Nation" is the next circumlocution in line for the absent name of country. The war is still on, the States still disunited, it's too early to go back to "the United States."

We discussed the term "nation" earlier this week, deriving it from a word meaning to be born. As such it extends to the place in which people are born or where a group of people are born together, usually in a certain location or territory, bound by blood or genetic kinship. No doubt about it, for a big gang of blood brothers "the Nation" was the appropriate term. Its history associates it with the idea of being born in the same blood pool and with the same spatial orientation.

As Lincoln speaks, what is now called the Old Immigration is arriving, 100,000 or more people a year. Population wends westward, past the Ohio Valley, past the Mississippi, strings of wagons driving on to California and Oregon. With these people in mind he raises the issue of blood descent from "the fathers," immersing himself thereby in the sticky theory of blood nationality.

If ever there were aborigines or original inhabitants of what is now called the Americas—that is, persons who came from nowhere else and were there as long as the land was habitable by *Homo sapiens*—we have no evidence of them. So far, no *Homo americanus* has been dug up. We know only of people who moved from elsewhere into two continents of unpopulated lands. Apparently the Indians of North and South America came from Asia, tens of thousands of years ago, crossing over a narrow passage far up north. The Mexica of Moctezuma's day, however, believed or half-believed that their ancestors were white and bearded, and took Cortés's party to be the long-absent descendants of their ancestors. As far as we know these virgin continents were deflowered by Asians, then raped by Spaniards on both continents, and in North America by French, Dutch, English, Swedes, Portuguese, and others.

With few exceptions, the Signers of the Declaration of Independence were English in origin. Yet Tom Paine pointed out that the population of Pennsylvania—the State in which the Declaration and later the two constitutions were drafted and signed—was not predominantly English. About a third of the population in that State was English, another third or so was German and Dutch, a fifth was Scots and Scotch-Irish, and the rest a mixed handful. Massachusetts had a higher percentage of English—over 80 percent. Virginia's was high too—almost 70 percent. But New York, New Jersey, and Pennsylvania had 50 percent or less, with relatively high percentages of German and Dutch, Scotch-Irish and Scottish, the last reaching proportions of one fifth to one quarter in the Carolinas and Georgia, too.

Aristocratically, the Signers of the Declaration of Independence married among their own families and with those of the drafters of the '77 and '87 Constitutions. The rest of the British population in North America was beneath them. Lincoln would have had a hard job branching himself back by blood to their tree trunks. These men did not marry women slaves but many enjoyed couching with them.

Debating with Stephen Douglas in campaign for the Senate, Lincoln opposed the "mixing of blood" and intermarriage. "I have never had the least apprehension that I or my friends would marry negroes if there was no law to keep them from it, [laughter] but . . . Judge Douglas and his friends seem to be in great apprehension that they might, if there were no law to keep them from it [roars of laughter]. . . ." Mary Chesnut, whose keen diary illustrates the South at mid-nineteenth century, testified against sanctimonious masters who kept harems of slave girls and women. "Any lady is ready to tell you who is the father of all the mulatto children in everybody's household but her own." Lincoln relied on the 1850 census statistics. There were 405,751 mulattos in the United States, nearly all in slave States, nearly all the issue of black female slaves and white male masters.

If there was in his time a non-English group in North America descended by blood from the signers of the various canonical documents of the United States, it was among the slaves. Even today you can guess the country of origin of slaveholders by the names of slave descendants. The slave owners whose names passed on to their slaves were mostly Celtic, with second place going to the English.

St. John looked at her tutee out of the corner of her eyes. "For instance, *Huggins* is a name that one would not be surprised to find borne by blacks."

"What about *St. John?*" countered Huggins. "What about St. John, spelled J-e-a-n in Louisiana, or Crèvecoeur?"

"Quite possibly also from former French islands like Martinique and Haiti. The white French and Spanish, whose religious rites were not so exclusive, followed a different practice: giving French and Spanish names to blacks and reds in Christian baptism."

————What's noteworthy about theories of extended or figurative blood descent as the basis for a country or nation's unity, she further observed, is that nationality is involuntary. Your ancestors fixed it for you and you're stuck with it. You are either flesh-and-blood related or not. If related, you, rich or poor, have no choice—you are part of this people and belong to this nation. Through no fault of your own, you are a national.

In social contract theory the people have certain characteristics that give them common interests which they seek to further by pooling some of their resources contractually. The entity they form by uniting is merely a means to their ends. If their interests are not secured, the contract is no longer useful, the deal is off. In a social contract as in a commercial contract the signers, whether people or States, give their consent; they sign voluntarily.

But the doctrine Lincoln proposes is that the people have one essential characteristic: they are related by blood or by a transubstantiation into blood. The entity formed by the existence of a blood-related people is the nation. It is *not* the means to an end. It is like a family whose end is its own well-being and whose relationships are determined less by interests than by sentiment, blood being thicker than water. In practice, this doctrine imparts a sense of belonging or identity to which the social contract theory cannot aspire. The contract deals with interests, not with blood relationship, kinship, or patriotism. In the First Inaugural, Lincoln rejects the contract theory: the United States is *not* "an association of States in the nature of a contract merely."

Although Lincoln brought the people to the fore, he attached them to a powerful, extra-constitutional president and bound them to involuntary membership in a great involuntary state.

He shook the voluntary basis of political unity not only by his ideas of national kinship, blood payment, baptism, and sacrifice but also by using force to prevent withdrawal from the association known as the United States. No matter how one looked at the outcome, a number of States and a substantial part of their peoples did withdraw from the United States and were forced back. A pretense of consent was later extracted from them by oaths taken under the threat of depriving them, among other things, of the right to vote and to hold property.

If substantial numbers of people wanted no part of the United States, would fight rather than be part of it, and yet were kept in by force of arms, it would seem that government of, by, and for the people had already perished from the earth. Membership in the United States of peoples or States was no longer voluntary or a matter of voluntary pact, covenant, contract, or consent.

In the matter of consent, "the Union" was now a more imperfect union.

In the matter of naming, "the Nation" that Lincoln saw arising in a new birth of freedom was no better off than before its reincarnation. "The Union," a collective common noun, had been an improvement only in that it was singular in number. It could not escape—no matter how much rhetoric Lincoln lavished on it—the plurality encased in its meaning: something composed of distinct parts. "The Nation," the second of Lincoln's circumlocutions, was an improvement over the Union because it was not just singular; it also did not imply distinct parts. You could have a nation without any States at all.

Both terms lacked the spatial location of "the United States of America." Nobody referred to "the Union of America" or "the Nation of America." The same goes for "the Republic," another circumlocution dear to postwar orators and embroidered, we'll see tomorrow, in a children's pledge of allegiance. As they were not proper nouns, they could refer to any union, nation, or republic on the planet.

The incorrigible Huggins stood up and gave a military salute. "Permission to speak, lieutenant?"

The relenting St. John waved a salute back and smiled. "At ease, private. Permission granted."

Huggins sat down. "Ma'am, if this nation was supposed to have a new birth of freedom, why didn't Father Abraham baptize it? Don't countries or persons, when shooting off in a new direction, change their names? Like Cassius Marcellus Clay, you know, the world champion heavyweight, changed his to Muhammad Ali."

"Yes, we talked about this before—remember? I can give you another example, the royal house of the United Kingdom. Breaking all association with cousin Kaiser Wilhelm's Germany, George V changed the dynasty's name from the House of Saxe-Coburg-Gotha to the House of Windsor. But since you once committed the Gettysburg Remarks to memory, how would you have worked in a proper name?"

"Let's see," began Huggins, nothing daunted. " 'Columbia' was still in the running, wasn't it?"

"Oh yes. Cartoons sketched the country comically as Uncle Sam, more seriously as the feminine Columbia. You may find this hard to believe: Columbia was sometimes identified in song as the daughter of Father Abraham."

"I see. In that case, he could have said"—Huggins beamed with mischief—"brought forth on this continent a new nation, my daughter Columbia."

St. John stared at him, then tilted her head back and laughed. Her chair started to wobble. She struggled to bring herself to order.

Huggins put on his blank look. "What?"

"Make another try, Oliver," she advised, fishing for a handkerchief.

"Lincoln could have said, 'that this nation, Columbia, under God shall have a new birth . . .' That's not too bad, is it?"

"Sounds okay. But Lincoln may have thought that would call for a mention of 1492. He didn't want to go back much further than 1776. Besides, a number of other Columbias had sprung up—remember?—including Columbia, the capital of the hated South Carolina."

"What about 'America'? He could have said 'brought forth on this continent a new America,' but that would have linked the name to continental North and South America or to Amerigo Vespucci."

"That's right. Moreover, Mexico and Canada, the other occupants of North America, may have concluded that the name 'America' reflected the United States's designs on their territory. Given the then recent United States military history and the size of its military establishment, who was to say their fears were unjustified? Perhaps several times Lincoln before the war in a version of 'We, the People' used the noun *Americans*:—'We Americans,' or following Daniel Webster used it as a term to include 'the Union' (composed only of new States and northern or Yankees areas) and the South. But he certainly could have said, 'testing whether this America or any nation so conceived . . .,' closing then with 'that this America under God . . .' Sounds just right to me."

"To me, too."

"Maybe to name the nation in dedicatory remarks at a mass burial ceremony might not have seemed propitious. Still, it does suit the death and rebirth theme that Lincoln was drawing on, a not uncommon motif of graveside orators and ministers.

"We have, it would seem, a once new nation, never baptized, about to be born again, as yet unbaptized. Or rather, we have two nations, the victor and the vanquished. One answers to 'the Union' or 'the Nation,' the other has now to be content with 'the South.'

"It begins to look like we shall have to search elsewhere than among our documents and presidents for a proper name. You know, a few replies to the New-York Historical Society's inquiry of 1845 had said that a name for country could no longer be enacted or officially proclaimed, that it was too late, that the name now had to arise from the people. For today, though, we've gone far enough."

Far enough? When had they gone far enough? Huggins was dying of longing or something.

St. John, still seated, in her short-sleeved blouse, stretched luxuriously. Huggins observed two channels of flesh on either side of her body starting from the insides of her upraised arms, flowing down into the sleeves of the blouse, disappearing (he imagined) along her ribs. When she wore something cut lower in the back he could see the beginning of another canal from the nape of her neck, running down the spine and (again, he imagined) down into a plump crevice. And yesterday as she bowed before him there was the suggestion of still another, beginning between two breasts, sliding down her belly, down past her navel. What about underneath her narrow knees? There must be short canals there, too, and elsewhere. She was a study in canals, a Venice, a Hangchow! Sometimes when she crossed her legs he glimpsed the insides of her flanks. Two other channels deepening as they ran toward each other to a hidden juncture. Not quite a juncture: they stopped three fingers wide of the mark. That, he knew, because when she stood up in a sheer skirt, light shimmered through.

St. John stretched once more, then collected herself and her things, stood up, and headed for the door. She turned the handle, the screen quivered but didn't budge. The door was stuck. She pushed again. It stayed stuck. The moist weather. Huggins knew this old door well. He jumped up. *He who hesitates . . .* He moved over to her right. She backed up a little to make room. He shoved his right foot on a pivot against the bottom of the door. It came ajar. Putting his right arm high and across he pushed it open a bit more than halfway. As she came alongside to pass through, he clamped his teeth on her ear, lightly, just in back of a carnelian earring rimmed in worked gold, and just for a second. St. John on her way out slowed imperceptibly, abstractedly touching her hand to her ear as if to check that the earring was still there. No hint of censure in her carriage. His eyes lusted down the path after her figure.

11

HOW HIGH THE TUNE: "THE STAR-SPANGLED BANNER" AND OTHER SOUNDS AND SYMBOLS

FRIDAY

Outside a blowing drizzle. Inside Huggins looking out one of the south windows again, engaged in a worried monologue. He had, he just had to make some declaration of his . . . what? Love? Starry-eyed admiration? Whatever it was, it had nothing to do with his appreciation of her as tutor, it had to do rather with her mind and body, with a desire to know that that admiration, that attraction, was mutual, that she too felt that longing to press bodies and bring lips together. She had given him enough cues. If she wanted to squelch him now, that was her business. Damned if he wasn't going to try at least. What could she do, slap his face? Kick him in the balls? He could block slaps and kicks. Tell his father? That wouldn't be the end of the world. Walk out on the tutorial altogether? Ouch, that would hurt. There were only these two days

left, two hours really. No, she couldn't run out. Still, she didn't
need the money, she dressed with expensive taste. Why tutoring?
Where had she been before these two weeks, where will she go afterward, before school starts? So what if he had nibbled at her ear
yesterday? She hadn't rebuffed him by so much as a glance. No, she
wouldn't run out on him. Yet where was she now—twelve minutes late already, she who was always early or on the dot?

Huggins had fastened back the screen door and shut the wooden
door against the blowing rain. Was that a knock? There it was again,
so soft you could hardly be sure. Strange. Claire never knocked.
She always walked straight in. Who was it? He opened the door.
Claire!—was it really her?—hair hanging straight down, rain dripping onto her face like a flood of tears, in a pale-green sopping wet
polo shirt double-collared—the inner one a faint blue—one hand
drawn in a limp fist and resting on her hip, the shirtsleeve drooping over it pathetically; the other—the sleeve pushed up, revealing
a fine wrist—loosely holding the strap of—of all things!—an
amber-clasped, cloth purse garishly brocaded with daisies and roses.
The knit shirt crumbled about the waist over the top of a skirt of
white batiste made gray and semitransparent by the soaking rain.
Through it, from left to right, Huggins could see an expanse of
thigh, a darker mid-terrain, and an expanse of the other thigh,
reaching down to the knee, the skirt drooping to the ankle and finished in . . . a scalloped hem. She was still in her nightgown! Her
feet were bare! This came as a shock to him, accustomed as he was
to seeing them wrapped in whispering calfskin. Bits of soil and grass
stubbed the tips of her painted toes.

Huggins raised his eyes. Her lowered eyelids were leaking fresh
and salt water over a sad face.

"Come in, come in! What's happened to you? You're soaked."

St. John slipped in without a word, stood in the middle of the
room shivering, dripping a puddle on the floor.

Rising to the crisis, Huggins flew to the bathroom and came out
with an old yellow chenille robe and a towel. He slipped the robe
around her shoulders and began drying her hair. She reached up
slowly and took the towel from his hands. He rushed over to a chest
in the bedroom, rummaged in a drawer. Pulling out ribbed cotton
briefs and undershirts, he thrust them into her hand and pushed her

into the bathroom, then dashed to a closet where he fumbled around till he located a threadbare long-tailed dinner shirt. The bathroom door was closed; he knocked. "Come in," said a weak voice. He opened the door. Her back to him, she had put the briefs on—they fit her better than him—and was just slipping the undershirt over her shoulders as she turned her head and flashed a grateful smile. He smiled back, tossed the shirt over the bathtub, and left, closing the door.

A jumble of thoughts crowded in on him: What the hell was this? She gave him no time to think. In two minutes she reappeared, dressed in the shirt; it reached just above her knees. Her legs, he observed, were no wider above than below the knee.

"Do you have a belt or something?" were her first words.

Another dash to the closet. Oliver snatched a necktie and handed it to her. She tied it round her waist.

Dropping herself down into one of the slatted steamer chairs and wearily lifting her legs onto its hooked extension, she finally raised her eyes to him.

"Well?" he said, crouching at her side.

No response. A tear coursed contrarily down her cheek. She brushed it angrily away.

"What's the story?" he persisted sympathetically.

"Nothing."

"Nothing?"

"They've rejected my thesis topic, that's what."

"Who's they?"

"My thesis committee."

"So?"

"You don't understand. They liked it at first, I worked on it for over a year, and now that I've drafted most of it, they say no."

"Why? Did they say why?"

"Not really. The topic is too broad, I use too much imagination, the sources are too few, too dubious, et cetera, et cetera."

"What was the topic?"

"I never told you?"

"You never tell me anything."

"Well, the title was, 'Threats of Secession from the United States.' "

"Ah."

"What do you mean, 'Ah'? They could have told me sooner, couldn't they? Now I have to start all over again, pick another subject—something they can grind their own axes on . . . or else leave school. Damn, I loved that topic."

"I could tell." Huggins had never seen her like this. Miserable. Furious. He considered licking away the little traces of salt under her eyes. The news of the rejected thesis sent his mind racing. He rose. Looking down at her he thought, What she needs is a shot of Wild Turkey, then recalling her Englishness, he substituted, booming heartily, "How about some hot tea?"

"Tea?" she queried weakly.

Oliver changed his mind again and darted off for something stronger.

It was now raining hard. You could hear the pounding on the porch roof.

Huggins came back with a glass on a small tray. Setting it on a hassock, he took her folded ankles, anklet and all—she had managed to wipe the mud and grass off her toes—and lifted them off the chair's leg rest and onto the floor. She looked at him inquiringly, still mournful. He unhinged the leg rest, kicked it away, and pushed the hassock closer. Dejectedly she took the glass, put it to her lips, and sipped.

"Listen," he said, oozing excitement. "I've got an idea."

St. John raised herself to put down the glass. "This chair is tippy," she whimpered.

"I know. Never mind, just look."

He went across the room and came back with the recorder that he had hidden away and left turned on last week. "Do you know what this is? . . . It's been here all the while . . . It's recorded all our words."

"What is it?" Unbelieving, beginning to understand. "You"—she didn't speak the next word, she mouthed it—"bastard."

"Easy, easy," Huggins placated.

"You can turn that damn thing off now!"

"No, no, Claire, wait a sec. This damn thing has recorded every moment, every sound in each of these hours since you first walked into the room. Why worry about a thesis? We've got something better here."

Claire didn't get it.

"Each night after you leave," explained Oliver, "I sit and take down everything off the machine, everything you and I said, and fill in just enough for background. Just enough and no more, I hope. I'm no Tacitus or Updike but I can write a simple declarative sentence."

Claire looked unconvinced.

"Look," exasperated, "I'll show you the first page or two."

"You mean you've started to write it already?"

"What do you think I've been doing these solitary nights—toying with Polly?" He walked over to the desk and began rummaging in one of the drawers.

"Oh, Oliver, really? That's wonderful. What do you say about me, I wonder?"

"Nothing 'cept what you've said. I've got a draft of our whole first week. Here, this is the first moment of Monday the first day. Read it out loud so I can hear how it sounds."

Claire took the page and read.

> "Good afternoon. I am Claire St. John, your teller of tales—"
>
> "My teller of tales?" said Oliver Huggins, shaking the outstretched hand. "I thought—"
>
> "I did not finish. In future, if I am to tutor you in history, in American history, please do not interrupt." She waited a moment, then went on.
>
> "My view of history is that it consists of tales. Tales must have a teller. I am your teller of tales. I have stored up a sequence of tales for our twelve sessions to come. Let's begin."

Claire glowed. "Oliver, that's not bad. Show me more."

He picked up a few sheets from the drawer and handed them over.

Liquid poetry flowed from her lips. Silently now, faster, she read through several more sheets, engrossed, unbelieving.

"Oliver, it's great. Do you think anyone will publish it?"

"One thing at a time. Leave that to me."

"Really? Can you . . . ?" Her astonished look melted into something more like admiration.

Oliver glowed. "You know, last weekend I looked some of it over and said to myself, 'Attaboy, Huggins, you son-of-a-bitch, attaboy.' "

"You didn't, not really, did you?"

"No, actually, I haven't looked it over yet."

"But you know it's good, you son-of-a-bitch, don't you?" Claire said, laughing.

Oliver mumbled something modest.

"I'd just love to see my committee's faces when the book comes out," she exulted. "I'll bet they won't even read it. It's not in thesis form. Anyway, who cares what academics think. Who cares, who cares?"

She must be drunk, Oliver judged. Authorship must be heady brew. In her white shirt she looked up to the ceiling, opened her arms wide, and intoned, "Oh Happy Book About to Be Born!" Then, seizing Oliver by both hands, she twirled him into a ring-around-a-rosy and sang out, Oliver piping in, "Happy Days Are Here Again," until, both dizzy, they plopped onto the sofa.

Oliver remembered something. "Should I turn off the machine?"

"No," said Claire, "let it go to the end."

"The end? The end's tomorrow."

They both sat up, sobered. With visible effort Claire the author shifted gears. Claire the tutor went back to work.

"Where were we?"

"We were going to look for a name for country in other things," prompted Huggins.

———Yes, in other things beside declarations, constitutions, speeches, and oaths. Last week we disposed of those things stamped with "U.S." or "U.S.A." representing the government of the United States or identifying its property. Consider, too, the private sphere—objects and persons not commissioned by the government, yet playing a symbolic role, due generally to their origin in the United States and their popularity, domestic or foreign: the female Columbia; the female Liberty (partly Indian, partly French Revolution); the Uncle

Sam cartoon; the Statue of Liberty; the Ford flivver in its day; perhaps the Colt six-shooter; transcontinental highways; railroads; the Sears Roebuck mail catalogs; the clean, white, bright, packaged, well-drawing cigarettes in World Wars I and II; Frank Sinatra in World War II through Europe and into the Soviet Union; jazz as a genre; and the widely popular sport of baseball, migrating to Cuba, the Philippines, Japan, and elsewhere.

"Don't forget Coca-Cola," prompted Oliver.

"How in the world did I forget Coca-Cola!" Claire wailed.

"Senility?"

"Turns you on, does it?" The coquette, with a smile, blinked once and glanced at him out of the corner of her eye.

"Not me," he disavowed, and to prove it, returned to the subject. "Do you remember Greta Garbo in *Queen Christina*, her despairing: 'I don't want to be a symbol, I want to be a human being'?"

Claire continued to look amused.

"What about the flag?" Oliver persevered.

"What flag?" innocently.

"You know what flag. Old Glory, the Star-Spangled Banner."

"Oh that. That oblong piece of bunting used for colorful display and decoration? I was going to discuss it separately. You know what the first official flag of the United States—the approved one, Continental Congress approved it in 1777—looked like, don't you? In the canton there was—"

"What's a canton?"

"Don't you remember? Oliver! A canton or union is the separate quarter carried by some flags next to the staff at the top."

————The ex-colonies had each devised their own flag—South Carolina flew a rattlesnake, New York a beaver, Rhode Island an anchor. In 1775, a committee of Congress charged with inventing a single flag for the government of the thirteen states proposed thirteen horizontal, alternating red and white stripes. In the canton rested two crosses—of Saint George and Saint Andrew, the patron saints respectively of England and Scotland. This happened to be exactly the same flag as that of England's East India Company.

In 1777, Congress came up with the circular star design in the canton, "representing a new constellation." This flag displayed thirteen stripes alternating white (maybe for purity), and red (maybe for courage, certainly not for revolution), and a canton of blue (for true blue?) bearing thirteen white stars (for the thirteen newly independent States) in a circle. As it happens, red, white, and blue are the colors of Great Britain's ingenious working of the three crosses of England, Scotland, and Ireland into the Union Jack.

But I like that circle constellation. The canton today is too crowded with row on row of stars, a square within a square. If the flag of the United States of America has an aesthetic defect, it is that impression of crowding. Compare the harmonious simplicity of the Union Jack.

"I'm beginning to think," said Huggins, grinning, "that you're a knee-jerk patriot."

"Oh, come on, Oliver. You don't know me well but you know me better than that. The thirteen stripes are too narrow to represent the sweep of great plains and mountain ranges. When Vermont and Kentucky joined the Union in 1790 and 1792, two stars were added, and another two stripes. This adding of stripes went on until there were twenty of them and flag-makers realized that at the rate of expansion the United States were going, the stripes on the bunting would soon be reduced to strips of ribbon. Imagine what it would be today with fifty stripes."

"Maybe we could reduce the stripes to nine, one for each of the first nine states to ratify the '87 Constitution," suggested Oliver.

"That would help, and at the same time we could restore the prettier circle of thirteen stars. The eleven States that seceded might like that better. It also would represent a time when they were equal political partners of the North. Besides, now that the 'new constellation' is gone, the canton looks more and more like a square of polka dots. But what about the other thirty-seven or more States?"

"Hmm. We *could* have three circles of stars." Oliver bent to make a sketch. "How's that look?"

Claire at his back, hands on his shoulders, looking over, nodding. "A big improvement."

It was all he could do to keep from pivoting around and grasping her at the waist (encircled by his necktie!).

But she had second thoughts. "Three circles make it look a lot like a target, a bull's-eye, don't you think?"

Prudence forced Oliver to agree. "You're right. Too many people shooting at us now as it is. Too bad. What about instead of stars, putting in white rows of ones and zeros, binary style?"

"Hmm. That would certainly express current foreign policy, American software domination of the world . . . But no, there's more to represent than that. Besides I prefer stars, don't you?"

"Yeah. Stars are cool."

——Flags, pennants, standards, crests, and banners are as old as warfare, that is, as old as humanity, said St. John, resuming her pedagogical posture. Among the inhabitants of the United States, the flag seems extraordinarily popular. A foreign observer notices it everywhere, not just over federal government buildings and military coffins. Only too well aware of the popular reverence for the flag, political protesters exploit it for publicity purposes, performing scandalizing acts like burning or pissing on it. More positively, advertisers fly the flag to draw attention to the pies they're peddling. Flags fly over gas stations, banks, department stores, private lawns, liquidation sales, become the theme of ballets and musical comedies, are depicted on walls at home, on toys, T-shirts, the seats of jeans, underwear, condoms, bikinis—the stripes on one breast, the stars on the other.

Out of breath, she paused.

"Anything to put condoms to good use," moralized Huggins.

Claire shot him a quizzical look.

". . . Until they discover a better system," he added. "You know, some time ago . . . when was it? . . . this winter in town, I was walking home one blowy night, passing by the hospital, and heard a snapping noise in the air. I looked up and saw an unlowered, unfurled Old Glory. I admit it disturbed me to see the Stars and Stripes flapping blind in the wind and the dark."

"That's the ticket, Oliver. They got to you while you were young. Who's the knee-jerk patriot now?" crowed Claire.

Oliver began a protest, but she ignored him. "Your reaction is probably due to one of two—no, let's make it three—factors. I was just about to talk about the first one: the Pledge to the Flag, or in full 'The Pledge of Allegiance to the Flag.' Last week I spoke of President Harrison and the Pledge. Do you know it by heart? Let's hear you recite it."

"That's easy: 'I pledge allegiance to the flag of the United States of America, and to the Republic for which it stands, one Nation under God, indivisible, with liberty and justice for all.' "

"Bravo," Claire applauded. "As you know, millions on millions of schoolchildren have recited this, week in, week out. Presidents do, too, on visits to high schools. Constitutionally and legally the pledge has no force: constitutionally, because the '87 Constitution does not require it of the people and according to the sovereignty of people doctrine the people bind their servants but not themselves; legally, because the recital in schools is not required by a United States law (which would presumably be unconstitutional) and also because the pledgers are not of legal age of consent."

Oliver started to reminisce again. "As kids, we must have felt the anthem and the pledge too solemn for us. So we made it fun—anything to keep from settling down to schoolwork—with inappropriate gestures behind teacher's back. The bad boys, encouraged by our smothered giggles, would start off the 'Star-Spangled Banner': 'O say can you see any bedbugs on me? If you do, catch a few and I'll fry them for you.' "

"Ugh!" said Claire.

"The words, *gave proof* sounded to a lot of us like *grapefruit*; 'grapefruit through the night,' we sang. Likewise for the Pledge of Allegiance. Who was the Richard Stans in 'I led the pigeons to the flag and to the republic for Richard Stans?' So, why make kids sing and pledge?"

"You've given the answer yourself. You are now of age and you remember by heart even the parodies. When you hear the flag flapping in the cold and dark, the religious solemnity resurfaces and your heart sinks."

"I guess it's an emotional business."

"Correct. I trust the words *indivisible* and *nation* have deeper sig-

nificance for you by this time. You can imagine how this pledge
was received in the South."

"It must have gone over big."

"While we're at it, I must add a caution to what we are saying
about the Star-Spangled Banner. In the South the so-called national
flag except in times of war has never generated the same enthusiasm; neither has a pledge with the words 'one Nation indivisible'
in it. Over the last century and a half a controversy crops up every
so often: the Federal versus the Confederate or a southern State
flag—which flies above the other? Which goes to which side of the
other? Which should be flown at all?"

"What would happen," asked Oliver, "if a State capitol flew its
own flag above that of the United States?"

"You can answer that better than I."

"I'd say, there'd be pole climbing and fights to pull the flag down
or keep it up. There'd be suits, the federal courts would 'decide'
that according to the flag code, the United States flag must fly on
top, and they would issue an injunction, backed by United States
marshals. If necessary, the president would call to colors the national
guard of that State."

"Something like that," Claire agreed. "The United States government is in the saddle and rides herd on the States. The eastern
seaboard States, South and North, have a lengthy history of colo-
nialism, war, diplomacy, and trade with England and Europe. The
new States have no such history to call their own. Seeking roots,
they planted and nourished stories of the cavalry versus the Indians
and of the cowboy code of honor—'When you say that, pardner,
smile!' and 'She wore a yellow ribbon.' "

Claire hammed it up: first, snarling, she drew a six-gun, then,
simpering, she tied a ribbon in her hair.

Oliver was glad to see her back in form.

"For the rest," she said, "they elaborated on their own northern
partisanship in the War of Secession. In Chicago there are Lincoln,
Seward, Stanton, and Grant parks, to mention a few of the com-
memorations you'll not often find in the South.

"As for factor two: The pledge is made to a flag. Don't you find
that curious? Why not to the country?"

"I know the answer to that," said Oliver.

"Yes?"

"The flag stands for an absent name."

"That's a good way to put it."

―――――The text, she observed, goes on to say that one also pledges allegiance "to the Republic for which it [the flag] stands." A republic is a form of government—we discussed it last week—but according to the pledge, this republic consists of one Nation "indivisible." In the eyes of the Confederate States of America and of those who argued for a federal union of States, this was patently false. The South accepted "one Nation indivisible" only because military might forced them, or as Lincoln affirmed, because "RIGHT MAKES MIGHT."

Congress and President Eisenhower in 1954 made the phrase "under God" official. The last words of the pledge further characterize the indivisible nation as a nation "with liberty and justice for all." If the nation does not act as a subject of God should, or does not provide justice and liberty for all, does the pledge still bind the pledger? No need to answer for as I just said, the pledge itself is not binding by law or constitution.

"But it can be binding by emotion," said Oliver.

"Sure. Look at your warbling in childhood. That's taking unfair advantage of children, isn't it? That may be the only way to make it binding, by sentiment. It doesn't conform to the voluntary or contractual constitution, though, does it? And, to take another line, where does reason come in, if sentiment for country has to be forced down the open throats of children in chorus?"

―――――Factor three: Remember we're trying to figure out why the flag is so popular. Factor three is the official national anthem, a song about the flag, "The Star-Spangled Banner." The words were written in 1814 by Francis Scott Key, a Maryland lawyer who for several years had been trying to find a popular martial subject to versify. He already had the tune, one that had been set to a variety of verses from the political to the bawdy. He may have first heard the mu-

sic in 1798 in the Federalist campaign song "Adams and Liberty."
Some years earlier one Englishman had composed the music and
another, the president of the London Anacreontic Society, had written the lyrics; music and lyrics together became "To Anacreon in
Heaven," the society's drinking song.

Anacreon is the ancient Greek poet of love and wine whom the
society celebrated in bibulous melody. Where you exalt "the land
of the free and the home of the brave," the society lauded "the
myrtle of Venus with Bacchus' vine."

"Anacreon is no mean poet. I'll give you a sample of a love lyric
of his." Claire took a deep breath. Oliver saw the bosom of his shirt
rise.

> *Thracian filly, watching me out of the corner of your eye, why do*
> *you run away? . . .*
> *Now you graze in the meadows and skitter playfully,*
> *for you have no expert horseman to mount you.*

"*I* should be spouting those lines," Oliver complained.

"You should but not yet. To catch a Thracian filly you have first
some catching up to do."

Before he could react she was back to the "Star-Spangled Banner."

————At the start Francis Scott Key tried writing new verses to
commemorate a United States naval triumph in the Mediterranean
war with Tripoli (1801–1805). That song was called "The Warrior's
Return," the warrior being the naval captain Stephen Decatur, who
later gave the famous toast: "May she always be in the right, but
our country right or wrong."

"By the way," said Claire, on a sidetrack, "what's the name of the
author of *The Great Gatsby*?"

"F. Scott Fitzgerald. Why?"

"What does the 'F.' stand for?"

"Francis."

"Is something missing?"

"I don't think so."

"Yes, there is. A *K* for Key. Francis Scott Key: the author of the verses of the 'Star-Spangled Banner.' "

"Were they related?"

"I doubt it. Anyway, the War of 1812 inspired Key anew with another set of verses for the old tune. Happening to witness the British naval bombardment of Fort McHenry (near Baltimore) and seeing in the morning that the flag still waved over the fort, he jotted down the new lines. He called the song 'The Defense of Fort M'Henry.' His brother-in-law, a judge, had it published right away as a broadside. Soon the title 'The Star-Spangled Banner' took over. The first edition, Baltimore 1814, imparted additional information: 'A Pariotic [*sic*] Song. Air. Anacreon in Heaven.' Key finally had a hit on his hands, at least for the time being. Out of a defeat in war, the song celebrates a victorious detail: Fort McHenry did not strike the colors.

"Over the long haul the song had to compete with other tunes, some already written, some not yet. When talking about George Washington, I gave a verse of 'Yankee Doodle'—"

Oliver interrupted. "Is that all you're going to say about the 'Star-Spangled Banner'?" He had done some thinking and tinkering with the song and didn't want to let the occasion escape.

"No, we'll come back to it in a minute." She must have noticed his suppressed excitement. "Why?"

"No reason. I just wondered."

————As I was going to say, where "Yankee Doodle" came from is unclear. Certainly the British sang the song in the French and Indian Wars to make fun of colonial soldiers. George Washington, who fought creditably in those battles, could not have liked it then but it may have filled him with pride on other occasions. I didn't tell you, did I, that when the British band played "The World Turned Upside Down" at the surrender of Yorktown, General La Fayette, with a sure touch, ordered the continental band to strike up "Yankee Doodle."

This irrepressible, brash, self-mocking, carefree, unpuritanical air with its bawdy refrain was the most popular fife-and-drum march of the Revolution. The first line of one of its earliest verses goes, "Columbians all, the present hour / As brothers should unite us . . ."

"The Liberty Song" written by John Dickinson in 1768 to the British tune "Hearts of Oak" carried as first line, "Come join hand in hand, brave Americans all." Americans signified British American subjects of George III. Throughout the Revolution, however, for every time we encounter "Brave Americans" in song we meet several times with "Brave Columbians" or "True Columbians" or "True sons of Columbia." Last week I mentioned Timothy Dwight of Connecticut and his "Columbia." Now I'll take up "Hail Columbia."

At a time of near war with France, voices in the streets, taverns, and theaters lifted to its "Hail Columbia, happy land." Joseph Hopkinson of Philadelphia, whose father Francis had signed the Declaration of Independence, wrote the words in 1798. A German violin virtuoso, band and orchestra conductor, and music teacher living in New York and Philadelphia wrote the music, which he seems to have composed earlier as "The President's March." He may not have been a citizen; his name which, with as many variants as Shakespeare's, had not yet jelled was Philip Pfyle, also known as Feyles, Fayles, Fyles, Phyla, Phyles, Phylo and Philo, Phayles, Phylz, Pfalz, Pfhylo, Pfyles, Pfeil, and Thyla. I should add "Philip Phile" to the list, for that was the name he himself used in advertising his services as music teacher.

The colonies and States were lucky to have good German musicians among their settlers.

Other songs like "Columbia and Liberty," "The Ladies' Patriotic Song" (first line: "Columbians arise Independence proclaim"), and "Rise Columbia," appeared at the same time to the tune usually of "Rule Britannia." In the undeclared war with France, 1798 to 1800, there also arose a "Hail! Columbia, Death or Liberty," and in the war with Tripoli, an "Arise, Arise Columbia's Sons, Arise." "Hail Columbia," though, had no real rivals for decades. Federal troops at Fort Sumter sang it under siege in December of 1861.

In song and story during the Revolution and probably up to the Civil War, the name of the country—of a country that existed or

not, but if not, then the name of that land extending from the Atlantic shores westward—was Columbia. The other two noteworthy
songs—"Yankee Doodle" and the "Star-Spangled Banner"—offer
us neither a proper noun like "Columbia" nor a common noun like
"the United States."

Many of the States boasted not only their own flags but their own
familiar songs. After Washington's presidency, it naturally fell to the
one-country advocates, the northeasterners and westerners, and the
party of John Adams, called by friends the Federalists, by enemies
the Anglo-monarchical party, to sing "Hail Columbia" with hearty
voices. It was first advertised with the title "The Favorite New Federal Song" and described as "A Patriotic Song"; the music also dou-
bled as a "President's March," of which at the time there were
several versions, all of minor quality.

While still colonies or provinces, the future thirteen States had
one national anthem in common—"God Save the King." As you
know, it is easier to write bad lyrics than good music. After colonial independence, "God Save the King" suffered several new sets
of words, some at the hands of women. The *Philadelphia Packet* in
1779 printed a Dutch lady's version of the hymn, with the title
"God save the thirteen States." Fifteen years or so later the *Philadelphia Minerva* published a poem by another lady to the same music.

"For your convenience I've memorized the opening words."

Claire raised herself upright, unbuttoned the two top buttons of
her shirt, and in a clear soprano, sang,

> *God save each Female's right,*
> *Show to her ravish'd sight*
> *Woman is free.*

"That last line feels good to the throat. Try it."

Oliver obliged. " 'Wo-man is free.' You're right, it does. But the
song is 'My Country 'Tis of Thee.' In school we used to say 'My
Country Tis-a-dee.' We thought it was the name of some Indian
territory maybe of Pocahontas or Hiawatha's tribe. We could never
figure out why teacher called the song 'America.' "

"Of course, you couldn't," said Claire. "It was and still is the

tune of England's 'God Save the Queen.' In 1831, the Reverend
Samuel F. Smith of Massachusetts set to it a hymn he called 'My
Country 'Tis of Thee.' His original draft carried no title or name,
even though in its second verse, no longer in use, the 'Of thee I
sing' line reads, 'Thy name I love.' "

————A decade or so later, "Columbia, the Gem of the Ocean"
appears on stage. Popular in military ceremonies, as the refrain
cheers "the army and navy forever," it is another flag song: "Three
cheers for the red, white, and blue." The flag in the song waves
over "Columbia's true sons" and Columbia's army and navy. Columbia's daughters are not mentioned but "Columbia" is a woman,
naturally, "with her flag floating proudly before her."

The "gem," though, was stolen goods. An English actor and mu-
sician who had emigrated to Philadelphia claimed he wrote the
words and music, but in England one Englishman seems already to
have composed the lively tune and another its lyrics, neither of
whom emigrated. It was called "Britannia, the Pride of the Ocean."
On reflection, a pride or a gem of the ocean would apply more naturally to the isle or island kingdom of Britain with a world-feared
navy and a world-famous admiral, Horatio Nelson. According to
heraldic rules, the color order in the song of "red, white, and blue"
fits the Union Jack, whereas Old Glory's stars and stripes would rank
as blue, red, and white. As for the tune, there is no doubt whatever: almost note for note the music is that of "Britannia."

Let's see now. Laying aside "Yankee Doodle" and the "Columbia" sung by Connecticut troops in 1775, we have as pretenders to
the throne of a national anthem, "Hail Columbia" in 1798, the
"Star-Spangled Banner" in 1814, "My Country 'Tis of Thee" in
1831, and "Columbia, the Gem of the Ocean" in 1843. The local
origin of these songs is Boston and Philadelphia. So far the only possible name of country is Columbia. Columbia was acceptable south
of Philadelphia too. South Carolina had already chosen to name its
capital Columbia, thus rivaling the District of Columbia. The War
of Secession approaches, a war of the two Columbias.

General Ulysses S. Grant once said, as far as music went he knew
only two songs: "One is 'Yankee Doodle' and the other isn't." That
other, I reckon, is "Dixie." Daniel Decatur Emmett, a celebrated

minstrel, composed its words and music and a Manhattan minstrel company sang it just before the war. "In Dixie land I'll take my stand . . . Away, away, away down south in Dixie." Down South may have got the name Dixie from the ten-dollar notes issued by a bank in prewar New Orleans. The reverse side of the notes was engraved in French. So on one side "ten," on the other, "dix." The South took up the tune. The band played it at the inauguration of Jefferson Davis, the South's one and only president, and the boys in gray sang it throughout the war, giving the South an unofficial proper noun name before the North had found one.

With the coming of disunion and war, the North scuttered to find an anthem. It turned up many songs to help recruiting, stoke sentiment, and enrich music publishers, and kept them all in the repertory to celebrate the triumphs of Union forces, but none survived the conflict or named the North as a country, or as Lincoln would have it, as the Nation.

"I suppose I'm not telling you anything new, Oliver. One little thing you may not know is this. By mid-century the rules of baseball, a game played in northeastern States, became fairly stable. Union troops played the sport throughout the war. Afterward in the North's eagerness for national symbols, baseball acquired the title of 'the national game.' Nowadays, although the sport has acquired various rivals, the federal government may step in to protect it whenever it may be menaced by scandal or strikes. At some point it became traditional for the president of the United States to throw the first pitch of the first game of the season. At another point it became traditional to start that first game with a rite. Men, women, and children stand, the men bare their heads, all place their right hands somewhere in the region of the heart, and burst into song. After which the public sits down, the president throws the ball to the pitcher, the umpire yells 'Play ball!' and the game is on."

"I do know all this," said Oliver, exaggerating. "But you forgot an important part of the ritual," he pointed out gleefully.

"I did?" Claire asked pleasantly. "What?"

"Before the game is on, the pitcher hoists his balls, spits, winds up, and throws. *Then* the game is on."

"I *knew* you wouldn't let me get away without mentioning that."

Oliver smirked. "That's why you left it out? Not out of delicacy? Balls!"

"Truly," said his unflappable tutor, "I was going to remind you. I'd heard that not so long ago the woman lead singer in the spotlight, having finished, grabbed her crotch and spat."

"It's 'balls,' not 'crotch,' observed Oliver, "as in 'Balls, said the Queen; had I two I'd be King.' "

"Not only that. Her mound was not the pitcher's mound. It was a shocking transgression. Many of the public objected, as would have Confucius, great arbiter of ritual."

"She might have hitched up her bra and started a different tradition," proposed Oliver with a cautious smile.

"Why not? Specially with a stars and stripes bra." Claire leaned forward in the chair, pulled her legs up and hugged her knees. Damn, thought Oliver, that silkiness of skin . . . Her heels held down the back tail of her borrowed shirt so that it wouldn't ride up, but it billowed at the sides up to her hips, uncovering flanks of smooth thigh.

"But of course you know the name of the song. Dating from its incorporation into the baseball ritual, the 'Star-Spangled Banner,' a song without a name for nation, was popularly called 'the national anthem.' "

"Sure," said know-it-all Oliver. "You know what they say are the last two words of the 'Star-Spangled Banner'?"

Claire waited.

"Play ball!"

A brief smile. "The song now opens every major sports event, not baseball alone." Her face lighted up with recall. "Speaking of the 'Star-Spangled Banner' and baseball, I've got a little personal tale.

"When I first came over to the States, to familiarize myself with the New World, I went to a baseball game. At the outset when everybody stood up and sang I was sitting in my seat in the stands munching a hot dog and swilling a beer. The loudspeaker blared, 'Please rise for the singing of the national anthem.' Everybody rose to their feet. Swallowing quickly, I rose too. Men with hats on took them off. Everyone placed their right hand over their heart. I followed suit, the loudspeaker struck up the national anthem, and all voices lifted powerfully."

Claire stood up, about to give voice, her right palm high on her chest, when Oliver objected.

"That's not your heart."

"It isn't?"

"No, it's lower down." Reaching out a tentative hand, "I'll show you."

Claire backed up a step. "Never mind, thank you. We're dealing with my patriotic heart, and that's what my hand covers. Now, if you'll allow me to proceed, sir . . . The loudspeaker struck up the song, all voices lifted powerfully . . .'"

Claire positioned herself to sing and to raise and lower her hand to and from her chest at each snatch of song. 'Oh—oh say can you see . . .' When they got to 'And the rocket's red glare,' " Claire tried to reach the "red glare" but couldn't make it. She lowered her voice an octave and repeated the phrase as a contralto. "When they got to these measures," she said, "the united volume broke, a few craned their necks for the sustained high notes, the rest weakly dropped to their knees. At 'Oh say does tha-at Star-Spangled Ban-an-ner-er ye-et wa-ave,' they reassembled their forces for a renewed assault o'er the la-and of . . . Unfortunately, they couldn't scale the heights. At the word 'free' they were routed, and slid down in a vocal scramble. Still on their feet stood the survivors—a few trained professionals, children under twelve, born coloraturas, and eunuchs. At the end, the others regrouped to join them in a feeble, chastised 'home uh-of the brave.' "

"Well, they're not going to have to suffer through that anymore," pronounced Oliver with finality.

"No? Why not?"

Claire had given him his opening. Quickly he launched into his tale.

"Speaking of the 'Star-Spangled Banner,' listen to *my* personal story. I never mentioned Richard Wagner's visit to Rossini in Paris, did I? Well, no matter, it must have been sometime after their meeting that I found myself in Paris again. I was living at home then with my parents in Sussex. At every opportunity I took a trip to Paris. The day was spring and sunny, the air like wine, the chestnut trees bursting with red buds and white blossoms. Walking along the Boulevard des Italiens, approaching the corner of Chaussée d'Antin—"

"Stealing a march on me, eh, Oliver?" Claire broke in.

"I have not finished," he said haughtily. "If I am to tutor you in history, in music history, pray interrupt not."

Claire, grinning, raised her hand, and without awaiting permission chimed in again.

"Turning the tables on me, too, eh?"

Ignoring her, he carried on.

I saw a man on the other side of the street waiting to cross. From sketches of him I'd seen in newspapers, I recognized the great maestro Gioacchino Rossini. Waiting till he crossed and drew near, I mustered courage and with a foreigner's innocence and cordiality greeted him: "*Bonjour,* Maestro. *Quel beau jour!*" He looked at me, taking in my accent, and returned my smile. "Good morning, young man. You are a stranger to these parts? From England, am I right?" I nodded a pleased assent. He'd had a little walk, he said, and felt like a chat; would I like to join him upstairs? Naturally I assented with pleasure. We were in front of his portal by now, and passing the concierge we climbed upstairs.

A maid opened the door to a spacious house and led us through a hall skirting the dining room into a study furnished only with a little table, a secretaire, a Pleyel upright piano, a small bed, and some chairs to sit on. The valet de chambre brought us a vermouth while I told the Maestro how much I loved *The Barber of Seville* and *La Cenerentola.* He sat and talked cordially about them and about contemporary opera in Italy, France, and Germany. About England, he apologized, there was not much to say. About the United States, he confessed to knowing next to nothing: they seemed deaf to good opera. He had heard "Yankee Doodle" played several times and also two pieces he called ceremonial, "Hail Columbia" and the "Star-Spangled Banner." "Yankee

Doodle" charmed him: he liked folk tunes and thought it might have originated in one of the British Isles. "Hail Columbia" didn't interest him, but the "Star-Spangled Banner" . . . ! He asked:

MAESTRO: Am I correct, monsieur, that like 'God Save the King,' it is to be sung by people generally?

MYSELF: Yes, Maestro. Many in the United States, I believe, prize it as a national anthem.

MAESTRO: Curious. What I write for my singers is often not easy. That song of theirs requires professional singers, too, for the range alone. As for beauty, it is simply not a beautiful air. I don't know the words. I've heard they too are not beautiful. They describe a flag, not a country: the land of the brave and the home of the free is a nice phrase but overused and vague. It fits England and Austria and France, also, no? And, the words seem just to ask one long question. The harmonic progressions are as uninteresting as the melodic line. I'll show you what I mean. Come over here.

He sat down at the small piano.

I'll play it. What key do you prefer? No, never mind, I'll play it in the ordinary tenor's medium range.

He played it by ear, from start to finish, *maestoso.*

Do you see the range?

With his left hand on the keyboard he showed that it was impossible for him to span a twelfth.

MAESTRO: Never write for ordinary voices without being able to span the range on the keyboard. That's a rule that amateurs like myself keep in mind. Where did this song come from, monsieur? Have you any idea?

MYSELF: Yes, Maestro, from my countrymen. It's the drinking song of a London poetry club.

MAESTRO: The drinking song has the same range?

MYSELF: Yes, I believe so.

MAESTRO: Unbelievable. You know, wine does not increase one's range. I can see the club members drunkenly supporting each other in a circle and, at the high notes, falling over each other onto the floor in one great heap, laughing uproariously.

His face took on a look of amused thought. Perhaps he saw the scene as part of a comic opera.

No, it's not even a good drinking song. As for a national anthem, the most beautiful is the Austrian, expressly composed by Haydn. You know it, of course.

The maestro played that too on the Pleyel, singing it in German, with gusto and an Italian accent.

Claire couldn't restrain herself. "You know why Haydn composed that song? Because he liked 'God Save the King' so much he thought that Austria should have a beautiful hymn, too."
Oliver cast her a terrifying look.
"If you wish to ask a question, Ms. St. John, raise your hand."
Claire was about to mutiny but her story-teller went on too quickly.

MAESTRO: Haydn loved that anthem, wrote variations on it. It was the last thing he played before dying. Truly it is a love song to country. Just what a national anthem should be, a love song.

He rose from the organ. We chatted a bit more, sipping another vermouth. I stood up to thank him for the honor granted me and handed him my card, ready to take my leave. He pressed my hand warmly. As the door opened and I stood in the hallway, he laughed and called out:

MAESTRO: They should cut it down a third, monsieur.
MYSELF: What did you say, Maestro?
MAESTRO: The "Star-Spangled Banner," they should cut it down a third. Or better yet, junk it. *Au revoir.*

The door closed. I went down the stairs with a project in mind.

By the tale's end, Claire was full of good humor. "What project's that?"

"To cut it down a third. Look, Claire, instead of junking it, let's revise the 'Star-Spangled Banner.' Right now! We'd be doing the people a great patriotic service, greater than a constitutional amendment."

She didn't need convincing. "How do we go about it?"

Oliver went over to the piano. He sat on the bench and patted it to invite her to sit down beside him. Claire sat, keeping her knees together.

"To cut it a third we have either to lower the top or to raise the bottom."

"Or to shave some off the middle," said Claire pretending to a bright stupidity.

Huggins laughed. "If all else fails, we'll do that. Here goes. Musically, the top part of the song has strength; it's the dull low register, as Rossini knew immediately, that has to go. I tried various versions last night and this is what I came up with.

"Don't forget, the only aim we have is to bring it within range of ordinary people. We can't correct its other faults. Else we really would have to take the Maestro's final advice. So, we'll bring it within range with the least change possible. We don't want anyone to think we're composing a different song.

"We'll put it in the easy key of G. This will be 'The Star-Spangled Banner,' Twenty-first Century.★

"Can you reach this D?" Oliver scaled up to D, a ninth above middle C.

Claire made it with ease. "Re-re-re-re-e-e."

"Good. The way I've figured it out we have to change the pick-up and first bar like this . . ." Oliver played the few notes. "The eighth and ninth bars like this . . ." More notes. "And the sixteenth bar like this . . ." More tinkling. "There, we've got it. Let's try it out all the way through. I'll play, you sing."

Oliver laid the sheet up against the piano rack. They put their heads together, rendering the song with charm, he thought:

★ Copyright applied for.

there. Oh, say, does that— star span - gled ban— ner— yet—

wave— O'er the land— of the free and the home of the brave?

"That's great." Claire's eyes shone. "At the end it was easy," she said. "Hardly sounded different at all."

"Funny, isn't it?" enthused Oliver. "Over the years there've been lots of changes made to it. The popular singing stars, generally, in contrast with concert and opera singers, can't bring it under voice control, and so each slips over a personal version. The public does not object because nothing has been done to bring it within its own range. The same was true for the Anacreonites. They kept falling over each other with tears in their eyes singing 'the myrtle of Venus.' Yet they never narrowed the range."

Claire nodded, got up, moved to her chair, clearing her throat noisily to regain tutorial authority, and resumed where she'd left off.

————Without question this song owed much of its first popularity to circumstances. The War of Independence, under the '77 Constitution, was won; the War of 1812, under the '87 Constitution, was lost. Not an auspicious military beginning. Both times the enemy was England. But the War of 1812 offered this consolation: it proved that the States, united or not, could lose a war and survive. The "Star-Spangled Banner" versified this consolation and intimated that the States and their flag might live to fight other battles together. And then along came baseball.

Still, not until World War I did President Woodrow Wilson, by executive order in 1916, declare the song the national anthem. In 1931, Congress was ready to grant the status of "official national anthem" to the song. The American Musicological Society protested. Congress paid little heed, and conferred the title.

"Couldn't we date the birth of the country from this date, 1916 or 1931," suggested Oliver, "when a national anthem was officially chosen?"

"We could, but that would just be a legal triviality," Claire tossed off, "and we've heard enough of that. Remember, the 'Star-Spangled Banner' gave the land of the free no name. Just hold on a bit, Oliver. Something important happened before then."

————You remember the attempt of the New-York Historical Society to fix a name for country, don't you? In some of the correspondence on the questions "America" was mentioned as a possibility. Unfortunately, as was recognized, it was the name of a continent in the title United States of America, and on the two American continents, several other independent countries were already located. But in the political circles of New York and New England the pre–Revolutionary War usage that influenced Washington persisted: America and Americans stood for former British America and British Americans.

Now, you said that as kids you couldn't understand why teachers called "My Country Tis-a-dee" "America." Its author, the Reverend Smith, spoke of "my hymn, my country 'tis of thee." And so the printers of 1831–32 titled it. When published again in 1861, the year of Lincoln's inauguration, the publisher inserted "America" before this title, and in the same year two other publishers dropped the "My country 'tis of thee" altogether, leaving as the title the single word "America" and forcing the Reverend Smith in later years to say that his hymn was "now styled 'America.' "

"Come round now and hear of the event of the century," invited Claire. "It is not a tale from the constitution. It's the marriage of Bates and Ward."

★ ★

————One fine day in June of 1893 a minister's daughter from Falmouth, Massachusetts, a professor of English literature at Wellesley College, having turned in her last student reports, put her household affairs in order, breathlessly finished her packing, and set out on her first trip west. She was to lecture on English religious drama at a new summer school in Colorado Springs. On the way, her New England eyes delighted in the endless wind-swayed plains of golden wheat. She had seen the Alps and the Pyrenees, but the Rockies, she discovered, were far more glorious. The summer school faculty consisted largely of eastern professors determined, as the saying goes, to scale "Pike's Peak or bust." Not on foot but by wagon, the last lap drawn by mules. Too bad Henry David Thoreau was not along. The astronomer in the merry party, a professor at Amherst, a dealer in rarefied atmospheres, insisted that everyone leave their lunch baskets untouched; he did not recommend eating above the clouds. On the "Gate of Heaven" summit, Katharine Lee Bates stood in wordless rapture. There the Muse wafted to her the opening lines of a hymn. Here she might have stayed to capture it all, but she had time for only "one ecstatic gaze." The astronomy professor had fainted. The party was "unceremoniously bundled into the big wagon" and headed down the descent. Back that evening in Colorado Springs she penciled in her notebook the whole verse in four stanzas. Suitably published on July 4, 1895, in *The Congregationalist* of Boston, the hymn won quick praise and immediate settings to music, over sixty at the author's last count.

Claire looked across at her tutee. "I've got a hunch you know what song I'm talking about."

"No, honestly I don't."

"Well, in telling how she came to write the verses, the author speculated that the reason 'the hymn has gained in these twenty odd years, such a hold as it has upon our people, is clearly due to the fact that Americans are at heart idealists, with a fundamental faith in human brotherhood.' "

"I've got it! *Brotherhood* gives it away."

"Quite, but you never marvel at the daring of plump Professor Bates, do you? Just think of the title. 'America,' not because a later generation pasted it in; 'America,' not because bombs were busting in air; 'America,' not because the name appears in the title: the hymn's original title was 'O Beautiful for Spacious Skies.'

" 'America' because at each refrain the cry arises 'America! America!'

"Mark the date in your calendar, Oliver." Suddenly she stopped herself. "No, wait, there's more to come. Do you know how the verses go?"

"Sure, at least the first stanza." Without coaxing he burst into song.

> O beautiful for spacious skies,
>   For amber waves of grain,
> For purple mountain majesties
>   Above the fruited plain!
>   America! America!
>   God shed His grace on thee
> And crown thy good with brotherhood
>   From sea to shining sea!

"Well done," said Claire. "Hand me my case, will you?"

"What case? You didn't bring it this time, remember?"

"That's right! You've made me feel so good, Oliver, I've forgotten my pitiful state on arrival. I was going to ask you to read over the other stanzas. No need; they can wait."

"The other verses aren't the world's best anyway, are they?"

"No, they aren't. You're probably thinking of strained phrases like 'impassioned stress' in stanza two, or 'human tears' in stanza four. Are there tears other than human? Animal tears? The poet labors for rhyme and meter. There are other defects, too. Some say—"

Huggins interrupted. "I remember one line so funny . . . I wonder whether it doesn't spoil the whole thing."

"What line?"

" 'O beautiful for pilgrim feet.' "

Claire showed charity. "I don't think we should let that spoil the whole thing. Let's tolerate Professor Bates's New England eyes. In good puritan form we'll censor stanza two, and while we're at it, three and four, also. A national anthem should be short. The first stanza is just the right length. It cries out America! Not because it's the world's leading military power, the land of economic opportunity, the New World fabled by Europeans, or the exemplar of lily-pure democracy. It cries out the name of country, America, for one reason alone and puts it on the side of the angels—because it's beautiful."

"I see an objection to that first stanza, though," Oliver said.

"Oh? What?"

" 'God shed His grace . . .' "

"It denominates a religion, you mean?"

"Yes it does, one with a masculine God who sheds *His* grace."

"One could add another note and change the line to 'Fortune shed her (or its) grace on thee.' The *thee*, one might argue also, should be changed: it hints of Quakerism. But an anthem is not part of an oath of office," she asserted with finality, "nor is it a government monopoly where public funds are spent on coins reading 'In God We Trust.' "

Oliver hooded his eyes. "And what about 'And crown thy good with . . . '?"

"I see. Well, let's not lay that time warp on Sister Bates, shall we? Whoever wants to sing 'sisterhood,' let him. Or 'siblinghood,' or 'brotherhood.' It's a free country, ain't it?"

"Did she write the music too?"

"I know what *you're* getting at, that the remarkable thing about 'America the Beautiful' is not its lyrics. Nor is it simply that it flings out the name of country, loud and unafraid. The marvel is the music—sublime, floating, with the greatest of ease, divine serenity. Not the miracle of Haydn's anthem, still, like his, a love song. Without that music the verse would have been as forgotten as 'God Save the Thirteen States.' And you notice the range? One note over an octave. Rossini's hand would span it easily. A good range for We, the People, in unison.

"Curiously, Bates seems to have had little taste in music. Among the sixty some tunes she heard as settings, she put a good, tearful, end-of-the-evening Scotch ditty on the same plane. 'Auld Lang Syne' is a lovely tune, of course, but lacks the uplifting crescendo at 'America! America!' Not one of the many musical settings, she complained, was composed expressly for her hymn. This time We, the People had the better taste: without voting they chose over all competitors, 'Materna.' "

" 'Materna'?"

" 'Materna' is the music composed by a music dealer of Newark, New Jersey, the organist of Grace Episcopal Church, a hero unsung, Samuel Augustus Ward. He wrote it ten years before Professor Bates climbed Pike's Peak. I'm ashamed to say I know nothing about Ward; so don't ask me, Oliver. I know only that he set the music to an old hymn going back to the 1500s called 'O Mother Dear, Jerusalem.' Where Bates's lines 'America! America!' now appear, the religious setting read, 'O happy harbor of the saints!' followed by 'O sweet and pleasant soil!' A nice equivalency, don't you think? Ward is supposed to have composed the music out of love for a deceased daughter. He himself died before Bates's words were finally set to the music. He died, but his music lived."

"If Bates had a good ear," said Oliver, "she would have thanked God that the two of them—her words and his music—had met."

"Yes, it was a providential marriage."

"Of two Americans."

"Correction, please. Of two *pre*-Americans who baptized the country 'America' on their secret wedding day. We don't know who first brought the couple together in a lasting romance. The earliest known publisher of music and verse was the YMCA Press of New York, New York, in a book of *Fellowship Hymns* edited by Clarence A. Barbour. The song appears as number 266."

"Was it really a secret marriage?" doubted Oliver. "In the ceremony the whole people—crowds pouring into the church, masses filling the streets outside throwing flowers, wildly, happily cheering the wedding—received a name in baptism." Oliver's imagery—a concoction of medieval throngs and cathedrals and revolutionary masses storming the palace—lifted him onstage. "From this day on, good People, you can say your country is America! Rejoice!"

"For the record the date of the marriage copyright was October 25, 1910," Claire said, shaking with repressed laughter. "Now can it—I mean, the film is ready for canning. I get your point. The people's clasping of the song to their hearts constitutes its ratification. The voice of the people, as we have heard at many intervals over thousands of years, is the voice of God.

"You remember, one or two replies to the New-York Historical Society letter of 1845 had wisely said that a name for country
could no longer be given by enactment or official pronouncement
but that it had to arise from the people. Bride, Bridegroom, and
best man came from the East, inspiration from the West. There were
no lines about vistas of puffy cotton and whiffs of fragrant tobacco.
The South was still out in the cold."

"The carpetbaggers have been gone, Claire, for over a century,"
as if she needed reminding.

"Yes, and you're right, the music at least is serene and pacific,
exalted, all-loving, all-embracing. To that tune, Canadians sing 'O
Canada, O Canada,' Mexicans sing 'O Méjico, mi Méjico.' Simply
by one's adding or subtracting an eighth note in the main line, the
possibilities become endlessly good and true. The song seems destined to rival the record of Haydn's anthem, which was sung in
eleven different tongues of the empire, and it leaves open an op-
tion: 'Columbia! Columbia'!"

Claire got up from her chair and started walking to and fro,
slowly, pensively, her shirttails swishing lazily.

————We have heard Lincoln set the birth of the country in 1776
("Four score and seven years ago"). Others have proposed different
dates. Without thinking, most historians and most people with them
take the date of the Declaration of Independence of 1776 or of the
drafting of the Constitution of 1787 or of its ratifying in 1789. Many
would select the time that Betsy Ross was supposed to have finished patching together the first flag. Along that line one author
chose the first flag salute given by a foreign port in response to a
gun salute from a ship of the Continental navy (November 16,
1776). Some take the date from the first use of "the United States"
as a singular noun, or with such postbellum usage (1866). Some
pick the date (1814) of the shelling of Fort McHenry. Some, R. E.
Lee's surrender at Appomattox (1865), or the end of Reconstruction (1877, *The Birth of a Nation*, Director: D. W. Griffith). Others, 1892, the Pledge of Allegiance ("one nation indivisible"); others,
the time when President James Monroe in his message to Congress
banned foreign intervention in Latin America (the Monroe Doctrine, 1823); still others, the formation of interstate political parties

(about 1840). And some when the National Association of Professional Base Ball Players was formed (1890).

America the Beautiful USA 15

"We know different, don't we, Oliver? We date the birth of the country from its naming in 1910. Mark the date. Conceived in the mating of music and verse, 'America the Beautiful.' "

Claire stopped pacing and took a stance in front of Oliver. Pause. He got up from his chair, too, and stood facing her.

"Oliver," she said tauntingly, trying to keep from grinning, "do you consider me an older woman?"

Showily Oliver drew his full six feet up in front of her, vaunting his inches of superior altitude. "No," haughtily. "I think of you as an adolescent, three years my junior. In other words, a broth of a girl."

"Idiot," laughed Claire, and gave him a push down in his chair. Bouncing up like a new tennis ball Oliver pushed her, gently, he thought. Stumbling back Claire hit a corner of the hassock with the back of her legs. She thrust out her arms for balance. Oliver reached to catch and steady them but she pulled him along to break the fall. The hassock slid to the side with a clatter of glass and tray. Oliver pitched forward, arms extended to avoid crushing her. Claire fell back flat, lungs whooshing air, head bouncing hard on the white, thickly shagged Polish rug, eyes closing. A second whoosh as Oliver landed on her stretched out length, breaking his weight with his forearms. Her shirt was thrown open, she lay there pale in his underwear. Opening her eyes, taking in the face breathing inches above her, mistaking the smile, the warm weight on her body, her throat and face turning red with fury—

"Get off me!" Taken aback, Oliver stuttered, "I was only trying to keep you from—" raising himself a bit more on his forearms. His words brought only a louder, more vicious "Get off of me, you son-of-a-bitch!" This was too much. Oliver caught her wrists and held them down stretched above her head; simultaneously, quickly and naturally, his knees pinned her thighs down flat. This time his smile was neither reassuring nor menacing, as she may have thought. It was appreciative: this beautiful woman in white underneath him, her thighs spread out, their canals running wide and deep, one burgundy nipple out of control posing alert on the top border of her (his) undershirt, too large, unwilling to slip itself back, the hot scent of her breasts rising up to bathe his face. Violently Claire twisted and turned, then quit, frustrated.

Oliver was holding himself suspended over her. He debated— with whom? with what? his conscience?—whether to rip the undershirt down to her navel. Instead—false to instinct, true to upbringing—he said, "Now what?"

Claire made a brave try at humor. She struck a Victorian attitude, turning her head to one side, closed her eyes, and unflexed. "Do with me what you will. I shan't resist."

Watching her every move, Oliver let his hips down slowly to settle over hers. He felt her mound rise to meet his groin, then subside deeply. Sensing what was coming, he jerked his rear back up just as she gave a bump of her hips, lunging into empty space. Unmoved and unmoving, he settled down over her again.

"What do you want?" Dumbly, out of breath.

"Isn't it obvious?"

"Isn't what obvious?"

"You've been talking for ten days. Now I want a chance to talk on a subject of my own."

"What? Are you serious?" she said.

"*Now* I'm not serious; a minute ago when you were scared I *was* serious. I might have been, too, seeing that you've done nothing but tease, cajole, and flirt for two weeks."

He let her wrists go and still seated on her, drew himself up, a blasé star of the old stage and screen, going through the motions of plastering back his hair. Then, inspecting the manicured nails of his curled fingers, he said superciliously, "I never bed a woman who wants to bed me."

"What rot!" she spat. Calling on all her strength she gave a huge push of hips and back, and rolled him over, ending up mounted on him, pinning down his wrists and thighs. She tried to look in his eyes, but they were fixed on her almost fully exposed breasts. He could bounce her off but didn't want to.

"You look too comfortable," she said, and ground her knees in his thighs. She succeeded only in amusing him.

"Well," he said, "you know what Confucius say, 'When about to be raped, relax and enjoy it.' "

"Does he? Well, he's assuming other things being equal."

"Is he? So am I. Other things *are* equal. I'm waiting . . ."

Pause. He lay there motionless. Straddling him, she too was still.

"So you're not going to rape me," he said. "Sorry 'bout that. Just like the Wife of Bath said. It must be power you're after."

"The Wife of Bath?"

Tutor was going to plead ignorance, was she? "You need prompting? They asked her, What is the thing women most desire? And she answered, To be above their lovers in mastery."

"I recall it . . . vaguely," she said.

What a liar! Oliver noted for future reference. "Now that you're on top, what are you going to do with your mezzo-soprano sovereignty . . . over your subject lover?"

Claire wavered. She was thinking of something, he was sure, but decided against it. She got up off quickly, brushed back her hair, straightened out her shirt, tied the belt tighter with an emphatic tug, her eyes brilliant.

"Where were we? Oh yes, you wanted to have your own little discourse. On what topic?"

"On the idea of consent."

Claire turned to look at him. "We've run out of time today. First thing tomorrow, okay?"

"No need," said Oliver. "I've already given it."

Claire's eyes widened. "Without words, you mean."

"That's right."

"In our Punch and Judy show?"

"Right again."

Suddenly she seemed concerned. Her head turned toward the desk. "Is that machine still recording?"

"Sure, you said to let it run. It doesn't record the action, though. That's up to me to fill in."

"Oliver, time is running me out of tales."

"Never," said he.

"One thousand and one," she mused. "Tradition has it that by the time Scheherazade told that many stories, she had three children by the king, all boys, one walking, one crawling, one sucking."

"You're nowhere near three hundred thirty-three and two thirds tales."

She retorted scornfully. "Just like a man. Never thinks of conception. She must have become pregnant within the first ten or twelve nights."

"In that case," parried Oliver, "we're behind schedule. Have to make up for lost time."

"Oliver, my dear, there is such a thing as spiritual conception, the conceiving of ideas. In that way I hope *you* have become pregnant."

"I *have* felt stirrings, mostly in the nether regions."

Claire seemed pleased. "Indeed."

"Could they have been quickenings?"

"Perhaps, but all stirrings, in case you didn't know, connect to the mind."

Suddenly her expression changed.

"Oliver," she said, serious with him for once. "It was the shock of falling . . ."

Silence.

"I've kissed lots of boys . . . men."

"What entertaining tales they must be!"

Claire hesitated two seconds, her eyes retrieving something from memory. " 'What are they compared with what I shall tell you tomorrow night,' Scheherazade replied. 'And what might that be?' said Dinarzad, her sister.' "

Oliver waited for the next line. Scheherazade lapsed into silence.

On a coatrack near the door hung his smudgy raincoat and a straw hat. Claire snatched them off, and newly clad, scooted out the door down the walk, painted toes plashing the puddles.

12

HOW TO GET RID OF

A CONSTITUTION

WITHOUT SAYING SO

OR MEANING TO

SATURDAY

Without knocking, St. John stormed in and handed Huggins a package. "Here's your shirt and coat all cleaned, washed, and ironed. Thanks."

Then, business-as-usual-like, "We've double-marched through pre-American history. From this point on, American history begins."

What *is* this? Huggins had been about to clasp her to his bosom. She must have sensed a forward leaning in his muscles: her face registered, "Back off me, Huggins." He sized her up.

Her dress, all in white, was of one tight piece in two fabrics. A slim belt with silver buckle encircled her waist. The V-neck bodice of finely ribbed gauze slid under the belt down to the beginning of her hips, at which point the other fabric came into play: satin in a chemise-skirt clinging to the thighs, widening slightly just below the knees, cascading over sheer stockings. Sleek lines. Not a ruffle to ruffle.

The bodice, too, was sheer. Was it transparent? Oliver couldn't tell. For cover Claire had hung over her shoulders an open linen jacket whose lapels annoyingly hid her breasts.

He decided to humor her, for now.

————There was no naming ritual, she was saying, like those presided over in person or in absentia by the crowned heads of Spain, France, and England, no official baptism, no gun salutes, no convention of delegates, no resolution of Congress. Two unsung heroes drafted "America the Beautiful," the people ratified it, lifting their voices.

Now Americans may speak and write of their country with a name, "America." Songwriters beseech "God Bless America" (Irving Berlin); poets dedicate themselves, "America I'm putting my queer shoulder to the wheel" (Allen Ginsberg); novelists never having visited America fabricate a visit to "Amerika" (Franz Kafka); settlers in the cities dance to "I'm Searching for America" (Ruben Blades); presidents and four-star generals sign off invoking "God bless America" (William Clinton, Colin Powell); and are buried to the music of "America the Beautiful" (Richard Nixon).

Time to dry up this rhapsody, thought Huggins, hoping to get around to a twosome named Oliver and Claire. "I seem to remember that our ambassador to Ethiopia was announced not as the 'Ambassador of America' but 'of the United States of America.' "

"And an ambassador is announced that way still," Claire chipped in, "although in conversation he may be referred to as the American ambassador. In the officialese of diplomacy and of federal transactions and property claims, the phrase refers to the government of the United States of America. Many historians, too, prefer 'the United States of America' and think of 'America' as a romantic name rather like 'Columbia.' " She carried cheerily on.

————But officially, though without intent, the Congress gave up the use of "America" as the location of the United States by admitting the first State situated outside of North America—Hawaii. No longer a location, America is now the name of the country in which fifty States are united. Mexico is the United States of Mexico. Brazil is the United States of Brazil, Venezuela is the United States of Venezuela, America is the United States of America. There is no continent named America. There is South America and North America, otherwise known as the Western hemisphere. And there is America, a country, that now extends beyond the Western hemisphere.

Nonetheless, because America is newly named we'll meet with a left-over mix-up for years to come. Sometimes it seems as if we hardly made any progress in the century and a half since the Committee on a National Name made its report. In the speech of foreigners, confusion remains. The educated classes, "the good People" of Jefferson's day, will in general say, "I'm going to the United States." In England, they will say—following George III's naming the thirteen States separately in the Treaty of Paris, "I'm going to the States." The French in their treaty listed the States separately, too, and otherwise—R. R. Palmer told me—referred to the rebelling colonists as *les Bostoniens* and later as *les Américains libres*. Like the English, they make a special case. Today if they don't say, 'I'm leaving for New York,' they will say, *Je vais aux États-Unis*. Elsewhere, prospective settlers will say as they have said since the 1880s, "I'm leaving for America." Except those from Mexico, Central and South America, where they say, "I am going to the North" (*voy al Norte*) or to *los Estados Unidos*.

Legal definition bases itself on formal citizenship. It would apply to someone who, like Saint Paul, needed to establish nationality. "I am an American citizen." But still confusing is the etiquette an American should follow in countries south of the border down to the Tierra del Fuego. He soon learns to pronounce "I am a United States citizen." As I say, usage remains in flux.

Inside the United States, the way I look at it, the perennial American concern over who is a real or true American is a legacy of the War Between the States, of the streams of settlers, and of the long history of timidity and uncertainty in naming the country.

By arriving early and staying long on the Atlantic seaboard the British-Americans managed to excise the *British* and the hyphen. A

Dutch American, Franklin D. Roosevelt, thirty-second president of the United States under the '87 Constitution, once poked fun at this history. Putting on his irresistible smile and tossing his head, he opened a talk to the Daughters of the Mayflower with the salutation, "My dear fellow-immigrants." The audience was not charmed.

Recent coinages have deprived British Americans of the full enjoyment of their unhyphenated name status. One is the acronym "WASP," White Anglo-Saxon Protestant, taken up by university students of the 1960s, often pejorative, and the other is "Anglo," a usage not necessarily unfriendly of Central and South Americans.

The English Pilgrims along with the Dutch and French can claim to be among the earliest *settlers* and therefore entitled to that term, whereas subsequent arrivals, though they also settle here, are called *immigrants*. By that logic, the Pilgrims, compared to the Mexica and their thousands of years of prior settlement, were immigrants.

There is yet another distinction. Early English settlers in the Northeast, it is said, were fleeing religious discrimination, whereas later settlers, the immigrants, were fleeing poverty, not an honest-to-God reason for flight. There might be something to this snobbery, were it not that religious persecution in England was meshed by law and custom with political and economic discrimination, too, such as exclusion from certain occupations, and restrictions on voting, on office- and property-holding and transfers. Bound labor and indentured servants made up 60 to 80 percent of British immigration to the colonies from 1619 to 1776. In the same period, Britain dumped fifty thousand convicts largely on Maryland and Virginia. Adventurers and speculators made for these shores also, out to make a fast buck.

Millennia ago the Stone Age people arriving in western North America via the Bering cross-over may have been seeking adventure, tailing the mammoth, or fleeing persecution, poverty, and punishment.

Let's settle for *settlers* all.

"We could have a Bureau of Settlement and Naturalization," suggested Huggins.

"Why not?" responded his tutor. "None of Franklin Roosevelt's audience nor he himself had the pedigree of earlier settlers like

Moctezuma and his black-haired, bronze-skinned people. Nor of his ancestors from across the eastern sea—Cortés and his bearded, mostly olive-skinned followers.

"Today, you know, America is slowly becoming darker skinned, thicker haired, darker eyed. Have you ever thought of that, Oliver? Something to look forward to. At least esthetically, don't you think? A darker shade of pale."

Oliver was dubious. Claire St. John, his true love, was a paleface, definitely, magnolia-white, well, creamy-white. As for esthetics! Who was more beautiful?

Something popped into his mind. "Claire, you're not Anglican by any chance?"

"Why? Do you want to marry me?"

"Not a bad idea. Will you be my lawful wedded wife?"

"Do you love me?" asked Claire, and before Huggins could shout "Affirmative!" added scornfully, "You don't know what love is."

"What is it, pray tell?"

"The desire for the everlasting possession of the beautiful."

The reply seemed suspiciously pat, but Oliver had no trouble adapting the formula. "You're beautiful and I want to possess you everlastingly."

"Hush, Socrates. You want to *possess* me everlastingly," she mocked, "but will you *want* me everlastingly? Anyway, you are going downward from the love of airy ideals like liberty and equality to the love of solid old me."

"So? Plenty of time to worry about liberty and equality."

"Before *we* run out of time," St. John ruled, "back to names."

————Prior to acquiring a name an infant is simply a member of the category "Infant." A name may indicate something of the infant's ingredients—egg of so-and-so and sperm of so-and-so. We talked the other day about white sperm joining with black egg to form British African offspring. As of now, in this part of the world the sound or sight of a name may reveal a person's parentage, sex, religion, and country of origin of family. It may disclose something of the family's occupational origins: Presidents Tyler and Taylor = tailor. Or ancestral class origins: noble versus commoner: Marie Joseph Paul Yves Roch Gilbert du Motier, Marquis *de* La Fayette.

Friedrich Wilhelm Ludolf Gerhardt Augustin, Baron *von* Steuben. Alexis Charles Henri Maurice Clérel, Comte *de* Tocqueville. Comte Donatien Alphonse François, Marquis *de* Sade. The pronunciation or spelling usually indicates the language and hence the country of origin: George versus Georges versus Jorge. The name may pinpoint a place name: Lincoln or Lincolnshire, England. A place name may indicate illegitimacy along the ancestral line. Leonardo born in the town of Vinci, hence Leonardo da [from] Vinci, a most illustrious bastard.

By revealing country of origin a name often reveals family religion. A Polish or Spanish name has the flavor of Roman Catholicism, as much as McGinnis and McCarthy. A Scottish name, you can bet odds, cloaks a Presbyterian. First names may support the indication of the last name: the Puritans liked the Old Testament as a source for first names. The other day you mentioned the name Cassius Marcellus Clay, English in spelling and pronunciation, hence presumably Christian, but indicating also an admiration for pagan Rome and perhaps, as a later acquisition, for Henry Clay, the orator Lincoln much admired. Muhammad Ali, the heavyweight champion boxer's new name, proclaimed his conversion to Islam. Malcolm Little was killed young, while speaking from the podium, but his name then was no longer Malcolm Little. Upon reflection, he had concluded that his great- or great-great-grandfather had his real name taken away from him and changed to that of a slave master of the past. With his real name lost, he felt cut off from history and ancestry. He chose as his name X, symbol of the unknown— Malcolm X. In "Malcolm" though, one recognizes a common Scottish and Christian first name (Gaelic *mael-Columb*, disciple of the Dove). Four kings of Scotland bore the name. Before he died Malcolm X changed his name again, to Al Hajj Malik Shabazz, to signify his conversion to Islam.

Last week I mentioned Phillis Wheatley, the young African slave poet who wrote a set of "Columbia" verses to George Washington. She acquired her name from John Wheatley, her Bostonian purchaser and master. The General, in his letter of thanks, addressed her as "Mrs. Phillis."

Names may also indicate an ancestor's affection for a particular religious figure. The unusual first name of Mayor La Guardia (the

Guard)—*Fiorello*—points to admiration for the *Little Flowers* (*I Fioretti*), tales of the life of Saint Francis of Assisi, founder of the Franciscan order. Saint Francis's baptismal name was Giovanni di Bernardone (John son of Big Bernard), but he was nicknamed "Francis"; his father, a wealthy trader, traveled constantly to France.

Charles Farrar Browne, who as "Artemus Ward" gave Lincoln more than a few chuckles, was born in Maine of Puritan stock. When asked once about his ancestry, he replied, "I think we came from Jerusalem, for my father's name was Levi and we had a Moses and a Nathan in the family, but my poor brother's name was Cyrus; so, perhaps that makes us Persians."

Not necessarily, Artemus, old boy. Cyrus is a Persian hero, true enough; but the Bible acclaims him for liberating the Jews from Babylonian captivity; he is the Lord's anointed and His pastor. So maybe you all did come from Jerusalem.

"If I were versed in speech sounds like Professor 'enry 'iggins, Oliver, I could place you within a stone's throw of your birthplace, your parents' homeland, your childhood neighborhood, and your schools. By the way, what happened to the family photos that were over there on the little cherrywood table?"

"I put them in the other room where they belong," said Oliver casually. "Anyway, you already know what my father looks like."

"That's right, I do."

"I learn more about him every day."

Claire raised and dropped her eyebrows, said nothing, looked down, shuffled papers busily, and resumed.

———We haven't yet abandoned the abstraction of names. The poet William Butler Yeats has a line, "I'll name the friends that cannot sup with us." Names can bring a person back. The pathos of monuments to the Unknown Soldier is that no one knows the names of those who are memorialized. Have you seen the Vietnam War memorial in Washington? Thousands on thousands of names of the fallen incised on black marble. Thousands on thousands of friends and relatives touching those names with their fingers.

Wherever in the world you may go, names and name-giving are important. To name is to possess, to have a name is to have a self, to belong, to be an individual, to have a center of sound and sight and smell to which a world refers itself and from which one can act.

A renewed awareness of proper nouns or names easily leads one to put certain philosophic terms and assertions through their grammatical paces. I'll touch on two: the *cogito* of René Descartes, French soldier, mathematician, and philosopher of the seventeenth century, and the general will (*la volonté générale*) of Jean-Jacques Rousseau, the Swiss-born French writer and philosopher of the eighteenth century

Descartes's proposition *cogito ergo sum* contains implicit in Latin the pronoun "I" in the first person singular form of the verb, which in French or English must be made evident: *I* think therefore *I* am." If you refer the pronoun back to its proper name, you get: "I, René Descartes, think, therefore I, René Descartes, am." Fleshing out the pronoun deprives the proposition of universality and, among other things, opens up genetic possibilities. René Descartes *is* because *Papa et Maman* Descartes made love one day, probably without thinking.

A similar grammatical approach would apply to Rousseau's *volonté générale*. The general will—I define it at considerable risk—expresses or embodies the will of everybody or the bulk of people (the generality) to act for the general (or common or everybody's or the generality's) welfare. The adjective "general" makes the general will a collective term. Who are the persons in these generalities or everybodies? Are they everybody in the whole world? If not, to distinguish them, tell us their names. Are they Genevans, Parisians, Frenchmen, Europeans? If they already possess names they have a community or a city-state, a sovereignty and a constitution reflected in their names.

The Descartes case elided the name of the speaker; the Rousseau case omitted the names of those who do the willing. Dispensing with names favors an illusory abstractness or universality and endangers further elaboration of philosophic arguments.

Huggins complained. "I didn't understand half of what you said."

"Don't worry about it," she said blithely, "until you enroll in Philosophy 201. Moving on now to Theology 101 . . ."

★ ★

————Descartes notwithstanding, there is nobody properly named "I" except God. Names of divinity are not to be taken lightly. In some cases they are not known or presumed not to be known. Who could bestow a name on the Lord? In the Bible the Divinity confers several names—Abraham, Sarah, John, Luke, and gives the task of naming the animals—not an easy one—to Adam, maybe to test his intelligence and ingenuity. Blasphemy is the sin of taking the Divinity's name in vain.

To a lesser extent, the names of parents and close relatives in Europe and the Americas are to be handled gingerly. Preferred usage is that their names be avoided and that they be called instead by their relationship or by name prefixed by their relationship—Father, Grandfather, Aunt Millie, Uncle Charlie. Using proper names alone is taken as a sign of disrespect.

The power of names and name-giving is so great that it lends itself to magical rites and to withholding one's name. Once at a dinner party in Oxford, the late anthropologist E. Evans-Pritchard, who had studied the Nuer of the upper Nile, told me the outcome of a chat he had had with a native. As I remember, it went something like this:

ANTHROPOLOGIST: Who are you?
NATIVE: A man.
ANTHROPOLOGIST: What is your name?
NATIVE: Do you want to know my *name*?
A: Yes.
N: You want to know *my* name?
A: Yes, you have come to visit me in my tent and I would like to know who you are.
N: All right. I am Coul. What is your name.
A: My name is Pritchard.
N: What is your father's name?
A: My father's name is also Pritchard.
N: No, that cannot be true. You cannot have the same name as your father.
A: It is the name of my lineage. What is the name of your lineage?

N: Do you want to know the name of my lineage?

A: Yes.

N: What will you do with it if I tell you? Will you take it to your country?

A: I don't want to do anything with it. I just want to know it since I am living at your camp.

N: Oh well, we are Lou.

A: I did not ask you the name of your tribe. I know that. I am asking you the name of your lineage.

N: Why do you want to know the name of my lineage?

A: I don't want to know it.

N: Then why do you ask me for it? Give me some tobacco.

————In aristocracies the protection of one's family name is a matter of honor. Andrew Jackson of Tennessee was held to be a Western democrat, but his gallantry with ladies and his dueling with men (including his killing of the man who had bandied his wife's name in disreputable surroundings) reflected the sense of honor of the southern aristocrat). The aversion to using family names in republics and democracies (we talked about it earlier) grows out of a different motive—to show that family and family influence play no part in one's personality and status, that one is self-made. That's why as I've heard it fragrantly phrased, "In America names don't mean shit."

Upon the reciting of that solemn fact, Claire looked around for her glass of water. Oliver was grinning, thinking he'd sure hate to see her clean up her act. Not seeing the water ready, she was about to go on without when he sprung up and made off to get it.

"Come here you," she ordered, addressing an unwashed boy. Stopped in his tracks, Oliver obediently turned back.

"Sit down."

He sat. If evidence was needed that he was still in thrall, this was it.

"You understand, Oliver, I'm giving you examples at random. The general subject of names is so complex it would take us well into next year to express it in fair and orderly fashion."

"What better way to spend our time?" asked Oliver, wader in the seas of knowledge.

"First we have to cap this book. Don't distract me. Please. What do settlers bring with them beside funny clothes, potatoes, rice, beans, and pasta?"

"What about germs?" Somewhere Oliver had read about the international spread of germs. "Don't new settlers bring germs too?"

"They certainly do, germs and viruses. Early English settlers killed more Massachusetts Bay natives with smallpox than they ever did with guns and knives, and gave thanks to God for thus opening up the territory to Pilgrim expansion."

————They also arrive with language, family, religion, dress, gait, skin, eye and hair color, teeth and head shape, a diet, habits, customs, attitudes, stories, legends, sports and games, fermented drinks, building techniques, beauty, art and music, a pharmacology, a sense of law, of community, of individuality, of fairness, and of right from wrong. In short, they bring their names. All this their names condense, define, and store in individual memory and muscle.

Would it be too much of an exaggeration to say that a name at any given time and place holds a constitution in storage, that the person possessing that name is an ambulatory constitution, that without it he is a mere non-furbearing biped?

"Well," Oliver hesitated, "I guess . . ."

"You wouldn't think it an exaggeration were I to say that many Americans treasure the '87 Constitution in their heart and mind, would you?"

"Hell no."

"Shall I recall what Thoreau said? You are to worry not about what any Jefferson and Adams wrote but to obey 'that eternal and only just Constitution, which He [capital *H*] has written in your being.' Remember when I asked you, Oliver Huggins, to write your own constitution, what did you do?"

"It seems to me I started off well with We, the People, didn't I? And a legislature, executive, and supreme court."

"That's what you did. You have had the We, the People, three-branches form of the '87 Constitution drummed into you. Is that the constitution written in your being? Imagine that an Oliver Huggins, probably of Sussex, England, passenger on the *Mayflower*—but mind you, not one of that undesirable London gang on board— were to write a constitution. He has a history of religious and political forms, oaths, covenants, charters, petitions to guide him. How would he start off? In the Name of God, Amen. We, whose names are underwritten, the Loyal Subjects of our dread Sovereign Lord King James by the Grace of God, et cetera, et cetera.

"Give your imagination a greater stretch. Suppose in 1620 a metamorphosis: a boatload lands on one or another of these shores, with more or less the same sort of crew and passengers who, however, bear Persian names, or Chinese, like Ma Yuanxing or Chen Youfang. Would they have written anything at all?"

"Hardly. A poem maybe."

"Would they have written anything resembling a constitution?"

"No."

"Would they have unwritten rules for living together?"

"Affirmative."

"Oliver, quit acting like a trained seal. You make me feel you're not taking me seriously."

"No, truly. I'm as enthralled by you as when you first walked in the door."

Claire yawned and stood up and gave herself a grand stretch. Her jacket started to slip from her shoulders. She shrugged it back on and continued.

————Well, then, these people would have never heard of a republic—at least not for a thousand years or more. Even today most of the world—including such entities as the United Nations and the International Monetary Fund—arrives at political decisions in some other way than republican elections and majority rule—in a way some describe as "arriving at consensus."

A country having to do with a lot of strange new names is a country whose constitution is undergoing change. How can a constitution withstand the encounter? The names of the Wampanoag like that of their chiefs Massasoit and Wanssutta reflected their unwritten constitution. They treated with the Pilgrims in 1631, and got used to hearing on their land the names of settlers like John Carver and Tim Tinker. In little more than a lifetime, the Wampanoag lost their constitution, their land, and their lives. In 1676 the new names, after a war without quarter, captured, drew, and quartered Chief Metacomet, known as King Philip, stuck his head on a pike, and displayed it in Plymouth square.

Much later, settlers from various States of the United States took up residence in a part of Mexico called Tejas. For a time the Mexicans welcomed the sound of strange names like Austin, Crockett, and Houston. Soon, strange names crowded out familiar names and set up a republic called Texas.

These examples illustrate merely the negative sides. After all, from the locals the Pilgrims learned to fertilize with fish and the Texans to eat chili. The things new settlers bring with them—including garlic, names, and constitutions—sooner or later, in small or great measure, permeate the older settlers, like it or not, reminding us that assimilation is never a one-way street.

One other thing: unlike what most Americans may think, migration is not and never has been directed uniquely at America. The face of the earth from time immemorial has been crisscrossed, and still is today, with trails of migration, forced or voluntary.

"Where did you learn all this? And you so young," Oliver asked in all seriousness.

"I've had good teachers from day one. Nothing I say is original. Remember that. For instance, I learned about constitutions from a teacher of politics when I was a schoolgirl."

Oliver protested. "You're still a schoolgirl."

"Not quite," came the quick correction. "He was from somewhere in Greece. He said he had left many years ago for reasons of health. We used to call him, among ourselves, 'the Philosopher.' He would spin these yarns about long ago while walking up and down the room, along the walls, between the rows in the back, in the front. He would stop at a window and gaze, thinking about something far off. If it was a cold, dreary gray day he would stare out for a long time without moving, and then wake up and begin pacing again. He was getting bald. A bit of a dandy. He cut quite a figure. I had a crush on him."

"How come the professors you know are all men?" Huggins teased.

Evidently St. John didn't hear him, for she went on. "As I was about to say, this teacher of mine wasn't quite sure the study of constitutions was important but he liked studying them. Years ago he directed a big research project analyzing over a hundred constitutions."

Huggins ever-practical asked, "Who financed it, a foundation?"

"I don't know for sure. A former tutee of his, I think, somebody Alexander or other. One study entitled *The Constitution of Athens* was published in English."

————Up to now, she proceeded, we have most often used the word *constitution* to mean, for short, a prescription for a frame of government. This would not differ from the Philosopher's usage, which draws the meaning out more fully. He said that the way they viewed constitutions in his younger days was through an analysis rather than a prescription, looking at the laws and customs of a country and selecting those that set the rules on obtaining important offices and powers, to see what sort of people held the important offices and powers—important in that these people would hold the authority to make decisions obligating the whole country. Keeping in mind, then, various sorts of people—the propertied rich, the middle class, the property-less, the military, artists and writers, the farmers, whatever groups the population divided up into—you could make a pie and think of each of them as constituting a slice, big or small, depending on the offices and powers each sort had acquired for themselves. Or you could think of a scale and each of them as differently graduated weights, adding up to a 100 percent balance.

In his most recent thinking the Philosopher had come to a conclusion about drafters of written constitutions. They think that what they are setting out to do is to draft the best possible constitution. And it may happen to be the best. Whether it is, though, and for the very reason that they really do believe it is the best, they try to make it a constitution for the ages. I mentioned this a few days ago. They try to stop time, to write in stone, to let the dead bind the living, to impose their arrangements of powers and offices on the future, to make the future in the image of what they would like today.

Assuredly, if they are in a position to prescribe a constitution, they do not come from the dregs of society, and their constitution, they cannot help but hope, will conserve their own position and that of those they favor from this time forward. The laws putting and keeping the constitution in operation they will call "fundamental" and hedge it with various protective devices.

But no one can freeze history, not even the Huaulu of eastern Indonesia, a people known best to themselves and to my friend the anthropologist Valerio Valeri. Something to keep in mind when dealing with written constitutions. Migration, immigration, or emigration can make over constitutions, defeat in war can annul them, so can threats of revolution, widespread disasters of any kind—epidemics, prospects of starvation, and so on, galloping with the Four Horsemen of the Apocalypse. Life produces many surprises, not all of them pleasant..

Written constitutions—these boastfully perpetual arrangements of powers and offices—would seem to be fragile things. Taking off from 1789, France's constitutions have swung among monarchies and empires, and a handful of republics. One French historian numbered his country's constitutions from 1789 to 1875. For this period of less than a century he counted thirteen.

Claire paused, fiddled among her papers, and started to hum a waltz.

"What's that you're humming? I don't recognize it."

"I can't think of the name myself," Claire admitted. "It'll come to me later."

"The last time I saw Paris," Oliver reminisced, "it was the capital of the Fifth Republic."

"And what's the number of the republic to whose flag as a boy you pledged allegiance?"

"The First, of course. We still have the same constitution."

Claire raised her eyebrows.

"Put my foot in it again, didn't I?" he said. "It's the Second Republic, isn't it? The first was the '77 Constitution, the Articles of Confederation and Perpetual Union."

"Doesn't it strike you as curious that the '87 Constitution of the

United States is still held to be one and the same? It's distinguished as being the oldest written constitution in the world. Why would the French have had thirteen constitutions while in the same span the United States had only one."

"Because the—"

"Stop!" Claire shot, her hand up in a traffic policeman's gesture.

Too pretty a hand for that, was Oliver's first thought, looking at her long white fingers, firm, oh so firm and authoritative. He waited.

"I know what you're going to say: 'Because the French are more excitable.' "

"I was *not*." Oliver was putting his foot down. "I was going to say, 'Because the United States Constitution is the *best* constitution,' that's why it's lasted over two hundred years."

"England's constitution still exists and has existed since time out of mind. Sparta's constitution lasted nine hundred years, Venice's one thousand years."

"I thought we were starting from 1789 or thereabouts."

"All right. Starting from then, why do you think it has turned out to be the best constitution?"

"For one thing, it is brief, a dozen pages or so."

Claire frowned. "You ought to know better than that. You make me think I've been wasting my time. If it takes forty-three pages to spell out the rules of poker, how can a constitution take less? Haven't I said more than once that the constitution you speak of includes whole bodies of law that are not written out in its few pages—common law and equity, admiralty and maritime jurisdiction, the law of nations, not to mention transcendent natural law, and a bagful of other things?"

Oliver, unabashed, looked pleased. "What about the amendment clause, then? The people don't have to resort to violence, as the French did, to amend their constitution. They can alter it by voting peaceably."

"I see what you're doing, Oliver, and it's okay. You're giving me the standard arguments. This one you can make only because of a case of national amnesia. You forget that, apart from the insurrections, separatist threats, and riots that have occurred under the '87 Constitution, you have had a War of Secession that took a million casualties, a far greater toll than all the violence brought on by changes and attempts at changes in the French, indeed in all the European constitutions put together. What happened to the United States' amending clause in 1861? There was a constitutional crisis and it did nothing to solve it. The issue was decided by force.

"Anyway, French constitutions typically contain a section on amendments or *revisions*."

"I'll make one more try," said Oliver. "I know already, though, that you'll shoot it down. The constitution of the United States is best because it is a *written* constitution."

"That won't wash, either. All the dozen or so French constitutions, in fact all constitutions of this period, were written. You remember that written-ness argument from the case of *Marbury* v. *Madison,* don't you?, that we took on at the beginning of the week. The 'greatest improvement on political institutions,' exaggerated the chief justice, 'a written constitution.' I'd like to review our general remarks and add a few that were not brought up in the mock trial or elsewhere."

———A constitution is not good simply because it is written. An unwritten constitution, such as the English is said to be, can claim greater flexibility. Also, it does not depend on the spread of literacy. The Mongolian Empire, embracing possibly the greatest territorial expanse of all time, must have had an unwritten constitution. It was ruled by Genghis Khan, an illiterate.

Furthermore there are no fully written constitutions. In general we overlook the many ways communities, literate as well as nonliterate, have for promulgating and preserving laws and constitutions, for demonstrating how powers and offices are arranged, through titles, insignia, apparel, art and architecture, processions and other ceremonies and rites. The '87 Constitution required a ceremony of spoken words and gestures, and objects—the oath of office. It instructed that the president "shall take" that oath. It did not say he "shall sign" it. Even signing it would amount to a performance.

We saw that Chief Justice Marshall, though committing himself to the written limits of the '87 Constitution, couldn't so confine himself. Weighted by the number of extra-constitutional sources he and other justices since have drawn on to buttress their decisions, the written words constitute a largely unpredictable part. One large unwritten part goes to the rights of the strongest or of the conqueror, admitted as law after the wars of the palefaces versus the redskins and of the Union versus the South. In the Cherokee cases Marshall asserted that "power, war, conquest, give rights which, after possession, are conceded by the world; and which can never be controverted." How does this square with what you said, John Marshall, that the United States government is emphatically a government of laws?

Given the prevalence from the 1770s or '80s, of written constitutions with amendment clauses, the question remains, Why is the '87 Constitution better than any other? Let's return to our earlier question of why the written constitutional score of France versus the United States is thirteen to one?

One possible answer is that France has had a monarchy floating in and out of its constitutions. To offset that, though, the United States has had the States coming in and going out of the '87 Constitution. Instead of asking why those constitution-mongers, the French, have had so many, the more instructive question may be, Why has the United States had only one constitution? Perhaps there are different constitutions hidden within.

"Of course," said Oliver, rising to the occasion, getting it right this time. "Like the Articles of Confederation and Perpetual Union. That was a written constitution, but nobody calls it that today."

Ms. St. John looked benevolently on teacher's pet. "They claim it was only a treaty, can you believe it?" she said, "a treaty between the States. Of Perpetual Union! This '77 Constitution, framing a republic, was thrown in the fire after ten years. From its ashes arose the republic that you as a child unreasoningly swore allegiance to—the Second Republic."

"That sounds awfully European."

Claire agreed. "It does, doesn't it?"

————You know, the heyday of written constitutions is over. It had one century of enthusiasm, roughly 1775 to 1875. By then the notion that a number of men of goodwill guided by their reasoning powers, by the Goddess of Reason alone, could get together, deliberate, and prescribe a government for the everlasting benefit of humankind, had sickened. Constitutions continued to be written and inaugurated with fireworks by participants, but nonparticipants looked on listlessly. The Weimar constitution in Germany, drawn up after World War I, had raised hope in some quarters. When that constitution fell, high hopes fell with it.

Except as we noted last week, in the United States. There *the Constitution* was more than a constitution. Drafted for a government without a country or a country without a name, it functioned—along with "the United States," "the Union," and "the Nation," as a common noun substitute for a much-desired country. It garnered unto itself much of the affection normally called love of country or patriotism. Constitution and country were the same. The equation—the Constitution = the country—persists although the country has found its name. The revised equation now reads: the Constitution = America. The fall of the Constitution would spell the death of America.

Not so. Written constitutions, new and old regimes, come and go; the country lives on in its name.

But as long as people believe that this constitution is the equivalent of America, they will persist in the illusion: *The* Constitution, its terms written in black and white, is one and the same, and so it must and will remain forever, just as it was proposed by the Framers in 1787.

"Including the amendments," Oliver inserted.

"Yes, we must consider the amendments, along with other things. Quite possibly amendments may conceal radical change in the arranging of powers and offices, and if so we may speak of a different constitution."

Oliver came up with a super-idea. "Why don't you take the Philosopher's conception of a constitution and apply it to the United States, and see how many constitutions you come up with?"

"Mmm," Claire mused. "That's a thought. You mean, do it, just like that, off the top of my head?"

"Sure."

"Sure," Claire echoed. "What have I to lose but my fair name? All right, here goes—The Tale of the Accordion Constitution."

The first constitution, that of 1777, the Articles of Confederation, composed in the spirit of '76 while most States were enlarging their electorates, was a democratic republic. The second in '87 we can designate an aristocratic republic or a republican aristocracy: its chief executive was to be nominated and chosen by that body of persons called the electoral college; the Senate was chosen by state legislatures, the supreme court was appointed by the president, and important political offices devolved among notable families.

Next came the first ten amendments, the Bill of Rights of 1791. Certainly in its language it is a separate constitution. The '87 Constitution does not mention *rights*. The Bill of Rights lists a number of rights that are out of the reach of the supreme law of the land and asserts that these rights and all others cannot be taken away by this constitution. They belong to the people, and all powers not mentioned in that constitution are reserved to the States or to the people. Among other things, they stipulated, the supreme law of the land cannot overturn the rules of common law in trials by jury.

These provisions were intended to reduce many of the powers and offices of the United States government and shift others to the States. In short, a radical and in many cases a contradictory change. If the '87 Constitution had framed a consolidated republic of powers, the '91 Constitution redesigned a federal republic of limited and divided powers and of untouchable rights of the people. This would mark the third, the Federal Republic. Thomas Jefferson symbolizes the change.

In 1792, Congress passed a law transferring to the president its power of calling forth the militias of the respective States into the service of the United States. Whether it was proper for it to delegate one of its constitutional powers, Congress did delegate that power. This left the States without control in the House and Senate of the military force they had retained in their militias. It gave the president a monopoly of military force in war and peace, strengthening that office so as to justify describing it as a republic with strong executive powers, a Monocratic Republic. Or, in light of the passing of the Virginia dynasty (Jefferson, Madison,

Monroe) and the downgrading of birth and education as qualifications for political office, the resulting constitution can better be called a Monocratic Democracy. Andrew Jackson represents the change.

The monopoly of military force in war or peace plus the president's arrogation of war powers during the South's secession led to instituting the Union Dictatorship. I am using the term without prejudice. The ancient Republic of Rome had an office of the Dictator, its incumbent chosen by the Senate only in time of crisis. On the whole, it had a good reputation. Its hero is Cincinnatus who, once he had as Dictator defeated the enemy, returned to the plow.

The Roman Dictatorship had a term of six months renewable only by decree of the Senate. The Union Dictatorship had no limits, and even when the crisis was over, many of its encroachments lived on to form standard powers of the presidency. After two centuries the Dictatorship of the Roman Republic had assumed an indefinite term, too, with Julius Caesar as its last incumbent.

The '87 Constitution does not provide for a dictatorship, yet Lincoln, you remember, claiming war powers under the constitution while at the same time insisting that the Union was not split in two by war but merely cracked by rebellion, did frame a new, unmentionable office of Dictator, which in time of domestic crisis could ignore supreme court rulings, suspend *habeas corpus*, let one part of a State secede from another, conscript armies, and issue proclamations and executive orders with the force of constitutional law. Our word *constitution* comes from the practice of Roman emperors to issue edicts or *constitutiones* with the force of supreme law.

After Lincoln's assassination as a tyrant—*Sic semper tyrannis,* cried his assassin—the Rump Congress, that is, the Congress remaining after the departure of southern members, carried on in the name of the Thirty-ninth and Fortieth Congresses. It changed the terms of its membership (Amendments XIV and XV), excluded representatives from eleven States, treated the South as a conquered territory, exacting from it "ironclad" oaths of allegiance, and admitted new States to an indissoluble union. South and westward the course of Empire!—inaugurating the era of the Imperial Republic or the Republican Empire.

Lincoln's Gettysburg remarks invigorated the saying in the Declaration of Independence that all Men are created equal. The Rump Congress broadened the class of citizens of the United States and of the States and, presuming that the unenumerated "right to vote" was within itself rather than in the people or the States, continued a trend (furthered by Amendments XIX, XXIV, and XXVI) toward universal suffrage, and, again, a Democratic Republic. The assumption was that getting the right to vote made anyone equal to the men who were created equal.

This review, you realize, is just a thumbnail sketch. One can easily classify these constitutions differently. To construe them I have mainly used constitutional amendments and laws. Were we to add the force of certain ideas, you might wish to make some revisions. Consider for a moment the ideas associated with Adam Smith—a world market economy governed by an "invisible hand"—and Charles Erasmus Darwin—"the survival of the fittest." This is the way the world goes, they taught, convincing many, including the supreme court and men of property. Late in the nineteenth century, corporations, maintaining that as persons at law they were entitled to the "equal protection of the laws" of Amendment XIV, used offshoots of these ideas effectively before the court. Armed with a judicial charter of corporate property, they proceeded to enslave working men, women, and children, especially those new to the cities. Ironically, Congress had originally designed the clause to provide equal protection for the new, ex-slave citizens. Amendment XIV eliminated chattel slavery and fostered wage-slavery.

What shall we call that frame of government legislated by the supreme court's standing by the books of Smith and Darwin? The Oligarchic Republic? A capitalist Republic? A commercial Republic? Or none of the above? Take your pick.

Whatever you call it, this particular constitution came to full flower at the end of the nineteenth century. About that time, in reaction, the labor force, as it came to be called, comprising the working men, women, and children packed in industrial cities, their numbers swelled by new settlers and new names, by people closer to the ideas that swept Europe in the 1848 revolutions . . .

Claire halted. "Whoa! I have said enough. We've gone past our base line. Looked at in this way the various constitutions up to 1875 give the United States a better record vis-à-vis France."

"I've been counting," said Huggins. "We're still losing, but it's more like a respectable thirteen to seven."

"That's a better score. John Adams, by the year 1808, had already lived under four of these seven, but they were enough to make him say, 'I have always called our Constitution a game of leapfrog.' "

————Of course, there are mixed elements and overlappings galore, continued Claire. My Philosopher told us that one of his former students living in Rome analyzed the constitution of the Roman Republic and concluded it was the best just because it was mixed. Some of the Framers knew of that theory, that a mixed constitution was best, and some defended the '87 Constitution for its similar mixture of offices: a president for a monarchy, a Senate and supreme court for an aristocracy, and a House of Representatives for a republic. The mixture is more complicated than that, as the simple classifications I have just used show.

These changes all brought new arrangements of powers and offices and yet took place without anyone's admitting a change of constitution, and as often as not without anyone's intending to change the '87 Constitution. What the United States has *not* had is a new constitution openly declared—such as that of Cromwell or Napoleon.

"Could we go so far as to adopt a *monarchical* form of government without saying so, I mean, without having to admit we have a new constitution?" inquired Oliver.

"You mean, if the president's accumulations of offices and powers doesn't classify it as a monarchy already, an elective monarchy?"

"No, I mean a monarchy that has got rid of elections by the people."

★ ★

————All right, but first let's note that Edward Gibbon, the expert on *The Decline and Fall of the Roman Empire*, defines monarchy as a state in which executing the laws, managing the revenues, and commanding the army are in the charge of a single person, whatever he may be titled.

Julius Caesar nursed a desire for kingship, perhaps dreaming of Alexander the Great. He knew the dangers, though. Whenever any of his followers would salute him as king—in Rome, hatred for the title "king" was endemic—he would snarl, "Don't call me Rex, call me Caesar." Thereby, for many powerful monarchs up to the last of the czars and kaisers, he changed the title of king to that of Caesar.

For transforming without saying so a republic into one-man rule Gibbon had a model, Octavian, later hailed by the Senate for his piety and love of peace as Augustus. His foster-father was Caesar, whose assassination taught his adopted son and heir a vivid lesson. Augustus, scribbled Gibbon, was aware that "mankind is governed by names." He learned how to slide republican words, titles, honors, and institutions around so that they seemed not only to be the same as before but to grow stronger, while he gathered the important offices and powers to himself, assuming the subtle, unofficial title of *princeps*, first among equals. At the end of his life he chose the son of his wife Livia by her first husband to succeed to his rulership. The Senate conferred on that son, Tiberius, the powers and offices of Augustus.

Huggins was listening with interest. "Why don't you take Augustus and guess how he might slip today through the '87 Constitution?"

"Want another flight of fancy, do you? Well, I'll try again. As long as you know what nonsense it is. If not instructive, it may be amusing. But we'll be brief, touching on just the constitutional or legal side, not going into (much as you might wish) husband and lovers, family and children, reporters, personal enemies, conspiracies, and underhand stuff. We first have to stipulate that the country is torn by crises. That's the way it was when young Octavian rose to power. It's not much of an assumption; if there is anything that one can predict offhandedly it is that this country will continue to be plagued by crises, real or conjured up and manipulated."

"Assumption granted." The eager drama student was bursting with ideas. "Why don't you start with Augustus as president? Or how about this? Why not make the president a woman?"

"Hmm. Why not? Too bad I'm not still wearing your shirt, Oliver. It's not the royal purple but would look more commanding than what I've got on."

Oliver considered what she had on to be so perfect as to make it a crime to muss up.

Claire arose, and warming up, turned herself into a portrait. She held her right hand above a book on the table and, brushing back her jacket, placed at her hip the other hand resting on the hilt of a broadsword.

"George Washington," murmured Oliver. Not for nothing had he played at charades.

That pose apparently not imperial enough for Claire, she struck another. Gazing out the dim distance she pulled up her skirt a bit, went into a half-crouch, and slowly extended her right arm, with the palm of her hand slightly upward. The authoritative blessing of the emperor Marcus Aurelius mounted on horse! Holding it for a full twenty seconds she let the arm slowly drop, straightened up, and announced take-off: The Tale of President Octavia.

Octavia liked that title more than just for the bowing and scraping that came with it. Its meaning could be stretched. Her new attorney general's staff well-supplied with handpicked constitutional lawyers reminded her that the Framers had transferred the title from the '77 Constitution where the president *presided* over Congress, to the '87 Constitution where he presided over nothing. The Framers thought that keeping the same title made the office seem like a familiarly weak one. Instead, that new constitution gave the executive total command of land and naval forces during peace as well as war, in a word, gave her *imperium*. Octavia was thankful for the 1792 law and for Lincoln's dictatorship that lent her authority to call up under her command the militias of all States. Gradually she reduced the armed forces, dismantled the draft system—a popular move—and substituted professional and specialized units.

Another job now was to secure control of revenue. Her legal advisers pointed out that she did have a hitherto little-considered constitutional power (Article II, Section 3): "On extraordinary occasions" she could adjourn Congress to such time as she "shall think proper." Starting with her existing veto power, she more and more often vetoed congressional legislation, line by line or in whole chunks, charging that Congress was locked into special interests, couldn't move fast or wisely enough, indeed had become inert, in these perilous, these desperate times.

Claiming that House and Senate couldn't agree, she adjourned Congress by proclamation and renewed for a year the already existing approved budget, thus giving her withdrawal of Treasury funds the necessary appearance of congressional authorization. Later she extended that budget indefinitely, funneling more and more funds to the executive branch, reducing Congress to penury, while praising the patriotism of a few of its members, heaping them with honors. In time she created a Rump Congress by convoking in special session the heads of important congressional committees, appointing some of them as members of her cabinet, which posts they could constitutionally accept, given that cabinet posts were not official.

She further enlarged the Rump Congress by bringing in state governors, slipping them executive patronage, and encouraging them to take steps similar to hers with their legislatures and constitutions. In effect, state governors eventually became Octavia's provincial governors. Now given the unitary proper noun name "America" for country, it was easier to deplete the residual power of the several States.

The Rump Congress for its first new budget proposed large tax cuts, gaining widespread approval and establishing a precedent for future budgets proposed by the president, rubber-stamped by Congress, and confirmed by the president.

"What about elections, and who was to succeed her? That's going to be a tough one," Oliver predicted.

Claire thought a moment. "President Octavia had her lawyers look into the matter. They quickly spotted the electoral college as the Achilles' heel of the constitution."

Originally this office was to be filled by "electors" chosen by state legislatures. The electors could nominate the president and vice-president of their choice. This provision soon changed. By about 1830 almost all States chose their electors by popular vote and obliged them to cast their choice according to the choice of the political parties. A momentous change, it came about not by amendment but by force of custom. In only a few cases have electors disobeyed their party's choice.

But Octavia, touting the need for reform and for returning to the Constitution's original principles, restored the electoral college's freedom from political parties (which were, after all, but groups of politicians, not entities empowered by the constitution). She then worked toward controlling its choices, which were of course *her* choices. Eventually she not only reelected herself—the no-third-term amendment having been repealed by her second term—but also at the appropriate time nominated a successor from her issue or family by birth or adoption or from other relationships. (Precedents already existed for obtaining office through family connections, not only among the families of the Framers but even in some prominent families of the twentieth century.)

All the while, with the solid tradition of Jackson, Polk, Lincoln, Woodrow Wilson, and the Roosevelts behind her, young Octavia represented herself simply as the defender of America, the only one with the mandate of the whole American people. The title "President" came to signify, as it almost does today, a single person enacting and executing the laws, managing the revenue, commanding all military forces, the one who presides over and defends Us, the People. The claim of presidential privilege changed smoothly into a version of lese majesty. President of the American people, as Napoleon was emperor of the French. She took care to modify old and introduce new emblems, ceremonies, celebrations (of her deeds, of her birthdays), and oaths, particularly military oaths wherein she quietly bound the allegiance of armed forces to "the President" and "the Commander in Chief."

Claire drew breath.

"You've made your point," Oliver commented.

"*My* point? *Your* point.

"This is only one course of action. One can think of a hundred others. A lot depends on luck. The Framers put in hard work and inspiration; even so, to overthrow the first constitution without saying so, but meaning to, they had to have luck.

"So before you place your bet, remember Lady Luck."

"One way or another, I guess there's constitutional change in the offing," said the uncertain Huggins. "I don't know whether to be glad or sad."

"Change, sure, but who knows where or when? So much depends on the nature of the crisis, the character of the person, and the condition of the people. I can understand that Americans believe their present constitution will last forever. Those I find hard to believe are those who say that all the rest of the world should and eventually will have a facsimile of that constitution. Some go even further and say that the world is inexorably climbing up toward its final form of government—universal democracy, Western-type."

"Didn't Karl Marx say that, too, except that in the end there would be universal communism?"

"Yes, similarly in the eighteenth century the best and the brightest believed that the ideal form of government was absolute monarchy and that was the super-highway the world should and would take."

"Did your Philosopher ever lecture on this?"

"Oh, yes. That former student of his, living in Rome, had concluded that constitutions or regimes followed each other in a certain order. There were the three main forms: monarchy, aristocracy, and democracy. (He and previous writers sometimes used different words for these types.) Each of the three had a degenerative variant, making six forms in all: kingship would degenerate into tyranny, tyranny would evolve into aristocracy which would degenerate into oligarchy which would generate a democracy which would turn into a mob-ocracy which would return to kingship.

"You see, if he's right, the future holds lots of changes."

"Did he give any details on how democracy would degenerate?" Oliver pursued.

"Some. Democracy, he said, sets a premium on equality and liberty of the citizen. Within a few generations, when the sovereignty of the people falls into the hands of its descendants, they'll have become so used to freedom and equality that they'll fail to appreciate them. Chiefly the sons of the wealthy, he remarked, fall into this error. They stupidly and greedily seek power and prestige by distributing largesse to the people, who thus corrupted become more and more difficult to govern. Ruling is replaced by unscrupulous force. Following such leaders, people degenerate. They ban other citizens, redistribute property, plunder, and kill, until they meet once more with a master who alone takes charge.

"This is the natural cycle in which constitutions change, disappear, and finally return to the point from which they started. He also said . . ."

Suddenly Claire lit up. "Now I remember that tune I was humming! Da da *da*, da da da da *dee* . . . It's 'La Ronde,' the roundabout, the merry-go-round, the song of a French film by Max Ophuls—delightful! The theme is that of a circle of loves: A seduces B, B makes love to C, C has an affair with D, and so on all the way round back to someone who beds with A."

The words, too, were coming back to Claire. "Round and round," she sang, "go my little actors, just as the earth spins day and night. Falling rain turns up in the heavens and then the clouds return as rain."

Oliver liked the song—it belonged in his repertory—and supplied what he thought to be the appropriate touch: "Love makes the world go round."

"Quite," said Claire.

———As I was about to mention, the Philosopher cautioned against taking the wheel of constitutions too literally—too many external events could stick a stick in the spokes. To that effect he liked to quote another student of politics, Niccolò the Florentine Secretary, who observed that almost no states lived long enough to pass through the cycle of governments, reach the starting point again, and stay on their feet. But surely change took place in some rough short sequence; of that my professor had always been convinced.

For the post-democratic stage he used the term "anarchy" in the sense that it was the form of no-rule, an unprincipled or lawless period. After which people seek a firm and just regal hand.

"Then there isn't any way of getting one of the good constitutions to last forever." Oliver was disappointed.

"If a perpetual motion machine is possible, so is a perpetual constitution," was tutor's dry remark.

Unwilling to let go, Oliver said, "I suppose the best thing that can happen is to be born in a country with a mixed constitution," then, exulting in new knowledge, "like the American Republic!"

" 'If you can keep it,' " Claire quoted. "Who said that? Let's see how much attention you've paid."

"John Calhoun?" Oliver asked tentatively.

Claire shut her eyes in dismay.

Oliver shouted with laughter. "Come on! I remember. It's Ben Franklin."

Claire took refuge in sarcasm. "Looks like without knowing it I've all along had a genius for a tutee."

She stood up and began pacing again.

"You seem nervous," Oliver observed.

"Who, me? Why should I be nervous?"

Huggins stood up too. In front of him she stopped, gave a great sigh, and yawned, rising on tiptoes, stretching her arms high, arching her back. Her jacket slipped from her shoulders, exposing the translucent blouse. With a jerk she brought down her arms and heels. Too late!

Oliver had reached out. Placing the backs of his hands on her chest, with second and third fingers he closed firmly on her nipples and pulled them forward. Claire gasped. She looked down at her breasts. Oliver had drawn them out taut. She took his wrists and held them steady. She shivered. She leaned over to his ear and murmured something. Gently she disengaged his fingers.

"Listen," he said smiling, "I'm sure the recording machine didn't catch your whisper in my ear. Just to keep a full account, shouldn't we put it on record?"

"Sure, why not?"

"For the record," Oliver announced, "Claire St. John whispered: 'Chill down, Oliver.' "

Claire howled with indignation. "I *did not*. For the record, *I*, Claire St. John said: 'How can you use a poor maiden so?' "

Laughing they gazed at each other with melting eyes. She picked up her jacket and threw it on a chair and came back before him. They joined hands.

"Oliver, you're one beautiful American."

"Claire, you're one beautiful spinner of yarns."

"Darling," she said softly. "Darling," he cried. They embraced tightly. They didn't kiss. Oliver felt the front line of his body disappear into hers, and his soul with it. They made one creature with two heads, four legs, four wrap-around arms, one hunger ready to roll.

For a full minute. Then with one will they came apart.

"Oliver," apologetically, "I've got a contract."

"An oral contract, wasn't it, with some fine unwritten print?"

"You know?" She seemed anxious. "You figured it out?"

Oliver nodded mysteriously.

"How?" Claire's eyes were round as silver dollars. "No, never mind." She looked at him incredulously. "It doesn't bother you? You're not cross?"

"Mmmm." Oliver began to hum. "Round and round, da da da da *dee*."

"It *doesn't* bother you!" She darted forward and hugged him. "God, I'm so relieved, I could just love you!"

She picked up a sheet of paper, tore it to pieces, tossed them in the air like confetti. "Whee!"

Oliver looked on, grinning.

Out of breath, gradually calming down, she turned to Oliver. "Look, there's no business like show business. We've got a book to top off."

"Let's do it."

————The imaginary paces you made me go through with the Philosopher and Octavia, if nothing else, must have convinced you that though chiseled in marble, written constitutions are slippery, fragile things. We've gone over the circumstances of the '87 Constitution. They illustrate some of its particular fragilities.

As did the revolutionary Congress, any outright opponents of the government would claim they were fighting against tyranny. To justify acts of resistance they would cite legal grounds among others. The law of the land is not supreme, is not above the higher law of natural rights, fundamental principles, conscience, or God. The supreme court's decisions are not the last word even in constitutional questions. Presidents—Jackson for one, Lincoln for another—have refused to obey the court. Lincoln said it was ultimately up to the people to approve or not its decisions. Opponents would declare that Congress exceeded its authority in delegating one of its constitutional powers to the executive—the power to call up the State militias—and seek to restore the power to the States. To split the country they could still claim that the original meaning of "We, the People of the United States of America" is "We, the Peoples of the signatory States." The president is authorized to speak not for America but only for this constitution, and even that's doubtful as presidents rarely if ever get a vote of more than one quarter of the electorate. Other opponents, once they think of it as no more than a couple of pages of vellum, might move to invalidate the '87 Constitution as a whole, citing the conspiratorial, illegal quashing of the '77 Constitution that invested a new, so-called federal government with false authority. They would call for a new constitution by convention or referendum.

"I take it this is a warning," said Oliver.

Claire did not pause.

————Speaking of We the People, there is another difficulty we've barely touched on. The preamble to the '87 Constitution, as you know by now, was drafted after the rest was completed. Its flowery statement of purpose would cheerfully be endorsed by any of the despots of history. Its chief legal accomplishment is in placing the source of authority in the We the People, an achievement of consummate ambiguity.

The main text gets down to business, however, lawyers' business. To avoid the sanctimonious theorizing of the Massachusetts Constitution, to make sure their constitution became law, the Framers drafted it in a closed language of powers. You will not find mentioned the rights of citizens. Nor their duties.

Hoping for assent to the draft, George Washington could speak of love of country but the text of the constitution he was promoting had no words for patriotism or loyalty of citizens. If they are disloyal, there is a law of treason, soon to be supplemented by a law of sedition. If they disobey, the courts guarantee justice. Citizens have no express *duty* to obey the law. Self-interest will keep them in fear of prison, of the stocks, the lash, the noose. Nor have citizens express *rights*.

To some of the States and their peoples this flat legal language smacked too much of the language of tyrannical kings and not enough like the Great Charter, the Bill of Rights and Petition of Right, nor like the Virginia Declaration of Rights of 1776. In the name of their peoples, these States protested that they would not assent to the '87 Constitution unless it contained a Bill of Rights.

Among the dissenters were Virginia and New York. Without these two great States, the Framers knew, there would be no point in going ahead, even if they could get the rest to ratify. But these two States and others as well were saying in effect that if you are going to propose a whole new constitution rather than just amend the existing, the '77 one, you should call a proper convention with an honest, open purpose rather than slip this one under the door.

The Framers were aghast. After a hot summer's hard work and quaffing in Philadelphia, the one thing the Framers did not want to do was to go back to the drawing board. They wanted to stay home for a while and sleep in comfortable beds. In convention they had got past a few roadblocks by the skin of their teeth. To try at this late date to insert new clauses would bring another bout of wrangling. Well then, should they give up and let the States convoke a new convention? Forget it. The States, it seemed, were raising ever more pointed questions. God knows what would happen in a new setting, with new delegates, and maybe without George Washington as presiding officer.

Adroit lawyers that they were, the Framers opted for quick settlement. *Que será será.* They struck a bargain. Once the draft was ratified they would add a Bill of Rights through the amendment process, just to humor the States, they said, for it really wasn't necessary. Even with this deal, ratifying was a close call. Getting the States to assent to the draft constitution brought out the convention's heavy artillery—Hamilton, Madison, and Jay for the newspapers and the stoutest chaps available for the streets and the meetings.

The promise was kept. It had to be kept, else the States involved would claim betrayal and withdraw, leaving Washington as president holding the bag, something he had feared from the start. The States submitted for inclusion in a Bill of Rights a mass of amendments—New York alone recommended thirty-two. The new Congress handed James Madison, the chief broker for a Bill of Rights, primary responsibility for paring the package down to manageable size. The Virginian knew the language of rights well. George Mason and Thomas Jefferson had been his mentors; he had worked with them on the Virginia Declaration. He and various committee members came up with twelve articles, Congress proposed ten of them as amendments, the States quickly ratified them.

This Bill of Rights ordains and establishes a new constitution, by our count the Third Republic. The Framers' '87 text proposed a constitution of tripartite *powers*, abstracted by Montesquieu as the legislative, executive, and judicial powers, and promulgated as supreme law. Along now come ten articles in the language of *rights*, natural rights of the people like those in the Declaration of Independence, rights that transcend so-called supreme law and cannot be touched by it, rights that are Creator-given. And whose law is higher than the Creator's?

The Bill enumerated explicitly certain of these rights—to assemble peaceably (Article I), to be secure against searches and seizures (Article IV), to a speedy and public trial by jury (Article VI), and to keep and bear Arms (Article II).

As rights are nowhere mentioned in the '87 Constitution, all rights of the people are protected by this defiant Bill of Rights. So we have two constitutions, the one of '87, of *powers* legally invested in the general government, side by side with the one of '91, of inviolate natural *rights* held by the people, both in the shade of one tree—*the* Constitution.

The courts have had the hardest time dealing with the anomaly. Typically they cope by conjuring up some extra-constitutional piety like, No government would subscribe to its own destruction. But that's exactly what the States intended to do through a Bill of Rights, to be able to subscribe to a potentially oppressive, consolidating government's destruction.

I've already shown that the addition of the Bill of Rights to the '87 Constitution created a stylistic break: it was written in an earlier language. Driven by your encouragement I speculated today that the import of its clauses established a different, a third constitution. I now point out that this deck of rights contains a wild card. Article IX: "The enumeration in the Constitution, of certain rights, shall not be construed to deny or disparage others retained by the people." The clause, similar to Article II of the '77 Constitution, holds that the United States government cannot deny to the people an *un*enumerated right. One of these unenumerated rights is the right to withdraw or secede, as States and individuals in both North and South have claimed at various times, and as the Colonies claimed in seceding from England.

Another is the right to vote, which the federal government itself by the acts of the Rump Congress of 1862 disposed of.

There is another unenumerated right, greater still—the right of revolution, the right of the people to rebel. The Declaration of Independence called it mankind's "Right and Duty." Many political philosophers have defended this right. Others have denied it. Written constitutions and laws invariably, expressly or not, deny it. This constitution, however, legally denies it in 1787, legally admits it in 1791, forcibly crushes it in 1861, and (il)legally denies it in 1862 (the Rump Congress's Amendment XIV). Yet as an unenumerated right it remains on the books, as Article IX of the Bill of Rights. People at times have in their hands enough *power* to effect a revolution. The American people, whether they know it or not, have a constitutional right to it.

In most of the time-span of this constitution, had you brought up Article IX, constitutional lawyers would have looked on you as though you had just sailed out of the clouds. It's a dead-letter law, they would have scoffed, everyone knows that. Let trouble brew, though, bad trouble, then the right of the people—to keep and bear arms, to rebel, to overthrow and change an oppressive government empowered under this constitution—cannot be denied.

"We the People," you know, are not bound by any oath. Nowhere have they sworn, "We the People do solemnly swear [or affirm] never to change this constitution in any way except as prescribed therein." If behind this constitution stands the sovereign We the People, they have the right to make and unmake it.

Historians will tell you that the colonists exercised that right in undoing their allegiance to the English Crown and Constitution; that the people exercised it again to ordain the '87 Constitution; that they took the power to legislate, to execute laws, and to judge away from England and gave it to the government framed by that constitution. And they can take it back again.

To this last remark some may object: *We*, organized as the United States of America, *are* the people. Who is this other "the People"? Without political organization they are just people, not *the* people. True by definition, but how were the people organized who ratified the '87 Constitution? By States. And are they no longer organized by States?

Suppose the people who rebel are not organized by States. They will always find leaders to assemble, organize, and direct them—and later perhaps to betray them—people under the sway (partisans will say "under the leadership") of a potential demagogue or tyrant, under a popular president or vice-president, a general, a senator, an ordinary citizen, having or claiming the support or acclamation of the people.

Written constitutions all have weaknesses. This constitution for the United States has peculiar frailties because of the origin of the old States in revolution, because of the revolutionary language of the Declaration of Independence and the persistence of that language in the Bill of Rights, because of the old names of these States and the tardiness of a counterpoise name for the general government and the larger country to which it aspired, and because of the resulting confusion in constitutional language and style.

But the larger point is that all written constitutions can have their writtenness turned against them. The chief minister to Louis XIII, Cardinal Armand Jean du Plessis, Duc de Richelieu, is reported to have said, "If one gives me six lines written by the hand of the most honorable of men, I will find in them something with which to hang him." The Cardinal was not boasting of his personal power over the courts; he was illustrating how far written words, like necks, could be stretched.

By now Oliver was ready for his own insurrection. "I can't figure this out. Is it a call to arms or a call to reform?"

"Neither," Claire said. "I'm a conservative. I stick with my Philosopher. 'Stay cool. Hold tight. Old laws are better than new,' he would say, and then add with a twinkle, 'other things being equal.' I did not come here, Oliver, to help you draft a manifesto or a declaration of independence."

"What *did* you come for?" A heavy question.

Claire looked him in the eyes but didn't answer.

"You weren't supposed to tutor me in American History, *were* you?"

"Not exactly," Claire replied seriously. "I was to tutor you in whatever I thought necessary."

"And do you think you've done it?"

She needed no reflection. "Yes. Yes, I have."

Time to lighten up, thought Oliver. "So you thought I needed tutoring in self-control, to resist temptation, like Saint Anthony."

Claire laughed. " 'Provoking Oliver Huggins.' How's that for a movie title? We can start the course all over again."

"No, we've done enough takes. Let's start shooting."

"Not today."

"Not today?"

"No, tomorrow. As of this moment I am no longer your tutor. We're equals in ignorance."

"Ignorance! You? I know you said that nothing you say is original, but I'm still amazed at how much you know."

"Me? If you still think so . . ." Claire's tone had suddenly taken on humility. Oliver marveled at the way the humble voice and lowered eyelashes contrasted with the svelte cosmopolitan figure, sitting with its mile-long silken legs crossed and thrust before his eyes. "I've been forgetting who I am," she recited, "I've overshot the mark. If I've said anything impudent or been talkative, you've got to remember it's Folly and a woman who's been speaking."

Before Oliver could decipher this sackcloth-and-ashes disclaimer, Claire jumped up.

"I'm going," she said.

Oliver jumped up too.

Slowly she picked up her bag and calfskin envelope, forgetting her jacket. For the first time she headed for the door without hurry and dawdled down the porch steps. At the bottom she stopped, fumbled in her envelope for something, and pulled out a piece of chalk, teacher's chalk! Lazily she tossed envelope and bag on the grass, kicked off one shoe, hesitated, put it back on. Intently she bent over to trace something on the walk. What was it? A grid? A hopscotch grid! She tossed the chalk on the grass, took her place at the starting line, drew her skirt up through her belt, blousing it like a peasant woman working the fields, thighs showing above her stocking tops, and began to hop—one, spread, two, spread, three. At the far end she stooped to pick up an imaginary marker, jumped about-face, and looked up. There at the top of the steps was Oliver, leaning against the porch post, looking down at her, smiling.

"What are you doing there, Oliver, waiting for me?"

Oliver nodded.

"Wanna play hopscotch?"

He shook his head.

"What then? What do you want to play?"

"Leapfrog."

A second's thought for it to sink in.

"Okay," she said eagerly. "First, turn off that fool machine! And gimme back your shirt." With her skirt still hiked up she bounded the stairs two at a time.

ACKNOWLEDGMENTS

Claire St. John wishes to thank:

—Her friend Margreta de Grazia, whose beautifully logical and literary mind traversed the entire manuscript with fulsome praise and gentle criticism.

—Those friends mentioned in the book's pages: Morton White and Valerio Valeri; and Robert R. Palmer and William Matson Roth, whose postprandial clouds of pipe and cigar smoke cleared the air. And Franco Aversa, for illuminating the incompatibilities of social contract theory with Justinian and Napoleonic law code traditions.

—C. Herman Pritchett, one of her good teachers from day one.

—Paola and Geoffrey Harris, for a taste of the problems of naming in current efforts at European unity.

—Julia Bernheim, for tracking elusive references and for preparing and pre-editing the manuscript with extraordinary skill and understanding.

—Marcia Tucker, for locating and calling up far-flung works of history and law.

—Alfred Joseph de Grazia III, for selecting and translating those taunting lines of Anacreon and for advice about North American Indians.

—Sebastian de Grazia, Jr., for permission to print his inspired "The Star-Spangled Banner: Twenty-first Century Version," and for acute comment on most of the manuscript.

—and her friend Lucia Heffelfinger de Grazia, for encouraging her to embark on this adventure and for cheering her on.

—The Twentieth Century Fund, an old friend, for supporting research in legal history and constitutional law.

—The Center for the Study of Human Values of Princeton University and Amy Gutmann, for a fellowship invitation at the right moment.

—The Historical Studies and Social Science Library of the Institute for Advanced Study and Elliott Shore.
—The Library of Congress and Constance Carter.
—The Princeton University Libraries and Dorothy A. Pearson.
—The New-York Historical Society.
—The Columbiana Collection at Columbia University and Hollee Haswell.
—The Historical Society of Washington, D.C.
—Archives, Margaret Clapp Library, Wellesley College, and Wilma R. Slaight.
—Talbott Library, Westminster Choir College, Princeton, New Jersey.
—Special Collections and Archives, W. E. B. Du Bois Library, University of Massachusetts at Amherst, and Ute Bargmann.

Oliver Huggins wishes to thank his father.

C.St.J.
O.H.